Gallery of Best Resumes

A Collection of Quality Resumes by Professional Resume Writers

by David F. Noble

Gallery of Best Resumes

Copyright ©1994 by David F. Noble

Published by JIST Works, Inc.
720 North Park Avenue
Indianapolis, IN 46202-3431
Phone 317-264-3720 • Fax 317-264-3709

Library of Congress Cataloging-in-Publication Data

Noble, David F. (David Franklin), 1935-

   Gallery of best resumes : a collection of quality resumes by professional
resume writers / David F. Noble.

     p.   cm.
   ISBN 1-56370-144-8 :
    1. Résumés (Employment)   I. Title.
HF5383.N62   1994
808' .06665–dc20   94-26608
                                               CIP

Cover Design: Robert Pawlak

ISBN 1-56370-144-8

Contents

This practical "idea book" of best resumes has three parts: 101 Best Resume Tips, the Gallery of over 200 resumes written by 79 professional writers, and 30 Best Cover Tips for polishing cover letters. With this book, you not only have a treasury of quality resume models but also learn how to use professional techniques in your own resumes and cover letters.

This book is for *any job searcher* who wants to know how the professionals write resumes. It's for *active job seekers* who want top-notch ideas for creating a first-rate resume in today's tight job market. It's for *all job searchers* who must have an ahead-of-the-pack resume— *from high school students* looking for their first job *to retired senior citizens* wanting to stay active. It's also for *career changers*, those *terminated* from downsizing, and the *overqualified* who must look in new directions and tailor their resumes in special ways.

This "idea book" can *transform your thinking* about resumes so that you have a better sense of what kind of resume is best for you and the interviews you schedule.

In this section, you learn experience-tested, resume-writing strategies, such as how to present *accomplishments in story form*, how to list your degree when you apply for work in another field, how to use a *resume as a marketing tool* rather than a job search document, how to appear less like a student and more like an experienced worker, how to indicate your jobs if you have had *no formal education* beyond high school, how to show your work experience if it is a liability when you compete with younger workers, and how to handle *stay-at-home years* of unemployment.

This section shows you effective design techniques, such as how to use *white space* for an uncluttered look; how to use as *testimonials* in a resume choice phrases from reference letters; how to use a resume as a marketing tool rather than a job search document; how to make decisions about *fonts and typefaces;* how to handle capital letters, underlining, italic, and boldfacing; and how to use *graphic elements* like bullets, horizontal lines, vertical lines, and shaded boxes.

To help you make your resume error-free, you learn in this section practical writing tips, such as how to use *capital letters* in computer terms; how to use *hyphens* in words and phrases; and how to use *commas, semicolons, dashes,* and *colons* correctly.

A quality resume can make a great impression, but it can be ruined quickly by a poorly written cover letter. This section shows you how to eliminate common errors in cover letters. It amounts to a *crash writing course* that you won't find in any other resume book. After you read the following sections, you will be better able to write and polish any letters you create for your job search.

In this section, you learn how to evaluate 25 sample cover letters. Many of them originally accompanied resumes in the Gallery. After you study this exhibit, you will have a better feel for designing your own cover letters to make them distinctive and effective.

Foreword

Y ou just have to ask whether the world needs yet another resume book. There are hundreds of them out there, and each year there is a new crop. So a legitimate question is, Why is this resume book worth while?

After looking at hundreds of resume books, I can tell you that most people who write them really don't know much about looking for work—and too few seem to know much about what makes a good resume. They often have backgrounds as personnel directors (who use resumes to screen people out, not in) or teachers (with little practical experience in actually looking for work). Nice people I'm sure, but not all that well qualified.

Gallery of Best Resumes is different from most resume books for two reasons:

  1. The resumes have all been created by people who write resumes for a living.

  2. David Noble.

I think that these two reasons make this a more useful and important book. Let me explain.

While most resume books are based on one person's opinion of what makes a good resume, *Gallery of Best Resumes* includes resumes written by dozens of professional resume writers. These people make their living helping others produce good resumes, and they sent us their best work. This approach allows for a wide range in writing styles, formats, and designs that just is not possible through any other approach.

But behind this extraordinary collection of resumes is the author, David Noble. Educated in the classics and a graduate of prestigious universities, he brings to this collection a discipline of thought and an understanding of good writing that is simply lacking in most resume books. When I asked him to explain to me how this book was developed, he used this analogy:

> If Plato had been asked, "What is a resume?" he would have asked the questioner what it was for, how it was used, and what it did. Plato would then have tried to imagine the ideal form that a resume should take to fulfill those functions. That, David explained, is deductive reasoning (an advanced form of intuition).

> Aristotle, a pupil of Plato, responding to the same question, would have asked, "Who makes resumes?" and then asked a number of those persons to show him examples. Aristotle would then have sorted through those examples and arranged them into types. From this, he would have determined what a resume is. That, David explained, is inductive reasoning (a scientific method).

Aristotle's method is the one that David Noble used to examine the question, What makes a resume a best resume?

There are, it seems, some things that make one resume stand out above others. Instead of just making assumptions, David Noble examined hundreds of professionally written resumes. After careful analysis, he presents his conclusions in this book—along with lots of outstanding resumes.

One good thing about this book is that you don't have to read either Plato or Aristotle to find out how to write a good resume. It's all here. You can examine carefully on your own the resumes presented in the Gallery or spend some time learning from David the principles of resume writing and, more importantly, how to *use* a resume.

J. Michael Farr

(Mike Farr is the author of several career planning and job search books including his own book on resumes, *The Quick Resume and Cover Letter Book*. Collectively, his books have sold more than one million copies.)

Introduction

Gallery of Best Resumes is a collection of quality resumes from professional resume writers, each with unique perceptions about resumes and resume writing. Unlike many resume books whose selections "look the same," this book contains resumes that look different because they are representations of *real* resumes prepared by professionals and used by actual job seekers throughout the country. Even when several resumes from the same writer appear in the book, the resumes are different because the writer has tailored each one to the needs of the client for whom the resume was written.

Instead of assuming that "one resume style fits all," the writers featured here believe that a client's past experiences and next job target should determine the resume's type, design, and content. The use of *Best* in the book's title reflects this approach to resume making. The resumes are not "best" because they are ideal types for you to copy, but because resume writers have interacted with clients to fashion resumes that seemed best for each client's situation at the time.

This book features resumes from writers who share several important qualities: good listening skills, a sense of what details are appropriate for a particular resume, and flexibility in selecting and arranging the resume's sections. By "hearing between" a client's statements, the perceptive resume writer can detect what kind of job the client really wants. The writer then chooses the information that will best represent the client for the job being sought. Finally, the writer decides on the best arrangement of the information, from the most important to the least important, for that job. With the help of this book, you can create this kind of resume yourself.

How This Book Is Organized

Gallery of Best Resumes consists of three parts. Part I, "101 Best Resume Tips," presents 29 resume writing strategies, 52 design and layout tips, and 20 resume writing style tips for making resumes visually impressive. Many of these strategies and tips were suggested by the resume writers themselves. When one of the writers is the source of a strategy or tip, the writer's name appears in brackets. A reference is given also to one or more Gallery resumes that illustrate the strategy or tip.

Part II is the Gallery itself, containing over 200 resumes and an Addendum from 79 resume writers. Included are five "before" resumes from clients so that you can see how the writers improved these resumes.

Resume writers commonly distinguish between chronological resumes and skills (or functional) resumes. A *chronological resume* is a photo—a snapshot history of what you did and when you did it. A *skills resume* is a painting—an interpretive sketch of what you can do for a future employer. A third kind of resume, known as a *combination resume,* is a mix of recalled history and self-assessment. Besides recollecting "the facts," a combination resume contains self-interpretation and is therefore more like dramatic history than news coverage. All three kinds of resumes are amply illustrated in the Gallery.

The Gallery opens with a special section of 16 resumes printed on quality paper of different colors. This section gives you a sense of how some of the resumes looked in their original form. The improved appearance of resumes on quality paper should encourage you to experiment in producing an outstanding resume of your own.

The resumes in the rest of the Gallery are presented in the following occupational categories:

> Accounting/Finance
> Administrative Assistant/Secretary
> Animal Care
> Career Change
> Communications
> Consultant
> Education/Training
> Graduating/Graduated Student
> Insurance/Real Estate
> Maintenance/Manufacturing
> Management
> Professional Service
> Sales/Marketing
> Technology/Engineering/Science

Within each category, the resumes are generally arranged from the simple to the complex. Most of the resumes are one page, but a number of them are two pages. A few are more than two pages. The names and addresses in the Gallery resumes have been fictionalized to protect the confidentiality of the original clients.

The Gallery offers a wide range of resumes whose features you can use in creating and improving your own resumes. Notice the plural. An important premise of an active job search is that you will not have just one "perfect" resume for all potential employers, but different versions of your resume for different interviews. The Gallery is therefore not a showroom where you say, "I'll take that one." It is a valuable resource of design ideas, expressions, and organizational patterns that can help make your own resume a "best resume" for your next interview.

Creating multiple versions of a resume may seem difficult, but it is easy to do if you have (or have access to) a personal computer and a laser printer or some other kind of printer that can produce quality output. You will also need word processing, desktop publishing, or resume software. If you don't have a computer or a friend who does, don't despair. Most professional resume writers have the hardware and software, and they can make your resume look like those in the Gallery. A local fast-print shop can make your resume look good, but you will probably not get there the kind of advice and service the professional resume writer provides. Of course, if all you have is a typewriter, you can still produce versions of your resume, but you will have to retype the resume for each new version.

Part III, "Best Cover Letter Tips" contains a discussion of some myths about cover letters, plus 30 tips for polishing cover letters. Much of the advice offered here applies also to writing resumes. Included in this part is an exhibit of 25 cover letters. Most of these letters accompanied resumes that appear in the Gallery.

Appendix A, "List of Contributors," contains the names, addresses, and phone numbers of those who contributed resumes and cover letters for this book. The list is arranged alphabetically by state and city. Although most of these resume writers work with local clients, some of the writers work with clients by phone from anywhere in the United States.

Note: Nearly all of the resume writers featured in this book are members of the Professional Association of Resume Writers. Some, through experience, a course of study, and an examination administered by the Association, have earned the designation CPRW, which stands for Certified Professional Resume Writer.

Who This Book Is For

Anyone who wants ideas for creating or improving a resume can benefit from this book. It is especially useful for active job seekers—those who understand the difference between active and passive job searching. A *passive* job seeker waits until jobs are advertised and then mails copies of the same resume, along with a standard cover letter, to a number of Help Wanted ads. An *active* job seeker believes that a resume should be modified for a specific job target *after* having talked in person or by phone to a prospective interviewer *before* a job is announced. To schedule such an interview is to penetrate the "hidden job market." Active job seekers can find in the Gallery's focused resumes a wealth of strategies for targeting a resume for a particular interview. The section "How to Use the Gallery" at the beginning of Part II shows you how to do this.

Besides the active job seeker, any unemployed person who wants to create a more competitive resume or update an old one should find *Gallery of Best Resumes* helpful. It shows the kinds of resumes that professional resume writers are writing, and it showcases resumes for job seekers with particular needs. Here are just a few examples:

- The Career Change resumes are for job seekers moving from one occupational field to another. Some of these resumes are appropriate for individuals trying to break into a field for which they have not been prepared through education or work experience. This category will be of special interest to discharged military personnel who want to reenter the civilian workforce.

- The Graduating/Graduated Student resumes are for anyone from high school juniors and seniors who are saving for college to a dental school graduate. This category includes college students about to graduate as well as those who have recently graduated and offers sample resumes for those seeking entry-level professional jobs in various fields.

- Several of the categories contain resumes for those who are "overqualified." To compete with less-experienced job seekers, these individuals must "tone down" their resumes in order to appear more on a par with other candidates. You will find these resumes particularly useful if you have been laid off because of workforce cuts and must look for a job that may not match your education, experience, or qualifications.

If you are a computer user and your system has desktop publishing capabilities, you can refer to the Gallery's state-of-the-art examples for ideas in desktop publishing your own resume. You do not have to be a computer user, however, to benefit from the examples. The information that you put in your resume is far more important than any design features you might introduce through desktop publishing.

What This Book Can Do for You

Besides providing you with a treasury of quality resumes whose features you can use in your own resumes, this book can help transform your thinking about resumes. If you think that there is one "best" way to create a resume, this book will help you learn how to shape a resume that is best for you as you try to get an interview with a particular person for a specific job.

If you have been told that resumes should be only one page long, the examples of multiple-page resumes in the Gallery will help you see how to distribute information effectively across two or more pages. If you believe that the way to update a resume is to add your latest work experiences to your last resume, this book will show you how to rearrange your resume so that you can highlight the most important information about your experience and skills.

After you have studied "101 Best Resume Tips" in Part I, examined the professionally written resumes in the Gallery in Part II, and reviewed "Tips for Polishing Cover Letters" in Part III, you should be able to create your own resumes worthy of inclusion in any gallery of best resumes.

Part I

101 Best Resume Tips

101 Best Resume Tips
at a Glance

Part I

101 Best Resume Tips

In a passive job search, you rely on your resume to do most of the work for you. An eye-catching resume that stands out above all the others may be your best shot at getting noticed by a prospective employer. If your resume is only average and looks like most of the others in the pile, the chances are great that you won't be noticed and called for an interview. If you want to be singled out because of your resume, it should be somewhere between spectacular and award-winning.

In an active job search, however, your resume complements your efforts at being known to a prospective employer *before* that person receives it. For this reason, you can rely less on your resume for getting someone's attention. Nevertheless, your resume has an important role in an active job search that may include the following activities:

- Talking to relatives, friends, and other acquaintances to meet people who can hire you before a job is available

- Contacting employers directly, using the *Yellow Pages* to identify types of organizations that could use a person with your skills

- Creating phone scripts to speak with the person who is most likely to hire someone with your background and skills

- Walking into a business in person to talk directly to the one who is most likely to hire someone like you

- Using a schedule to keep track of your appointments and callbacks

- Working at least 25 hours a week to search for a job

When you are this active in searching for a job, the quality of your resume confirms the quality of your efforts to get to know the person who might hire you, as well as your worth to the company whose workforce you want to join. An eye-catching resume makes it easier for you to sell yourself directly to a prospective employer. If your resume is mediocre or conspicuously flawed, it will work against you and may undo all of your good efforts in searching for a job.

The following list offers 101 ideas for making resumes visually impressive. Many of the ideas are for making resumes pleasing to the eye, but a number of the ideas are strategies to use in resumes for special cases. Other ideas are for eliminating common writing mistakes and stylistic weaknesses.

Nearly half of the ideas have come from comments of the professional resume writers who submitted resumes for the Gallery in Part II of this book. As mentioned in the Introduction, the name of the writer appears in brackets. Gallery resumes that illustrate the ideas are referenced by resume number.

Some of these ideas can be used with any equipment, from a manual typewriter to a sophisticated computer with desktop publishing software. Other ideas make sense only if you have a computer system with word processing or desktop publishing. Even if you don't have a computer, take some time to read all of the ideas. Then, if you decide to use the services of a professional resume writer, you will be better informed about what the writer can do for you in producing your resume.

Best Resume Writing Strategies

1. **Although many resume books say that you should spell out the name of the state in your address at the top of the resume, consider using the postal abbreviation instead.** The reason is simple: it's an address. Anyone wanting to contact you by mail will probably refer to your name and address on the resume. If they appear there as they should on an envelope, the writer or typist can simply copy the information you supply. If you spell out the name of your state in full, the writer will have to "translate" the name of the state to its postal abbreviation.

    Not everyone knows all the postal abbreviations. and some abbreviations are easily confused. For example, those for Alabama (AL), Alaska (AK), American Samoa (AS), Arizona (AZ), and Arkansas (AR) are easy to mix up. You can prevent confusion and delay simply by using the correct postal abbreviation. As resumes become more "scannable," the use of postal abbreviations in addresses will become a requirement.

    If you decide to use postal abbreviations in addresses, make certain that you do not add a period after the abbreviations, even before ZIP codes. This applies also to postal abbreviations in the addresses of references, if provided.

    Do not, however, use the state postal abbreviation when you are indicating only the city and state (not the mailing address) of a school you attended or a business where you worked. In these cases, it makes sense to write out the name of the state in full.

2. **Adopt a sensible form for phone numbers and then use it consistently.**
    Do this in your resume and in all of the documents you use in your job search. Some forms for phone numbers make more sense than others. Compare the following forms:

123-4567	This form is best for a resume circulated locally, within a region where all the phone numbers have the same area code.
(222) 123-4567	This form is best for a resume circulated in areas with different area codes.
222-123-4567	This form suggests that the area code should be dialed in all cases. But that won't be necessary for prospective employers whose area code is 222. This form should be avoided.
222/123-4567	This form is illogical and should be avoided also. The slash can mean an alternate option, as in ON/OFF. In a phone number, this meaning of a slash makes little sense.
1 (222) 123-4567	This form is long, and the digit 1 isn't necessary. Almost everyone will know that 1 should be used before the area code to dial a long-distance number.

Note: For resumes directed to prospective employers *outside* the United States, be sure to include the correct international prefixes in all phone numbers so that you and your references can be reached easily by phone.

3. **Make your Objective statement focused, interesting, and unique so that it grabs the reader's attention.** If your Objective statement fails to do this, the reader might discard the resume without reading further. An Objective statement can be your first opportunity to sell yourself. For examples of effective Objective statements, see Resumes 11, 18, 22, 23, 34, 39, 41, 47, 59, 61, 63, 64, and many others.

4. **Omit an Objective statement when your goal is to work in another field but you have not determined the kind of job or position you want.** See Resume 62. [Lowry]

5. **In the Experience section, state achievements, not (or not just) duties or responsibilities.** Duties and responsibilities tend to be boring. Achievements can be exciting. The reader probably considers life too short to be bored by lists of duties and responsibilities in a stack of resumes. See Resumes 3, 4, 26, 31, 34, 37, 54, 56, 59, 63, 64, 69, 79, 86, 93, 95, 104, 107, 109, 111, 113, 115, 122, 123, 124, 125, 127, 128, 129, 130, 132, 139, 147, 152, 156, 157, 158, 166, 170, 171, 173, 174, 176, 178, 180, 182, 185, 187, 188, 190, 192, 193, 195, 197, 204, 206.

6. **If you feel you must indicate duties, call attention to special or unusual duties you performed.** For example, if you are an accountant, don't say that you prepared accounting reports and analyzed income statements and balance sheets. What else is new? That's like being a dentist and saying, "I filled cavities and made crowns." What did you do that distinguished you from other accountants? To be noticed, you need to stand above the crowd in ways that display your individuality and work style.

7. **Focus on achievements the reader wants to hear about.** This simple approach is better than the use of "gimmicks." Employers aren't impressed with cuteness but are impressed with a polished, professional presentation that calls attention to your achievements. See Resume 160. [Barr]

8. **Use a series of achievement statements to indicate accomplishments beyond a 9-to-5 workplace.** Compare Resumes 145 and 146. [Busby]

9. **Instead of just listing your achievements, present them as very brief stories, perhaps indicating what you did when something went wrong or needed fixing.** See Resume 107. [Young]

10. **When your work experience is varied, group the entries according to recognizable categories instead of listing all of the entries chronologically.** Within each group, however, list the work experiences by order of importance (from greatest to least) or chronologically (from most recent to earliest). See Resumes 83, 101, 110, 139, and 140.

11. **To make your promotions stand out, list your work experiences chronologically, with the range of dates for each position.** See Resume 25. [Baskin]

12. **Summarize your qualifications and work experiences to avoid having to repeat yourself in the job descriptions.** See Resume 62. [Lowry]

13. **Divide your resume's overall content into three or four categories.** Consider using the following categories:

Professional Qualifications	To highlight skills, knowledge, and experience
Work History	To support the qualifications and provide key job duties and accomplishments
Education	To show fields of study, degrees, grade point average if high, honors, and awards
Activities/Affiliations	To show leadership or excellence outside the workplace

See Resumes 46, 125, and 177. [Wohl]

14. **When your college or university degree is not in the field you are exploring, indicate only your degree but not your field.** For example, indicate Bachelor of Art or Bachelor of Science, but do not include history, English, art, or geology. See Resume 103. [Lawrence]

15. **To appear less like a student and more like an experienced candidate for a specialized job, play down typical education information and play up any experiences related to your job objective.** Distinguish those experiences in a separate section apart from college/university experiences. Consider using the heading Leadership Experience. Instead of listing related courses (a section commonly found on resumes of graduating students), call attention to "areas of emphasis" that seem relevant to the targeted job. See Resume 92. [Ferrell]

16. **Use concrete, specific examples that illustrate possible contributions or benefits you may offer to a new employer.** See Resume 178. [Veith]

17. **Use the resume as a marketing tool rather than a job search document.** A resume that emphasizes experience and accomplishments can easily be made into a marketing or promotional instrument. See Resume 60. [McGoldrick]

18. **If you have had no formal education beyond high school, use a functional-chronological format, which accentuates job titles and includes dates to indicate any positive progression of employment.** See Resume 134. [Lawrence]

19. **To ensure that your profession is not confused with some other profession of a questionable nature, emphasize professional terms, accrediting, special training, and professional experience and skills.** Consider using conservative paper for the resume. Include along with the resume any testimonials, a list of references, and a resume cover so that potential employers have no doubt that you are an ethical, professional worker. See Resume 12. [Styer]

20. **Mention throughout the resume the main theme of your career goal, particularly for a career change.** See Resume 123. [Ferrell]

21. **When many years of work experience are a liability in competing with younger workers, list only your recent work experience but indicate that your prior employment history is available by request.** See Resume 172. [Lawrence]

22. **If you have noticeable periods of unemployment, list relevant community activities during your stay-at-home years.** Also consider listing education before work experience if further education occurred during those years. See Resume 64. [Lawrence]

23. **To diminish the negative impact of a gap in your employment, omit the dates of employment and consider listing employment in some order other than chronological.** See Resume 103. [Lawrence]

24. **If you are a senior citizen wanting to tutor children and educationally deprived adults, omit dates and emphasize areas of expertise, special**

skills, licensure, education, and selected work experience and accomplishments. See Resume 66. [Ferrell]

25. **Create a prominent Skills and Abilities section that draws together skills and abilities you have gained in previous work experience from different careers.** If you have worked for the same company over an entire career, use this section to showcase the skills and abilities you have acquired in different positions with that company. See Resumes 163 and 206. [DiGiorgio]

26. **Indicate on a subline the former name of a company if its name has changed.** See Resume 172. [Lawrence]

27. **Avoid using the archaic word *upon* in the References section.** The common statement "References available upon request" needs to be simplified, updated, or even deleted in resume writing. The word *upon* is one of the finest words of the 14th century, but it's a stuffy word on the eve of the next century. Usually, *on* will do for *upon*. Other possibilities are "References available by request" and "References available." Because most readers of resumes know that applicants can usually provide several reference letters, this statement is probably unnecessary. A reader who is seriously interested in you will ask about reference letters.

28. **Consider presenting a list of projects in a table as an addendum.** See Resume 151. [Culp]

29. **Consider creating an addendum to the resume.** In the addendum, you might highlight your skills, including job-related and transferable skills. Use the addendum *after* an interview and include it with a thank-you note. See Addendum 208. [Bernstein]

Best Resume Design and Layout Tips

30. **Use quality paper correctly.** If you use quality watermarked paper for your resume, be sure to use the right side of the paper. To know which side is the right side, hold a blank sheet of paper up to a light source. If you can see a watermark and "read" it, the right side of the paper is facing you. This is the surface for typing or printing. If the watermark is unreadable or if any characters look backward, you are looking at the "underside" of a sheet of paper—the side that should be left blank if you use only one side of the sheet. For examples of watermarked paper, see the Special Paper section at the beginning of the Gallery in Part II.

    Why should you use the right side of a sheet of paper, with the watermark facing up? You want to show a prospective employer that you are someone who pays attention to details. If you were creating a resume just for yourself, it wouldn't make any difference which side of the sheet you used. But if you go to the trouble of using special paper to impress someone, why not use the paper correctly? If the person who interviews you seems not to notice such things, perhaps you have higher levels of awareness than the interviewer. That insight might give you more confidence during the interview.

31. **Make a resume that matches your personality.** If you are a quiet, reserved person, create a more traditional resume that displays restraint and good taste. If you are a flamboyant person, create a flamboyant resume, using drawing and desktop publishing programs, if possible. Your resume then sends the right signals to the reader to help that person assess you accurately. See Resume 166. [Young]

32. **Use special paper that matches your personality or target profession.** If you are a recent graduate from a law school and are looking for a position with

an established law firm, brilliant white paper may be most fitting for your resume. If you have a sunny disposition, are always optimistic about the future, and are looking for an upbeat job in an exciting new venture, putting your resume on rainbow-colored paper is worth considering. See Resume 74. [Young]

Note: Many designer-type papers, such as those with a rainbow, a marbleized border, or a simulated torn edge, are precut to 8 1/2″ by 11″. For this reason, they could not be included in the Special Paper section of the Gallery. But you might consider such paper for your resume as you look for a type of paper that is suitable for you.

33. **Use adequate "white space."** A sheet of white paper with no words on it is impossible to read. Likewise, a sheet of white paper with words all over it is impossible to read. The goal is to have a comfortable mix of white space and words. If your resume has too many words and not enough white space, the resume looks cluttered and unfriendly. If it has too much white space and too few words, the resume looks skimpy and unimportant. Make certain that adequate white space exists between the main sections. For examples that display good use of white space, see Resumes 2 (through line spacing), 13, 14, 15, 16, 28, 49, 50, 83, 90, 91, 105, 142, 150, 170, 183, and 190.

34. **Make the margins uniform in width and preferably no less than an inch.** Margins are part of the white space of a resume page. If the margins shrink below an inch, the page begins to have a "too much to read" look. An enemy of margins is the one-page rule. If you try to fit more than one page of information on a page, the first temptation is to shrink the margins to make room for the extra material. It is better to shrink the material by paring it down than to reduce the size of the left, right, top, and bottom margins. If you do your resume on a computer, lowering the point size of the type is one way to save the margins.

35. **Be consistent in your use of line spacing.** How you handle line spacing can tell the reader how good you are at details and how consistent you are in your use of them. If, near the beginning of your resume, you insert two line spaces (two hard returns in a word processing program) between two main sections, be sure to put two line spaces between main sections throughout the resume.

36. **Be consistent in your use of horizontal spacing.** If you usually put two character spaces after a period at the end of a sentence, make certain that you use two spaces consistently. The same is true for colons. If you put two spaces after colons, do so consistently.

Note that an em dash—a dash the width of the letter *m*—does not require spaces before or after it. No space should go between the *P* and *O* of P.O. Box. Only one space is needed between the postal abbreviation of a state and the ZIP code. You should insert a space between the first and second initials of a person's name, as in I. M. Jobseeker (not I.M. Jobseeker). These conventions have become widely adopted in English and business communications. If, however, you use other conventions, be sure to be consistent. In resumes, as in grammar, consistency is more important than conformity.

37. **Make certain that characters, lines, and images contrast well with the paper.** The quality of "ink" depends on the device used to type or print your resume. If you use a typewriter or a dot-matrix printer with a cloth ribbon, check that the ribbon is fresh enough to make a dark impression. If you use a typewriter or a printer with a carbon tape, make certain that your paper has a texture that allows the characters to adhere permanently. (For a test, send yourself a copy of your resume and see how it makes the trip through the mail.) If you use an inkjet or laser printer, check that the characters are sharp and clean, without ink smudges or traces of extra toner.

After much use, a cloth ribbon in a typewriter or a daisywheel printer may cause some characters (especially *a, e, o, g,* and *p*) to look darker than others. The reason probably is that ink has collected in the characters on the type bars or print wheel. To fix this problem, use a toothbrush and a safe solvent to clean the type.

38. **Use vertical alignment in stacked text.** Resumes usually contain tabbed or indented text. Make certain that this "stacked" material is aligned vertically. Misalignment can ruin the appearance of a well-written resume. Try to set tabs or indents that control this text throughout a resume instead of having a mix of tab stops in different sections. If you use a word processor, make certain that you understand the difference between tabbed text and indented text, as in the following examples:

   Tabbed text: This text was tabbed over one tab stop
                         before the writer started to write the sentence.

   Indented text: This text was indented once before the
                         writer started to write the sentence.

   Note: In a number of word processing programs, the Indent command is useful for ensuring the correct vertical alignment of proportionally spaced, stacked text. After you issue the Indent command, lines of wrapped text are vertically aligned automatically until you terminate the command by pressing Enter.

39. **For the vertical alignment of dates, try left- or right-aligning the dates.** This technique is especially useful in chronological resumes and combination resumes. For examples of left-aligned dates, see Resumes 2, 22, 25, 28, and 35. Compare these resumes with Resume 1, in which left-aligned dates are indented slightly. For right-aligned dates, look at Resumes 3, 4, 10, 13, 14, 17, and 18. See also Resume 64, which uses both left- and right-aligned dates.

40. **If you must specify two addresses, such as those for home and school, left-align one address and right-align the other for a balanced look at the top of the page.** See Resumes 40 and 82. Compare these with Resumes 84, 92, 98, and 111, in which an address is at the right margin but not right-aligned.

41. **For an unconventional, eye-catching look, place the name, address, and phone number farther down on the page.** See Resumes 53 and 189. [Busby]

42. **Use as many pages as you need for portraying yourself adequately to a specific interviewer about a particular job.** Try to limit your resume to one page, but set the upper limit at four pages. No rule about the number of pages makes sense in all cases. The determining factors are a person's qualifications and experiences, the requirements of the job, and the interests and pet peeves of the interviewer. If you know that an interviewer refuses to look at a resume longer than a page, that says it all. You need to deliver a one-page resume if you want to get past the first gate. It *is* possible to compress a great deal of information into a small number of pages. See Resume 68, which was originally a 27-page curriculum vitae and is now just two pages!

43. **Even though it is not a good idea to use one sheet of paper for a two-page resume, consider using both sides of a single sheet in special cases.** See, for example, Resume 76. This style can be used by someone who does "cold calling" to look for a job, or who distributes resumes (containing a personal profile) without a cover letter or other enclosure. [McNamee]

44. **If you want to make a one-page resume "space efficient" but comfortable, try writing most of the way across the page, but use short paragraphs.** Long paragraphs extending across the page take up valuable space and seem lengthy. See Resume 177, which has short paragraphs. [Wohl]

45. **Use a two-page resume to expand a list of achievements important for a position.** This style might be appropriate if you are seeking a job within the same company under new ownership. See Resume 23. [Nieboer]

46. **Instead of following a one-page rule, consider using two-page brochure style for a detailed work history when you want to include every job in a career or mention extensive training and many personal accomplishments.** See Resumes 130 and 131. [Lichtenstein]

47. **For a striking, unusual look, try experimenting with border designs.** If you don't have a computer system that can handle graphic lines, you may need the help of someone who does. See Resume 150.

48. **When you have letters of recommendation, use quotations from them as testimonials in the first column of a two-column format.** Devoting a whole column to the positive opinions of "external authorities" helps to make a resume convincing as well as impressive. See Resume 185. [Culp]

49. **Consider using three-column newsletter style to give your resume a distinctive and different look.** See Resume 54. [Young]

50. **Unless you enlist the services of a professional printer or skilled desktop publisher, resist the temptation to use full justification for text.** The price that you pay for a straight right margin is uneven word spacing. Words may appear too close together on some lines and too spread out on others. Although the resume might look like typeset text, you lose readability. See also Tip 4 in Part III of this book.

51. **If you can choose a typeface for your resume, use a serif font for greater readability.** Serif fonts have little lines extending from the top, bottom, and end of a character. These fonts tend to be easier to read than sans serif (without serif) fonts, especially in low-light conditions. Compare the following font examples:

Serif	**Sans Serif**
Century Schoolbook	Franklin Gothic
Courier	Futura
Times New Roman	Helvetica

Words like *minimum* and *abilities* are more readable in a serif font.

52. **If possible, avoid using monospaced type like this Courier type.** Courier was a standard of business communications during the 1960s and 1970s. Because of its widespread use, it is now considered "common." It also takes up a lot of space, so you can't pack as much information on a page with Courier type as you can with a proportionally spaced type like Times Roman.

53. **Think twice before using all uppercase letters in parts of your resume.** A common misconception is that uppercase letters are easier to read than lowercase letters. Actually, the ascenders and descenders of lowercase letters make them more distinguishable from each other and therefore more recognizable than uppercase letters. For a test, look at a string of uppercase letters and throw them gradually out of focus by squinting. The uppercase letters become a blur sooner than lowercase letters.

54. **Think twice about underlining some words in your resume.** Underlining defeats the purpose of serifs at the bottom of characters by blending with the serifs. In trying to emphasize words, you lose some visual clarity. This is especially true if you use underlining with uppercase letters in centered or side headings. Of course, if you have no way to use italic characters, you may have to underline some words, such as titles of books in a Publications section of a curriculum vitae.

55. **If you have access to many fonts through word processing or desktop publishing, beware of becoming "font happy" and turning your resume into a font circus.** Frequent font changes can distract the reader adversely, **AND SO CAN GAUDY DISPLAY TYPE.**

56. **To make your resume stand out, consider using a nonstandard format with the headings in unconventional display type.** See Resume 156. When you compare this idea with the preceding idea, you can see that one of the basic rules of resume making is, "Anything goes." What is usually fitting for resumes for most prospective jobs is not always the most appropriate resume strategy for every job opportunity. [Busby]

57. **Be aware of the value differences of black type.** Some typefaces are light; others are dark. Notice the following lines:

    A quick brown fox jumps over the lazy dog.
    A quick brown fox jumps over the lazy dog.

    Most typefaces fall somewhere in-between. With the variables of height, width, thickness, serifs, angles, curves, spacing, ink color, ink density, boldfacing, and typewriter double-striking, you can see that type offers an infinite range of values from light to dark. Try to make your resume more visually interesting by offering stronger contrasts between light type and dark type. See Resumes 2, 19, 29, 106, 185, and 190.

58. **Use italic characters carefully.** Whenever possible, use italic characters instead of underlining when you need to italicize the titles of periodicals or books. See, for example, Resumes 36 and 48. Think twice about using italic throughout your resume, however. The reason is that italic characters are less readable than normal characters. You might consider using italic to call attention to achievements. See Resumes 3, 38, 115, and 122.

59. **Use boldfacing to make different job experiences more evident.** You might use this strategy if you are trying to open as many doors in a field as possible. When a typewriter or dot-matrix printer is the only printing device available, try combining underlining with boldfacing to make different career experiences stand out. See Resume 175. If the underlining impairs the readability of the boldfacing, use only boldfacing. [Markman]

60. **For attention-getting headings, make them white on black if you use software that has this capability.** See Resume 55.

61. **If you use word processing or desktop publishing and have a suitable printer, use special characters to enhance the look of your resume.** For example, use typographic quotation marks (" and ") instead of their typewriter equivalents (" "). Use an em dash (—) instead of two hyphens (--) for a dash. To separate dates, try using an en dash (a dash the width of the letter *n*) instead of a hyphen, as in 1993–1994.

62. **To call attention to an item in a list, use a bullet (•) or a box (□) instead of a hyphen (-).** Browse through the Gallery and notice how bullets are used effectively as attention getters.

63. **When it is not possible to type or print bullets, use an alternative symbol, such as side-by-side hyphens (--).** See Resumes 27 and 140.

64. **Use bullets to combine skills and accomplishments with duties and responsibilities.** This approach is better than a "laundry list" of duties in selling talents to a prospective employer. See Resume 178. [Veith]

65. **For variety, try using bullets of a different style, such as diamond (◆) bullets, rather than the usual round or square bullets.** Examples with diamonds are Resumes 22, 28, 120, 126, 130, and 131. For other kinds of "bullets," see Resumes 11, 23, 31, 37, 53, 57, 63, 93, 102, 135, 144, 170, and 173. [Hosek]

66. **Make a bullet a little smaller than the lowercase letters that appear after it.** Disregard any ascenders or descenders on the letters. Compare the following bullet sizes:

· Too small   ● Too large   ● Better   • Just right

67. **When you use bullets, make certain that the bulleted items go beyond the superficial and contain information that employers really want to know.** Many short bulleted statements that say nothing special can affect the reader negatively. Brevity is not always the best strategy with bullets. For examples of substantial bulleted items, see Resumes 99, 111, and 193. [Noonan]

68. **If possible, visually coordinate the resume, cover letter, and envelope with the same graphic to catch the attention of the reader even before that person sees the resume.** See Resumes 90 and 167. Each of these resumes was sent in an envelope that displayed the graphic shown in the resume. [Robertson]

69. **Use a graphic motif (such as a torn edge) throughout a system of boxed headings to unify the resume visually.** See Resume 55.

70. **When the amount of information justifies a longer resume, repeat a particular graphic, such as a filled square bullet (■) or a round bullet, to unify the entire resume.** See Resumes 118, 161, and 207.

71. **Try to make graphics match the subject of the resume.** For example, see Resume 154 for Madd Maxx Hammer. Four 3-D "boxes" move away to four different vanishing points on three different horizons. Such an approach is experimental and innovative from an artistic point of view. This playful "madness" seems to match Madd Maxx, who is noted for discovering new rock "talents before their time."

72. **Substitute a Profile statement for an Objective statement and use attention-getting, side-by-side boxes for a special effect.** See Resumes 145 and 146. Compare these resumes with Resume 164. [Busby]

73. **Use a horizontal line to separate the name and address from the rest of the resume.** If you browse through the Gallery, you can see many resumes that use horizontal lines this way.

74. **Use horizontal lines to separate the different sections of the resume.** See Resumes 10, 15, 50, 55, 81, 83, 115, 122, 128, 142, 143, 190, and 201. See also Resume 203, whose lines are interrupted by the section headings.

75. **To call attention to a resume section, use horizontal lines to enclose it.** See Resumes 26, 48, 53, 65, 66, 74, 92, 98, 102, 128, 148, 173, 175, 176, 184, 189, 192, and 202. See also Resumes 130 and 164, in which two or more sections are enclosed by horizontal lines.

76. **Change the thickness of part of a horizontal line to call attention to a section heading below the line.** See Resume 15.

77. **Use horizontal lines between sections and then vary the positions of the section headings along the lines. To help the reader locate a heading quickly, thicken each horizontal line at the position of the heading.** See Resume 91.

78. **Use a vertical line with two-column format to include testimonials with your resume.** See Resume 185.

79. **Use a vertical line to spice up your resume.** See Resumes 84, 117, 137, and 185. See also Resumes 54, 65, and 119, which use both vertical and horizontal lines to define areas of the resume.

80. **Use diagonal lines to give the resume a different look.** See Resumes 107, 150, and 154.

81. **Use shaded boxes to make a page visually more interesting.** See Resumes 132 (a shaded column with shaded top and bottom borders), 153, 165 (shaded column), and 188 (originally the entire area in the box). Compare these boxes with the *shadow* boxes in Resumes 119, 145, and 146.

Best Resume Writing Style Tips

82. **Check that words at the beginning of lists are parallel.** For example, notice the bulleted items in lists in Resume 1. In the first list, *assist* and *receive* are in present tense. These verbs are used for duties in the current job. In the third list, *recruited, contacted, conducted, assisted,* and *received* are in past tense. These verbs are used for duties in a previous job. This kind of parallelism makes each list easy to read and visually appealing. If the parallelism is disrupted by a change in tense, such as using *received* after *assist* in the first list, the list would have a hitch in it and be harder to read.

83. **Check that words or phrases in a list are parallel.** For example, notice in Resume 61 the list of positions in the Summary of Experience section. All of the entries begin with nouns. To begin one of them with a verb form would be jarring.

84. **Use capital letters correctly.** Resumes usually contain many of the following:

    • Names of people, companies, organizations, government agencies, awards, and prizes

    • Titles of job positions and publications

    • References to academic fields (such as chemistry, English, and mathematics)

    • Geographic regions (such as the Midwest, the East, the state of California, and Oregon State)

    Because of such words, resumes are mine fields for the misuse of uppercase letters. When you don't know whether a word should have an initial capital letter, don't guess. Consult a dictionary, a handbook on style, or some other authoritative source. Often a reference librarian can provide the information you need. If so, you are only a phone call away from an accurate answer.

85. **Check that capital letters and hyphens are used correctly in computer terms.** If you want to show in a Computer Experience section that you have used certain hardware and software, you may give the opposite impression if you don't use uppercase letters and hyphens correctly. Note the correct use of capitals and hyphens in the following names:

LaserJet III	Hewlett-Packard
PageMaker	MS-DOS
WordPerfect	PC DOS

    The reason that many computer product names have an internal uppercase letter is for the sake of a trademark. A word with unusual spelling or capitalization is trademarkable. When you use the correct forms of these words, you are honoring trademarks and registered trademarks.

86. **Use all uppercase letters for most acronyms.** An *acronym* is a pronounceable word usually formed from the initial letters of the words in a compound term, or sometimes from multiple letters in those words. Note the following examples:

BASIC   Beginner's All-Purpose Symbolic Instruction Code
COBOL   COmmon Business-Oriented Language
FORTRAN   FORmula TRANslator

An acronym like *radar* (*ra*dio *d*etecting *a*nd *r*anging) has become so common that it is no longer all uppercase.

87. **Be aware that you may need to use a period with some abbreviations.** An *abbreviation* is a word shortened by removing the latter part of the word or by deleting some letters within the word. Here are some examples:

adj. for *adjective*   *amt.* for *amount*
adv. for *adverb*   *dept.* for *department*

Usually, you can't pronounce an abbreviation as a word. Sometimes, however, an abbreviation is a set of uppercase letters (without periods) that you can pronounce as letters. AFL-CIO, CBS, NFL, and YMCA are examples.

88. **Be sure to spell every word correctly.** A resume with just one misspelling is not impressive and may undermine all the hours you spent putting it together. Worse than that, one misspelling may be what the reader is looking for to screen you out, particularly if you are applying for a position that requires accuracy with words.

If you use word processing and have a spelling checker, you may be able to catch any misspellings. Be wary of spelling checkers, however. They can detect a misspelled word but cannot detect when you have inadvertently used a wrong word (*to* for *too*, for example). Be wary also of letting someone else check your resume. If the other person is not a good speller, you may not get any real help. The best authority is a good dictionary.

89. **For words that have a couple of correct spellings, use the preferred form.** This form is the one that appears first in a dictionary. For example, if you see the entry **trav•el•ing** *or* **trav•el•ling,** the first form (with one *l*) is the preferred spelling. If you make it a practice to use the preferred spelling, you will build consistency in your resumes and cover letters.

90. **Avoid British spellings.** These slip into American usage through books published in Great Britain. Note the following words:

British Spelling	American Spelling
acknowledgement	acknowledgment
centre	center
judgement	judgment
towards	toward

91. **Avoid hyphenating words with such prefixes as *co-, micro-, mid-, mini-, multi-, non-, pre-, re-,* and *sub-.*** Many people think that words with these prefixes should have a hyphen after the prefix, but most of these words should not. The following words are spelled correctly:

coauthor	microcomputer	minicomputer
coworker	midpoint	multicultural
cowriter	midway	multilevel

| nondisclosure | prearrange | reenter |
| nonfunctional | prequalify | subdirectory |

Note: If you look in a dictionary for a word with a prefix and can't find the word, look for the prefix itself in the dictionary. You might find there a small-print listing of a number of words that have the prefix.

92. **Be aware that compounds (combinations of words) present special problems for hyphenation.** Writers' handbooks and books on style do not always agree on how compounds should be hyphenated. Many compounds are evolving from *open* compounds to *hyphenated* compounds to *closed* compounds. In different dictionaries, you can therefore find the words *copy editor, copy-editor,* and *copyeditor.* No wonder the issue is confusing! Most style books do agree, however, that when some compounds appear as an adjective before a noun, the compound should be hyphenated. When the same compound appears after a noun, hyphenation is unnecessary. Compare the following two sentences:

> I scheduled well-attended conferences.
> The conferences I scheduled were well attended.

For detailed information about hyphenation, see a recent edition of *The Chicago Manual of Style.* You should be able to find a copy at a local library.

93. **Be sure to hyphenate so-called *permanent* hyphenated compounds.** Usually, you can find these by looking them up in a dictionary. You can spot them easily because they have a "long hyphen" (–) for visibility in the dictionary. Hyphenate these words (with a standard hyphen) wherever they appear, before or after a noun. Here are some examples:

all-important	self-employed
day-to-day	step-by-step
full-blown	time-consuming

94. **Use the correct form for certain verbs and nouns combined with prepositions.** You may need to consult a dictionary for correct spelling and hyphenation. Compare the following examples:

start up	(verb)
start-up	(noun)
start-up	(adj.)
startup	(noun, computer industry)
startup	(adj., computer industry)

95. **Avoid using shortcut words, such as abbreviations like *thru* or foreign words like *via*.** Spell out *through* and use *by* for *via.*

96. **Use the right words.** The issue here is correct usage, which often means the choice of the right word or phrase from a group of two or more possibilities. The following words and phrases are often used incorrectly:

alternate (adj.)	Refers to an option used every other time. OFF is the alternate option to ON in an ON/OFF switch.
alternative	Refers to an option that can be used at any time. If Cheerios and Wheaties are alternative cereals for breakfast, you can have Cheerios three days in a row if you like. The common mistake is to use *alternate* when the correct word is *alternative.*
center around	A common illogical expression. Draw a circle and then try to draw its center around it. You can't. Use *center in* or *center on* as logical alternatives to *center around.*

For information about the correct usage of words, consult a usage dictionary or the usage section of a writer's handbook.

97. Use numbers consistently. Numbers are often used inconsistently with text. Should you present a number as a numeral or spell out the number as a word? One approach is to spell out numbers *one* through *nine* but present numbers 10 and above as numerals. Different approaches are taught in different schools, colleges, and universities. Use the approach you have learned, but be consistent.

98. Use (or don't use) the serial comma consistently. How should you punctuate a series of three or more items? If, for example, you say in your resume that you increased sales by 100 percent, opened two new territories, and trained four new salespersons, the comma before *and* is called the *serial comma.* It is commonly omitted in newspapers, magazine articles, advertisements, and business documents; but it is often used for precision in technical documents or for stylistic reasons in academic text, particularly in the Humanities.

How the serial comma began to disappear is unknown. One story is that two typesetters agreed to omit serial commas when they ran out of commas in their type drawer. They continued to leave out serial commas, and the practice spread. Whether you use the serial comma should depend on your occupation and where you plan to work. Consistency is what matters. If you use the serial comma some of the time in your resume, you should use it all of the time.

99. Use semicolons correctly. Semicolons are useful because they help to distinguish visually the items in a series when the items themselves contain commas. Suppose that you have the following entry in your resume:

> Increased sales by 100 percent, opened two new territories, which were in the Midwest, trained four new salespersons, who were from Georgia, and increased sales by 250 percent.

The extra commas (before *which* and *who*) throw the main items of the series out of focus. By separating the main items with semicolons, you can bring them back into focus:

> Increased sales by 100 percent; opened two new territories, which were in the Midwest; trained four new salespersons, who were from Georgia; and increased sales by 250 percent.

Use a semicolon even if just one item in the series has an internal comma.

100. Avoid using colons after headings. A colon indicates that something is to follow. A heading indicates that something is to follow. A colon after a heading is therefore redundant.

101. Use dashes correctly. One of the purposes of a dash (an em dash or two hyphens) is to introduce a comment or afterthought about preceding information. A colon *anticipates* something to follow, but a dash *looks back* to something already said. Two dashes are sometimes used before and after a parenthetical remark—a related but nonessential remark such as this—within a sentence. In this case, the dashes are like parentheses, but more formal.

Part II

The Gallery

The Gallery at a Glance

Part II

The Gallery

How to Use the Gallery

You can learn much from the Gallery just by browsing through it. To make the best use of this resource, however, read the following suggestions before you begin.

Examine the resumes on special paper at the beginning of the Gallery. These 16 examples show how quality paper can enhance the appearance of a resume. The papers range in color from whites to blues and include ivory, brown, gold, a warm gray, and a couple of cool grays. Some of these papers are watermarked, and most are laser compatible. Paper that is not laser compatible can be used if a resume is printed professionally. Most of the papers have a weight of 24 lb., which is widely used for resumes. Some of the paper samples have texture that you can feel or view by holding the sheet up to a light source. Notice what colors are not included: pink, orange, green, purple, and darker values of any color.

Look at the resumes in the category containing your field, related fields, or your target occupation. Notice what kinds of resumes other people have used to find similar jobs. Always remember, though, that your resume should not be "canned." It should not look just like someone else's resume but should reflect your own background, unique experiences, and goals.

Use the Gallery primarily as an "idea book." Even if you don't find a resume for your specific occupation or job, be sure to look at all of the resumes for ideas you can borrow or adapt. You may be able to modify some of the sections or statements with information that applies to your own situation or job target.

Study the ways professional resume writers have formatted the names, addresses, and phone numbers of the subjects. In most instances, this information appears at the top of the first page of the resume. In a couple of resumes, you will find this information in the middle of the first page. Look at type styles, size of type, and use of boldface. See whether the personal information is centered on lines, spread across a line, or located near the margin on one side of a page. Look for the use of horizontal lines to separate this information from the rest of the resume, or to separate the address and phone number from the person's name.

Look at each resume to see what section appears first after the personal information. Then compare those same sections across the Gallery. For example, look just at the resumes that have a Goal or an Objective statement as the first section. Compare the length, clarity, and use of words. Do these statements contain complete sentences, or one or more partial lines of thought? Are some statements better than others from your point of view? Do you see one or more Objective statements that

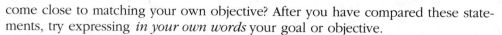

come close to matching your own objective? After you have compared these statements, try expressing *in your own words* your goal or objective.

Repeat this "horizontal comparison" for each of the sections across the Gallery. Compare all of the Education sections, all of the Qualifications sections, and so on. As you make these comparisons, continue to note differences in length, the kinds of words and phrases used, and the effectiveness of the content. Jot down any ideas that might be true for you. Then put together similar sections for your own resume.

As you compare sections across the Gallery, pay special attention to the Career Highlights, Qualifications, and Experience sections. Notice how skills and accomplishments are worked into these sections. Skills and accomplishments are *variables* that you can select to put a certain "spin" on your resume as you pitch it toward a particular interviewer or job. Your observations here should be especially valuable for your own resume versions.

After you have examined the resumes "horizontally" (section by section), compare them "vertically" (design by design). To do this, you need to determine which resumes have the same sections in the same order, and then compare just those resumes. For example, look for resumes that have personal information at the top, an Objective statement, an Experience section, an Education section, and finally a line about references. (Notice that the section heads may differ slightly. Instead of the word *Experience,* you might find *Work Experience* or *Employment.*) When you examine the resumes in this way, you are looking at their *structural design,* which means the order in which the various sections appear. The same order can appear in resumes of different fields or jobs, so it important to explore the whole Gallery and not limit your investigation to resumes in your field or related fields.

Developing a sense of resume structure is extremely important because it enables you to emphasize the most important information about yourself. A resume is a little like a newspaper article—read quickly and usually discarded before the reader finishes. That is why the information in newspaper articles often dwindles in significance toward the end. For the same reason, the most important, attention-getting information about you should be at or near the top of your resume. What follows should appear in order of descending significance.

If you know that the reader will be more interested in your education than your work experience, put your Education section before your Experience section. If you know that the reader will be interested in your skills regardless of your education and work experience, put your Skills section at or near the beginning of your resume. In this way, you can help to ensure that anyone who reads only *part* of your resume will read the "best about you." Your hope is that this information will encourage the reader to read on to the end of the resume and, above all, take an interest in you.

Compare the resumes according to visual design features, such as the use of horizontal and vertical lines, borders, boxes, bullets, white space, graphics, and inverse type (light characters on a dark background). Notice which resumes have more visual impact at first glance and which ones make no initial impression. Do some of the resumes seem more inviting to read than others? Which ones are less appealing because they have too much information, or too little? Which ones seem to have the right balance of information and white space?

After comparing the visual design features, choose the design ideas that might improve your own resume. You will want to be selective here and not try to work every design possibility into your resume. As in writing, "less is more" in resume making, especially when you integrate design features with content.

Resumes on Special Paper at a Glance

Note: The resumes in this section were submitted originally on special paper different from the paper samples provided here. The original paper and these samples correspond in quality but differ in other respects, such as brand, name, color, texture, and weight.

SUSAN R. SMOAK

400 Newtonia Circle ● Beauview, SC 00000 ● (000) 000-0000

CAREER OBJECTIVE: Seeking an entry-level Human Services position with the goal of moving into management.

EDUCATION: Winthrop College, Winthrop, South Carolina
Bachelor of Social Work

WORK EXPERIENCE:

March 1993 - Present
BLUETOWN COUNTY HEALTH DEPARTMENT (Particular Department)
Beauview, South Carolina
Job Title: Administrative Assistant B (Temporary)
- Assist with purchase requisition
- Receive and verify small parcel

June 1992 - March 1993
EARL T. BROWN VETERAN MEMORIAL
Lancaster, South Carolina
Job Title: Medical Social Worker
- Assist patients and family with discharge planning
- Communicate and work with physicians and significant others for an appropriate discharge plan
- Schedule and arrange all nursing home and rehabilitation transfers
- Refer patients to appropriate agencies upon their request

June 1991 - June 1992
BRIGHTWELL HEALTH CARE CENTER
Any Town, South Carolina
Job Title: Admissions Coordinator/Social Worker
- Recruited potential candidates for nursing home placement
- Contacted various agencies and family members
- Conducted and finalized the admissions process
- Assisted up to 149 residents on routine basis
- Received and investigated all client and family grievances

August 1989 - May 1990
DEPARTMENT OF SOCIAL SERVICES
Some City, South Carolina
Job Title: Intern Student
- Interviewed clients
- Evaluated home settings
- Attended court hearings and staffings
- Monitored visitation among clients

October 1987
SOME AVENUE DAY CARE CENTER
Winthrop, South Carolina
Job Title: Volunteer Worker
- Conducted arts and crafts
- Assisted in preparing lunches
- Monitored clients during activities

REFERENCES FURNISHED UPON REQUEST

Chronological. *Nancy P. Stein, Columbia, South Carolina.*
Chronological format shows continual work since graduation. Positions easy to find through use of italic for Job Title. Duties for each job are grammatically parallel.

1

THOMAS S. MORROW

2200 Willow Street . Newington, Pennsylvania . 00000
(000) 000-0000

OBJECTIVE   Position as electrician in electrical construction

ACHIEVEMENTS

"Outstanding Senior Award." Electrical Occupations
Parliamentarian for Opening/Closing Competitions
President. Some Very Important Clubs of America

EMPLOYMENT HISTORY

May 1989   JOHN J. SMITH AND SONS - Newington, PA
to Present

Electrician
Perform electrical construction procedures in residential, commercial,
and industrial installations. Applied OSHA safety standards.

May 1988   NEWINGS ELECTRIC COOPERATIVE - Some Town, PA
to May 1989

Hydro Plant Operator
Charge of start-ups and shut-downs, meter readings, piezometer
readings. Performed general maintenance.

1986   BROWN PAPER PRODUCTS - Newington, PA
and 1987

Machine Operator/Hand Packer
Summer employment through college program. Operated Staple
Machine, "L" Sealer, Padline. Packed notebooks and folders.

EDUCATION

August 1986   SOME VILLAGE COMMUNITY COLLEGE - SOME VILLAGE, PA
to April 1988

Associated Degree - Electrical Occupations
Troubleshooting/Safety, English Composition I, Construction Labs
I, II, III, and IV, Residential, Commercial, Industrial Wiring, AC/DC
Fundamentals, Industrial Motor Control, Programmable Logic Control.

"On The Job Training"
Selected by the instructor to participate in the program because of
dependability and accuracy displayed on lab projects.

September 1983   NEWINGTON AREA HIGH SCHOOL - NEWINGTON, PA
June 1986

Diploma - General Curriculum
Basketball Manager, Member of the Soccer Team
Mathematics, Science, English, U.S. History

NEWINGTON AREA VOCATIONAL TECH. SCHOOL - MUD CREEK, PA

Diploma - Electrical Occupations
Theoretical and practical background in electrical circuitry and
terminology. Learned to handle tools and material properly.

REFERENCES   Available upon request

Chronological. Margaret M. Hilling, Huntingdon, Pennsylvania.
Person's name, section heads, positions, educational degree, training program, and diplomas
are all easy to see at a glance because of boldfacing and line spacing.

2

Christopher T. Smart

1304 Valley View Drive
Oakton, Ohio 45000
(614) 555-5555

OBJECTIVE

To obtain a challenging position as a Social Studies teacher of grades 7-12.

EDUCATION

OHIO UNIVERSITY, Oakton, Ohio - June 1993
Bachelor of Science in Education - Social Studies Comprehensive
Certified Government and History, Grades 7-12
Associate Degree in Communications

**RELATED
EXPERIENCE**

Student Teacher   3/93-6/93
HAMILTON HIGH SCHOOL, Beaver, Ohio

*Effectively combined classroom management and instructional
skills to teach Social Studies while encouraging students to strive
for maximum individual success.*

- Developed innovative learning strategies and designed lesson
  plans for government and history classes
- Independently taught classes
- Supervised and managed class to facilitate individual and group
  learning

Tutor   1/93-3/93
ABLE (Adult Basic Literacy Education) LAB, Oakton, Ohio

*Encouraged adults to attain educational goals by designing and
implementing individualized programs to teach basic reading,
writing and mathematical skills while bolstering self-confidence
and commitment to learning and personal growth.*

- Developed individualized learning program for students
- Interacted with adults gaining skills necessary for GED
- Tutored on a one-to-one basis
- Encouraged continued commitment to education

Student Observer   12/92
SMITH HIGH SCHOOL, Sandhill, Ohio

*Attained expanded understanding of special needs and
challenges to be met in rural school systems.*

- Analyzed effect of rural environment on educational process
- Assessed differences between students in rural and city schools
- Evaluated escalating need for quality teachers in impoverished
  school systems

Field Experience   9/91-11/91
OAKTON MIDDLE SCHOOL, Oakton, Ohio

*Expanded foundation of practical classroom experience while
developing improved interaction and teaching skills.*

- Assisted teacher with 7th grade Social Studies class
- Coordinated learning programs for challenged students
- Motivated and tutored students on individual basis

References Available Upon Request

Chronological. *Melissa L. Kasler, Athens, Ohio.*
Recent graduate's training experiences made to look like job experiences to offset lack of
employment. Italicized achievements and bulleted duties build the person's image.

3

JASON DEAN

(209) 222-2222 • 5000 West Blue • Athens, CA 93000

EXPERTISE: Sales Management ... Marketing ... Account Management

SUMMARY OF QUALIFICATIONS:

Over 14 years' successful experience in sales management and sales. Consistently made significant contributions to corporate goals for business growth and profits. Created, implemented, and managed productive marketing programs for tangibles and intangibles.

Customer-driven focus: Built strong business partnerships, maximized account retention, and improved customer loyalty. **Team-oriented:** Recruited, motivated, and managed productive sales and sales support teams.

PROFESSIONAL EXPERIENCE:

<u>GENERAL SALES MANAGER</u> -- Special Sales, Athens, CA   4/92 - Present
                                                                                   and 2/80 - 11/87

- Promoted from Sales Manager to General Sales Manager in less than one year.
- Directly accountable for sales management, marketing, promotions, and programming.
- Manage national accounts. Negotiate co-op advertising and sponsorship packages.
- Was recruited to **revitalize sales** -- accomplished this goal through restructuring sales force, conducting intensive sales training, and implementing successful incentive programs.
- Personally **generated significant new business.**

<u>AGENT MARKETING COORDINATOR</u> -- Village Sales, Athens, CA   10/89 - 3/92

- Liaison between Village Sales and 30 retail outlets to coordinate indirect distribution channel for cable service.
- Motivated and trained sales force; created successful incentive programs.
- **One of 20 nationwide** to earn "Manager Achievement Award" (awarded for design of successful promotions and management of outside agencies in a highly regulated market).
- Selected to **"Circle of Excellence"** (awarded to one per market nationally for overall performance).
- Featured in national monthly newsletter for consistently exceeding monthly goals.
- Won numerous incentive awards (including trip to London) for quota achievement.

<u>GENERAL SALES MANAGER</u> -- New Town Leasing, Athens, CA   11/87 - 2/89

- Managed and motivated sales team. Coordinated marketing strategies.
- Personally sold to and serviced regional accounts.
- Increased sales 500%; advanced from 15th to 3rd highest billing station in market among 30 stations.

EDUCATION:

DEGREE PROGRAM: A.S., Business Merchandising & Management, California City College

Sales and Sales Management Seminars:
- Smith & Associates: "Fundamentals of Consultant Sales," "Leading High Performance Sales Teams"
- IBM Training: "Selling Technology," "Selling Naturally," "Retail Sales Skills and Management"
- CareerTrack Seminars: "High Impact Communication Skills"

Combination. *Susan B. Whitcomb, CPRW, Fresno, California.*
Expertise statement, strong qualifications, and significant achievements in current and
previous jobs offset limited education. Note boldfacing and good use of parallel verbs.

4

LEONARD A. GETREADY

2000 Wellview Drive Suite A-1234, Orlando, GA 30000 **(000) 000-0000**

SUMMARY OF QUALIFICATIONS

Over seven years of successful management primarily in the banking and the financial industry. Acquired competent knowledge in consumer/ commercial lending and cost accounting of financial portfolios. Highlights:

- Recognized for efficient and accurate management control methods that were consistently rated at grade "A"
- Established marketing strategies that resulted in 60% increase of client portfolios

EXPERIENCE

Associate Account Executive

CCC TELECOMMUNICATIONS, Beauville, NC 1990 - 1991

Evaluated market potential, developed effective marketing strategies and increased overall revenues. Attained strong product knowledge and expanded client base while maintaining excellent customer relations.

Financial Service Manager

NEW INVESTOR BANK, Somerville, NY 1987 - 1989

Researched and implemented business developmental plans. Executed marketing strategies and achieved business objectives. Initiated forecast, budgeting, and coordinated plans with Area Sales Manager. Administered various financial seminars and supplemented product knowledge. Acted as a Consultant and interacted daily with diverse clients on financial planning.

Operations Manager/Financial Sales Support Officer

FIRST COUNTY BANK, Albany, New Jersey 1986 - 1987

Monitored branch performance, trained and motivated staff, and maintained efficient operations. Developed a minority business plan that was later implemented throughout the company.

Assistant Branch Officer

THRIFT SAVINGS BANK, Albany, New Jersey 1983 -1986

Directed up to twenty employees and provided on-going guidance. Conducted training sessions and maintained staff support.

EDUCATION

B.A. Pre-Law/Business 1981
UNIVERSITY OF SOUTH CAROLINA, Columbia, SC
4 Years Naval ROTC - Honorable Discharge
Skills: IBM AT, HP PC, Unisys, Microsoft Excel

ASSOCIATIONS

URBAN BANKERS ASSOCIATION

REFERENCES FURNISHED ON REQUEST.

Combination. *Terek A. Jabali, CPC, Atlanta, Georgia.*
An executive logo stands out and calls attention to the person's name. In the Experience section, descriptions of the positions include achievements as well as duties.

Mr. DO EVERYTHING

3000 Wellview Drive B-000, Orlando, GA 00000 **(000) 000-0000**

CAREER HIGHLIGHTS

Extensive and successful background in sports promotions with emphasis on sales and client development. Managed sales staff, provided direction, and ensured on-going motivation. Conducted interviews, selected qualified candidates and administered training sessions. Developed promotional advertising materials, implemented assertive campaigns, and achieved overall objectives. Conducted field sales and expanded sales revenues. Acknowledged for meeting sales goals while maintaining excellent client relations.

EXPERIENCE

RED EAGLES, Charlotte, NC 6/91 - Present

Manager of Client Relations

Oversaw overall ticket sales responsibilities. Supervised sales staff, provided direction, and maintained on-going support. Developed season ticket programs and composed marketing brochures. Administered sales contests and maintained a motivated environment. Provided courteous customer service and implemented professional guidelines. Corresponded with clients and maintained excellent client relations.

Manager of Client Relations 6/91 - 9/92

Supervised the customer service department. Analyzed customer needs and developed targeted programs. Launched assertive campaigns and increased seasonal ticket values.

Account Executive 6/90 -6/91

Performed field sales and sold tickets to individuals, groups, and corporations. Met and exceeded sales quotas and accomplished delegated objectives.

CONTINENTAL BASKETBALL ASSOCIATION, Santa Barbara, CA

Director of Sales and Promotions 8/89 - 4/90

Directed all sales and promotional operations. Supervised inside and field sales staff. Solicited corporate sponsorships and established an expanded client base. Coordinated entertainment functions and conducted extensive public relations activities.

EDUCATION

Bachelor of Arts Degree - Radio/Television 1986
EASTERN OREGON STATE COLLEGE, La Grande, Oregon

OTHER

Participated and presented in the following functions: Sports Career Conventions, NBA Stay in School program.

Combination. *Terek A. Jabali, CPC, Atlanta, Georgia.*
A general-purpose resume. Career Highlights section focuses on sales, client development, supervision and training of staff, and development of promotional materials.

6

MARTIN SMITH
2000 Fleming Avenue
Elliott Rocks, PA 00000
412-000-0000

OBJECTIVE

Full or part-time position in Sign Painting with emphasis on lettering, design, layout and type finishing.

WORK HISTORY

ELLIOTT W. EVERTON - New Town, PA
Owner/Operator . Self-employed from 1970 to Present
Provides dependable, honest, and personal service throughout the Harrisburg and surrounding areas.

- Maintenance of daily operations at shop facility
- Developed clientele and maintains personal contact
- Assesses clients' specific needs for visual promotion and recommends suitable solution
- Directs promotion, sales and service of products
- Prepares bids, invoices and assists in bookkeeping

Sign Painter . 1952 to Present
Experience in lettering, design, layout and fabrication. Uses safety practices in painting, building, and sign erecting.

- Use various types of paints compatible with sign material
- Hand letter commercial/standard vehicles including trucks, trailers, cars, and boats
- Custom letter windows, office doors, and store fronts
- Experienced in gold leaf techniques
- Constructs sign material to client's specifications

SPECIAL PROJECTS

* Designed and created televised CBN banner
* Presently paints logos for worldwide soft drink company
* Selected to refurbish existing signs for hospitals, business, industry
* Sign painter for charitable organizations

MILITARY EXPERIENCE

UNITED STATES ARMY - NC and SC
Communications Specialist, Rank of Sergeant: 1956-1962
Responsible for transmitting and receiving radio and teletype communications. Selected for special service work in sign painting.
- Recipient of military commendation for sign painting completed at various Army facilities
- Utilized artistic abilities when requested

EDUCATION

Harrington Hall Community College - Harring Town, PA
Graduated in the top 3rd of class
Received special recognition for artistic abilities

REFERENCES

Available upon request

Chronological. Margaret M. Hilling, Huntingdon, Pennsylvania.
An unusual chronological resume in which both positions over a 40-year work history are still current positions. Military experience was an episode within that history.

7

HEATHER BROWN
500 New City Avenue
Newton Town, Pennsylvania 00000
(000) 000-0000

OBJECTIVE

Part-time position as a medical secretary/receptionist with emphasis on processing insurance forms, finance/accounting, bookkeeping, and general office support.

WORK EXPERIENCE

DR. JOHN R. DOE - NEWTON TOWN, PA
Medical Secretary/Receptionist . June 1988 to Present

Demonstrate proficiency in clerical/administrative secretarial skills. In-depth knowledge of medical terminology. Also serve as full-time bookkeeper and financial manager. Process all types of insurance forms including Blue Cross and Blue Shield, Medicare, Medical Assistance.

Accurate and thorough ICD-9-CM coding for physician payment. Working knowledge of Physicians' Current Procedural Terminology listed by the American Medical Association CPT Code.

DR. DONALD R. DOE - NEW VILLAGE, PA
Medical Secretary/Receptionist . January 1969 to 1988

Demonstrated skill in supervising an efficient, well-run office. Oriented new employees; allocated jobs and monitored distribution of work load among professionals. Greeted patients, answered phone, scheduled appointments, and typed correspondence.

Maintained bookkeeping records of accounts payable/receivable. Computed employee hours and did payroll. Kept detailed records and updated files. Prepared insurance forms. Assisted physician as needed. General working knowledge of business machines.

EDUCATION

Attend bi-yearly insurance meetings at Allegheny Memorial Hospital. Purpose: To learn about changes in the insurance industry and processing forms correctly for prompt payment to the Physician.

Subscribe to St. Anthony Hospital Publications. Receive updated replacement pages containing new additions, deletions and revisions made to ICD-9-CM by the Health Care Financing Administration

Newton Town Area High School - Newton Town, PA
Academic and Business Curriculum

REFERENCES

Available upon request

Chronological. Margaret M. Hilling, Huntingdon, Pennsylvania.
After steady work in the same kind of position for over 25 years, this person now seeks a part-time position. Indenting two paragraphs gives visual relief from block-style paragraphing.

8

John Richardson — *Hospitality Executive Management*

15 Maple Way
Redwood City, California 94000
Telephone (000) 000-0000

Background includes practical experience and education, which have provided good working knowledge of these key areas:

Restaurant & Club Operations	**Cost Controls Management**
Profit/Loss Responsibility	**Strategy Planning**
Business Development	**Fine-dining Ambiance**
Inventory & Purchasing	**Food & Service Quality**
Staff Motivation & Training	**Marketing & Advertising**
Menu Development	**Remodels & Expansions**

Deliver highly motivated and effective performance in all areas of hospitality operations management. Experienced with multiple-site operations. Provide strong leadership and staff motivation. Excellent communications, presentation and promotions abilities. Exceptionally guest oriented.

Operations Director
WELLINGS RESTAURANT CORP.　　Redwood, California August 1987 - Present
Report to the owner/CEO and to the senior vice president of this company that has 55 restaurants in nine states—with a $33-million sales budget for 13 of the properties. Joined Wellings as an assistant manager in Arlington and was promoted to general manager of flagship restaurant in 1989, Named to current post in May 1993. Key areas of accomplishment and responsibility include:

*   Strengthened controls and accountability, reduced costs, and improved profits by 25%.
*   Oversaw re-opening of a property that involved development of a new concept and name.
*   Direct-reports include three division managers and 14 general managers; responsible for recruiting, hiring, training, performance evaluations and relocations.
*   Manage promotional activities to achieve market recognition and increased sales; pro-active in menu planning & design, food testing and quality assurance.
*   P/L responsibilities include budget forecasts, and cost controls.

At the Villa and Valley restaurants, which had dining room, banquet and lounge facilities, played key roles in organizing catered events, promoting patio dining, and installing a national reservation system.

Director of Food & Beverage
KEY VIEW INN　　Harvey, Louisiana 1986 - 87
Managed all restaurant, banquet and room service sales and personnel at this 200-room property operated by Vista Host, Inc. Launched a promotional drive to attract business lunches, dinners and catering that increased sales by 15 percent.

General Manager
BEST EVER ENTERPRISES　　Boca Raton, Florida 1982 - 86
Successfully managed three restaurants in College Station and Houston, including planning and managing the openings of the bar/restaurant operations for Sam's Cantina and Zephyr Annex for this rapidly expanding restaurant chain.

BA Degree Program - Business Administration
FLORIDA A&M　Boca Chica

Extensive Food & Beverage Management seminars and workshops

Combination. *Ted Bache, Palo Alto, California.*
Smaller size of type keeps extensive background, key accomplishments, and wide range of responsibilities on one page. Job experience viewed as more important than college degree.

9

ANDREA MAY CHAPPELLE
100 Southview Drive • Easton Downs, ST 00000 • (000) 000-0000

OBJECTIVE

To obtain a position as a software or hardware support agent with a computer service firm. I would prefer limited out of town travel so I can pursue a college degree in computer science or network management.

EXPERIENCE

Computer Sales   Easton Downs, ST
Sales Counselor   **April 1993 - Present**
• Advise customers on computer systems and accessories that are suitable for their needs.
• Consult with customers on the use of home office equipment such as fax machines, and telephone systems.

Computer Systems, Inc.   Arlington, ST
Technical Support Specialist   **January 1992 - April 1993**
• Responsible for providing technical support on the use of specific accounting and law firm software packages.
• Provided technical service on hardware such as hard drives, disk drives, printers, controller cards and network interface cards.
• Setup, configured and gave support on the use of local area networks.
• Created training manuals and presentations for various software bundles.

Bushert, Baggett & Greenly, CPA P.A.   Easton Downs, ST
Network Manager   **Febuary 1987 - January 1992**
• Supervised and maintained a fourteen station Novell network.
• Setup and deleted users; wrote login scripts; installed proper hardware.
• Responsible for monitoring and troubleshooting LAN problems.
• Installed and upgraded specific software packages.
• Performed some data entry and administrative duties.

SPECIFIC SOFTWARE EXPERIENCE

• A-plus Tax Accounting Software
• Novell Netware Operating System
• Creative Solution's Depreciation Solution II
• WordPerfect 5.1 / Lotus 1-2-3
• Best Program's Fixed Asset System
• Mountain Tape Drive Programs
• Pro System's Payroll Checkwriting
• PC Anywhere / Norton Utilities
• Software Technology's - Time Accounting & Billing, General Ledger, Accounts Payable, Critical Date and Trust Accounting systems.

EDUCATION

Airport High School
Graduation Date: 1986

REFERENCES AVAILABLE UPON REQUEST

Chronological. Nancy P. Stein, Columbia, South Carolina.
Person with only a high school diploma but a wealth of computer network experience wants a job with minimal travel in order to get a college degree in field of experience.

10

B. SMITH HORTON

200 Edward Place ● New City, SC 29000 ● (123) 555-0000

CAREER OBJECTIVE:

Seeking responsible position in areas of maintenance and/or project management. Past experience covers wide range of responsibilities in heavy industrial manufacturing.

EXPERIENCE HISTORY:

WEST SHORE PHOTO COMPANY   1966 - Present
Division of National Photo Company
New City, South Carolina

∞ Strategic Planning: (Present Assignment) Involved in dismantlement and transfer of filament and staple manufacturing facility to a foreign location. Assignment responsibility includes transfer of staple technology and assistance in startup of reassembled plant. Includes advise and consultation in the setting up of a maintenance organization for the chemical operation.

∞ Maintenance/Shops: (5 years) Responsible for mechanical and electrical forces in DMT, TPA, PTA production. Implemented quality management program that improved maintenance service acceptance significantly.

∞ Construction: (6 years) Project Manager responsible for $43M expansion of polyester staple plant and subsequent $20M modernization. Both projects completed on schedule and under budget. Also, involved in the successful startup of both projects.

∞ Production: (10 years) Experience ranged from staff engineer to supervisory responsibilities in production of polyester fiber. Achieved significant experience in polyester fiber manufacture, i.e., spinning, drawing, and baling.

∞ Engineering: (2 years) Responsible for mechanical and civil engineering group.

NATIONAL ALUMINUM COMPANY
Bamton operations, Appleton, Illinois   1963 - 1966
Torro Operations, Torro, Mississippi   1962 - 1963

∞ Experience began in machine design on small maintenance projects then progressed to rolling mill design. Assisted in the successful startup and checkout of continuous cold mill used in production of can stock aluminum. Later assigned responsibility in the furnace area.

EDUCATION:

Some Important State University, Newton, North Carolina
B.S. Degree in Mechanical Engineering, 1962
Post graduate work at University of Mississippi, Mississippi State University, University of Maryland and Carolina College

PROFESSIONAL INFORMATION:

Past Member ASME ∞ Registered Professional Engineer in South Carolina

REFERENCES AVAILABLE UPON REQUEST

Chronological. *Nancy P. Stein, Columbia, South Carolina.*
Chronological format supports emphasis on five different areas of responsibility over 27+ years with the same company. Achievements included with description of duties in each area.

11

JAMES SMITH
100 Peachtree Street • Atlanta, Georgia 30303
(404) 111-1000

OBJECTIVE: Professional Massage Therapist position.

MEMBERSHIP: American Massage Therapy Association

EDUCATION: Atlanta School of Massage
(Meets requirements of the Georgia Department of Education for approval pursuant to the Georgia Proprietary School Act. The curriculum is approved by The American Massage Therapy Association, and is accredited by the Accrediting Commission for Trade and Technical Schools of the Career College Association.)

Relevant Training:
- Functional Anatomy
- Deep tissue training
- Myofascial massage using significant pressure and consideration of muscle fiber direction — a technique originated at Atlanta School of Massage.
- Advanced myofascial techniques.
- Theory and practice of basic cross fiber techniques.
- Joint movements.
- Theories, concepts and applications of myofascial trigger points.
- Orthopedic assessment, postural analysis, hydrotherapy/heliotherapy.
- Swedish friction, effleurage, petrissage, vibration, tapotement
- Japanese massage — Shiatsu
- Temporomandibular joint work (T.M.J.)
- Sports massage

CLINICAL EXPERIENCE:

Internship, Atlanta School of Massage, Student Clinic
Performed seventy-two massages that were reported as effective and successful. Different methods and skills were implemented over the course of the internship.

OTHER EXPERIENCE:

Buyer, Peachtree Florist and Bridal Shoppe.
Atlanta, Georgia. 1980 to 1990.

Heavily involved buying for specific, client-centered business. Interacted with clients on one-to-one basis to discover and meet particular needs. Initiated marketing strategies for the business as needed.

REFERENCES Furnished upon request.

Combination. *Charles H. Styer, Tifton, Georgia.*
Skills are evident in Education and Clinical Experience sections. Testamonials and references were included with actual resume to prevent association with "massage parlor operators."

12

Thomas J. Thurgood

444 E. Cincinnati
Fresno, CA 93000
(209) 222-2222

■■ **Career Focus: International Business** ■■

EDUCATION

CALIFORNIA STATE UNIVERSITY, FRESNO

B.S., Business Administration (12/92)
Emphasis: **International Business**

REPRESENTATIVE COURSEWORK

Intro to International Business	International Finance
Management of Multinational Enterprises	International Marketing
World Commerce and Development	International Management

RELATED EXPERIENCES

- **Pacific Rim Trip:** Visited Hong Kong, Bangkok, Thailand, Singapore, and Seoul, Korea in connection with CSUF coursework. Opportunity provided exposure to conducting business in the Pacific Rim.

- **International Business Internship:** Under direction of CSUF Department Chair, worked with entrepreneurs from Ireland in researching, identifying, and contacting companies offering potential for import/export business.

- **Import Experience:** Presently employed with Trade International which specializes in importing watches from Hong Kong, Malaysia, and India; make buying recommendations and organize shows for sales in five western states.

COMPUTER

Extensive computer coursework (60+ hours) with knowledge of various desktop hardware and software applications, including Lotus 1-2-3, WordPerfect, and dBASE III+ and IV.

EMPLOYMENT SUMMARY

Personally financed 100% of education through the following employment:

Import/Sales: Trade International	1992-Present
Assistant Manager/Driver: Best Courier Services	1989-1990
Shift Supervisor/Waiter: Holiday Inn	1988-1989
Banquet Supervisor: The Marriott	1986-1988

AFFILIATIONS

International Business Association
Central California International Trade Association
Toastmasters International

Available for Relocation • References Upon Request

Combination. *Susan B. Whitcomb, CPRW, Fresno, California.*
Degree emphasis, relevant coursework, and related experiences are featured early for this
graduate. Limited work experience is downplayed later in an Employment Summary.

13

MELINDA M. CHAMPION

3000 West Shaw Avenue
Fresno, California 93000
(209) 222-2222

CAREER GOALS

Association with an organization that will benefit from my initiative, capabilities, and contributions, ultimately qualifying for advancement and increased decision-making responsibilities.

EDUCATION

CALIFORNIA STATE UNIVERSITY, FRESNO

Degree: Bachelor of Science (December 1993)
Major: Economics
Emphasis: Political Science and International Economics

FRESNO CITY COLLEGE

Degree: Associate of Arts (December 1991)
Honors: Participated in the college's Honors Program

SUMMARY OF SKILLS

- Extensive general office experience encompassing administrative, secretarial, computer data entry, light bookkeeping (A/P, A/R, payroll), and special projects.

- Proficient in IBM computer environment; familiar with WordPerfect, Quattro, MultiMate, Q & A, One-Write Plus, Lotus 1-2-3, Org Plus, and DOS.

- Exceptional organizational/planning skills; simultaneously managed and monitored multiple tasks; developed new systems and forms to increase office efficiency.

- Excellent computer keyboard skills; typing speed of 85 wpm; composed correspondence and memoranda; word processed lengthy proposals/reports (60+ pages), legal documents, and architectural specifications.

- Maintain composure under pressure; able to work autonomously with little direct supervision.

PROFESSIONAL EXPERIENCE

Personally financed majority of education, holding part-time or full-time employment while maintaining above average GPA and completing degree in 4½ years:

Office Manager/Secretary -- Barry T. Thornton, Attorney at Law	8/90 to Pres.
Temp Office Worker/Secretary -- Newton Personnel	5/90 to 7/90
Temp Office Worker -- On-Call Temporaries	12/89 to 4/90
Legal Secretary -- Bart Smith, Attorney at Law	5/89 to 1/90
Telex Typist -- Far East Corporation	11/88 to 5/89

Combination. *Susan B. Whitcomb, CPRW, Fresno, California.*
Featured early for this graduate are career goals, two degrees, and a Summary of Skills section. Downplayed later is professional experience that includes temporary work.

14

Andrew R. Thompson

2000 S.W. Linwood Lane #12
Portland, Oregon 97000
(503) 555-5555

Profile

Multi-disciplined graphics designer with award-winning experience in design and illustration, print advertising, packaging design and typography. Skilled in managing all phases of the creative process, from concept through delivery.

- Experienced in designing brochures, catalogs, logos, fliers and other types of marketing communications.
- Proficient in budgeting, bidding, scheduling and project management.
- Able to consistently produce high quality work—*on time and within budget*.

RELATED SKILLS: Lettering; black & white line art; airbrushing; photo retouching and proofing; 3-D modeling; technical drawing and illustration.

Awards

Certificate of Merit	Art Directors of Portland
Certificate of Excellence	Los Angeles Design Association
Certificate of Distinction	*Art Director* Magazine
Award of Merit	Society of Technical Communicators
Design of Excellence Award	*Print* Magazine
Award of Merit	ADDY
Award of Excellence	Pacific Printing Industries
Award of Excellence	*American Corporate Identity*

OTHER ACHIEVEMENTS: Appeared in *Print* Magazine, *American Illustration* (Book #3) and *American Corporate Identity* (Book #7).

Education

MUSEUM ART SCHOOL – Portland, Oregon
Bachelor of Fine Arts, Design (1979)

Experience

EVERTON ILLUSTRATION & DESIGN – Portland, Oregon (1986-Present)
Free-lance Illustrator / Designer
Complete various types of graphic design and illustration projects for clients such as Tektronix, Xerox, Nike and Intel Corporation.

ART DESIGN, INC. – Portland, Oregon (1981-1986)
Illustrator / Designer

ADVO LTD. – Portland, Oregon (1980-1981)
Illustrator / Designer

References

References and portfolio available upon request.

Combination. Pat Kendall, CPRW, Aloha, Oregon.
Use of Ventura Publisher enabled the writer to thicken horizontal lines over the side headings to call attention to them. Skills and awards emphasized. See also Resume 91.

15

GEORGE A. WHATMAN

1111 East New Lane
Fresno, California 93700
(209) 111-1000

QUALIFICATIONS

Accomplished 17-year career encompassing strengths in:

♦ Administration/Management
♦ Resource Development/Fundraising
♦ Human Resources/Personnel

PROFESSIONAL EXPERIENCE

Administration/Management:

• Planned and managed business operations for non-profit organizations, including finance, budgeting, facilities management, staffing, programming, and public relations.
• Prepared comprehensive business operating plan with short-range and long-range goals.
• Negotiated contractual agreements pertaining to purchase of property, rental of facilities valued at $2 million, refinancing, and construction/remodel projects.
• Balanced budget after long history of deficits.
• Supervised seven department directors and support staff.

Human Resources/Personnel:

• Managed all facets of Human Resource Department including start-up of new department.
• Experienced in recruiting, interviewing, placement, and evaluation of personnel (program managers, departmental supervisors, construction/trades, educators, and support staff).
• Conducted orientation and wrote curricula for training.
• Researched, presented for CEO approval, and administered employee benefits program.
• Wrote policy and procedures manual.
• Developed personnel forms.

Resource Development/Fundraising:

• Directed resource development programs for multi-state region.
• Targeted untapped cities through direct mail, generating $25,000 in revenue.
• Achieved $10,000 through direct mail alone, using segmented list with genesis series of letters.
• Developed prospect lists and data files for new donor acquisition.
• Took over planning for annual banquet and generated $25,000 (prior year's event lost money).
• Assisted in developing a deferred giving and financial counseling program.

EDUCATION

Master of Arts Degree, Famous University
Bachelor of Science Degree, Some University

EMPLOYMENT HISTORY

Director of Personnel/Resource Development: New Services, Inc., Fresno, CA	1991-Pres.
Senior Administrative Pastor: Important Services, Village, ST	1988-1991
Senior Administrative Pastor: Important Endeavor, Village, ST	1981-1988

Combination. Susan B. Whitcomb, CPRW, Fresno, California.
The three strengths in the Qualifications section are the criteria for the Professional Experience section for this former pastor seeking to transfer skills to another field.

16

Special Paper Information

Resume 1
Brand: Neutech
Parent Company: Mead
Paper: 100% Cotton White Wove
Color: White
Weight: 24 lb.
Watermarked: Yes
Laser compatible: Yes

Resume 2
Brand: Beckett Paper
Parent Company: International Paper Company
Paper: Cambric Writing
Color: White, Linen finish
Weight: 24 lb.
Watermarked: Yes
Laser compatible: Yes

Resume 3
Brand: Beckett Paper
Parent Company: International Paper Company
Paper: Cambric Writing
Color: Ash
Weight: 24 lb.
Watermarked: Yes
Laser compatible: Yes

Resume 4
Brand: Neenah Paper
Parent Company: Kimberly-Clark Corporation
Paper: Classic Laid Laser
Color: Baronial Ivory
Weight: 24 lb.
Watermarked: Yes
Laser compatible: Yes

Resume 5
Brand: Gilcrest
Parent Company: Mead
Paper: Recycled, Laiser Laid
Color: Fiber Cream
Weight: 22 lb.
Watermarked: Yes
Laser compatible: Yes

Resume 6
Brand: Beckett Paper
Parent Company: International Paper Company
Paper: Cambric Writing
Color: India, Linen Finish
Weight: 24 lb.
Watermarked: Yes
Laser compatible: Yes

Resume 7
Brand: Simpson
Parent Company: Simpson Paper Company
Paper: Valley Forge Parchment
Color: Antique Gold Text
Weight: 60 lb.
Watermarked: No
Laser compatible: No

Resume 8
Brand: Hopper Papers
Parent Company: Georgia-Pacific Corporation
Paper: Skytone
Color: Natural Text
Weight: 60 lb.
Watermarked: No
Laser compatible: Yes

Resume 9
Brand: Hopper Papers
Parent Company: Georgia-Pacific Corporation
Paper: Skytone
Color: Brown Text
Weight: 60 lb.
Watermarked: No
Laser compatible: Yes

Resume 10
Brand: Beckett Paper
Parent Company: International Paper Company
Paper: Cambric Writing
Color: Bamboo
Weight: 24 lb.
Watermarked: Yes
Laser compatible: Yes

Resume 11

Brand: Beckett Paper
Parent Company: International Paper Company
Paper: Cambric Writing
Color: Frost
Weight: 24 lb.
Watermarked: Yes
Laser compatible: Yes

Resume 12

Brand: Gilbert Paper
Parent Company: Mead
Paper: Gilcrest Recycled, Laser Laid
Color: Fiber Blue
Weight: 22 lb.
Watermarked: Yes
Laser compatible: Yes

Resume 13

Brand: Beckett Paper
Parent Company: International Paper Company
Paper: Beckett Enhance!
Color: Marble Gray, Wove
Weight: 24 lb. Writing
Watermarked: No
Laser compatible: Yes

Resume 14

Brand: Simpson
Parent Company: Simpson Paper Company
Paper: Valley Forge Parchment
Color: Script Blue Text
Weight: 60 lb.
Watermarked: No
Laser compatible: No

Resume 15

Brand: Beckett Paper
Parent Company: International Paper Company
Paper: Beckett Enhance!
Color: Marble Blue
Weight: 70 lb. Text
Watermarked: No
Laser compatible: No

Resume 16

Brand: Neenah Paper
Parent Company: Kimberly-Clark Corporation
Paper: Classic Crest Writing
Color: Ember Blue
Weight: 24 lb.
Watermarked: Yes
Laser compatible: Yes

Accounting/Finance
Resumes at a Glance

ICAN ACCOUNT
Telephone: (444) 666-8888

1234 Bookkeeping Place
My Town, USA 55454

OBJECTIVE: Position as a Comptroller utilizing successful accounting and managerial experience.

HIGHLIGHTS:

- In-depth knowledge of accounting procedures including accounts payable/receivables, payroll and related taxes, and preparation of financial statements.
- Resolved problems of a financially troubled company and restructured it into a stable position.
- Proven ability to effectively manage daily office operations including hiring, training, and supervising staff, purchasing equipment and supplies, and obtaining and overseeing insurance and benefits plans.
- Very accurate and detail-oriented individual with excellent communication skills.
- Experienced in use of WordPerfect, dBASE, Excel, Lotus 1-2-3, Framework, Windows, and DOS.

EXPERIENCE:

Comptroller, Tops at Bookkeeping, Inc., This City, USA   1990 - present

Report directly to President of company. Responsible for overseeing all accounting operations as well as ensuring office is running efficiently, i.e., supervise employees, purchase supplies and equipment, and make decisions affecting daily operations.

- Began position while company was experiencing financial difficulties. Through effective management and negotiations, resolved all problems and significantly improved company's financial status.
- Full responsibility for P&L of company with a sales volume of over $4 million annually. Prepare all financial reports, establish budgets/projections, etc.
- Ensure all reports and taxes are filed in a timely manner.
- Review status of invoices to ensure payments are paid in accordance with terms thereby taking advantage of discounts and averting penalties.
- Assist in developing and implementing company policies and procedures.

Accountant, The Best Accounting Firm, My Town, USA   1985 - 1990

Fully responsible for all facets of accounting practices for six corporations and one partnership. Designed and implemented computerized analysis program which resulted in financial statements being produced in a faster and more accurate manner.

- Improved closing date time by 22%.

Office Manager / Bookkeeper, Tip Top Tax Service, Any Town, USA   1982 - 1984

Responsible for daily management of 6 bookkeepers. Set up job descriptions and standards of performance for all office positions. Handled payroll taxes, year-end adjustments, and tax returns.

- Successfully guided new business to a 91% increase while adding only 3 new employees.
- Decreased office supply expense by 13% through improving forms and strict inventory control.

EDUCATION:

B.A., Business Administration, Accounting, Great College, My Town, USA   1981

Continuing Education

- Partnership Corporation and Estate Tax Course, H & R Black Tax Company
- Various computer courses including WordPerfect, Lotus 1-2-3, and DOS 5.0, Area Community College

REFERENCES: Excellent professional and personal references available upon request

---

Combination. Susie Brady, CPRW, Virginia Beach, Virginia.
A considerable amount of information fits on one page because of long bulleted items, narrow margins, and small point size. Some achievements are quantified in percentages.

17

PATTY PERKY
3160 Friendly Road
Any City, USA   23332
(804) 444-6666

OBJECTIVE: Customer Service-oriented position where excellent supervisory, communication, and problem solving skills can be utilized.

HIGHLIGHTS OF QUALIFICATIONS:

- **Customer Service Skills**: Ability to communicate effectively and establish excellent rapport with clients from diverse socio-economic backgrounds. Serve as liaison between clients and insurance companies to resolve accounts. Handle problems which staff members cannot reconcile.

- **Problem Solving Skills**: Routinely mediate problems concerning financial issues. Negotiate payment plans and resolve account discrepancies to the satisfaction of both the client and the company.

- **Supervisory Skills**: Supervise up to 15 employees including financial counselors, bookkeepers, account representatives, insurance billers, and collectors. Responsible for interviewing, hiring, scheduling, assigning tasks, training, counseling, and terminating. Counsel employees on work performance, infractions of company policy (absenteeism, tardiness, etc.), personal matters, and substance abuse problems.

RELATED EXPERIENCE:

Office Supervisor, Fantastic Company, My Town, USA   1990 - present

Responsible for managing daily activities of a medical practice with a volume of 8,000 accounts monthly. Regularly make on-the-spot management decisions. Supervise and train 15 staff members whose daily tasks include third party and self-pay billing and collections as well as routine clerical functions.

- Handle accounts payable and payroll functions as well as delinquent and accounts receivable reports.
- Monitor efforts of outside collection agencies as well as payments by major 3rd party payors for correctness and timeliness of payment.
- Responsible for weekly updates and revised reports.

Finance Manager, The Best Health Center, This City, USA   1988 - 1989

Responsible for all billing and collection efforts of this 500 bed long-term care facility. Supervised receptionist and bookkeeper (including accounts payable and payroll functions).

- Served as liaison between family members and other healthcare facilities. Position required ability to work with and relate to family members under extreme stress due to illness of loved ones.

Credit Manager, The Local Hospital, My City, USA   1985 - 1987

Responsible for training and supervising of four collectors and three financial counselors. Managed all inpatient and outpatient self-pay receivables. Monitored efforts of three outside collection agencies. Reviewed accounts for possible charity write-off or potential bad debt.

- Utilized excellent interpersonal skills in dealing with family of critically or terminally ill patients. Position required ability to empathize with family members while maintaining a profitable collection department.

Billing Supervisor, In Town Hospital, Any City, USA   1982 - 1985

Began as Billing Clerk and advanced to supervisory position within 1 year. Monitored special service accounts. Responsible for supervision, training, and performance evaluations of one verification clerk and six billing clerks. Coordinated all financial activities of the Unit.

REFERENCES:

Excellent professional and personal references available upon request.

18
***Combination.** Susie Brady, CPRW, Virginia Beach, Virginia.*
The Objective statement and Highlights of Qualifications section focus the dominant skills in this resume: those for customer service, supervision, communication, and solving problems.

CHARLES A. MILLER
441 Allegheny Street . Huntingdon, Pennsylvania . 00000
(000) 000-0000 or (000) 000-0000

QUALIFICATIONS

Ambitious, results-oriented individual with over 4 years of experience in accounting and financial analysis. Excellent analytical and problem-solving skills. Experienced in computer software applications.

PROFESSIONAL EXPERIENCE

Accountant January 1989 to Present
FIRST NATIONAL BANK - Hesston, PA
* Run asset/liability simulation model for executive management
* Input information pertinent to cost accounting system
* Daily operations management of investment portfolio
* Conduct research analysis for internal reports
* Gather, calculate and process data for Federal Call Report

Clerk Summers of 1989, 1990, and 1991
HOLLIDAYSBURG TREASURERS OFFICE - Hollidaysburg, PA
* Responsible for tax computations
* Received and processed payments for back taxes
* Resolved wide range of taxpayer problems
* Balanced tax ledger and recorded on master docket
* Reimbursed state for sales of various licenses

Cashier October 1985 thru April 1988
HOSS'S STEAK AND SEA HOUSE - Duncansville, PA
* Helped finance college education through employment
* Assisted manager in closing up procedures
* Performed minor maintenance on equipment
* Oversaw coworkers in work performance
* Adhered to prescribed food service regulations

EDUCATION/ HONORS

Bachelor of Science Public Accounting May 1991
PENN STATE UNIVERSITY - University Park, PA
Dean's List graduating **Cum laude** [GPA 3.656]
Charles Rice Outstanding Senior Accounting Award
Recipient of Outstanding Business Student Scholarship
Textbook Scholarship for achievement in business

Diploma Academic Curriculum June 1987
HOLLIDAYSBURG AREA HIGH SCHOOL - Hollidaysburg, PA
Graduated **High Honors** top 5% of class
Award for Excellence in Chemistry
Received U.S. Army Reserve Student Athletic Award
Member of District Championship Football Team

SEMINARS

DAYS INN - Altoona, PA
Updated education involving FASB Regulations

CENTURY CORPORATION - Belleville, PA
Indepth training on asset/liability simulation model

HOLLIDAYSBURG HIGH SCHOOL - Hollidaysburg, PA
Securities Processing - Sponsored by American Institute of Bankers

VOLUNTEER

Tutoring, Little League Baseball, Biddy Basketball, Special Olympics

---

Combination. *Margaret M. Hilling, Huntingdon, Pennsylvania.*
White space and short bulleted items make this an easy-to-read resume for a bank accountant looking for his second job since graduation.

19

MANNATEE A. FISH

1234 Any Street • Some Town, State 12345

Office: (000) 555-1234
Home: (000) 555-1234

PROFILE

CPA • Financial Manager • General Manager • MS Accounting/Finance
Results-oriented financial manager seeking senior level general management, financial management, or business development position.

SUMMARY OF EXPERIENCE

- General manager experienced in operations, finance, and marketing
- Demonstrated abilities to improve profitability
- Comprehensive financial and management experience including financial planning, capital budgeting, internal audits, forecasting and accounting
- Direct control of operations management, asset utilization, operations analysis, management of divested assets
- Initiated, negotiated and closed acquisitions and divestitures
- Controlled financial operations of multi-plant international companies

SIGNIFICANT ACHIEVEMENTS

- Designed and implemented a financial control system and strategic plan for a Fortune 500 company that was instrumental in its turnaround from a loss operation to one of the 20 most profitable in the decade
- Reduced costs and improved profitability by over 50% for a service company
- Acquired and divested over 30 domestic and international privately held and NYSE companies ranging in size from $1 million to $700 million
- Raised funds for working capital, fixed assets, real estate and acquisitions
- Initiated public offerings of wholly owned subsidiaries in Brazil and Sweden

EXPERIENCE

General Manager (xxxx - Present)
PERSONAL BUSINESS, INC., Anytown, State/Some Town, State
Reorganized operations and marketing efforts. Since xxxx in Some Town, opened three satellite units and restructured branch management that resulted in an 18% increase in sales, increased profits 53% while reducing receivables 40%.

Senior Vice President, Corporate Development (xxxx-xxxx)
COMPANY, Anytown, State
Successfully restructured the Company-owned bank from a significant loss with severe regulatory problems to a profit and no regulatory restrictions.
Restructured two partnerships, eliminating losses of over $5 million/year.

Staff Vice-President
Director, Operations Analysis Acquisitions & Divestitures (xxxx-xxxx)
LARGE CORPORATION, Another Town, State
Instrumental in downsizing company and restructuring of over $1 billion in debts while funding $600 million in losses. Conceived and implemented an asset redeployment program and divested operations with sales of over $1.2 billion; directed and negotiated the sale of 15 units which generated over $300 million in proceeds.

20

Combination. *Linda Morton, CPRW, Lawrence, Kansas.*
Achievements appear not only in the Significant Achievements section but also in the statements about the five positions held. Person's name and lines are used as header on p. 2.

MANATEE A. FISH   *Page 2*

Vice President, Administration (xxxx-xxxx)
VERY BIG CORPORATION, Eastern City, State
Directed a program that resulted in acquisition of a major NYSE company and the divestiture of ten divisions constituting over 30% of the company. Stabilized three failing businesses and assisted in privatizing company. Initiated a Washington lobbying effort to bolster defense marketing operations. Reduced corporate administration costs by 17%.

Director of Financial Control (Controller) (xxxx-xxxx)
LARGE COMPANY SYSTEMS, INC., Yet Another Town, State
Developed and implemented an MIS system which reduced reports and provided management with timely, all-inclusive information. Reduced administrative costs by 29%. Created standardized operating procedures in all U.S. and Canadian plants and parts of Europe. Restructured European financial functions in Paris at a savings of $1 million annually.

EDUCATION

B.S. Accounting, University of State
M.S. Accounting and Finance, Some University

LICENSE

Certified Public Accountant

Paragraph style is used for these five statements, which display clearly and repeatedly the person's skills in lowering costs, restructuring, eliminating losses, and generating proceeds.

JOHNATHAN BROWN
33-34 18th Street • *Bensonhurst, New York* • *(222) 222-1111*

OBJECTIVE   To obtain employment in the world of Corporate Finance where my experience would prove useful.

SUMMARY of QUALIFICATIONS

Interpersonal Abilities
- As a member of management team, taught seminars to new employees — the basics of how to interpret and understand the financial pages.
- Interfaced with new and out-going members, reviewing their status through direct communications (one-to-one), resolving all problems.
- Organized committees for purposes of dealing with larger organizations, meeting with others for roundtable discussions.
- Intercommunicating with other department heads (computer department) and employees to ensure the smooth flow of daily operations.

Management Skills
- Responsible for hiring, firing, assigning raises, setting policy, and drafting job evaluations of employees under my direct supervision.
- Completed research projects which involved drafting proposals for International and Statewide non-profit foundations.
- Managed three departments, interacting daily with personnel for various banking functions.
- Excellent communication skills, both oral and written.

EMPLOYMENT HISTORY

BARBARY STREET BANK & TRUST CO., Brooklyn, NY   1991 - 1993
Project Coordinator Assistant - Reconciled, collected and researched open receivables for the Coupon Processing Department.

NEW YORK STOCK EXCHANGE, New York, NY   1987 - 1990
Manager/Treasury Operations - Assisted the Treasurer with a broad range of financial responsibilities related to exchange activities.

FIRST BANK OF NEW YORK, New York, NY   1985 - 1987
Senior Custody Administrator - Responsible for overseeing the daily activity of corporate accounts, interacting with other department heads to ensure the timely and accurate operation.

CENTRAL HOSPITAL FUND of NEW YORK, NY   1979 - 1984
Assistant Director of Development - Researched information and organized committees; organized roundtable discussions. Worked closely with volunteers on matters relating to fund-raising activities. Drafted proposals for foundations and corporations.

UNITED STATES SECURITY COMPANY of NEW YORK, NY   1970 - 1979
Corporate Custody Officer (1974-1980) / **Tax Coding Specialist** (1968-1973)
Interacted with Treasurers, Controllers and Investment Advisors regarding all administrative functions of clients' accounts.

EDUCATION   FORDHAM UNIVERSITY, Bronx, NY
B.S. Degree in Finance, 1977

SEMINARS   Certificate in Trust Banking, Cash Management, Risk Management, Interviewing Skills, Lotus 1-2-3, WordPerfect.

21   ***Combination.*** *James Voketaitis, Flushing, New York.*
Underlining, bullets, uppercase letters, boldfacing, and recognizable sections make this resume easy to grasp for this person, wanting to change from banking to corporate finance.

John Doe
555 Merry Lane ◘ Player, Ohio 00000 ◘ Telephone: (000) 555-0000

OBJECTIVE: To secure the challenging position of the **Sales and Use Tax Consultant** within your organization that will utilize my education, experience, and unique abilities to further my career opportunities.

SUMMARY OF QUALIFICATIONS:

- ♦ Possesses over **16 years** experience in accounting, auditing, and financial management. **Eleven** years as an Auditor for the Cool Money Department.
- ♦ Outstanding **management and supervisory** skills - the ability to coordinate multi-faceted activities; determine, analyze problems; and develop and implement productive corrective actions.
- ♦ Outstanding **Communication** skills - proficiently utilizes inter-personal skills in relating with others.
- ♦ Effective **Planning and Organizational** skills - Expertise in business administration, recordkeeping, planning, policies and procedures, researching, scheduling, and related acts to ensure productive operations.
- ♦ In-depth knowledge of automated accounting system design and set-up.

EDUCATION: PLAYERSTATE UNIVERSITY, Player, Ohio
Bachelor of Applied Science in Management - 1978

PLAYERCOMMUNITY COLLEGE, Player, Ohio
Associate in Applied Science in Business Management - 1976

**Additional
Training:** JOE DEERECAREER CAMPUS:
Operation Lotus 1-2-3   Certificate, March 1987
Business Writing Skills   Certificate, March 1987

CADRE PROGRAM (8/85-11/87)
This program was devoted to training in managerial skills, human resources development and behavioral sciences.

EXPERIENCE:

November 1987
to November 1993

DECORATOR INC., Cowtown, Illinois
   President/CEO
Successfully managed the overall activities of an automobile leasing operation. Responsible for the day-to-day operations, personnel administration, sales, accounting, ordering, purchasing, budgeting, advertising, marketing, and customer service.
- ♦ Recognized in Who's Who.
- ♦ Recipient of the Business-of-the-Month Award.

August 1978
to November 1987

COOL MONEY DEPARTMENT, Cool, Pennsylvania
   Revenue Senior Auditor
Expertly conducted and/or reviewed selected, highly complex Pennsylvania and out-of-state audits of multi-national corporations, businesses, partnerships, and individuals to ensure compliance to tax regulations. In charge supervising and training an audit staff of 3-4 auditors. Coordinated, assigned, directed, and reviewed the activities of the audit team. Effectively conferred and corresponded with taxpayers and/or representatives regarding various issues and findings. Thoroughly interpreted and resolved technical problems and prepared/reviewed/approved audit reports. Testified as an expert witness at informal hearings or in court. Meticulously researched tax laws, rules, regulations and other resources in relation to applicable cases.
- ♦ Progressed through the ranks from Auditor A, to Auditor B, to Auditor C, to finally Revenue Senior Auditor.

PERSONAL: Hobbies/Interests: Tennis, Basketball, Travel, Reading, and Community Involvement.
Willing to travel.

REFERENCES: Available upon request.

Combination. *Laura G. Lichtenstein, Springfield, Illinois.*
Use of small type size enables much information to be kept on one page. White-on-black bullets at the top of the page and diamond-shaped bullets add visual interest.

22

June Knape

21 West Shefield Street ● Fremont, Michigan 40000
home (555) 555-5555 ● (555) 555-0000 work

CAREER SUMMARY

Excellent track record and outstanding performance in all aspects of banking industry. Began banking career as receptionist and continued to accept added responsibilities and promotions before being appointed *Auditor and Compliance Officer*. Recognized ability to go beyond designated responsibilities resulting in evaluations, suggestions, and implementations to better the working environment. Supervisory experience.

CAREER OBJECTIVE

An opportunity where a competent individual whose loyalty and successful approach to banking procedures and operations can continue to contribute the knowledge and expertise of an experienced professional.

CAREER ACCOMPLISHMENTS

☞ Recommendation of compliance resource materials purchased by bank
☞ Recommendation of hiring the services of Compliance Consultants and Company.
☞ Wrote new compliance policy and presented new Conflict of Interest policy and questionnaire to management for approval
☞ Coordinated a task force to address record retention needs, rewrite the Record Retention Manual, and supervise all aspects of the project
☞ Presented a new Audit Policy to management and Audit Committee for approval and proceeded to rewrite audit work programs for each audit performed
☞ Enjoy a successful working rapport with EDP firms of Thompson & Crowe and Delaware Touche for past six years
☞ Served as coordinator in assembling information in preparation for examiners and CPAs
☞ Increased personnel awareness of banking regulations regarding loans and the reporting of large currency transactions
☞ Instituted annual report of large currency transaction exemption list
☞ Initiated teller training to increase awareness of security procedures and improved security policies and procedures through consultation with law enforcement officials and security specialists

continued . . .

23
Combination. *Patricia L. Nieboer, CPS, CPRW, Fremont, Michigan.*
Person applying for another position at same place of work under new ownership. Two-page format chosen so that a whole page could be devoted to the person's accomplishments.

June Knape, continued . . .

CAREER HISTORY

Auditor and Compliance Officer

Old Independent Bank, Fremont, Michigan   1987 - present

☞ Report directly to audit committee submitting regular reports of audit activities and findings. Meet with audit committee semi-annually to present audit plan for approval and discuss audit findings. Work independently of operations. Serve in capacity of compliance coordinator or supervisor with each department and independent compliance consultant.

Officer of Operations, Security and Compliance

Old Kent Bank, Fremont, Michigan   1972 - 1987

☞ Responsible for maintaining operational controls over all areas of bank including general ledger. Oversaw adherence to operational procedures and policies and evaluated and updated as necessary. Evaluated equipment needs, inventory, and maintenance. Complied with IRS investigation requests. Filed required reports of supervisory agencies and insured adherence to security policies by bank personnel. Monitored cash flow. Initiated teller meetings as required.

☞ As Officer of Auditing, worked with bank examiners and outside auditors. Investigated problem areas and devised and applied solutions. Supervised maintenance of record retention. As Supervisor of Auditing, assisted in balancing accounts, balancing problems, and customer related problems.

CAREER EDUCATION AND TRAINING

MBA Internal Audit Seminar, 1988, 1989, 1993
Auditing School, 1992
Various Compliance and Auditing Seminars, 1988 - 1992
Speak Up with Confidence Seminar, Carol Kent, 1989
MBA Compliance Implementation Seminar, Steve Hughes & James Conboy, Jr., 1988
MBA Consumer Compliance Institute Seminar, Steve Hughes & James Conboy, Jr., 1988
Completion of Audit Training Program, Sponsor NBD, 1987
Leader Effectiveness Training, Steve Crandell, 1986
Audit Consultation and Training Seminar, Norman Morris, 1979
Accounting, Jordan College, 1978
Principles of Banking, American Institute of Banking, 1969
Trust Department Services, American Institute of Banking, 1968

REFERENCES AVAILABLE UPON REQUEST

Job descriptions contain duties and responsibilities, but Career Summary, Career Objective, and Career Accomplishments sell the person. Index (finger) bullets tie the pages together.

ANDREW ST. JAMES

890 Windswept Circle
Friendswood, TX 00000
000-000-0000

CAREER SUMMARY

Senior accounting professional with eleven years of total retail accounting experience, including five years of Corporate Controllership for entities with up to $30 million in sales volume and 40 locations. Heavy experience in implementation of automated P.O.S. systems, inventory control, personnel selection and management, distribution management, crisis management, and direction of all financial functions and related operational activities.

EDUCATION

University of Kansas   1982
Bachelor of Business Administration   Accounting G.P.A. 3.0

CAREER HIGHLIGHTS

- Developed budgets and forecasts, (including 5-year business plans), for internal use, as well as for presentation to potential lenders and outside investors.

- Developed and directed a crisis management plan which resulted in a $400K/yr. (38%) expense savings in home office expense.

- Merged three Corporations, resulting in $60K/yr. in state and local tax savings.

- Directed implementation of three integrated P.O.S. retail systems from start up to completion.

- Obtained outside lines of financing for operating and capital leases to fund operational cash needs and equipment purchases. Negotiated leases and related addendums to reduce rent and expenses for store locations.

- Responsible for physical inventory functions in retail stores, distribution centers, and warehouses, using both automated and manual count methods to determine inventory shrinkage.

- Performed and supervised internal audits of large-to-medium volume retail locations, as well as individual home office departmental audits to improve productivity and loss prevention. Directed year-end outside audits, with emphasis on problem resolution and GAAP compliance to improve net profit.

24
Combination. *Nell Turk, Houston, Texas.*
A Career Summary sets the tone for this resume. This Summary and a Career Highlights section work together to produce a strong first page.

Andrew St. James   Page 2

EMPLOYMENT HISTORY

Gibson & Shuller, Inc. - Hemstead, NJ   1/90 - 2/93
Corporate Controller
Retailer of upscale and designer women's shoes and accessories. Operated in 40 locations, both in owned stores and in leased departments located in major markets across the U.S., with $28 million in sales volume. Reported directly to the two owners of the family-owned business who held the positions of President and Executive Vice President. Gained heavy experience in banking negotiations and crisis management, was responsible for personnel administration in the home office and in the stores, (personnel selection, salary administration and performance appraisals). Directly supervised 17 employees.

Lee - Stein, Inc. - Houston, TX   5/88 - 8/89
Corporate Controller
Owned and operated nine Lee - Stein retail stores, doing $20 million in sales volume. Assumed the responsibilities of the C.F.O. subsequent to his resignation and as a result gained extensive working knowledge of managing cash in a negative cash flow scenario. Internalized financial reporting and progressively reduced internal staffing which resulted in a $105k annual savings. Remained with parent after store segment of company was purchased, gaining heavy experience in liquidating the assets and liabilities of the parent.

Jamestown Department Stores - Laurel, MS   7/82 - 5/88
Accounting Systems Manager (4 yrs)
Internal Auditor (2 yrs)
A 160 store, $325 million chain, specializing in moderate to budget family apparel. Recruited as Internal Auditor. Gained experience in new store set ups, chain wide P.O.S. installation and training, as well as achieving the status of an extremely successful auditor, prompting promotion to Accounting Systems Manager. Was the accounting liaison for E.D.P. development gaining heavy experience in automated accounting systems and controls thereof, assisted outside auditors in year-end and interim audits, and was responsible for physical inventory.

The square filled bullets are fitting for the block-style paragraphs throughout. The equal length of paragraphs on p. 2 makes the shortest job (5/88-8/89) seem of equal importance.

JAMES L. GREGG
89 Glenwood Road
Marlboro, New Jersey 00000
(908) 000-0000

SUMMARY OF QUALIFICATIONS

Twenty years of financial management experience encompassing a steady progression of increasing accomplishments and responsibilities and active involvement in many major strategic decisions. Background also includes International Finance and management of a data processing organization. Primary strengths are excellent leadership, analytical, communication, and interpersonal skills.

EXPERIENCE

1975-Present   **H&H CHEMICALS, INC.** - A diversified International chemical company with sales of $500 million.

1986-Present   **VICE PRESIDENT, FINANCE & CONTROLLER**
Responsible for all finance and control functions, including data processing. **CHIEF FINANCIAL OFFICER** and member of the Executive Committee, which sets policies and strategic direction for the Corporation. Supervises several departments including 65 employees.

1979-1985   **CORPORATE CONTROLLER**

1977-1978   **DIRECTOR OF COST ACCOUNTING AND DATA PROCESSING**

1975-1976   **MANAGER OF COST ACCOUNTING**

ACCOMPLISHMENTS

- Significantly upgraded the Company's information systems (EDP) capabilities while at the same time reducing data processing costs by more than 20%.

- Initiated and led a program that reduced working capital by 5% of sales, thereby lowering interest and operating expenses by $3 million.

- Analyzed and participated in negotiation of many major acquisitions and divestitures which enhanced the strategic thrust of the Company.

- Significantly reduced accounting errors, accelerated the monthly closing cycle, and eliminated "surprises." Consistently had clean audit reports.

- Implemented financial statement reporting by major product line. This enhanced decision-making and focused business managers' attention on the "bottom line" for their products.

- Streamlined and enhanced the Corporate budgeting process and made it the cornerstone upon which the Company's operations are measured.

25

Combination. Beverly Baskin, CPRW, Marlboro, New Jersey.
The subject of this resume wanted his promotions within the current company to stand out. Putting an extensive Accomplishments section after these promotions calls attention to them.

JAMES L. GREGG   Page 2

<u>**ACCOMPLISHMENTS**</u> (Continued)

- Restructured foreign subsidiaries' balance sheets and updated transfer prices and management fees so that the Corporation's tax payments were reduced by over $1 million.

- Significantly improved the financial reporting systems to make them more responsive to the needs of the Business.

- Standardized cost accounting practices at all locations. This greatly enhanced controls and aided in decision-making.

- Developed and conducted financial seminars for Business Management to aid them in the use of financial concepts for decision-making.

1973 - 1975   **LONDON CORPORATION - ESSEX DIVISION**

> **MANAGER OF FINANCIAL PLANNING & ANALYSIS** - Supervised a department of eight. Responsible for preparation and review of the annual budget and long-range plans; operational analysis of monthly results and trends; preparation and analysis of capital expenditure requests; monthly closings.

1966 - 1973   **STAMCO, INC.**

> **SENIOR FINANCIAL ANALYST (1970-1973)** - Analyzed and prepared all major capital expenditure requests for submission to the Board of Directors; learned both FORTRAN and BASIC programming languages and developed timesharing computer models such as plant production simulation studies and Monte Carlo investment risk analysis.

> **CHEMICAL ENGINEER (1966-1969)**

EDUCATION

MASTER OF BUSINESS ADMINISTRATION, 1975 - Rutgers University

BACHELOR OF CHEMICAL ENGINEERING, 1966 - City College of New York (CCNY)

- Captain of City College Tennis Team
- President of Omega Tau Alpha Fraternity

PERSONAL

Married, two children, excellent health, likes to participate in athletic activities.

The 10 items in the Accomplishments section exhibit careful use of parallel verb forms. Although usually omitted nowadays, the Personal section ends the resume on a light note.

DAVID R. IRVING, CPA

635 Lakewide Drive
Millersville, Kentucky 00000
(000) 000-0000

CORPORATE ACCOUNTING & FINANCE EXECUTIVE

Corporate Controller with over 15 years experience building and leading high-caliber accounting, finance and administrative organizations. Combine strategic planning and business development expertise with strong technical qualifications to establish finance operations responsive to long-range corporate objectives for growth and profitability. Extensive background in real estate finance, budgeting, SEC reporting, corporate tax, credit/collections, acquisition analysis and executive negotiations.

PROFESSIONAL EXPERIENCE:

REYNOLDS MANAGEMENT CORPORATION, Philadelphia, PA   1990 to Present
(Residential & Commercial Property Development & Management Firm)

CONTROLLER

Senior Finance Executive with full responsibility for the strategic planning, development, implementation and management of all corporate cash management, treasury, accounting, financial reporting, financial analysis, and property/capital budgeting operations. Concurrent executive responsibility for corporate administration and human resources. Manage relationships with vendors, bankers, accountants, legal counsel and mortgage companies. Prepare detailed financial reviews and projections for potential acquisitions. Direct a staff of four.

- Reduced annual audit fees by 42% through improved recordkeeping procedures and development/implementation of a complete portfolio of internal controls.
- Automated a diversity of accounting, analysis and reporting systems, eliminated several accounting positions, and saved the corporation over $64,000 in annual payroll expenses.
- Increased monthly rent collections from 94% to 99% of billings through integration of improved credit and collection procedures.
- Decreased energy and water usage 12%-30% through implementation of utility conservation programs.
- Increased lease renewal by 14% at one property, saving more than $140,000 in turnover costs.

WYLIE PHARMACEUTICALS, INC., Greenwich, CT / Fort Washington, PA   1986 to 1989
(Publicly Traded, Start-Up Pharmaceutical Company)

CONTROLLER (1987 to 1989)

Promoted within one year of joining the company and accepted senior management assignment directing corporate accounting, budgeting, financial reporting and administrative functions. Managed corporate relationships with NASDAQ, outside legal counsel, external auditors and bankers, working to position Greenwich as a growth-oriented pharmaceutical products development and manufacturing organization.

- Worked in cooperation with CFO to develop a top-down $20 million annual operating budget and performance analysis program.
- Designed, implemented and oversaw accounting operations at multiple facilities (e.g., corporate HQ, administration, R&D).

ACCOUNTING MANAGER (1986 to 1987)

Prepared SEC filings, private placement documents, financial statements, and Federal and state tax returns.

- Led the automation of accounting and management information systems.

26

Combination. *Wendy S. Enelow, CPRW, Forest, Virginia.*
Horizontal lines enclose a capsule profile of this resume's senior executive. A solidly designed resume. Each position on a line is preceded and followed by blank lines.

DAVID R. IRVING, CPA - Page Two

TOUCHE ROSS & COMPANY (Deloitte & Touche), Stamford, CT   1981 to 1984
(International Public Accounting & Consulting Firm)

SENIOR ACCOUNTANT / MANAGEMENT CONSULTANT

Planned, executed and supervised audits of national, privately held and public companies. Prepared financial statements, parent company reporting packages, SEC filings and corporate tax returns. Consulted with corporate executives to evaluate financial condition, current assets and liabilities, long-term debt obligations and strategies to improve net profit.

- Wrote detailed performance improvement plan (emphasis on production cost reductions and operating efficiency improvements) for a $20 million manufacturer. Client accepted and implemented 98% of recommendations, successfully repositioning company for long-term profit improvement.
- Directed design/implementation of an improved credit and collection program that increased turnover of clients' accounts receivable from 4 to 9 times a year.
- Championed the introduction of microcomputer technology into the audit practice.

SMITH, BROWN, GREENE & CO., CPA's, Albany, NY   1978 to 1981
(Regional Full Service Public Accounting Firm)

CERTIFIED PUBLIC ACCOUNTANT

Specialized in corporate accounting, auditing, financial statement and tax return preparation. Industry experience included hospitality, health care and manufacturing.

RELATED PROFESSIONAL EXPERIENCE:

OMNI SYSTEMS CONSULTING INC., West Chester, PA   1989 to Present
(Software Development Consulting & Training Firm - Fortune 500 Clients)

CONSULTANT

Part-time consulting position providing strategic planning, financial and human resources support to the principals of this high-growth venture. Supervise the entire accounting operation, issue monthly financial reports and prepare detailed profit/performance analyses. Consult regarding long-range business development and market positioning.

- Worked with the President of the firm to develop and implement strategic plan which has expanded product line threefold and increased revenues by more than 35%.
- Directed the selection, installation and ongoing operations of automated accounting systems for A/R, A/P, G/L, Payroll and Financial Reporting.

EDUCATION:

UNIVERSITY OF PENNSYLVANIA - WHARTON SCHOOL OF BUSINESS
Small Business Development Program Management Certificate (1993)

PENNSYLVANIA STATE UNIVERSITY - SMEAL SCHOOL OF BUSINESS
MBA - Finance & Management (1986)

STATE UNIVERSITY OF NEW YORK - ALBANY
MS - Accounting (1981)
BS - Accounting (1977)

Certified Public Accountant

After each position, a paragraph describes duties and responsibilities. After each paragraph, a bulleted list presents achievements. Almost all of these are quantified.

ARLO B. TWAIN, CPA, CIA
600 E. Glenview
Some City, ST 00000
(000) 000-0000

PROFILE

Outstanding analytical skills; demonstrated ability to interpret and summarize data into meaningful information. Vast knowledge of and experience in reviewing the design of internal financial control and administrative systems. In-depth exposure to all facets of a Famous University and the Famous University Hospitals and Clinics. Extensive experience in preparing financial reports and narrative reports to State officials, upper management and others.

PROFESSIONAL EXPERIENCE

OFFICE OF STATE OFFICIAL - FAMOUS STATE, Some City, State

State Task Manager - 19XX to 19XX
-- Manage and assign daily workloads to professional staff of 10 workers.
-- Review operational systems and procedures of various University departments to assess viability and efficiency.
-- Develop and maintain cordial working relationships with U of X and XUHC administrators on various levels.
-- Budget manpower and resources in organizing tasks; assign responsibilities, delegate authority, and review documents for accuracy and completeness.
-- Conduct analytical procedures on financial data to determine reasonableness of amounts reported.
-- Contribute to development of goals and priorities of Official of State office through participation in annual management retreat.
-- Selected to participate on internal quality review team. Review was designed to improve operations in preparation for external review to be performed Fall, 19XX.

State Task Supervisor - 19XX to 19XX
-- Led task team of 5-6 workers in performing various assignments at the Famous University and the Famous University Hospitals and Clinics.
-- Interpreted and applied Federal and State laws and regulations in testing compliance of grants and contracts.
-- Evaluated the Famous University's internal task control systems in recommending updates or improvements.
-- Authored management letters containing comments and recommendations highlighting system improvements.
-- Studied Medicare/Medicaid programs at a famous institution in Some City.

Senior Official - 19XX to 19XX
-- Oversaw and assigned duties to task crew of two or more assistants.
-- Prepared annual financial statements for review and publication.
-- Studied sampling approach on study tests performed at assigned state and local governmental units.

Assistant Official - 19XX to 19XX
-- Performed tasks on municipalities and smaller school districts under close supervision.

---

27 *Combination. Elizabeth J. Axnix, CPRW, Iowa City, Iowa.*
The Profile sells the person at the beginning. The Professional Experience section displays a steady rise to higher positions. Lists for each position present duties and achievements.

ARLO B. TWAIN, CPA, CIA
Page Two

CAREER-RELATED EXPERIENCE

FAMOUS STATE SPECIAL BOARD
> *Committee Member* - Special Management Systems Group, 19XX to 19XX
>> -- Appointed by Special State Official to serve on committee charged with determining need for and costs of new administration systems for state universities and XUHC.

NATIONAL STATE OFFICIALS ASSOCIATION
> *Team Leader* - Special Review Team, Month, 19XX
>> -- Recommended policy and procedure improvements to increase quality of work produced by the Famous State Official's Office.

> *Team Member* - Special Review Team, Month, 19XX
>> -- Evaluated special system of State Official's Office.
>> -- Recommended as Team Leader for future reviews.

EDUCATION

Bachelor of Science degree in **Industrial Administration** (Special Field)
Famous University, Some City, State, 19XX

MEMBERSHIPS AND ACCREDITATIONS

Certified State Official, State Officials' Institution, 19XX
Certified Special Worker, State Board of Special Work, 19XX
State Group of Special Workers, 19XX to 19XX
> *Member* - Special Committee
> *Member* - Another Special Committee, 19XX
> *Member* - Important Professional Group

COMPUTER EXPERIENCE

Use Lotus 1-2-3, Word for Windows, Volkswriter, Easy Flow (flow chart) and Desktop Publishing on IBM PC and laptop. Design Lotus macros for office-wide use. Act as computer resource person. Experienced in networking by modem.

COMMUNITY SERVICE

Instructor - Famous University Special Club, 19XX to 19XX

Treasurer - Sebastian Protestant Church, Some City, State, 19XX to 19XX
> -- Designed a computerized financial system to produce accurate financial statements in a timely manner using Lotus 1-2-3.
> -- Chaired Task Committee

Volunteer - Big Brothers/Big Sisters Program of Gaither County, 19XX to 19XX

This diversified page displays breadth in team leadership, professional memberships, computer literacy, and community service. Note how the use of italic unites the first two pages.

ARLO B. TWAIN, CPA, CIA
Page Three

AWARDS
Named to Who's Who Among Rising Young Americans (19XX, 19XX)
Awarded Famous Award, 19XX

CONFERENCES ATTENDED
Group of College and University Officials
19XX Annual Conference, Some City, State
19XX Annual Conference, Some City, State

National Special Officials Group
Special Annual Conference, Some City, State, 19XX

Organization of Famous Officials
Famous Officials in Government Conference, Some City, State, 19XX

CONTINUING EDUCATION

Course	Date	Provider	Location
Procedures Update	3/XX	In-house	Another City, ST
Course #XXX	3/XX	In-house	Another City, ST
Manager as Coach	3/XX	Career Track	Famous City, ST
Overview of Course #XXX	3/XX	In-house	Another City, ST
Management Round Table	7/XX	In-house	Another City, ST
Human Resource Management (Graduate level)	8/XX	Famous University	Some City, ST
Quantitative Methods (Graduate Level)	5/XX	Famous University	Some City, ST
Special Procedures IV	5/XX	In-house	Another City, ST
An Assertive Manager	5/XX	In-house	Another City, ST
Compliance Tasking	5/XX	In-house	Another City, ST
Official of State	12/XX	In-house	Another City, ST
County Activities	11/XX	In-house	Another City, ST
Ethics	5/XX	Group of Governmental Personnel	Another City, ST
One-Minute Manager	2/XX	Career Track	Famous City, ST
19XX Revisions of Special Book			Teleconference
How to Supervise People	5/XX	In-house	Another City, ST
Relevant Controls	4/XX	Group of Governmental Officials	Another City, ST
Special Implementation	4/XX	Famous Firm	Another City, ST
Lotus Advanced	10/XX	Special Group	Some City, ST
Lotus Intermediate	10/XX	Special Group	Some City, ST
Microcomputer Tasking	5/XX	Group of Special Officials	Another City, ST
Computer Training	3/XX	In-house	Another City, ST
Task Sampling	11/XX	In-house	Another City, ST

The substantial entries here justify the inclusion of a third page. Extensive participation in continuing education offsets the lone Education entry on the second page.

Administrative Assistant/Secretary Resumes at a Glance

FRANCES SMITH
123 Main Street
San Diego, CA 00000
(619) 555-0000

CAREER
SUMMARY

◆ Experienced highly competent administrative assistant and secretary.
◆ Strong interpersonal and communication skills.
◆ Computer knowledgeable.

EXPERIENCE
1992-1993

RANCHO BERNARDO INN, San Diego, CA
Catering Administrative Assistant

◆ Worked directly with vendors to ensure accuracy and completeness.
◆ Worked with clients on final requirements for their functions.
◆ Daily distribution of activity reports, function sheets, memos, etc.
◆ Weekly distribution of prospectus packet to clients and hotel departments.
◆ Provided secretarial and administrative support services.

1987-1991

SHOWTIME NETWORKS INC., New York, NY
Secretary/Sales Reporting and Analysis

◆ Collected data from regional offices for national distribution; located, researched and resolved discrepancies.
◆ Assisted in preparation of weekly and monthly reports.
◆ Tracked distribution of national monthly report.
◆ Maintained library of departmental reports; input in WordPerfect.
◆ Provided secretarial and administrative support services.

1985-1987

AMERICAN SAVINGS BANK, East Meadow, NY
New Business Assistant, AmWide Inc.

◆ Acted as liaison between life insurance agents and Savings Bank Life Insurance Fund.
◆ Provided administrative assistance to senior executives.
◆ Contacted agents regarding application status.
◆ Determined that requirements were met without delays; reviewed, investigated and resolved related problems.
◆ Prepared periodic sales reports.

1984-1985

NOBLE LOWNDES INTERNATIONAL, INC., New York, NY
Secretary/Word Processor - Computer Software Company

◆ Performed word processing, administrative support and switchboard duties.
◆ Generated correspondence and financial reports.
◆ Greeted visitors, screened telephone calls.

REFERENCES

Available upon request.

Chronological. Ruth L. Binder, CPRW, San Diego, California.
This resume's design can be comprehended at a glance. Diamond-shaped bullets lead the
reader's attention down through the resume. Good use of blank lines for white space.

28

JUANITA Q. PUBLIQUE

123 Main Street • Anytown, USA 12345
555-123-4567 • 555-234-5678

OBJECTIVE

To work in a challenging position that would assist your company in achieving growth
and profits through maximum use of my experience and qualifications.

EXPERIENCE

Administrative Assistant • Realtor
Summer Properties, Menlo Park, CA • 1990 to 1993

Assisted top producing realtors and brokers in the following: Handled all marketing,
escrow and property appraisal administration. This position required extensive
customer and co-worker interaction.

Realtor
Little Known Real Estate, Palo Alto, CA • 1989 to 1990

Marketed, administered, and successfully sold real property.

Director of Marketing Services • Production Coordinator for Syndication Division
LFC Financial Corporation, San Mateo, CA • 1983 to 1988
Real Estate Investment Company, Division of John Jones Companies

Worked for national real estate developer:
Managed production of all marketing materials. Handled project development with
production vendors, including graphic designers, photographers, editors, while
ensuring all deadlines and budgets were met. Coordinated site selection. Developed
and negotiated entire travel and function budgets for meetings, seminars and
promotional trips. Designed and implemented display booth for trade shows.

Sales Associate • Office Administrator
Smith & Associates, Palo Alto, CA • 1981 to 1983

Established and serviced advertising accounts for two trade publications. Maintained
office production. Responsible for marketing products at trade shows.

ADDITIONAL EXPERIENCE & ATTRIBUTES

- 15+ years administrative experience
- Coordinate and attend trade shows
- Type 70+ WPM

- Interview and supervise personnel
- Work well under deadlines
- Computer literate

EDUCATION

AA–Office Administration • *Division of Indiana/Purdue University, Ft. Wayne, IN*
California Real Estate License • *Anthony Schools, Menlo Park, CA*
Travel Career and Continuing Education • *Foothill College, Los Altos, CA*

REFERENCES AVAILABLE UPON REQUEST

29

Combination. Elaine Jackson, Boulder Creek, California.
The Objective statement exhibits confidence, and the Experience section displays movement
toward higher levels of responsibility. Original resume on sharp designer paper.

S. OLIVIA HANSON
4444 Kitz Road
Evansville, Indiana 47711
(812) 555-5555

PROFILE

Highly skilled Executive Secretary with outstanding, professional experience including:

▸ Ability to communicate with all levels of management and employees.
▸ International communication liaison with subsidiary companies.
▸ Contract Negotiation Bargaining Team member.
▸ Use of word processing, Windows and training on Lotus 1-2-3.

EXPERIENCE

PIONEER CORPORATION Evansville, Indiana
Executive Secretary 5/88 - 8/93
• Served as secretary to the Director of Plant Operations and to the Director of Engineering.
• Assisted in start-up of two branches of the company (Brazil, S.A., Ft. Smith, AR).
• Arranged all aspects of international and domestic travel for Engineering Department.
• Member of bargaining unit representing the Company during contract negotiations.
• Maintained executive calendars, scheduled appointments, and fielded phone calls.
• Prepared draft of monthly reports regarding current capital engineering projects.
• Routed all incoming company mail to appropriate department.
• Assisted in the preparation and editing of the company newsletter.
• Provided visitor assistance and arranged departmental luncheons.

SEIGNMAN ENGINEERING Evansville, Indiana
Part-Time Secretary/Receptionist 1983 - 1985
• Assisted with compiling legal data and putting it in chronological order.
• Prepared court exhibits.
• Typed correspondence and legal documents.
• Answered phones and greeted clients.

CENTRAL SERVICE Evansville, Indiana
Customer Service Representative 1978 - 1980
• Located overages/shortages at main store.
• Answered service calls, scheduled appointments, and resolved customer complaints.
• Performed clerical and cashier duties.

PET MEDICAL CENTER Evansville, Indiana
Veterinarian Assistant 1972 - 1978
• Assisted in surgery with anesthesia and instruments.
• Provided pre- and post-operative animal care.
• Performed administrative clerical and reception duties.

EDUCATION

INDIANA VOCATIONAL TECHNICAL COLLEGE Evansville, Indiana
Professional Secretary Certification November 1993

References Available Upon Request

Combination. *Teresa Collins, CPRW, Evansville, Indiana.*
This clean-looking resume has distinctive touches: the horizontal line interrupted by the phone number, and right-pointing bullets that highlight skills and achievements.

30

Marion Jones

500 Maple Lane, Wind Haven, New Jersey 00000   (000) 000-0000

Efficient Administrative Assistant skilled in coordinating functions, developing/promoting programs and servicing clients. Accustomed to handling diverse responsibilities resourcefully. Excellent writing and communications skills. Expertise includes:

Customer Service	Public Relations	Office Administration
Order Processing	Special Events	Meeting Planning
Marketing	Newsletters	Supervision

CAREER EXPERIENCE:

THIRD UNION BANK, Princeton, New Jersey   1992-Date
Customer Service Representative
- Resolve customer inquiries by referencing computer records and reconciling differences.
- Market accounts and other bank products. Consult with clients and interact extensively by phone.

R. & J. SMITH DISTRIBUTORS, INC., New Hope, Pennsylvania   1985-1992
Office Manager for Manufacturer's Representative Firm   1981-1982
- Set up and managed work flow of corporate office including order processing, invoicing, correspondence and bookkeeping.
- Liaison with suppliers. Expedited deliveries to ensure customer satisfaction.

MANHATTAN DEPARTMENT STORE, New York, New York   1983-1985
Buyer's Assistant
- Bought and priced occasional/accent furniture with sales volume of over $50 million.
- Developed catalog line and marketing strategies. Coordinated merchandising programs.
- Organized and presented furniture catalog pages at divisional meetings. Resulted in increased catalog pages for occasional furniture.
Special Accomplishments: Received cash award for outstanding marketing presentation. Composed instruction letter about shipping/handling, which is still used to guide vendors.

FAMILY SERVICE, INC., New York, New York   1975-1981
Public Information Coordinator
- Supervised and trained clerical assistants for public information department. Oversaw PR projects by volunteers in the U.S. and Canada, including 20 national exhibits annually.
- Coordinated the participation of 10,000 people in the 1980 International Convention. Guided the Canadian, Australian and New Zealand services. Prepared and chaired workshops.
- Supervised the creation and publication yearly of 6,000-circulation newsletter as well as an in-house publication for membership. Developed articles, brochures, kit materials and other literature.
- Developed and supervised direction and casting of TV and radio commercials.
Special Accomplishments: Won New York Art Director's Award for Best Public Information Poster Campaign. Featured speaker at American Psychiatric Convention, Rutgers University and conferences.

EDUCATION:

Garden State University, Chatham, New Jersey - B.A., Sociology
Columbia University/School of Sociology, New York, New York - Certificate

SKILLS: WordPerfect (5.1), Data Entry, Typing

---

31 *Combination. Vivian P. Belen, CPRW, Fair Lawn, New Jersey.*
An easy-to-read scanning list at the top makes this worker's areas of expertise readily visible to the reader. Special Accomplishments follow duties and other achievements.

SUSAN WHITAKER
1227 Juniper Drive
Bloomington, Indiana 00000
(812) 555-5555

HIGHLIGHTS OF QUALIFICATIONS

- Four years experience in administrative/clerical support positions.
- Easily establish rapport with managers, staff, and customers.
- Proficient at analyzing statistics and market trends to develop accurate forecasts and effective sales presentations.
- Excellent problem-solving, project management and decision-making skills.
- Proven ability to prioritize and complete multiple tasks.

COMPUTER SKILLS

Software:	WordPerfect, Microsoft Word for Windows
Graphics:	Harvard Graphics, PowerPoint for Windows
Database:	Telemagic
Hardware:	Apple IIE, HP and most IBM compatibles
Spreadsheets:	Lotus 1-2-3, Microsoft Excel, Quattro Pro

OFFICE SKILLS

65+ wpm typing, 75 wpm word processing, 70+ wpm shorthand, CRT, dictation, 10-key adding machine, statistical analysis

PROFESSIONAL EXPERIENCE

PEPSI-COLA COMPANY, Indianapolis, Indiana   1988 - Present
Administrative Assistant

- Analyze sales volume and profit.
- Finalize and package forecasting reports for more than $100 million in annual sales.
- Monitor monthly spending and reconciliation for $8 million budget.
- Manage $300,000 in advertising and promotional materials.
- Interact with sales staff impacting service to 1200 customers.

EDUCATION

Executive Secretarial Certificate, 1988
ITT TECHNICAL INSTITUTE, Indianapolis, Indiana
- Dean's List, 3.7/4.0 GPA
- Maintained perfect attendance record

REFERENCES AVAILABLE UPON REQUEST

Combination. *John A. Suarez, CPRW, St. Louis, Missouri.*
Qualifications and skills dominate this resume. Computer skills are categorized, and office skills are quantified. Bullets in several sections unify the resume visually.

32

MOTHER GOOSE

Administrative Assistant

6500 Shier Rings Road • Amlin, OH 00000 • 000/000-0000

SUMMARY OF EXPERIENCE

Office Experience

- Experienced word processing knowledge in WordPerfect, IBM
- Knowledge of Lotus 1-2-3 and dBASE; DOS computer system; typing (90 WPM); transcribe from transcription equipment
- Order office supplies, organize office, maintain filing, handle incoming telephone requests, compose letters, prepare reports (ensuring confidentiality), and bookkeeping

Office Coordination/Scheduling

- Oversee day-to-day management of office to ensure all activities are running smoothly
- Assist in planning jobs, setting goals, and ensuring work is completed in a timely manner
- Arrange conferences, airline and hotel reservations, plan itineraries, schedule appointments
- Proficient in handling simultaneous projects and meeting deadlines effectively
- Proven ability to interact with clients and staff at all levels

Administrative Support Projects

- Prepare and submit budgets
- **Offer extensive Human Resource assistance**
- Work within safety committee; promotions committee
- Conducted seminars for staff on Management Training on Property
- Attended management conferences
- Obtained sponsors for March of Dimes

EXPERIENCE

ABC HOTEL • Anytown, OH • June 81 to Present
First class hotel and restaurant chain consisting of 40 hotels throughout U. S. and Mexico.

1990	Executive Secretary	1983	Assistant Front Office Manager
1985	Front Office Manager	1981	Reservation Manager

Highlights:

- Letter composition, typing, filing
- Forecasting, budgeting, payroll
- Control and selling of guest rooms; conducting tours of guest rooms, checking in and checking out guests, reservations
- Supervise and schedule employees
- Interview prospective employees; hire needed personnel; terminate and conduct exit interviews
- Ensure ADA Compliance in the workplace
- Successful handling of guest complaints

ATTORNEY FIRM • Anytown, OH • September 1979 - June 1981
Law firm representing trucking firms.

Legal Secretary
Typed contracts, wills; filing; general office duties.

EDUCATION

ANYTOWN TECHNICAL INSTITUTE • Associate Degree • 1987
Secretarial Science/Legal/Basic Accounting

TECHNICAL COLLEGE • Anytown, OH • January 1977 - June 1979
Major: Court Reporting

33

Combination. *Susan Higgins, Amlin, Ohio.*
The Summary of Experience section is conveniently divided into three areas for easy recognition. Almost 90 percent of the resume is devoted in some way to experience.

Animal Care
Resumes at a Glance

SPOTSWOOD BRAVO

265 Charlotte Street
Asheville, NC 00000
000/000-0000

Office Cat

Seeking a career of challenge and service in professional environment. Documented competence and initiative; promotion to high-visibility position on executive desk (in Out-Box) gained through merit and softness of fur. Highly unusual markings. Dedicated; often asleep.

EXPERIENCE

GATEHOUSE BUSINESS SERVICES, Asheville, NC
Supervisor/Mouse Patrol
- Initiated and implemented program of systematic reduction of staff in mouse department; 75% reduction in record time.
- Enthusiastic purring, adaptability, and open-door accessibility resulted in marked improvement in office morale.

JOHN JONES HOUSEHOLD, Asheville, NC
House Cat
- Consistently met mouse quota while maintaining appearance of complete ease.
- Liaison to dog, successfully representing 2 other much-older cats in difficult negotiations.
- Communications ability, far-sightedness (can see in the dark), combined with excellent climbing and decision-making skills, led to rapid promotion as Top Cat.

HUMANE SOCIETY, Asheville, NC
Kitten
- Instrumental in bringing record number of potential adopters to kitten section during open house.
- Outstanding good looks resulted in adoption of mother as well as siblings.

EDUCATION

Graduate, The Silent Miaow, Paul Gallico course on how to become an indispensable member of a human household.

REFERENCES

Excellent, perhaps overly enthusiastic references available on request.

Chronological. Dayna Feist, Asheville, North Carolina.
This easy-to-read resume, making good use of white space, is for a real cat that probably couldn't care less about relocation or a new career.

34

Lola A. Mueller

_____Professional Profile

5000 Shenley Drive
Erie, Pennsylvania 00000
(000) 000-0000

**Summary of
Qualifications:**
Administrative Skills:
Recruit volunteers, write subpermits, inventory control, organize and
conduct fund-raising events, coordinate and schedule staff
Communication Skills:
Prepare and design hand-outs, write news releases, sales experience and
receptionist duties
Educational Skills:
Prepare and conduct training sessions, work with interns perusing the
wildlife field
Writing Skills:
Grant writing for a non-profit organization, file year end reports and request
up-to-date permits

**Professional
Highlights:**
10/91 - present
Erie Animal Hospital, Erie, Pennsylvania
Veterinarian Receptionist
Responsible for extensive Receptionist duties. Handle incoming calls, direct
calls, assist customers with situations, file, type, data entry, dispense
medicines and bill patients. As a Veterinarian Technician, restrain animals,
draw blood, assist doctors, check laboratory specimens and perform
various other duties as assigned.

03/90 - 09/91
Canine Control Division, Woodbridge, Connecticut
Canine Control Officer
Responsible for pet therapy at nursing homes, daily record keeping, license
survey, issue infractions for dog law violations and answered dog
complaints. Also impound stray dogs, handle dog adoptions, euthanize
dogs and attend special educational / training programs.

10/88 - 03/90
Bethany Veterinary Hospital, Bethany, Connecticut
Veterinary Technician Assistant
Responsible for prescription dispensing, prepare vaccines, assist surgeons
during surgery, clean cages, feed animals and autoclave surgical
instruments. Also assume all Receptionist duties.

06/86 - 06/88
Connecticut Audubon Society, Fairfield, Connecticut
Educator / Assistant
Responsible for the environmental education for K-6 grade. Also wildlife
rehabilitator, fund-raiser for wildlife program, coordinate volunteers and
oversee the Foster Family Program.

Education:
08/85
The Pennsylvania State University, State College, Pennsylvania
Master of Science in Recreation and Parks

06/82
Mercyhurst College, Erie, Pennsylvania
Bachelor of Arts in Environmental Studies

References:
Available upon request

35

Combination. _Wendy A. Lowry, Erie, Pennsylvania._
A difficult resume for a multitalented person who, with education and experience in one
field, wants to expand into some other field but hasn't chosen it yet. Boldfacing is effective.

COLLEEN M. VALLIERE

55 Beatle Road
Union, Maine 55555

Call (000) 555-5555   Fax (000) 888-8888

CURRICULUM VITAE

EDUCATION:

Bachelor of Science Degree   **Animal and Veterinary Sciences**
University of Maine,Orono, Maine (May 1989)

Associate of Science Degree   **Animal Medical Technology**
University of Maine, Orono, Maine (August 1988)

CERTIFICATIONS & LICENSURE:

AALAS Certified, Laboratory Animal Technologist   **October 1993**
AALAS Certified, Laboratory Animal Technician   **March 1992**

Licensed Animal Technician, State of Oklahoma   **June 1988**
State Board of Veterinary Medicine (No. 123)

PROFESSIONAL EXPERIENCE:

The Miller Laboratory, Boothbay Harbor, Maine   **1991-1993**
Research Assistant (1992-1993)
• Researched mouse models for Alopecia Areata and Inflammatory Bowel Disease.
• Research involved colony management, record keeping, and specialized techniques.
• Techniques included necropsy, surgery, bacterial culturing, and tissue freezing.
• Presented research data to the scientific community.

Senior Laboratory Technician II, Animal Health Department (1991-1992)
• Examined animals and collected biological specimens.
• Prepared surgical packs and schedules for animal and environmental monitoring.
• Conducted follow-up investigations.
• Collected, analyzed, and entered computer data.
• Taught and oriented students.

Hurtz Dairy, Norway, Maine   **1989-1991 (On Call 1991-Present)**
Herdsperson
• Manage Holstein herd; directly involved in all areas of herd health.

Curriculum vitae. Rolande L. LaPointe, CPC, CIPC, CPRW, Auburn, Maine.
Usually longer than a resume, a curriculum vitae (course of one's life or career) often includes
certifications, publications, memberships, activities, and references. Original had a cover sheet.

36

COLLEEN M. VALLIERE   **Curriculum Vitae (Page Two)**

PROFESSIONAL EXPERIENCE: (continued)

- Responsible for overall disease prevention and treatment.
- Work in all aspects of husbandry, milking, record keeping, and sanitation.
- Perform field work including heavy equipment operations.
- Supervise dairy farm and co-workers during owner's absence and on call.

University of Maine, Augusta, Maine   **1989**
Dairy Research Technician
- Collected blood samples via the jugular and coccygeal veins from over 50 Holsteins and Jerseys.

- Obtained regular weight and temperature readings.
- Processed blood samples in the laboratory.

J.T. White Center, University of Maine, Augusta, Maine   **1989**
Farm Hand
- Position involved milking and routine care of Holsteins and Jerseys.

Rumford Veterinary Hospital, Rumford, Maine   **1988**
Animal Medical Technologist Internship
- Performed laboratory techniques.
- Assisted in surgical procedures.
- Provided animal nursing of both large and small animals.

Med-Pro Laboratory, Harrison, Maine   **1988**
Laboratory Animal Technician Internship
- Performed regular plasmapheresis along with routine care of goats, sheep, and rabbits.

- Processed blood in the laboratory and maintained records.

Harmon's Hill Dairy, Marsh, Maine   **Summer 1987**
Farm Hand
- Position involved milking and routine care of Holsteins.

Charles Veterinary Hospital, Freeport, Maine   **Summer 1986**
Veterinarian's Assistant
- Position involved laboratory, surgical assistance, animal husbandry and receptionist duties.

Professional Experience section includes university student summer work and shows the progression from a veterinarian's assistant to a certified laboratory animal technologist.

COLLEEN M. VALLIERE   *Curriculum Vitae (Page Three)*

ABSTRACTS, PUBLICATIONS & ACKNOWLEDGMENTS:

Valliere, C.M., Sundberg, J.P., and King, L.E.

- Poster presented "An Alopecia Areata-Like Disease in Aging C_3H/Hej Mice."

- The Genetic Short Course, The Jefferson Laboratory, Port Clyde, Maine, July, 1993.

Valliere, C.M., Sundberg, J.P., and King, L.E.

- "An Alopecia Areta-Like Disease in Aging C_3H/Hej Mice."

- Abstract presented at the 44th AALAS meeting in Nashville, TN, November, 1993.

Sundberg, J.P., Valliere, C.M., and King, L.E.

- "Alopecia Areata in Aging C_3H/Hej Mice," *Mouse Mutations with Skin and Hair Abnormalities: Animal Models and Biomedical Tools.*

- Book in press, 1993.

Sundberg, J.P., Cordy, W., and King L.E.

- "Alopecia Areata in Aging C_3H/Hej Mice," *Journal of Investigative Dermatology,* submitted 1993.

MEMBERSHIPS:

American Association for Laboratory Animal Science
Member, (AALAS)   1992 & 1993

Ellsworth Concert Band, Ellsworth, Maine   1992 & 1993

National Block and Bridle "Maine Animal Club," Member
University of Maine, Orono, Maine   1988-1989

Abstracts, Publications, & Acknowledgments section displays the subject's growing involvement with an article. Both undergraduate and postgraduate memberships given.

COLLEEN M. VALLIERE

Curriculum Vitae (Page Four)

RELATED ACTIVITIES & VOLUNTEER WORK:

Heifer Project International Volunteer	**April, 1993**
Raised backyard flock of Rhode Island Reds	**1990**

Judging Team, Maine Animal Club
• Contest held at Cornell University, New York   February, 1989

Orono Royal Livestock Show
University of Maine, Orono, Maine
• Dairy Show   April, 1989
• Sheep Show   April, 1988

S.P.C.A. Volunteer   **1979-1981**
Society for the Prevention of Cruelty to Animals, Auburn, Maine
• Position involved daily care, grooming, and feeding of dogs, cats and some wildlife.

REFERENCES:

Dr. Terrie Harrison
Animal Health Department Clinical Medicine
The Jefferson Laboratory
000 Main Street
Port Clyde, Maine 00000   Telephone: (000) 000-1111 Ext. 0000

Dr. Barbara A. Bailey
Manager, Dairy Research
Oak Mills, Inc.
Box 67812
St. Louis, Missouri 00000   Telephone: (000) 000-1111

Dr. Allan Carrigan
Animal and Veterinary Science Department
University of Maine
Orono, Maine 00000   Telephone: (000) 000-1111

Tom Blynn
Blynn's Dairy
Box 0000
Carthage, Maine 00000   Telephone: (000) 000-1111

Related Activities & Volunteer Work section shows a long-time interest in, and diversified involvement with, animals. References span work, education, and postgraduate research.

Career Change
Resumes at a Glance

Any Street   (000) 000-0000
Any Town, USA 00000

RESUME
of
JANICE DOE

***   Twenty years of experience as an Administrative Specialist with the United States Army.

***   Effective trainer and leader accustomed to ensuring correct training procedures, encouraging professional growth of trainees through continuation of education.

***   Demonstrated skills in promptly completing assigned tasks, initiated methods to improve section, and proven commitment to mission accomplishment.

EXPERIENCE

8/73 - 9/93   United States Army
                   Administrative Specialist

                   Accomplishments:

                   ✓ Supervised one NCO and three enlisted soldiers responsible for providing personnel services to 4,000 soldiers.
                   ✓ Provided personnel support services which included: processing all promotion worksheet data for initial evaluations and follow-up reevaluations, and point adjustments for promotions.
                   ✓ Ensured promotion packets were filed and orders published by deadline.
                   ✓ Served as Assistant Squad Leader.

EDUCATION/ TRAINING

                   Clerk Typist - eight weeks
                   Personnel Management Specialist - six weeks
                   Personnel Senior Sergeant - five weeks

                   Additional Military Courses: Administration, Primary Leadership, Medical Records, Medical Specialist, Criminal Investigation, Senior Sergeant, and Veterans Food Inspector.

REFERENCES AVAILABLE UPON REQUEST

Combination. *Claudia Stephenson, Bismarck, North Dakota.*
A "first-timer" resume for someone who joined the Army after high school and served for 20 years. She now must show how skills learned in the Army can benefit the private sector.

37

JAMES ROBERT JONES

| 2400 Rising Trail | Atlanta, Georgia 00000 | (000) 335-0000 |

OBJECTIVE

To secure a Teaching or Counseling position in a High School or Technical School specializing in Industrial Arts Education.

SUMMARY OF QUALIFICATIONS

Eleven years experience in training, counseling, and participation in various educational activities including classes for a wide range of audiences on multiple topics. Completed Practical Teaching at Madison County Technical School and participated as a substitute teacher in Madison County, Alabama. Currently hold *Conditional Certification for State of Georgia.*

Counseling

Fostered congenial, productive atmosphere for 115 employees. Formulated new ideas; updated old procedures. Counseled and scrutinized employees regularly; set training goals and monitored progress. Implemented changes which allowed intellectual growth.

Training

Prepared and scheduled training for small organization. Implemented safety practices. Established and evaluated training and performance of tasks.

Personnel

Interviewed and counseled over 2500 clients seeking security clearances. Obtained information to assist in conducting background checks and investigations. Apprised unit executive of best qualified individuals. Managed sensitive files and records. *Acknowledged for high-level performance.*

Administrative

Defined detailed guidelines and supervised full maintenance program services; *received Unit Award in recognition of performance.*

Personal endeavors were recognized with The Department of the Army Customer Service of Excellence Award.

EMPLOYMENT HISTORY

U.S. ARMY, 1982 to 1993, *Honorable Discharge*

EDUCATION

ALABAMA A&M UNIVERSITY, Normal, Alabama
Bachelor of Science with Honors, Industrial Arts Education

Kappa Delta Pi, National Educational Honor Fraternity
Alpha Kappa Mu, National Honor Society - President
Sigma Tau Epsilon, Education and Business Fraternity - Founding Father

38 *Functional (Skills). Carol Lawrence, CPRW, Snellville, Georgia.*
Another resume for a person leaving the military. An extensive Summary of Qualifications section describes four groups of activities displaying skills that can transfer to civilian life.

JOHN ROBERT BURNS, JR.

0 Academy Cove • Oxford, Mississippi 38655 • (601) 555-5555   Hermland Plantation • Gibson, Mississippi 39150 • (601) 555-5555

OBJECTIVE: Obtain an administrative or managerial position with a technical firm utilizing my leadership, technical, and business skills.

EDUCATION: **Master of Business Administration**
University of Mississippi, Oxford, Mississippi
Completion: December 1992

Bachelor of Engineering
University of Mississippi, Oxford, Mississippi
Emphases: Telecommunications and Business
Completion: December 1991

WORK EXPERIENCE:

November 1989 - Present   Communications NCOIC
Mississippi Army National Guard, Jackson, Mississippi
- Responsible for 21 subordinates, 3 vehicles and all communications equipment

December 1988 -   DMZ Sincgars Trainer
October 1989   **United States Army**, Camp Howze, South Korea
- Taught DMZ battalion the characteristics, use and maintenance of Sincgars
- Responsible for $1.5 million in secret radio inventories

December 1988 -   Communication Security Custodian
October 1989   **United States Army**, Camp Howze, South Korea
- Responsible for security, destruction, and dissemination of materials to subordinate units

July 1888 - December 1988   Radio Section Sergeant
United States Army, Camp Howze, South Korea
- Responsible for all communications equipment, 15 radios, 4 vehicles, and 12 people

July 1986 - April 1988   Radio Team Chief
United States Army, Fort Bragg, North Carolina
- In charge of Radio/Teletype team, 3 people, equipment, vehicle, and generator

April 1984 - April 1985   Maintenance Manager
Southwest Supply Company, Laurel, Mississippi
- Maintained efficient warehouse
- Operated heavy transportation equipment

May 1981 - December 1982   Skilled Labor
Summers 1980 & 1983   **Arrow Contractors**, Venice, Louisiana
- Served as lead-off hand on maintenance crew, crane operator, and pipe fitter
- Responsible for tools, equipment, and crane

HONORS & ACTIVITIES:
Academic
- Chancellor's Honor Roll
- Dean's List

Military
- United States Paratrooper
- 2 Army Achievement Medals
- 2 Army Commendation Medals
- Honors Graduate of Primary Leadership Development Course
- Honors Graduate of Basic Non-Commissioned Officer Course

Chronological. Leo J. Lazarus, Oxford, Mississippi.
The Objective statement focuses on leadership, technical, and business skills for this former paratrooper with an engineering degree, communications experience, and a recent M.B.A.

39

OUTSTANDING FLYBOY

Current Address	**Social Security Number**	**Business Address**
590 Airport Drive	000-00-0000	Directorate of Plans, Training,
Enterprise, AL 00000-0000		Mobilization, and Security
(000) 000-0000		Fort Rucker, AL 00000
FAX (000) 000-0000		(000) 000-0000

OBJECTIVE: Career pilot/instructor pilot employment

FLIGHT RATINGS:
- Airline Transport Pilot: Airplane Multiengine Land
- Commercial Privileges: Airplane Single engine land; Rotorcraft Helicopter, Instrument
- Written Exam: Flight Engineer Turbojet (02/93, 96%)
- Medical Certificate: FAA Class I, no limitations, 20/20 uncorrected vision
- Radiotelephone Operator Permit: Restricted

FLIGHT TIMES:

	Total	PIC	Multi Eng	Single Eng	Instructor Pilot	Cross Country	Instrument Actual	Sim	Night
FixedWg	1761	1527	1541	220		1466	247	45	151
RotaryWg	3381	2580	70	3311	1489	2331	14	139	533
Total	5142	4107	1611	3531	1489	3797	261	184	684

AIRCRAFT QUALIFICATIONS:

- C12-C/D/F (King Air 200)
- U21-H (King Air 100)
- PA 44 (Seminole)
- T42A (Baron 55)
- PA28 (Arrow)
- UH1B/H (Bell 205)
- CH-47B/C/D (Chinook)
- AH-1G/Q/S (Cobra)
- OH-58A (Bell 206)
- TH-55 (H300)

WORK EXPERIENCE: *U.S. Army, Major/Pilot/Staff Officer*

Nov 91 - Present   **Director of the Aviation Division.** Directorate of Plans, Training, Mobilizing and Security, U.S. Army Aviation Center, Fort Rucker, Alabama. Manage airspace, aviation safety, noise mitigation, installation aircrew training program and command aviation policies and procedures. Direct supervision of 10 personnel and indirect control over 2500. Pilot-in-command in King Air 200 and instructor in Bell 205.

Nov 90 - Nov 91   **Assistant Installation Commander.** HHC, 17th Avn Bde, Yongsan, Korea. Managed the maintenance and upkeep of the buildings and grounds valued over $80,000,000. Responsible for the safety and welfare of 850 soldiers and civilians living and working on the installation. Assured armed security of the installation. Pilot-in-command in King Air 200.

Oct 86 - Nov 90   **Accident Investigator,** U.S. Army Safety Center, Fort Rucker, Alabama. President of major Army aviation and ground accident investigation boards for 32 class A accident investigations worldwide. Pilot-in-command in King Air 200 and Bell 205.

Feb 84 - Oct 86   **Assistant Commander,** Phillips Army Airfield, Aberdeen Proving Grounds, Maryland. Assisted and advised the commander in technical and flight aspects of administration, training, safety, operations, and maintenance. Pilot-in-command in King Air 200, 100, and instructor in Bell 205.

Jul 83 - Feb 84   **Safety Officer/Instructor Pilot.** Phillips Army Airfield, Aberdeen Proving Ground, Maryland. Developed and managed the air and ground safety program. Trained and evaluated 17 UH-1 pilots in all phases of flight and ground school. Pilot-in-command in King Air 200, 100, and instructor in Bell 205.

40

Combination. Penny J. Rotolo, Enterprise, Alabama.
Extensive military training, diversified experience in the United States and Korea, and skills evident in Flight ratings, Flight times, and Aircraft qualifications make this resume unique.

OUTSTANDING FLYBOY   2

Jul 82 - Jun 83   **Flight Operations Officer**, Troop E (AIR) 1st Cav, Fort Wainwright, Alaska. Planned, developed, and executed training programs and all unit operations for 230 soldiers/aviators. Supervised and assured the flight standardization program. Pilot-in-command in Bell 206.

Apr 82 - Jul 82   **Assistant Commander**, Troop E (AIR) 1st Cav, Fort Wainwright, Alaska. Assisted the commander in all areas of command and responsible for all the logistics of the Calvary Troop and maintenance of all aircraft and vehicles in excess of $35 million. Pilot-in-command in Bell 206.

Dec 80 - Apr 82   **Utility Helicopter Platoon Commander**, Troop E (AIR), 1st Cav, Fort Wainwright, Alaska. Responsible for all platoon duties including supervision and training of up to 18 personnel; planning and conducting missions; and aircraft maintenance valued at $5 million. Pilot-in-command in Bell 205.

Jun 80 - Dec 80   **Attack Helicopter Section Commander/Troop Supply Officer**, Troop E (AIR), 1st Cav, Fort Wainwright, Alaska. Conducted individual and crew proficiency training and responsible for maintaining all logistics to include fuel, ammunition, and equipment. Pilot-in-command in Cobra.

May 78 - Oct 79   **Test Operations Coordinator/Instructor Pilot**, U.S. Army Aviation Board, Fort Rucker, Alabama. Coordinated support for operational testing of aircraft, components and equipment for the Training and Doctrine Command. Pilot-in-command in Cobra, Chinook, Baron 55 and instructor in Bell 205.

Nov 76 - May 78   **Standardization Instructor Pilot/Flight Commander**. Advance Div, Dept of Undergraduate Flight Training (UH-1H), U.S. Army Aviation Center, Fort Rucker, AL. Trained Initial Rotary Wing students in all phases of UH-1 helicopter training, to include academic, flight instruction and night vision goggles. Instructor in Bell 205.

Oct 75 - Oct 76   **Attack Helicopter Section Commander**, Co B, 2d Avn Bn, 2nd Inf Div, Camp Casey, Korea. Trained and supervised flight crews; maintained training and combat load of ammunition. Pilot-in-command in Cobra.

Apr 74 - Jul 74   **Assistant Personnel Manager**, HHC, The School Brigade, U.S. Army Infantry School, Fort Benning, Georgia. Supervised the personnel functions and duties of permanent party and student officers.

EDUCATION:

   Bachelor of Arts, Industrial Arts/Industrial Technology, Penn State University, University Park, Pennsylvania, 1973

MILITARY EDUCATION/TRAINING:

- Command and General Staff College, 1989
- FAA Rotorcraft Safety and Accident Investigation School, 1988
- Joint Firepower and Control Center, 1982
- UH-1 Instructor Pilot Course, 1977

- Crash Survival Investigation School, 1989
- U.S. Army Safety Officer Course, 1986
- Infantry Office Advance Course, 1980
- Initial Rotary Wing Training, 1975

PERSONAL DATA:

   Born: April 7, 1950; 75"/195 lbs.; excellent health (Non-Smoker); Medical Certificate, First-Class; married 21 years with two children. Interests include: flying, family activities, auto repairing/upkeep, and woodworking. Department of Defense top secret security clearance.

                                      AVAILABILITY: February 1, 1994

Narrow margins, long lines, and small type provide space for 13 brief descriptions of military assignments and duties. Boldfacing of positions makes these descriptions easy to scan.

MARY ANDERSON
1234 Nevada Avenue
Colorado Springs, Colorado 00000
(719) 555-0000

CAREER OBJECTIVE: A position in a results-oriented company that requires an ambitious and career conscious person where acquired skills and education will be utilized toward continued growth and advancement.

SKILLS:

10 key	Filing
Payroll	Purchasing
WordStar	Typing 45 wpm
MS-DOS	Word Processing
Cash Register	Customer Service
Spreadsheets	Office Management
Office Machines	Computer Accounting
IBM, Wang Computers	Accounts Receivable / Payables

EXPERIENCE:

•**Clerk/Cashier** - Army and Air Force Exchange Service, Peterson Air Force Base, Colorado
August 1993 to Present
Responsible for cash handling, customer service, cash register operation, TRW verification of credit cards, answering telephones, and reconciliation of cash drawers.

•**Theater Supervisor** - AAFES, Kaiserslautern, Germany
October 1992 to June 1993
Duties included interviewing, training, scheduling, evaluating, hiring and supervising personnel. Ordered, received merchandise and performed end-of-month inventory. Verified, consolidated and submitted personnel hours to payroll department. Scheduled movies, typed calendars and posted advertisement posters.

•**Secretary / Receptionist** - Recreation Center, Sembach Air Force Base, Germany
April 1992 to October 1992
Responsible for incoming and outgoing correspondence, answered phones, and scheduled appointments for the Director. Typed contracts, documents, various correspondence and maintained files. Prepared purchase orders, and performed end-of-month inventory. Responsible for funds and financial accountability for Air Force entertainment such as Top & Blues and USAFE Showcase.

•**Purchasing Agent** - Financial Branch, Sembach, Germany
August 1991 to April 1992
Responsible for Air Force Non-Appropriated Funds (NAF) and Morale, Welfare and Recreation (MWR) facilities. Procured merchandise, prepared and typed purchase orders, received shipping documents and prepared discrepancy reports. Established and maintained concessionaire contracts, individual service contracts, and nonpersonal service contracts. Maintained official files for purchasing department. Data entry of financial end-of-month reports.

•**Inventory Technician** - NAF, Sembach Air Force Base, Germany
March 1991 to August 1991
Verified prices and coded receiving reports and invoices. Data entry of receiving reports and invoices into the computer system. Prepared end-of-the-month inventory control ledgers; observed and inspected MWR facilities inventory procedures.

41

Combination. Gina V. Bump, Colorado Springs, Colorado.
The two-column scanning list of skills arranged from shortest to longest provides an impressive mix of skills derived from courses and Air Force base work experiences.

Page Two - Continued
RE: Mary Anderson

•Child Care Giver - NAF, Sembach Air Force Base, Germany
April 1990 to March 1991
Supervised and interacted with children to enhance growth and development. Ensured safety and conducted daily health checks. Led children in play activities such as songs and fingerplays. Guided children in positive behavior and conducted parent conferences to review the progress of the children.

•Accounts Receivable/Payable - Vestcap Financial Group, San Ynez, California
July 1987 to January 1990
Interacted daily with property managers and tenants. Data entry of general ledger, maintained rent roll and verified invoices. Responsible for end-of-month financials and reports; performed receptionist duties. Promoted to Payroll Clerk in April of 1989. Maintained time sheets, verified and consolidated employee hours and data entry into the computer. Created new employee files, monitored health benefits, vacation, sick leave and workman compensation claims.

EDUCATION: **Santa Barbara Business College,** Santa Maria, California, September 1986 to July 1987. Received a Diploma in Business Administration. Courses Studied: Ten Key, Business Math, Computer Concepts, Computer Accounting, Data Base Management, Accounting I, II, III, Electronic Spreadsheet, Introduction to BASIC Programming, Keyboarding, Typing I, Business Law, Business Communications, Payroll Accounting, Marketing, Lotus 1-2-3 and Business Management.

Allan Hancock College, Lompoc, California, August 1984 to December 1984.
Courses Studied: Introduction to Business and Sociology.

Lompoc Adult Education, Lompoc, California, April 1982 to July 1982.
Received a certificate in Keypunch I & II.

United States Air Force, April 24, 1990. Received a certificate in Customer Service.

AWARDS: **Outstanding Performance Award,** June 1993, AAFES, Theater Supervisor.
Certificate of Achievement, April 1992, NAF, Purchasing Agent.
Certificate of Achievement, July 1992, Recreation Center, Secretary.
Employee of the Month, April 1991, NAF, Inventory Technician.
Perfect Attendance - 10 months, July 1987, Santa Barbara Business College.

REFERENCES: Excellent References Available upon Request

Indented descriptive paragraphs help make the positions stand out. The list of five awards at the end of the resume is a strong note that should catch the reader's attention.

CAREER CHANGE

6500 Shier Rings Road
Amlin, OH 00000

(000) 000-0000

OBJECTIVE

To obtain a position that offers challenge, growth and career opportunity.

EXPERIENCE

Nationwide Insurance, IPO Nationwide Pension Services
December 1991 to Present

Plan Document Technician

- Perform restatements of pension contracts using dBASE III Plus
- Input and manage all client information in dBASE
- Perform quarterly billing invoices on R&R
- Create quarterly billing reports for PPA Support
- Input and manage all client billing information in dBASE
- Answer telephone inquiries from clients regarding their restatements
- Mass mail restatement letters to all clients
- Generate Adoption Agreements for the Proposal Center
- Create Client's Employee Contribution Reports using the Paycheck System
- Answer and direct incoming calls to the 800 line

Nationwide Insurance, IPO Pre-Need Administration
December 1990 to December 1991

Processing Clerk

- Processed all deposits on the Wang System
- Balanced deposits on a Lotus spreadsheet
- Balanced Deptrans and Aggregate Report to the Prelim Report
- Logged in all incoming mail
- Checked Aggregate Deposits on the PALLM System for accuracy
- Assisted in the monthly Money Movement
- Assisted in the mass mailings of quarterly reports
- Processed all withdraws on the WANG System
- Calculated John Deere death benefits
- Sent surrendered information to Huntington National and Washington National
- Balanced daily on a Lotus spreadsheet suspense report
- Researched missing claims to determine their sources
- Processed all Nationwide variable fees
- Verified flow for accuracy
- Received supply orders by phone for the Customer Service Area

42
Chronological (Before). Included by Susan Higgins, Amlin, Ohio.
The subject created this resume herself, wanting to leave the insurance industry for some other field. The Objective statement is unfocused, and the lists are long and uninviting.

CAREER CHANGE
Page 2

Nationwide Insurance, COLRO Accounting
July 1989 to December 1990

Accounting Clerk

- Input and balanced all accounting jobs
- Processed all Traveletters
- Balanced Cash Receipts to the General Ledger
- Checked endorsements on claim drafts
- Balanced claim drafts to bank statements

Software: Lotus 1-2-3, WordPerfect 5.1, Fastback, dBASE III Plus, R&R Report Writer, Paycheck

Accomplishments: 1991 United Way Lieutenant, 1991 Unit Representative for IIP's Birthday
                   Recognition Organization, 1990 Soar Award, 1992 Soar Award

The small amount of information on this page could have been put on the first page, and
the whole resume could have been put on one page.

CAREER CHANGE
6500 Shier Rings Road
Amlin, OH 00000
(000) 000-0000

Administrative Assistant

STRENGTHS

Ability to create and present an excellent image of the company and its services to customers, and to coordinate and communicate well with clientele and management at all levels and efficiently meet objectives.

CAREER SKILLS/KNOWLEDGE

- Create and type reports
- Cash management
- Office management
- Office machines
- Data entry

- Balancing statements
- Computer-based accounting systems
- Customer relations and service
- Lotus 1-2-3, WordPerfect 5.1, Fastback dBASE III Plus, R&R Report Writer, Paycheck

CAREER EXPERIENCE

NATIONWIDE INSURANCE • July 1989 - Present

IPO Nationwide Pension Services
Plan Document Technician
December 1991 to Present

- Perform restatements of pension contracts: requires extensive use of dBASE III Plus, ability to answer client inquiries, mass mailing of restatement letters to all clients
- Input and manage all client information and invoicing into dBASE
- Create reports using dBASE III Plus and Paycheck System and R&R Report Writer

IPO Pre-Need Administration
Processing Clerk
December 1990 to December 1991

- Processed all deposits and withdrawals on the WANG System
- Balanced deposits on Lotus spreadsheet
- Balanced Deptrans and Aggregate Report to the Prelim Report
- Ensured accuracy of Aggregate Deposits on the PALLM System
- Assisted with mass mailings of quarterly reports

COLRO Accounting
Accounting Clerk
July 1989 to December 1990

- Input and balanced all accounting jobs
- Processed all Traveletters
- Checked endorsements on claim drafts

SPECIAL RECOGNITION

1991 United Way Lieutenant
1991 Unit Representative for IIP's Birthday Recognition Organization
1990 and 1992 Soar Award

43

Combination (After). Susan Higgins, Amlin, Ohio.
This remake of Resume 42 limits it to one page, focuses on strengths, collects skills in a separate section, reduces the number of listed items, and shortens them for faster reading.

JANE SMITH
Any Street
Any Town, USA 00000
(000) 000-0000

OFFICE COORDINATION/SKILLS

- Organize and set up meeting rooms for Social Security hearings, and serve as clerk reporter.
- Answered telephone for a 24-hour crisis help line including recruiting and training volunteers.
- Identified emergency referrals for individuals in distress.
- Functioned as clerk reporter for hearings.
- Developed and maintained office filing system.
- Assisted accountant at Iowa State University, including resource referral for students.
- Performed various banking transactions for Ft. Dodge National Bank.
- Possess typing skills.
- Capable of efficiently handling 10 telephone lines with 130 extensions.
- Experienced in operating most general office equipment (photocopier, adding machines, etc.).

SPECIAL SKILLS

- Presented grief seminars to clubs, service groups, classrooms, church groups, and organizations to increase awareness of grief-related issues.
- Coordinated fundraising for community programs.
- Serve as advocate for suicide survivors.
- Initiated and facilitated "Suicide Survivors Support Group."
- Developed brochure for support group.
- Taught self-esteem class to third grade students to enrich their individuality.
- Developed "The Celebration of Lights"--a statewide fundraising and awareness program for Iowa Mental Health Association.

HONORS/AWARDS

- Received Peterson Award for the state of Iowa - 1988
- Received Woman of the Year award for the Iowa Mental Health Association - 1989

EDUCATION

1992   **Iowa State University** - Ft. Dodge, IA
                Introduction to WordPerfect 5.1

1960 - 1962   **Iowa Business College** - Ft. Dodge, IA
                Clerical

WORK HISTORY

1991 - Present **Clerk Recorder;** Department of Health and Human Services, Social Security Administration; Office of Hearings and Appeals - Ft. Dodge, IA

1983 - 1989   **Volunteer Coordinator/Special Events Chair;** Mental Health Association of Iowa Ft. Dodge, IA

1966 - 1968   **Clerk Accountant;** Iowa State University - Ft. Dodge, IA

1960 - 1964   **Bookkeeper/Teller;** Ft. Dodge National Bank - Ft. Dodge, IA

REFERENCES AVAILABLE UPON REQUEST

Combination. Claudia Stephenson, Bismarck, North Dakota.
A resume for a homemaker with little recent experience who now must work. Skills (with achievements) and awards are featured rather than education and work history.

44

JANINE E. ROSSIER
200 **Longwood Terrace**
Long Island, N.Y. 00000
(000) 000-0000

SUMMARY OF QUALIFICATIONS

Provided executive support in areas including:

- Office Administration
- Translation
- Project Management

- Research/Technical Writing
- Training and Supervision
- Page Layout

PROFESSIONAL ACCOMPLISHMENTS

Administrative Management

- Currently hold the position of Executive Administrative Assistant to three Vice-Presidents of Bankers Trust World Assets, New York, N.Y.

- Responsible for extensive proofreading and editing of business reports. Provide daily executive support through the creation of graphs, spreadsheets, charts, and slide presentations for simultaneous projects.

- Researched and accurately summarized technical data pertaining to specifications of a new computerized system account.

- At Magnavox Computer Europe Inc., researched and wrote bi-weekly reports on the free flow of electronic data transfer in the European Community and upcoming European Legislation regarding software copyrights.

- Liaised daily with European offices during projects and wrote project reports. Attended meetings, wrote meeting minutes and managed meeting agenda.

- Managed the department's hardware equipment and lab equipment.

Translation

- Translated daily from French into English legal documentation and legal contracts at Magnavox Computer Inc. Translation documents included leases, exclusive and non-exclusive dealership, various agreements, and trademark infringements.

Training

- Taught basic, intermediate, and advance French as a Foreign Language to senior executives of General Electric Company, Thomas Cook, and Woodgundy.

- Taught basic and intermediate Business English to graduates at Universite Rueil Malmaison, Rueil, France.

EDUCATION

M.A., International Journalism
City University of London, London United Kingdom, 1988

B.A., Cum Laude, Journalism
Hofstra University, Hemstead, N.Y. 1986

45

Combination. *Beverly Baskin, CPRW, Marlboro, New Jersey.*
This person did not want a secretarial job but also did not want to seem too high-powered. Qualifications and Accomplishments (categorized) still show expert French-English skills.

Janine E. Rossier

Page 2

EMPLOYMENT

BANKERS TRUST CO., New York, N.Y. 1993-Present

<u>**Executive Administrative Assistant**</u>

MAGNAVOX COMPUTER EUROPE, INC. , Paris, France, 1992-1993

<u>**Translator**</u>, Legal Department

TEACHER OF FRENCH AS A FOREIGN LANGUAGE, Paris, France, 1990-1993

Conversational and Business French for Senior Executives Level I, II, III, Individual and group classes.

UNIVERSITE RUEIL MALMAISON, Rueil, France, Summer Session, August 1991

<u>**Teacher of English as a Foreign Language**</u>

MAGNAVOX COMPUTER EUROPE INC., Paris, France, 1986-1990

<u>**Executive Bilingual Assistant, European Research and Development**</u>

SKILLS

French-English: fluent

COMPUTERS

Word for Windows, WordPerfect, Excel, Powerpoint, Persuasion, Harvard Graphics.

PERSONAL

French and United States Citizen

The person's fluency in French and English is evident in almost every section on this page. The section where language is not mentioned displays the person's computer skills.

LEON JEFFREYS   *8000 Pineview Lane*
(000) 000-0000   *Gastonia, NC 28000*

PROFESSIONAL EXPERIENCE

ELECTRONIC TECHNOLOGY
   Familiar with oscilloscopes, volt-ohm meters, TV color generators, external power supplies, isolation transformers, digital/analog circuits (discrete and integrated), computer-controlled components, and parts for a wide range of consumer electronic products.

TECHNICAL SERVICE
   Experienced in field and in-shop service on televisions, VCRs, CD players, turntables, audio cassette decks, and stereo amplifiers. Perform board- and component-level repairs and maintenance. Strong diagnostic abilities; can take items from initial testing and analysis through complete restoration to manufacturers' specifications.

COMMUNICATION & INTERPERSONAL SKILLS
   Good at customer service -- i.e., answering technical questions, via phone or in person, related to equipment use and installation. Have trained service technicians and delivery personnel (in installations). Have received customer letters praising professionalism, punctuality, and product and systems knowledge.

WORK HISTORY

Clayton Electronics (Gastonia, NC) -- *1993 to Present*
Queen City TV & Appliance (Charlotte, NC), Murphy's Video (Shelby Township, MI), and Colortyme Rental (Warren, MI) -- *1985-93*

Electronic Service Technician. Perform warranty/nonwarranty maintenance and repairs on consumer electronic products. Deal with a wide variety of technical problems.

EDUCATION

B.A.S. in Electronic Engineering Technology, Siena Heights College, Southfield, MI -- 1991

   Curriculum included a range of liberal-arts classes, along with technical courses. Earned and paid 100% of college expenses.

Certificate in Electronic Engineering Technology, National Education Center (a college-level technical institute), East Pointe, MI -- 1985

   Courses included engineering drafting, technical writing, mathematics (through calculus), industrial electronics, and computer electronics and programming.

46 *Combination. Barry Wohl, Charlotte, North Carolina.*
The person fixed TVs, VCRs, CDs, etc., but wanted to work in automotive technology. Breadth in experience, work, and education is therefore emphasized throughout the resume.

VALERIE FRANCIS
7000 Hallers Street
Bronx, NY   10000
(000) 000-0000

OBJECTIVE
- A position as a Word Processing Secretary which will utilize my computer knowledge, strong people skills, organizational abilities and business experience.

OVERVIEW
- Experienced, organized, take-charge office professional with demonstrated ability to successfully overhaul procedures, thereby increasing productivity.
- Able to coordinate multiple projects; can shift to cover a multitude of positions as needed.
- Detail-oriented person with exceptional follow-through abilities; able to oversee projects from concept to finished product.
- Able to work well with individuals on all levels.
- People person, sensitive and perceptive; extensive customer/client contact.
- Demonstrated ability to develop and maintain sound relationships with customers, anticipating their needs.

AREAS OF EFFECTIVENESS

Organizational Ability - Successfully revamped inventory/supply and purchasing systems which eliminated over-ordering by 31%. Received credit for returned supplies. Comparison shopped for best prices when purchasing, thereby cutting monthly expenditures by 28%. Increased efficiency allowed for a greater number of clients to be serviced.

Finance - Attention to detail, communication with clients and contact with insurance companies generated an additional $3,000 per month in revenue while decreasing overdue payments by 8%.

EXPERIENCE
1989 - 1991
DR. PAUL S. TAXIN, New Rochelle, NY
Dental Assistant in a four-handed expanded dental practice.
- Oversaw scheduling and ordering of supplies.
- Provided training to office personnel.
- Coordinated patient care.

1986 - 1989
DR. BARRY JASON, Mt. Vernon, NY
Office Manager in a practice with six locations plus a mobile unit.
- Scheduled appointments in multiple locations.
- Handled insurance, accounts payable, accounts receivable.
- Assisted dentist in direct patient care.

ADDITIONAL SKILLS
- Experience in mainstream Word Processing packages; knowledge of **DisplayWrite 4** and **MultiMate.**
- Computer literate; hands-on experience in Lotus 1-2-3 with macros, using **Allways** to generate business graphics.
- Significant expertise in dBASE III.
- Working knowledge of DOS.
- Familiarity with WordPerfect.

EDUCATION
1992 - Present
B.O.C.E.S. SOUTHERN WESTCHESTER, Valhalla, NY
Majoring in: Computerized Information Technologies

1978 - 1980
BRONX COMMUNITY COLLEGE, Bronx, NY
Major: Business Communications

REFERENCES
Available upon request.

Combination. *Mark D. Berkowitz, N.C.C.C., Yorktown Heights, New York.*
The hybrid chronological-functional format of a combination resume enabled this person to emphasize skills and abilities in searching for a job to use newly learned computer skills.

47

FRED J. BOYNTON

Staff Writer / Contributor

3000 Starling Lane
Pleasant View, California 93000
(000) 000-0000

- **AUTHOR** of 35 articles relating fictional, mythical and sometimes true experiences working as a cop, which have appeared in over 100 law enforcement publications around the U.S.

- **CO-AUTHOR** of *How To Get Into Law Enforcement*, a 146-page, frank, funny and very user-friendly book on becoming a law enforcement officer and what it's like after you're there.

- **WRITING INSTRUCTOR** of Law Enforcement Reports for Police Officer Standards Training at San Simeon College.

- **GUEST** on area radio talk shows, including The Cary Uptown Show (KOO), and Matty Bernard's Consumer Affairs program (KYI-FM), as well appearances on local cable television shows.

Patrolman
City of Pleasant View, California
• SWAT Team Member
• Field Training Officer
1987-Present

Deputy Sheriff
San Simeon Sheriff's Dept.
1986-87

Fiction Writing
San Jose State University

Associate Degree - English & Journalism
San Jose City College

48

Combination. *Ted Bache, Palo Alto, California.*
This talented patrolman sought to leave law enforcement and become a full-time writer. The casual resume features the person's success as a communicator (both written and oral).

Communications
Resumes at a Glance

JIM T. ANNOUNCER

(000) 555-1234 Business
(000) 555-1234 (Home)

EDUCATION

B.S., Journalism (xxxx-xxxx), *University,* Anytown, State
Major: Broadcasting; Minors: English, Political Science, Economics
Relevant coursework included:

Broadcast Newswriting	Composition I and II
Mass Media	Broadcast Programming
Music Theory	Private Voice Lessons
Music History	Participation in top choirs

Honors: Alpha Epsilon Rho (Broadcast honorary)

State College, Another Town, State (xxxx-xxxx)
Major: Communications; Minor: Music
Relevant coursework included:

Music Theory	Private Voice Lessons
Music History	Participation in top choirs

Received training in WordPerfect Computer Software (xxxx)

PROFESSIONAL EXPERIENCE

Classical Radio, Some City, States (xxxx-Present)
Morning Show Host and Production Director.

The Bird, Anytown, State (xxxx-Present)
Writer and Reporter.

A Philanthropy, Anytown, State (xxxx-xxxx)
Consultant/Supervisor to groups needing to raise money.

XXXX Radio, Anytown, State (xxxx-xxxx)
Acting News Director, news writer, reporter, morning anchor/personality.

KLIN Radio, Place, State (xxxx-xxxx)
News writer, reporter, announcer, and disc jockey.

University Radio & TV, Place, State (xxxx-xxxx)
News writer and reporter.

Telemarketing, Place, State (xxxx-xxxx)
Sales Operator

ORGANIZATIONS

President, Knights of Columbus Council xxxx; Church Pastoral Council; Announcer at University of State, former member of Association of News Broadcasters of State, former Associated Press Stringer, Member of Toastmasters.

Chronological.* *Linda Morton, CPRW, Lawrence, Kansas.
Clean design and white space make this resume easy to read. Courses in two columns display the person's music background and suitability for hosting a morning classical radio show.

49

Lance R. Ellery

222 North Shaw #222
Fresno, California 92222
(222) 222-2222

TARGET

Television Newscasting/Programming, anticipating future on-camera responsibilities.

PROFESSIONAL STUDIES

B.A., Communications with Specialization in Forensics (1992)
University of California, Santa Barbara

Educational Highlights
- *Mass Communications*
- *Group Discussion*
- *Persuasion*
- *English*

- *Reporting*
- *Debate*
- *Argumentation*
- *Forensics Lab*

PROFILE and REPRESENTATIVE EXPERIENCES

- *Articulate and persuasive public speaker, both extemporaneously and from script.*

- *Television and radio spokesperson; made presentations before company owners and decision-makers to promote business trade.*

- *Presented well-received stand-up comedy routine at UCSB in connection with Communications coursework.*

- *Traveled independently throughout Europe, concurrently working to support myself. Visited England, Ireland, France, Belgium, Germany, Holland, Spain, Italy, Greece, Egypt, Hungary, and Austria.*

- *Other work experience comprises employment with Santa Barbara Unified School District, Soup Plantation, and Macy's of California.*

- *Recipient of Steinbeck Contest 1st place award for creative writing.*

- *Published author, with short story represented in an anthology of children's stories.*

- *Reared in the Bay Area; received well-balanced exposure to both commerce and culture.*

- *Avid reader of newspapers, biographies, and authors such as Irving and Goethe.*

Work Samples and References Available upon Request

50

Functional. Susan B. Whitcomb, CPRW, Fresno, California.
Seeking to become a TV newscaster, this recent graduate with little work experience features instead a medley of education, public speaking, travel, publication, and reading experiences.

LAURA EWEN

111 Best Way
City of Angels, CA 91111
(213) 111-1111

EXPERIENCE, STRENGTHS, TALENTS

PROGRAMMING & SPECIAL EVENTS

- As **Programming Assistant for the ABC affiliate**, worked as programming contact with executive office, sales, news, promotions, production, and engineering departments.

- Liaison between station's Programming Department and *Los Angeles Times* and *TV Guide*.

- Created concept for new late night program targeting 18-25 year old market.

- Used planning skills to help coordinate special event in honor of corporate CEO; event was attended by 1,000+ including film producers, directors, athletes, celebrities, officials.

ORGANIZATIONAL STRENGTHS

- Assisted directors as **Script Supervisor** for multiple feature films (one which earned honors as Best Film at the Cannes Film Festival), as well as commercial spots, PBS special, video tests, three-camera video, and American Film Institute student films.

- Worked closely with producers, directors, actors, and techs, suggesting techniques for acting, directing, set decoration, etc. to enhance film continuity.

- Position required exceptional attention to detail, ability to "think on your feet," tact and diplomacy, a self-starting temperament, and mental/physical stamina to withstand 85-hour work weeks.

THE ARTS

- **Writer:** Excellent command of the English language; good proofreading and editing skills ... capable of producing a proliferation of alliterations (captivating copy, jazzy jingles, lovable lyrics).

- **Film:** Basic knowledge of production (pre-planning, actual production, post-production analysis), film editing, and programming (from concept through airing). Capable photographer (B&W, color).

- **Musician:** Five years of classical studies in voice. Considerable on-stage experience as singer/songwriter.

EDUCATION

B.A. DEGREE, ENGLISH -- University of Massachusetts at Amherst

PROFESSIONAL SUMMARY

Programming Assistant, KZZZ TV Channel 6 (ABC Affiliate)	1991-1993
Special Assistant to CEO, Entertainment Production Associates	1988-1990
Script Supervisor for various feature films, specials, commercials (details available)	1985-1988

References upon Request

Combination. *Susan B. Whitcomb, CPRW, Fresno, California.*
The prominent skills section has ABC A+B+C structure. Labeled Experience (A), Strengths (B), Talents (C), the section then illustrates each of these three areas in turn.

51

HEES A. WRITER

1234 Any Street • Anytown, State 12345 • (000) 555-1234 (h) • (000) 555-1234 (w)

SUMMARY OF QUALIFICATIONS

- **Over five years professional experience** holding a variety of responsible positions in communications.

- Experienced in **both national and international public contact roles**; able to cultivate and maintain relationships with a wide variety of individuals.

- **Conversant with federal and state regulatory agencies**; proven ability to establish and maintain important professional relationships with key personnel.

- Extensive **oral and written communication skills.**

- **Perform well under pressure**; accustomed to working with deadlines.

- **Creative and innovative professional**; prepared to adapt a variety of talents toward a new challenge.

PROFESSIONAL EXPERIENCE

A BIG GROUP ASSOCIATION OF PEOPLE, Anytown, State
Manager of Government Relations (x/xx-Present)
- Coordinate with counsel and Director of Communications to analyze and summarize information on federal regulations, administrative rules and environmental initiatives. Write/produce Government xxxxxxxx, bulletins, position papers and presentations to keep membership apprised of new laws, administrative regulations, government relations policies and relevant environmental topics. Create key contacts with EPA, OSHA, Labor, congressional offices. Formulate and recommend courses of action for association.

Staff Writer (x/xx-x/xx)
- Researched, developed and wrote original feature material for Group Association magazine, both on assigned and enterprise basis. Written material also ranged from straight news stories and departmental material to complex feature articles covering such subjects as association activities, something operations and management methods and current technology.

ANYTOWN DAILY PAPER, Anytown, State
Area Reporter (x/xx-x/xx)
- Covered a four-county area that included: 10 city councils, 9 school districts, 1 four-year college, sheriff and police departments. Reported agriculture, weather, general assignments, and spot news.

ANOTHER COUPLE OF NEWSPAPERS , Sometown, State
Reporter (x/xx-xx/xx)
- Reported all newsworthy activities and events in county and city government, courts, community corrections, county hospital and school district. Photographed events for news stories and wrote a bi-monthly column.

UNIVERSITY PAPER, Anytown, State
Columnist (x/xx-x/xx)
- Researched and created a weekly humor and entertainment column.

Reporter (x/xx-xx/xx)
- Established and implemented beat coverage of physical operations at the University. Additionally covered general assignments.

EDUCATION   **B.S., Journalism; B.A., English** (xxxx), University, Anytown, State

---

52

Combination. *Linda Morton, CPRW, Lawrence, Kansas.*
Summary of Qualifications section emphasizes breadth (national/international, federal/state, oral/written). Experience section displays career growth from college reporter to manager.

Profile: Presenting an extensive experience as a COMMUNICATIONS SPECIALIST, with expertise in:
- PROMOTIONS & SPECIAL EVENTS
- PUBLIC & GOVERNMENT RELATIONS
- PRINT & ELECTRONIC MEDIA
- MARKETING & SALES
- BUSINESS DEVELOPMENT
- PRODUCTION COMPANY ORGANIZATION
- STAFF TRAINING & MANAGEMENT

Achievements:
- Created Special Interest Women's Expo (Two local counties), enlisted sponsorship, exhibitor/advertiser/major media/corporate interest.
- Devised sales plan to promote Sailing Prize '92.
- Developed sponsorship for the Aerobat Air Show.
- Increased corporate sponsorship 100% for the "Accolades '92" Some Branch military honors presentation.
- Secured noted personalities for keynote addresses (e.g., noted actors/actresses).
- Produced three annual Congressional Technology Conferences Conferences on Global Interests and North American Trade Alliance (featured high-level government officials).
- Planned and assisted Presidential and Congressional candidate fund raising planning and development.
- Served House and Senate subcommittees on Education and the Department of Education.

Mary Anne Smith

1212 East Street
Some City, California 90000
111/555-1212

Career History:

1989-Present	President & Founder - Interest Concepts International, Some City, CA
1988-1989	Director, Public Relations - Congressman Jim Smith, Some City, CA
1987-1988	Special Assistant, Administration & Program Services - Center in the National Interests, Major University Program, Near the Nation's Capitol.
1984-1986	Congressional Aide - Congressman John Smith, Washington, D.C.

Education:

1987	M.A., International Affairs, Major University, East Coast, USA
1984	B.A., Political Science, Good College, City of Honors, PA
1984	University of Florence, Florence, Italy
1983	Universite Francois Language, Provence, France

Memberships: Big World Trade Organization; Big World Affairs Council; Fund raising Chair, United Nations Association, San Diego; Meeting Planners International; Some County Convention & Visitors Bureau, Membership Committee.

References: Available upon establishment of mutual interest.

Combination. Nita Busby, CPRW, Placentia, California.
Placement of the name below center gives prominence to Profile and Achievements sections.
All uppercase letters and oval bullets make the Profile section stand out further.

53

SALLIE YOUNG

2797 La Jolla Avenue · San Jose, CA · 95124

(408) 978-7278

Objective: Your Resume Writer.

HIGHLIGHTS OF QUALIFICATIONS

- ♦ Creative idea generator.
- ♦ Finely tuned sense of the English language and its usage.
- ♦ Flair for graphic design.
- ♦ Pride in achieving the best possible results.
- ♦ Thrive on helping clients get the results they want.

EDUCATION

B.A., Journalism
San Jose State University

3rd Degree
School of Hard Knocks

The Wordsmith
Writing & graphic design

TECHNICAL SKILLS

- ♦ Type 90 wpm in Microsoft Word on Macintosh SE.
- ♦ Can operate any Mac word processing or desktop publishing program.
- ♦ Also have IBM and Atari capabilities.
- ♦ Can produce final copies with print shop-quality results.

PROFESSIONAL EXPERIENCE

Writing & Editing
- ♦ Penned dozens of interesting and lively features from interviews of amazingly diverse people during five-plus years as a professional reporter.
- ♦ Discovered gold mine of bright bits to write about people, programs and occupations, through informational interviewing, to publish in district newsletters and local news media during five-plus years in school district public information.

Graphic Design & Layout
- ♦ Created graphic design and layout of posters, flyers, programs, brochures, booklets and resumes for a family-owned print shop.
- ♦ Conceived ideas in a variety of media, on a limited budget, for newsletters, flyers, programs, manuals, full-color brochures and other publications for public school districts.

Resume Results
- ♦ Crafted several resumes published in "Resume Round-Up: A Nationwide Sampler of Successful Resumes," compiled by resume guru Yana Parker, printed by Ten Speed Press.
- ♦ Fashioned dozens of resumes for family and friends throughout the past 15 years that secured interest, interviews, and ultimately, jobs.

© THE WORDSMITH, Sallie Young, 1991

WORK EXPERIENCE

Present	Proprietor	The Wordsmith, San Jose, CA
1991	Freelance Writer	Various publications, Santa Clara County
1990	Reporter	Los Gatos Weekly-Times, Los Gatos, CA
1987-89	Staffperson	Santa Clara County Supervisor Dianne McKenna's Office, San Jose, CA
1989 (Fall)	News Editor	Spartan Daily, San Jose State, San Jose, CA
1989 (Spring)	Reporter	Spartan Daily, San Jose State, San Jose, CA
1987	Freelance Writer	Indio Moneysaver, Indio, CA
1984-87	Public Information Specialist	Desert Sands Unified School District, Indio, CA
1983	Reporter	Palm Springs Desert Sun, Palm Springs
1981-83	Public Information Technician	Bakersfield City School District, Bakersfield, CA
1980	Graphic Artist	Hall Letter Shop, Bakersfield
1978-79	Reporter	Yuma Daily Sun, Yuma, AZ

54

Combination. *Sallie Young, San Jose, California.*
This eye-catching newsletter-style resume was created by the resume writer for herself to market her skills. Diamond-shaped bullets guide you to the beginning of items in columns.

G I N G E R
MAHON

1234 Dailey Street
Sunnyvale
California   **(408)**
95054   **555-7278**

OBJECTIVE

Temporary creative position
using desktop publishing and/or writing skills.

HIGHLIGHTS OF QUALIFICATIONS

✓ 15 years' experience in the writing field; 7 years in graphic design and desktop publishing.
✓ Sharp, innovative, quick learner; ability to adapt quickly to a challenge.
✓ Diplomatic, tactful; communicate well with a wide range of personalities.
✓ Finely tuned sense of the English language and its usage.
✓ Enthusiastic, creative idea generator; flair for graphic design.
✓ Able to meet deadlines and maintain sense of humor under pressure.

PROFESSIONAL EXPERIENCE

Writing & Editing

- Wrote freelance feature cover stories about local citizens and took photos for weekly advertising mailer.
- Penned dozens of interesting and lively news and feature articles derived from interviews of diverse people in an array of activities for newspaper and magazine publication.
- Coordinated yearbook publication for quality control department of international computer workstation corporation, becoming familiar with corporate structure and technical jargon.
- Edited community college campus literary magazine, supervising eight editors of various departments to produce a nationally award-winning publication.

Desktop Publishing & Graphic Design

- Fashioned dozens of fliers for variety of activities and events, using graphics, typefaces and unusual layout elements for eye-catching display.
- Designed mass distribution promotional materials and business brochures for small-business clients such as a dry cleaner, fashion consultant and piano teacher, capturing the right "look" for their individual needs.
- Designed and supervised production of full-color K-12 certificated personnel recruitment brochure.
- Separated, resized and duplicated two-color layouts for labels in Aldus FreeHand, completing an estimated two-week job in one-and-a-half days.
- Perked up otherwise plain-looking resumes by using desktop publishing programs to import text and graphics for more versatile layouts.

Computers

- Developed good working skills with variety of computer software programs for Macintosh, IBM and Atari computers, including (but not limited to) Microsoft Word, WordPerfect, PageMaker, Quark Xpress, Aldus FreeHand and Photoshop.
- Chaired word processors' users group: answered questions and solved software-related problems for staff; trained staff on IBM mainframe system using Word-11 software.
- Conducted staff training on the Apple Macintosh for Santa Clara County Supervisor McKenna's office.

WORK HISTORY

1990-91	*Reporter*	LOS GATOS WEEKLY-TIMES, Los Gatos, CA
1987-90	*Staffperson*	SUPERVISOR DIANNE MCKENNA'S OFFICE, Santa Clara County, CA
1989	*Publication Editor*	SUN MICROSYSTEMS, Mountain View, CA
1987	*Freelance Writer*	INDIO MONEYSAVER, Indio, CA
1984-87	*Public Info Officer*	DESERT SANDS UNIFIED SCHOOL DISTRICT, Indio, CA
1983	*Account Executive*	GRATTAN ADVERTISING, Palm Springs, CA
1981-83	*Public Info Technician*	BAKERSFIELD CITY SCHOOL DISTRICT, Bakersfield, CA
1980-81	*Graphic Artist*	HALL LETTER SHOP, Bakersfield, CA
1979	*Assistant Editor*	SOUTHWEST SPORTING NEWS, Yuma, AZ
1976-78	*Asst. Public Info Officer*	ARIZONA WESTERN COLLEGE, Yuma, AZ

EDUCATION

San Jose State University, San Jose, CA
BA, Journalism

Arizona Western College, Yuma, AZ
AA, Mass Communications

American International School
Kabul, Afghanistan

Work samples shown upon establishment of mutual interest.

© THE WORDSMITH, *Sallie Young, 1992*

Combination. *Sallie Young, San Jose, California.*
The same resume writer created this resume for getting temporary work. The name, address, and headings are white-on-black with a torn edge. Horizontal lines separate sections.

Thomas Paul Gajda—Technical Writer

108 Kathleen Street • Springfield, Massachusetts 01119 • 413–782–0401

Objective

Contract or permanent technical writing assignment

Areas of Expertise

Writing expertise includes ISO 9000 and FDA GMP documentation, training manuals, and engineering proposals. Technical expertise includes papermaking, chemical processing, process engineering, and mechanics.

Writing Experience

Contract Technical Writer, 1991 to present. Assignments include:

- Polaroid, Norwood, MA (current assignment) — write all levels of ISO 9000 and FDA GMP documentation for film coating plant. Supervise four college interns and contribute to project development and planning.
- Decorative Specialties International, Johnston, RI — wrote ISO 9000 quality policy manual for web coating operation.
- Rhinelander Paper Company, Rhinelander, WI — wrote training manuals on stock preparation and chemical makeup systems, steam and condensate system, dryers, size press, calender, reel, and winder.
- St. Joe Forest Products, Port St. Joe, FL — wrote training manuals on stock approach system, headbox, fourdrinier, and wet press.
- Weyerhaeuser Paper Company, Columbus, MS — wrote manuals on chemical makeup, chlorine air-padding, and vaporization systems.

Staff Specialist, Simons-Eastern Consultants, Decatur, GA, 1989 to 1991. Simons-Eastern provides consulting engineering services to the pulp and paper industry. I edited and coordinated the production of engineering proposals for large ($50 to $500 million) capital cost projects.

Computer and Documentation Skills

Expert word processing and page layout skills using WordPerfect and Microsoft Word for Windows. My software experience also includes: Microsoft PowerPoint for Windows, Aldus PageMaker and Adobe Illustrator for Windows, and DrawPerfect. I have used many of these software packages on Macintosh systems.

My documentation skills include program development, document design, and conceptualizing and drawing illustrations. My office has an IBM computer, full range of software, modem, and laser printer.

(CONTINUED)

56

Combination. *Thomas Paul Gajda, Springfield, Massachusetts.*
Another resume writer's own resume. Wide margins and reduced point size create ample white space. The 4 5/8-inch lines are readable because they are not too long.

RESUME   PAGE 2
THOMAS PAUL GAJDA   MARCH 1994

Technical Experience

Research Scientist, Kimberly-Clark, Roswell, GA, 1986 to 1987. Working in a corporate research environment and at mills, I sought new ways to process fibers and manufacture specialty papers. Team member on a patent disclosure.

Technical Services Supervisor, Kimberly-Clark, Spotswood, NJ, 1984 to 1986. Supervised eight professionals; together we provided process engineering and laboratory support to a six-machine paper mill. Negotiated a wastewater treatment program that saved $35,000 a year.

Senior Technical Assistant, C.H. Dexter, Windsor Locks, CT, 1981 to 1984. Dexter operates ten nonwoven machines. I developed specialty grades through laboratory and pilot machine studies. Developed a quality assurance test used to control the manufacturing of a new grade.

Chemical Operator, Monsanto, Springfield, MA, 1972 to 1975. Operated control room and field equipment in a large chemical processing plant. Set a production record.

Special Training

Attended *Documentation for ISO 9000 Compliance* seminar, presented by ISO-NOW Corporation, Natick, MA, 1992

Attended a series of in-house seminars on ISO 9000 at Polaroid, 1993

Participated in comprehensive workshops in statistical process control and quality management process at Kimberly-Clark

Education

M.A. in Journalism, Northeastern University, 1989
B.S. in Wood Science (Cum Laude), University of Massachusetts, 1979

Memberships

Society for Technical Communication
International Society for General Semantics

The writer's science degree, technical experience, master's degree in journalism, computer documentation skills, and writing experience support the objective of technical writing.

Susan J. Search

(000) 555-1234   1234 Some Street • Anytown, State 12345

PROFILE
- Talented reporter with extensive **administrative, writing** and **research** skills
- Self-motivated and able to work independently
- Excellent organizational and analytical skills; able to focus on the important aspects of information
- Extensive government and legal contacts in Northeast State
- Consistently recognized by peers for superior writing ability
- Some editing experience

PROFESSIONAL EXPERIENCE

THE ANOTHER TOWN PAPER, Another Town, State   (xxxx-Present)
Anytown Bureau Chief/Staff Writer (xxxx-Present)
Supervise stringers and interns in Anytown-County area. Assign stories; assist with background information and contacts; direct story compilation. Cover city/county government and other news.

State Staff Writer/Anytown Bureau (xxxx-xxxx)
Researched, investigated and wrote news stories and feature articles throughout Northeast State. Tracked all news items in three county area. Specialized in coverage of law enforcement, crime and courts at all levels. Organized election news reports in the paper's 23-county circulation area.

Intern/Part-time Writer (xxxx-xxxx)

EDUCATION

B.S. Journalism, *cum laude* (xxxx)
State University, Some Town

ADDITIONAL EDUCATION

Basic Photography, Continuing Education
Editing I (Dr. Professor), University, Anytown

PROFESSIONAL AFFILIATIONS

National Federation of Press Women
- Conference Director for National Conference, Some City, State
State Press Women
- Freedom of Information/Legislation Director
- Northeast District Director

AWARDS

NATIONAL FEDERATION OF PRESS WOMEN COMMUNICATIONS CONTEST
- **News Reporting Awards:**
  First Place, 1992
  Second Place, 1981

STATE PRESS WOMEN COMMUNICATIONS CONTEST
- First, Second, Third Place and Honorable Mention Awards in **News Reporting, Feature Story, Interview, News Photography** and **Special Articles-Education** Categories

WRITING SAMPLES AND REFERENCES AVAILABLE UPON REQUEST

57

Combination. *Linda Morton, CPRW, Lawrence, Kansas.*
Resume of an award-winning news reporter who has worked for the same paper since undergraduate days. Pen-tip "bullets" direct attention and fit the person's career.

Consultant
Resumes at a Glance

JULIE E. SWARINGEN

280 North Second Street
Albemarle, NC 28000

(000) 000-0000 (H)
(000) 000-0000 (M)

CAREER OBJECTIVE:

Challenging computer position with progressive opportunities where proven skills and talents in . . .
MONEY MANAGEMENT
COMPUTER APPLICATIONS
ACCOUNTING
. . . will be of mutual benefit.

EDUCATION:

September 1989 to August 1990	**American Business & Fashion Institute**, Charlotte, NC
	Diploma: Travel/Business GPA: 3.72
	  Internship: 100 hours
	    World Travel of Albemarle - Albemarle, NC
	    Carol Shank, Manager

June 1990	**System One Training School** - Houston, TX Certificate: Conversion-Level III
October 1985 to December 1985	**Stanly Community College** - Albemarle, NC Major: Business GPA: 3.5
December 1984 to September 1985	**Stanly Technical College** - Albemarle, NC Diploma: Adult High School

EXPERIENCE:

August 1992 to Present	**Carolina Motor Club - AAA Travel** - Charlotte, NC *(Apollo/Focal Point System)*
	Executive Corporate Travel Consultant - Lou Lyons, Manager
	Airline, hotel and car reservations for all corporate accounts, enter client profiles.
	  First Union Corporation - Charlotte, NC
	  Travel Services Department (February 1992 to Present)
	  Airline, hotel and car reservations for First Union accounts only at a high productivity level.

July 1991 to August 1992	**Custom Cruises & Travel** - Albemarle, NC *(Apollo)* *Travel Consultant* - Maura Eberhardt, Manager Reservations & ticketing, issue boarding passes, complete ARC Sales Report, operate IBM PC, phone and walk-in sales and some outside sales experience.
May 1990 to July 1991	**World Travel of Albemarle** - Albemarle, NC *(System One)* *Travel Consultant/Accountant* - Carol Shank, Manager Process airline reservation, issue boarding passes, operate Telex 080A, operate IBM PC, complete ARC reports, money management, phone and walk-in sales.
June 1990 to July 1991	**Paramount Realty** - Albemarle, NC *Secretary/Bookkeeper* - Dewey Sides, Owner/Manager Accounting and bookkeeping, Type: 48 wpm, payroll, contracts/letters, record data, operate machinery.
November 1985 to May 1990	**Pizza Hut, Inc.** - Albemarle, NC *Food Server/Hostess/Cashier* - Doug Cleveland, Area Supervisor Greet customers, prepare food and beverages, operate register.

PERSONAL ATTRIBUTES:
Career focused, self-motivated, strong-management skills. Ability to organize people and process information.
Enjoy working independently and as a team.

REFERENCES AVAILABLE UPON REQUEST

Chronological. Julie S. Thompson, Albemarle, North Carolina.
Having worked as a travel consultant and for corporate clients, this person now features computer experience and management skills to find a position with a growing business.

58

MARIAN J. KNIGHTS

1000 Christiana Drive
Lawrenceville, Georgia 30000
(000) 000-0000

PROFESSIONAL OBJECTIVE

To provide leadership and guidance in the area of **Professional Image**, utilizing international training and 12 years' distinguished experience in the field.

SUMMARY OF QUALIFICATIONS

Certified International Image Consultant, accomplished **Trainer, Speaker, Workshop Leader**, and **Consultant**, offering over 12 years' leadership experience to business and industry, academia, professional and volunteer organizations.

- **Programming and Public Speaking Skills:** Developed and presented professional seminars and workshops in Germany and the USA in the areas of Professional Presence, Successful Image, Interview Presentation, Image and Communication, Dressing for Success, Wardrobing with an International Flair, and The Professional Woman.

- **Consultation Services:** Offered personal and professional consultations to private individuals and business/professional organizations in academia, law, retail and fashion.

- **Program Development and Coordination Skills:** Planned, organized and coordinated special events and fundraisers for volunteer and retail organizations, including Fashion Shows.

- **Professional attributes:** Self-motivated, innovative, organized, with excellent communication skills and proven ability to work well with others. Elegant, polished professional appearance, with finesse and highly developed facilitation skills.

PROFESSIONAL EXPERIENCE

1988 to 1992   SELF-EMPLOYED IMAGE CONSULTANT   Newville, PA
Provided workshops, presentations, and individual/corporate consultation on topics related to image and professional presence.
- Led in-service workshops for teachers and administrators through the local school board.
- Served in an advisory role to the Fashion Archives and the local University, providing consultation, workshops, and coordinating special events.
- Received certificates of appreciation from the Central Pennsylvania Association of Women Executives and Shippensburg University for outstanding seminars on women's issues in business and academia.
- Organized and presented a program to the Women's Law Caucus for Dickinson School of Law on "Professional Dress within the legal profession."
- Presented workshops within the Home Economics department for local colleges and universities.

59

Combination. *Julianne S. Franke, Lilburn, Georgia.*
A resume whose wealth of information justifies the use of two full pages, narrow margins, and single-spacing.

PROFESSIONAL EXPERIENCE (Continued)

1986 to 1988   SELF-EMPLOYED IMAGE CONSULTANT   Bamberg, Germany
                 Managed home-based consulting business, working primarily
                 with military organizations, professional organizations, and
                 women's groups, including the Federal Women's Program,
                 Army Community Services, and the Association for American
                 Women's Activities in Germany (AWAG).
                 • Successfully completed international training in London.
                 • Received certificate of appreciation for presentation at
                   the annual AWAG conference.
                 • Designed and presented programs on "Professional Presence,"
                   "Successful Dress for Interviews," and "Wardrobing on a Budget."

1981 to 1989   Leadership positions in Professional, Civic and Community
                 Volunteer Organizations, including the following:

                 • Board of Directors, Vice President and Program Chairman
                   for the Officer's Wives Club, Carlisle, PA, 1989.
                 • President, Student Advisory Council, Bamberg, Germany, 1986-1988.
                 • President and Program Chairman for Health Services, Ft.
                   Knox, KY, 1984-1986.
                 • Board of Directors for MEDDAC-DENTAC, Ft. Hood, TX, 1981-1984.

1975 to 1981   **Nursing** positions in medical, dental, and surgical environments.

EDUCATION   Pennsylvania College of Technology, 1974
                 Nursing

CERTIFICATION AND TRAINING

                 The Professional Woman's Network, Advanced Corporate Training, 1991
                 Total Image Consultant - Color Me Beautiful (USA), 1990
                 Advanced Color and Makeup - Color Me Beautiful (USA), 1990
                 Total Image Consultant - Color Me Beautiful (USA), 1989
                 Total Image Consultant - Color Me Beautiful International,
                 London, England, 1986-1988.

PROFESSIONAL DEVELOPMENT SEMINARS ATTENDED

                 Color Me Beautiful National Convention, Scottsdale, AZ (1/90)
                 Image and Communication Skills for Women, National Seminars, Inc.
                 Leadership and Communication, U.S. Army War College, Carlisle, PA
                 Leadership and Supervisory Skills for Women, National Seminars
                 How to Handle Difficult People, The National Seminars Group
                 How to Make Presentations that Win Approval, Career Track
                 Strategic Selling Workshop, Slight Edge, Inc.
                 Community Leadership Development, Department of the Army

PROFESSIONAL AFFILIATION

                 National Association of Female Executives
                 The Professional Woman's Network
                 American Association for Training and Development
                 Atlanta Network Executive Women

REFERENCES   Excellent professional references available upon request.

Nurse's training is downplayed because of limited nursing career. Image consultant's training, experiences, and qualifications are played up because this role has become the chief career.

PROFESSIONAL PROFILE

CHARLES B. RILEY, CEI/CES
(Address on cover)

BACKGROUND

Charles B. Riley has had over 25 years of diversified experience in the technical and engineering field. His qualifications include having worked in Manufacturing/Industrial Management, Engineering Sales and Management; in addition to his positions as a Management Consultant Engineer, Safety Director, and more recently, Environmental Consultant.

PROFESSIONAL EXPERIENCE

A Professional Environmental Consultant since 1988, Mr. Riley specializes in the marketing of services related to:

- Contamination Assessments and Remediation at Hazardous and Non-hazardous sites.
- Underground Storage Tank (UST) Evaluations.
- Phase I, II and III Assessments.
- Asbestos Abatement/Radon Testing.
- OSHA 40-Hour Haz-Met School.
- Personnel Placement of Engineers and Technicians.

Mr. Riley's professional background includes prior employment with the following companies:

Donahue Groover & Associates, Staff Engineer/Consultant. Coordinated financial budget (P&E); marketing and logistics; Industrial Relations; general overall monitoring of organizational activities.

INA Insurance Company of North America (now Cigna), Senior Marketing Technical Representative. Responsible for monitoring total loss control, in conjunction with 30 insurance agencies. Instructed insurance officials, their insureds, and prospective clients on the OSHA Regulations and the implementation of safety programs to insure governmental compliance.

Hayes Aircraft, Senior Project Engineer. Supervised eight engineers. Coordinated research and design problems on Saturn V Swing Arms. Worked closely with NASA Engineers in reviewing and resolving problem areas.

Bendix Corporation, Supervisor of 50 personnel at John F. Kennedy Space Center, Florida. Coordinated refurbishment of Saturn V Swing Arm. Supported NASA Contractors and directed all operations. Training instructor for mechanical and pneumatic personnel involved in Swing Arm project. Instructor at Ground School for Heavy Equipment and Launch Control Systems.

Honeywell, Inc., Industrial Engineer/Cost Estimator. Worked on various "classified assemblies" and military electronic devices. Prepared cost estimates for bidding.

EDUCATION

Mr. Riley studied Industrial Engineering at Ohio University and is also a graduate of the International Safety Academy. In July, 1992, he received a 40-Hour OSHA Certification from the Technical Environmental Training Institute. During his career, he has participated in a variety of certified, specialized training and management programs; together with being an instructor for a Welding School and the Saturn V Ground Support School. He has conducted seminars and given speeches on OSHA Regulations and Procedures; Safety Programs to Insure Compliance with OSHA; Environmental Work - Air Quality, Smoke Stack Emissions, and Water Contamination.

PROFESSIONAL MEMBERSHIPS/AFFILIATIONS

- Environmental Asssessment Association (EAA)
- Environmental Conservation Organization (ECO)
- Lifetime Member - Methods Time Management Association (MTM)

60 *Functional. Diane McGoldrick, Tampa, Florida.*
Not a typical resume, this resume is a profile of a person's credentials and was created as a marketing tool. A useful format for professionals in business. Note the limited use of dates.

Education/Training
Resumes at a Glance

SAMPLE RESUME - TEACHER'S AIDE

HOPE I. CANAIDE
2 Kindergarten Lane
Readiness, NH 00000
(000) 000-0000

OBJECTIVE

A teacher's aide position in the school system for the opportunity to utilize and build on previous experience in education and demonstrate a caring for young people with special needs.

SUMMARY OF EXPERIENCE

<u>Substitute Teacher</u> for the Greater Academic Learning Collaborative working with special students on elementary, junior high, and secondary levels (1993-).

<u>Leader, Co-Leader</u> for Girl Scout Troop 14 coordinating workshops and activities, including merit badge advancement programs, arts and crafts and costume making, plus special weekend outings at Camps Whinneehaha and Minniehaha (1987-).

<u>Room Mother</u> for Grades 2 and 5 at Don Sparetherod Memorial School, Readiness, NH (1990-)

RELATED ACTIVITIES

Volunteer, Readiness Recreation T-Ball Program.
Assistant at Progressive School, Readiness
Member Readiness Parent-Teacher Association.

EDUCATION

Graduate Area Regional Cooperative High School, Readiness, NH - Business Course
Enrolled in Early Childhood Education Certification Program, Field Day, NH

TRAINING

Essentials of Leadership - Sweetbriar Girl Scout Council
Children as People - Bye For Now Mommy Child Care Center

OTHER WORK EXPERIENCE

9/90-9/91 First Money Bank, Readiness, NH - Bank Teller

8/88-9/90 Hinge On Success Door Company, Readiness, NH - Office Assistant

---

Combination. *Stephen H. Mazurka, Exeter, New Hampshire.*
Indented paragraphs, all uppercase side headings, and adequate white space make this resume easy to grasp at first glance.

61

RHONDA L. RESUME

PROFESSIONAL PROFILE

1300 Wellington Place
Some City, Pennsylvania 00000
(000) 000-0000

SUMMARY OF QUALIFICATIONS:

Excellent administrative, interpersonal and communication skills . . . Experience in negotiating, teaching, project and behavioral management . . . Counseling and training abilities . . . Spanish speaking ability . . . Excellent motivator and people person . . .

EDUCATION:

Famous Pennsylvania University, Somewhere, PA

19XX - 19XX   **30 graduate hours in Special Education**

19XX   **Master's in Education**

19XX   **Bachelor of Science in Elementary Education**

Concentration in English Literature: Completed requirements for Master of Educational Psychology; Pennsylvania Teacher's Certification

TEACHING QUALIFICATIONS:

Responsible for monthly reports and daily lesson plans. Extensive experience with learning and emotional support students. Developed and implemented a foreign language program (Spanish) within first grade classes, enabling children of migrant worker families to assimilate into the school environment. Experienced in behavior modification and control therapy.

TEACHING HIGHLIGHTS:

Some Place, Lancaster Intermediate Unit, Some Name, Another Name, Harrington and Meadville Schools, PA

1987 - present   **Substitute Teacher, K-12**

Harcourt Elementary School, PA

1969 - 1980   **First Grade Teacher**

Brunette Elementary, PA

1968 - 1969   **First Grade Teacher**

Cavendish Elementary, PA

1967 - 1968   **Fifth Grade Teacher**

COMMUNITY SERVICE:

Famous Charity, **Volunteer; support to ill patients**
Harrington / Meadville Schools, **Fund-raising Committee**

REFERENCES: Available upon request

62

Combination. Wendy A. Lowry, Erie, Pennsylvania.
Boldfacing in the Summary of Qualifications section is a strong opener. The Teaching Qualifications section reenforces it. Note the imbalanced format at the top of the page.

JANE HALE

3000 Briarwood Lane • Marlboro, MA 00000
(000) 000-0000

OBJECTIVE To obtain a position as an *Elementary School Teacher* in which a strong dedication to the total development of children and a high degree of enthusiasm can be fully utilized.

EXPERIENCE
9/90 to Present

Mary Finn School, Southboro, MA
First Grade Teacher
- ✏ Participated in the design and development of a **Whole Language Reading** curriculum that included large and small group instruction. Participated in the development of assessment tools to evaluate Whole Language.
- ✏ Adapted the Whole Language Program to meet individual needs by using elements of a basal and/or a phonetic reading program.
- ✏ Implemented DMP (**Developmental Math Process**) which is a hands-on approach to problem solving through the use of math manipulatives.
- ✏ Developed learning centers based on the needs of a heterogeneous class. Utilized a **thematic approach** to the curriculum.
- ✏ Have stressed an individual approach to learning by providing enrichment as well as modification based on a particular student's needs.
- ✏ Participated in organizing curriculum units including Chinese New Year, Ecology, and Weather.
- ✏ Fostered ongoing communication with parents through the use of a monthly newsletter detailing thematic units.
- ✏ Involved parent volunteers to assist the children in classroom enrichment activities such as the use of computers and numerous whole class projects.
- ✏ Contributing member of Building Based Support Team pilot program, a 3-year grant funded by the State Department of Education.

COLLEGE RELATED TEACHING ASSIGNMENTS
Fall 1989

Mary Finn School, Southboro, MA
First Grade--Student Teacher.
- ✏ Developed teaching units on the seashore and trees, and utilized advanced teaching methods including Whole Language and math manipulatives. Developed and implemented learning centers.

Spring 1989

Warren School, Ashland, MA
Second Grade--Field Study II.
- ✏ Developed plans for individual and group use on Time and Money.

Fall 1988

Framingham State College Nursery School, Framingham, MA
To Fulfill Requirements for Curriculum I.
- ✏ Developed extensive observation and management skills.

Spring 1988

Lilja Elementary School, Natick, MA
First Grade--Field Study I; Teachers Aide

EDUCATION Framingham State College, Framingham, MA
B.S., Early Childhood Education. Minor: Psychology. 1990.
Workshop: American Sign Language. Sponsored by Mary Finn School.

AWARDS AND ACHIEVEMENTS
Dorothea J. Kunde Memorial Award For Excellence In Teaching 1989-1990.
President's List, 1989-1990; **Dean's List**, 1988-1990.

Combination. Steven Green, CPRW, Northboro, Massachusetts.
Pencil-shaped bullets call attention to this innovative teacher's achievements as she looks for her second teaching position to implement her new Whole Language Reading curriculum.

63

ALICE WONDERLAND
1500 Tricky Card Trace
Snellville, Georgia 30000
(404) 000-0000

OBJECTIVE:

To secure a teaching position for gifted elementary students where I can make a positive contribution to their education by establishing a creative and stimulating classroom environment through which they can develop and grow to their full potential.

EDUCATION:

UNIVERSITY OF GEORGIA GRADUATE SCHOOL, Athens, Georgia
M.Ed., Reading, 1978
Gifted Endorsement, June 1993

UNIVERSITY OF GEORGIA, Athens, Georgia
B.S., Elementary Education, Magna Cum Laude

Honors
   Participated in a pilot program, "Competency Based Teacher Education" utilizing clinical experience in schools for four quarters while attending education classes.

   Phi Kappa Phi Honor Society
   Kappa Delta Pi Honor Society

EXPERIENCE:

1979 to 1987   **ISLAND ELEMENTARY SCHOOL, Island, South Carolina**

3rd Grade Lead Teacher   *1984 to 1987*
   • Developed an Environmental Study Unit integrating science, anthropology, archeology, South Carolina history, ecology and environmental awareness. This utilized a local wetland conservancy and was adopted by the local Audubon Society.
   • Charleston Trip Coordinator for study of South Carolina History.

Served on:
   • Elementary School Discipline Policy Committee
   • Building Committee for Architectural Design of the New Elementary School
   • Island School Council
   • Essential Skills Committee

2nd - 3rd Grade Combined, Lead Teacher   *1983 to 1984*
   • In-service Meeting Coordinator for in-school staff development.
   • Designed unit on South Carolina history involving a three-day overnight trip for students visiting historic sites in Charleston and Fort Sumter, South Carolina.
   • Awarded Scholarship to attend Audubon Ecology Camp for Teachers at the University of Connecticut during the summer.

Chronological. Carol Lawrence, CPRW, Snellville, Georgia.
Progression of teaching experience in another state is listed in detail to help a teacher away from the workforce for six years compete for a much-desired position in the current state.

ALICE WONDERLAND   **Page 2**

EXPERIENCE (Continued)

ISLAND ELEMENTARY SCHOOL (Continued)

4th - 5th Grade Combined, Lead Teacher   *1979 to 1983*
- Designed a "Health by Agreement" Drug Unit for fifth graders which the county incorporated into the health curriculum guide.
- Worked with Savannah Morning News on an in-school newspaper project.
- Coached Continental Mathematics League and County Spelling Bee, using the team teaching approach.
- Wrote "Barrier Island - Environmental Study Unit" with a colleague for fourth grade.

Served on:
- Local School Advisory Council
- Principal's Evaluation Committee

1978 to 1979   **MIDDLE SCHOOL, Athens, Georgia**

Reading Specialist
- International Reading Association
- Volunteer at IRA Spring 1979 Conference, Atlanta, Georgia

COMMUNITY SERVICE:

Cultural Arts Coordinator, Hometown Elementary School   1989 to 1992
Instituted Artist-in-Residence Program for the school

Junior Service League   1988 to 1992
- Ways and Means Committee
- Event Coordinator and Monitor for the Young Audiences of Atlanta Concert

Council of Arts   1990 to Present
- Coordinator of "Festival of Nations" - International Embassy Exhibits
- Arts Guild for Hometown - Promoting Civic Center activities

REFERENCES:

Available upon request.

Putting Education first (showing Gifted Endorsement) and listing education-oriented community activities during stay-at-home years help to offset not working for six years.

SCHOOL TEACHER
6500 Shier Rings Road
Amlin, OH 43000
(614) 000-0000

"Every leader a teacher, every teacher a leader, every student a success."

PHILOSOPHY

A professional who strives to create a positive classroom environment, a community of learners, in which each student's heightened self-esteem leads to higher achievement and a desire to be a lifelong learner.

EDUCATION

THE OHIO STATE UNIVERSITY (1971-1975)
Bachelor of Science in Education, summa cum laude
Major: English Communications (English, Speech, Journalism)

Graduate Work

Ashland University, Ashland OH (1980, 1983, 1992, 1993)
The Ohio State University (1975, 1993)
- Gifted Education
- Computer Literacy
- Writing Workshop
- Reading
- Cooperative Learning

Honors
- 3.96 GPA Overall, 4.0 GPA College of Education, 4.0 Graduate Work
- Alpha Lambda Delta Freshman Honorary
- Summa Award
- Chi Delta Phi English Honorary
- President's Undergraduate Leadership Award
- President's Senior Scholarship Award
- Graduated 1st in class in College of Education at OSU and top 1/2 of 1% of all OSU graduates
- Phi Kappa Phi National Scholastic Honorary

CERTIFICATION

Current Ohio Certificate: Secondary 7-12
Areas: English, Comprehensive Communications

Ohio Provisional (July 1, 1993 - June 30, 1997)

65

Combination. *Susan Higgins, Amlin, Ohio.*
Out of the job market for some time, this teacher lists features to make an early impression: a quotation, Philosophy statement, recent graduate courses, high GPA, awards, and honors.

SCHOOL TEACHER   Page 2

TEACHING EXPERIENCE

DUBLIN CITY SCHOOLS
Dublin OH
1993-Present
Substitute Teacher
Grades 7-12

HILLIARD CITY SCHOOLS
Hilliard OH
1993-Present
Substitute Teacher
Grades 7-12

LEXINGTON HIGH SCHOOL
Lexington OH
1977-1983
English and Journalism Teacher (Grades 9-12)
School Newspaper Adviser
Junior Class Adviser
Quill and Scroll Journalism Adviser

- Representative to Richland County English Curriculum Revision Committee
- Steering committee member for North Central evaluation
- Levy renewal committee representative

CENTERBURG HIGH SCHOOL
Centerburg OH
1975-1977
English and Journalism Teacher (Grades 9-12)
School Newspaper Adviser
Y-Teens Adviser
Quill and Scroll Adviser

RELATED EXPERIENCE

1992-1993
Private Tutor in grammar, composition, and vocabulary for Watterson High School student

1989-1993
Part-time Team Teacher
DUBLIN COMMUNITY PRESCHOOL
Dublin OH

LIFE EXPERIENCES COMMUNITY INVOLVEMENT

Lifelong learner, lover of books, children, teaching, life

School
Scottish Corners Elementary
Dublin OH
- Head room mother (1989-Present)
- Classroom volunteer (1989-Present)
- PTO board member (Visiting Author committee chairperson 1993-1994)
- School levy campaign volunteer

Girl Scouts
1989-Present
Girl Scout Troop Co-Leader
Dublin OH
- Girl Scout Leadership Development Recognition Award (1991, 1992, 1993)
- Girl Scout Day Camp Unit Leader Camp Kenjockety, Galloway, OH (1991, 1992, 1993)
- American Red Cross First Aid Certified

Church
Indian Run United Methodist Church
Dublin OH
- Publicity Chairperson (1988-1991)
- Sunday school volunteer and teacher (1986-Present)
- Vacation Bible School teacher (1987-1991)

Other
- Attendee at Upper Arlington Summer Institute for Educators (1992)
- Attendee at Dublin Literacy Conference (1993)
- Ohio State University Alumni Association Life Member
- March of Dimes volunteer (1986 - Present)
- Memorial Tournament volunteer (1992, 1993) PGA Tournament Players Child Care

This two-column page shows that this person was not inactive but did substitute teaching, private tutoring, and part-time team teaching and was involved in a variety of community activities.

Elizabeth Williams

Professional Tutoring for Educationally Deprived Adults
Math   •   Reading   •   Communications   •   Life Skills

1001 McDonald Street   (317) 555-1212   West Lafayette, IN 47000

Elizabeth Williams

An experienced educator with a sensitive interest in educationally deprived adults, especially those with learning difficulties. Her established instructional abilities are complemented by the enriching experience of international travel and cultural involvement in Africa, Europe, and the Far East.

Areas of Expertise

- Remedial Math
- English and Reading Skills
- English as a Second Language

- Writing Skills
- Verbal Communication Skills
- Interpersonal and Life Skills

Special Skills

- Effective with adults impaired by dyslexia, physical handicap, or mild developmental disability. Patient and focused on building self-worth.

- Effective with foreign nationals making cultural and language transition to the United States.

Licensure

Indiana State Board of Education -- Life License
- High School English and Social Studies, Option 1

Indiana Library Certification Board -- Life License
- Certified to head libraries for populations to 300,000

Education

Ph.D. program in Special Education (in progress), Purdue University
- Teaching English as a Second Language
- Teaching Methods for Persons with Learning Disabilities
- Group Therapy

Master of Science in Education, Purdue University
- Also completed major coursework in Sociology

Master of Science in Advanced Library Science, University of Pittsburgh
- Carnegie Fellowship; Kappa Delta Pi Education Honorary

Bachelor of Science in Library Science, Douglass College, New Brunswick, NJ

International: Africana, French, and Japanese studies, Purdue University
Certificate in French, University of Grenoble, France

Selected Experience and Accomplishments

Acme Adult Reading Academy
- Reading tutor for the 1993 Outstanding Learner for the State of Indiana

Organized and managed libraries in Indiana elementary and high schools
- John Cotton Dana Award for the development of school libraries

Former Chairperson, Tippecanoe Area English Council

Served as cultural liaison for foreign employees at Continental Book Publishers, Chicago

References and Additional Information Available

66

Functional. *Alan D. Ferrell, Lafayette, Indiana.*
Nothing in this resume gives away the age of this 70+-year-old retired librarian who, with considerable education, travel experience, and verbal skills, wants to tutor others.

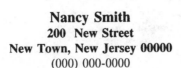

Nancy Smith
200 New Street
New Town, New Jersey 00000
(000) 000-0000

PROFILE:

Highly motivated individual with art background and strong interpersonal and communication skills. Diversified work experience covering Education, Personnel and Sales/Service. Noted for my resourcefulness, ability to handle diverse situations with ease and explain material in an interesting and clear manner.

PROFESSIONAL CAPABILITIES:

Interact effectively with people on a one-on-one and group basis. Taught and counseled students in both multi-cultural inner city and suburban schools.

Research a subject thoroughly and prepare well-documented reports. Conducted original research on historic homes in Newington as part of a graduate studies project.

Evaluate and draw inferences through careful listening and observing. Noted for my ability to absorb and retain detailed information and read the nuances of a situation.

Organize and coordinate a multitude of arrangements. Successfully planned and produced an art auction to raise funds for local school. Handled all publicity, advertising and financial arrangements. Rated as one of the top fund-raisers for the organization.

Create artistic displays and craft unique fabric collages using a combination of antique and modern materials. Commended for use of color and design sense. Work was shown at a local gallery and cultural center.

EDUCATION:

NEW YORK UNIVERSITY, New York City, New York
B.A. degree with concentrations in History and English
Summer Internship - New York Department of Labor & Industry
TRENTON STATE COLLEGE, Trenton, New Jersey
Master's degree studies in Art History (in progress)

WORK EXPERIENCE:

SOCIAL STUDIES TEACHER/SECONDARY LEVEL - Taft High School, Bronx, NY; Marsh Junior High School, Bronx, NY; and Chatham High School, Chatham, NJ
SALES CONSULTANT - Silver Crafters (New Craft Gallery), Nyack, NY
OFFICE ASSISTANT - Newcomb School of Politics, Princeton University, Princeton, NJ

COMPUTER SKILLS: Macintosh Plus; Microsoft Word and MacWrite

PERSONAL: Travelled extensively in Europe and Asia.

Functional. Vivian Belen, Fair Lawn, New Jersey.
No dates appear on this resume, which highlights the transferable skills of a mature woman with little work experience and emphasizes her art background—her strongest credential.

67

SUZIE JOBHUNTER
8555 West Cactus Road #00
Phoenix, Arizona 85000
(602) 000-0000

ARIZONA CERTIFICATIONS

	Expiration Date
• Standard Elementary - (K-8)	7/1/94
• Standard Special Education - (K-12)	7/1/95
• Supervisor - (K-12)	7/1/94
• Principal - (K-12)	7/1/94
• Superintendent - (K-12)	7/1/94
• Reading - Learning Disabled - Emotional Handicapped (K-12)	7/1/94

EDUCATION

Arizona State University - Ed.D in progress - Educational Administration - 1984 to present
Arizona State University - Master's - Elementary Education - 1979 to 1980
Arizona State University - Master's - Special Education - 1976 to 1979
Grand Canyon College - Bachelor of Science - Elementary Education - 1970 to 1972
Northern Arizona Univ. - Bachelor's in progress (completed at Grand Canyon College 1972) -1968 to 1970

SUMMARY OF ADDITIONAL TRAINING

■ Outcome Base Education National Conference, 11/91 ■ State Department of Education Summer Leadership Academy Faculty Member, 89, 90 ■ State Department of Education - Summer Principal's Academy Attendee, 85, 86, 87 ■ National Association Elementary Educ. Principal National Conference attendee, 1987, 1988 ■ State Department of Educ. Summer Superintendents Academy attendee, 1986 ■ Clinical Supervision Workshop with Sue Wells, 1985 ■ Advanced Essential Elements of Supervision, 1986 ■ Cooperative Learning, 1988 ■ True Colors, 1992 ■ Gang Prevention, 1991 ■ Family Math ■ Non-Graded Institute, 1992 ■ Reality Therapy, 1991 ■ Quality Schools, 1991 ■ Assessment as Learning - N.C.A. Institute, 1992 ■ Assertive Discipline, 1986 ■ S.R.I. Teacher Perceiver, 1986

HIGHLIGHTS OF QUALIFICATIONS

▶ 20 years experience in the educational field in a diverse multi-cultured urban environment, consisting of 8 years in administration and 12 years in teaching.

▶ Proven skill & experience in the planning; programming & building of a new $5.8 million facility.

▶ A visionary, with *proven* capability to create new programs for the benefit of children.

▶ Effective problem-solving skills, with demonstrated ability to identify and analyze problems and bring them to successful conclusions.

▶ An accomplished *change agent,* with an established track record in getting positive results working with community-based organizations, parents, and neighborhood groups in a multi-ethnic community.

▶ Proven communication that is straightforward, honest, and articulate, yet tactful and diplomatic as appropriate; active listening and consultation skills with ability to listen to, respect, and respond to divergent opinions and interests; ability to establish rapport with diverse individuals and groups.

▶ Caring, empathetic, friendly, positive, approachable, available, possessing strength of character and sincere sensitivity to unique needs and aspirations of all segments of the community.

▶ Strong academic background and well-grounded educational philosophy which allow for flexibility and tolerance for others; driven by a belief that *all* children can learn and a passion for learning that inspires.

▶ Courage, risk-taking, and an entrepreneurial spirit in exploring new frontiers and new school-business partnerships in education to effect what is best for students.

continued - page two

68
Combination. Bernard Stopfer, Phoenix, Arizona.
A 27-page curriculum vitae compressed into a 2-page resume! Different formats for the different sections help to break up the amount of information and provide a sense of variety.

SUZIE JOBHUNTER - page two

SUMMARY OF PROFESSIONAL EXPERIENCE

- Supervised daily operations of school with population of 880 pre-school to 6th grade pupils, **45 teachers** and 40 school personnel (Longview Elementary School - Osborn District).
- *Solid experience* in working with programs such as Chapter I, Indian Education, English as Second Language (students and adults) Free/Reduced federal food programs, K-3 At Risk Program, City of Phoenix Percent for Art, Head Start programs, Artist in Residence, Peer Mediation, and **Extended Day** Care Programs, to meet the needs of disadvantaged and low-income populations.
- Chaired School Site committee in passing 2 budget overrides & a $27 million Bond Issue.
- Hired, assigned, trained, motivated, and evaluated certified teachers and classified staff.
- Demonstrated competencies in teacher supervision, knowledge of instructional strategies, educational goals, policies, procedures, learning principles, curriculum development, and in-service planning.
- Ability to act as liaison, harmoniously and effectively between parents, school, and community.
- Prepared, submitted and oversaw budgets and procurement of supplies and materials.
- Charged with the discipline and safety of the student body; organized all aspects of security procedures.
- Successful in reshaping the school and its staff into a solid, dedicated team committed toward students and quality education.

PROFESSIONAL ACTIVITIES, AWARDS, AND HONORS

AWARDS

- Who's Who Of American Women, 1989 • Who's Who In American Education, 1992 • City Of Phoenix Neighborhood Partnership Award, 1992 • City Of Phoenix Special Achievement Award-Neighborhoods That Work, 1992 • Outstanding Curriculum Program Award - "R.A.F.T.," 1989
- Distinguished Administrators Award, 1989 • Mentor Award, 1987 • Venture Grants 1986-1992

PRESENTATIONS

- Principal's Academy, 1985 • ASA Promising Administrators Conference, 1986
- AWARE Spring Conference, 1987 • ASA Fall Conference, 1988 • Leadership Academy, 1988, 1989 - ASCD Fall Conference, 1989 • Spring National Women's Executive Conference, 1990 • Arizona Board of Regents, Dec. 1990 • Phoenix College Re-entry Conference, 1992

ACTIVITIES

ARIZONA SCHOOL ADMINISTRATORS - • Member 1982 to present (Also AASA member since 1985) • Minority Affairs Committee 1988-1990 • Minority Affairs "Enhancing Educational Leadership" Conference, 4/90 (Mentor)
ARIZONA AWARE • Member 1980 to present • Board Member 1987-1988, 1988-1989
ASSOC. SUPERVISION AND CURRICULUM DEVELOPMENT - • Member 1982 to present • Board Member, 1987-1988, 1988-1989, 1989-1990
NAESP - • Member 1984 to present • Conference attendee 1987, 1988
ARIZONA PRINCIPAL'S ACADEMY/LEADERSHIP ACADEMY (Summers) • Participant - 1985-1987 • Speaker - 1985 • Faculty - 1989, 1990
SUPERINTENDENTS' ACADEMY - • Participant - Summer 1986
PHI DELTA KAPPA - • Member 1983 to present • Interview team 1986, 1987

COMMUNITY SERVICE

Glendale Leadership Advancement Development, Class of 1993
Arizona State University West - Faculty Associate - 1992-present
Grand Canyon College - Adjunct faculty member - 1980-81 & 1984 - Asian Advisory Board - 1992
Longview Neighborhood Advisory Council - • Board Member 1991, 1992
Bear Essential News - • Advisory Board Member 1991 to present

REFERENCES FURNISHED UPON REQUEST

Because of the compression, information in the Professional Activities, Awards, and Honors section is not arranged strictly chronologically but with a view also to order of importance.

Suzanne P. Keating
61 Branford Street
Needham, MA 00000
(617) 444-4444

Objective	To obtain a position as a *Principal* utilizing demonstrated expertise as an educational leader and effective organizer.
Summary	• Demonstrated ability as an effective educational leader and manager. • Excellent knowledge and experience of the significant trends in education including Whole Language, Process Writing, Cooperative Learning, Learning Centers and the use of techniques promoted by the National Council of Teachers of Mathematics. • Outstanding parent, staff and student communication skills.
Experience 1992 to Present	**DOVER ELEMENTARY SCHOOL**, Dover, MA *Principal* • Effectively manage a school with almost 500 students in grades 1-5, and a professional staff of 40.
Curriculum Innovation	• Instituted quarterly curriculum updates to evaluate effectiveness of all programs. • Developed new math curriculum to meet the recommendations of the National Teachers of Mathematics national agenda. • Pioneered a multi-age classroom for first and second grade. • Integrated a variety of disciplines including art/music/library and gym. • Initiated the "Poetry Corner" to promote literature and poetry. • Brought in enrichment programs including expanded use of computers.
Communication	• Created the concept of "The Principal's Coffee" to encourage greater community/parental participation in the school. • Regularly publish a newsletter called "It's Elementary" to keep parents informed about school activities, events and general information. • Developed good working relationships with the local news media and regularly issue press releases to assure positive and recurring coverage of the school.
Staff Development	• Hired a number of new staff including specialists. • Conduct regularly scheduled performance reviews using the Skillful Teacher model. • Work closely with new teachers to instill the confidence necessary to perform effectively. • Use site-based management principles to have teachers feel a part of the decision-making process and take ownership for school results. • Providing common planning time for staff to better coordinate curriculum.
School Organization	• Eliminated a punitive discipline program and replaced it with a conflict resolution approach that gives each student responsibility for their actions. • Reorganized bus schedules to allow children more quality time while awaiting the beginning of the day and the time for dismissal. • Revamped the PTO in an attempt to revitalize the program.
Plant Management	• Managed the process of installing a new $125,000 roof. • Redefined performance standards for custodial staff.

69

Combination. *Steven Green, CPRW, Northboro, Massachusetts.*
Side subheadings in italic in the Experience section are useful categories for grouping the person's many achievements in her current position.

Suzanne P. Keating   **Page Two**

1985 to 1992   **MARLBORO PUBLIC SCHOOLS**, Marlboro, MA
                       Director - STEP Program
                       Head Teacher
Administrative   *First Grade & Fourth Grade Teacher*
                       • Organized and supervised teachers and students in an after-school program.
                       • Member, Teacher Interview and Selection Committee.
                       • Organized and implemented Professional Development Program for staff.
                       • Successfully implemented Whole Language Program in first grade,
                         developed method of evaluation and collected data for the assessment.
                       • Chairperson, School Based Support Team (SBST) Pilot Program.
                         Wrote handbook entitled, "Helping Teachers Help Children."
                       • Designed parent survey focusing on language development in kindergarten for
                         Chapter I grant.
                       • Designed and delivered science workshop for MESPA
                         (Massachusetts Elementary Schools Principals Association).
                       • Developed effective relationship with local newspaper to publicize school events.
                       • Supervised Student Teachers.

Classroom   • Utilize activity-centered learning.
                       • Integrated Whole Language throughout curriculum.
                       • Implemented DMP (Developmental Math Process) which uses a hands-
                         on-approach to problem solving and emphasize process in math.
                       • Organize cooperative groups in a heterogeneous self-contained class.

1975 to 1985   **FOXBORO PUBLIC SCHOOLS**, Foxboro, MA
                       Grade Leader - Third Grade
                       Kindergarten & Third Grade Teacher
                       • Successfully organized an intergenerational Thanksgiving Dinner
                         involving students and senior citizens.
                       • Developed an integrated day curriculum using contracts (scheduled
                         programs of classwork) to foster student independence.
                       • Member of Grant Writing Committee that acquired funding for the integration of
                         arts in the curriculum.
                       • Created new curriculum units based on student interests including Poetry,
                         Genealogy, Endangered Species, and Outer Space.
                       • Participated in organizing a Gifted Committee consisting of parents,
                         teachers, and administrators. The system's first Gifted Program resulted from this
                         effort. Approached by the Superintendent to accept the directorship of the
                         program.

1970 to 1975   **NEW YORK CITY PUBLIC SCHOOLS**, Brooklyn, NY
                       First Grade Teacher, Bilingual
                       Kindergarten Teacher

Education   City University of New York, Queens College
                       M.S., Early Childhood Education. 1975
                       B.S., Early Childhood Education. 1970.

                       Worcester State College, Worcester, MA
                       Principal Certification Program. 1990.
                       C.A.G.S., Leadership and Educational Administration. 1991.

Other   • **Selected**, Steering Committee, Principals Center, Worcester, MA
                       • *Business Advisor* for Junior Achievement.
                       • **Appointed**, Board of Directors, Learning Experience School, Marlboro, MA.

The bullets across two pages help to unify this resume visually. The dates of employment
show no gap and display steady progress from kindergarten teacher to school principal.

J. C. CAUSELAND
7 Savoy Court
Iowa City, Iowa 57777
(319) 777-7777

TEACHING EXPERIENCE

THE UNIVERSITY OF IOWA, Iowa City, IA
   Visiting Assistant Professor - Theater Department   1974 to Present
      Courses (undergraduate)
         Acting with Verse
         Acting I

MIDDLEBURY COLLEGE, BREAD LOAF SCHOOL OF ENGLISH, Middlebury, VT
   Professor of Theater - Summers   1965 to Present
      Courses (graduate)
         Actor's Perspective: Embodying the Text
         Introductory Acting
         Connections: Improvisation and Writing
      Honors
         Named 1975-76 Merino Professor of Literature

PRINCETON UNIVERSITY, Princeton, NJ
   Guest Director - Program in Theater and Dance   1963 to 1973
   Lecturer - Program in Theater and Dance   1963 to 1972
   Lecturer - Department of English   1962 to 1973
      Courses (undergraduate)
         Women in American Theater
         Modern Drama
         Introductory Acting
         The Processes of Theater
      Honors
         Profiled in Ken Macrorie's *Good Teachers Good Deeds* (Oxford University Press,
            1967) as one of twenty outstanding teachers in the United States and Great Britain.

WESTMINSTER CHOIR COLLEGE, Princeton, NJ
   Lecturer - Theater   1964 to 1971
      Courses (undergraduate)
         Improvisation and Movement for Singers
         Introductory Acting for Singers

RUTGERS UNIVERSITY, MASON GROSS SCHOOL OF THE ARTS, New Brunswick, NJ
   Graduate Teaching Assistant   1963
      Courses (undergraduate)
         Beginning Acting

NEW HAMPSHIRE SCHOOL SYSTEMS
   English and Drama Teacher   1956 to 1962
      Honors
         Pacesetter Award: Teacher of the Year, New Hampshire State Department of
            Education, 1961.
         Highest Teaching Award, New Hampshire Council for Better Schools, 1961.

70 *Curriculum vitae. Elizabeth J. Axnix, CPRW. Iowa City, Iowa.*
Prominence is given to the names of the prestigious institutions where this theater professor
has taught or is teaching, rather than to the ranks or positions held at these institutions.

J. C. CAUSELAND
Page Two

DIRECTING EXPERIENCE

Equity Theater

McCarter Theater, Princeton, New Jersey, Director's Laboratory
House of Bernarda Alba
Lorca, 1970

Theater of the Open Eye, New York City, New York
The Sixteen Appropriate Steps For Viewing Your Grandfather In An Open Coffin
Billy Aronson, 1969

University Theater

The Scarlet Letter	Carol Easton	The University of Iowa, 1976
	Ellen Laver	
The Emperor of the Moon	Aphra Behn	The University of Iowa, 1975
Sean, The Fool, The Devil	Ted Hughes	The University of Iowa, 1974
The Pregnant Pause	George Feydeau	Rider College, 1974
A Doll House	Henrik Ibsen	Princeton University, 1973
Rococo	Harry Kondoleon	Princeton University, 1971
Cloud Nine	Caryl Churchill	Princeton University, 1970
Measure for Measure	Wm Shakespeare	Princeton University, 1969
Miss Furr and Miss Skeene	Gertrude Stein	Bread Loaf, 1969
The Rover	Aphra Behn	Princeton University, 1968
Love's Labor's Lost	Wm Shakespeare	Princeton University, 1967
Vinegar Tom	Caryl Churchill	Princeton University, 1967
A Midsummer Night's Dream	Wm Shakespeare	Princeton University, 1966
Ethel and Julie: The Rosenbergs	Alec Baron	Princeton University, 1966
The Fifteen Minute Hamlet	Tom Stoppard	Princeton University, 1965
The Seagull	Anton Chekhov	Princeton University, 1964
Everyman	Anonymous	Princeton University, 1964
The Imaginary Invalid	Moliere	Princeton University, 1963
The Good Person of Setzuan	Bertolt Brecht	Princeton University, 1962
Aeneas In Flames	Billy Aronson	Princeton University, 1962
Play Without Words II	Samuel Beckett	Princeton University, 1961
The Bear	Anton Chekhov	Princeton University, 1961
On The Harmfulness of Tobacco	Anton Chekhov	Princeton University, 1961
No Trifling With Love	Alfred de Musset	Rutgers University, 1961
Killer's Head	Sam Shepard	Princeton University, 1960
Crocodiles (adapted: Pynchon's *V*)	Alan Mokler	Princeton University, 1960
Offending The Audience	Peter Handke	Bread Loaf, 1960

Edinburgh Festival Fringe, Scotland

Action	Sam Shepard	1965
Delearium	Billy Aronson	1965
Christopher Columbus	Michel deGhelderode	1964
Three Pieces By...	Gertrude Stein	1963

Centered headings—all uppercase, underlined, and in italic—tie together this four-page curriculum vitae. The extensive list of plays, playwrights, places, and years is impressive.

J. C. CAUSELAND
Page Three

GUEST ARTIST ROLES

Role	Work/Playwright	Company
Regan	*King Lear*/Shakespeare	Bread Loaf, 1974
Various Roles	*Caucasian Chalk Circle*/Brecht	Bread Loaf, 1973
May	*Footfalls*/Beckett	Princeton, 1972
Sonnerie	*Red Noses*/Barnes	Bread Loaf, 1971
Lady Macduff	*Macbeth*/Shakespeare	Bread Loaf, 1970
Hermione	*A Winter's Tale*/Shakespeare	Bread Loaf, 1969
Edward/Betty	*Cloud Nine*/Churchill	Bread Loaf, 1968
Joyce	*Top Girls*/Churchill	Princeton, 1968
Olivia	*Twelfth Night*/Shakespeare	Bread Loaf, 1967
Chorus leader	*Oedipus the King*/Sophocles	Princeton, 1966
Maggie	*American Days*/Poliakoff	Princeton, 1965
Varya	*The Cherry Orchard*/Chekhov	Bread Loaf, 1964
Amy	*The War Widow*/Perr	Princeton, 1963
Nina	*The Seagull*/Chekhov	Bread Loaf, 1962

RELATED THEATER ACTIVITIES

National Endowment for the Humanities Institute: Visiting Artist, 1976.

National Endowment for the Humanities Institute: Master Teacher of Acting, Bread Loaf School of English, Middlebury, Vermont, 1975.

Children's Theater of The University of Iowa: Founded, organized, produced, and directed, 1975.

National Endowment for the Humanities Institute: Visiting Fellow, led workshops and taught classes at high schools through the United States, 1972 to 1973.

The Acting Ensemble: Member of this Equity company which performs at Bread Loaf and whose members assist in course in literature, writing, and theater, 1968 to Present.

Princeton to Edinburgh Project: Founded, organized, produced, and directed productions which represented Princeton University at the Edinburgh Fringe Festival, 1963 to 1965.

BBC 2: Filmed and aired *Three Sisters Who Are Not Sisters,* 1963.

ARTS (Arts Recognition and Talent Search): Theater Adjudication Panel, National Level, 1963 to 1968.

Educational Testing Service: Theater Consultant, 1962 to 1969.

Children's Theater: Founded, organized, produced, and directed original theater pieces for children performed by high school students. These pieces toured the state of New Hampshire and were presented on New Hampshire educational television, 1957 to 1959.

The equally impressive lists of Guest Artist Roles and Related Theater Activities sustain interest and help to display a high level of expertise and accomplishment throughout.

J. C. CAUSELAND
Page Four

PROFESSIONAL TRAINING

Acting and Directing	Joseph Cates, Robert Smith, Bill Enson
Improvisation	Bill Ashes, Steve Cayan
Dance and Movement	Adam Zeller, Eva Cahen
Voice	Joan Smooth
Set Design	Doug Fein

EDUCATION

Master of Arts degree in **English and Dramatic Arts**   1966
   MIDDLEBURY COLLEGE
      Middlebury, Vermont

Bachelor of Arts degree in **English** with Honors   1956
   NOTRE DAME COLLEGE
      Manchester, New Hampshire

By the time you get to this fourth page, the smaller amount of material is acceptable as a fitting conclusion to the first three substantial pages.

FUNCTIONAL FORMAT
Accurate Writing & More
P.O. Box 1164
Northampton, MA 01061-1164
(413) 586-2388/(800) 683-WORD

SUMMARY:
- Consultant offering site-specific group and individual training to enhance workplace productivity and office functionality
- Skilled in wide range of modalities and techniques, emphasizing self-esteem through physical, mental, and emotional repatterning
- Diverse experience in administration, supervision, program development and management, sales and marketing

SKILL AREAS:
Training/Facilitation:
Workshops, classes, and individual lessons targeted to each client's needs. Holistic, systems-oriented approach. Topics include but are not limited to:
- Employee motivation and cooperation
- "Win-win" conflict resolution and other communication-oriented problem-solving strategies
- Personal empowerment, creativity, and self-esteem building
- Stress management/wellness education
- Peak performance and productivity
- Learning tools
- Therapeutic movement and fitness

Counseling/Teaching:
- Group and individual communication
- Dance/movement and other expressive therapies (certified Kripalu DansKinetics instructor)
- Psychosynthesis, Gestalt, Neuroassociative Conditioning, vocational training, and other modalities
- Experience with variety of mainstream and special needs populations, including business, new immigrants, mental health clients, children and adolescents

Management:
- Business concept development and coordination from initial idea through test marketing, site selection and design, production, retail and wholesale sales, and follow-up
- Full personnel, financial, and operations responsibilities
- Management experience in retail and human service settings
- Event organization and logistics, including publicity and marketing through media exposure and advertising

EDUCATION:
- **M.Ed. In Management**, Cambridge College, Northampton, MA, 1990
- **B.A. In Social Work**, minor in psychology, University of Wisconsin, 1972

WORK HISTORY:
Consultant/Trainer, freelance, 1993–present.
- Clients include Baystate Medical Center, Greenfield YMCA

Manager, A New Leaf, Holyoke, MA, 1988–93.
- Created new retail program: developed made-from-scratch product line; located and coordinated renovation of storefront, etc.; successfully marketed bulk-ordered handcrafted items by creating new distribution channel
- Instituted team-building strategy resulting in 30% decrease in absenteeism and tardiness

Service Coordinator, Mount Tom Institute, Holyoke, MA, 1985–88.
- Promoted three times from original hire as direct-care provider

Community Health Educator/Counselor, CHOICE, Philadelphia, PA, 1980–84.

Dance-Movement Therapist, Northeast Community Center for Mental Health, Philadelphia, PA, 1977–80.

References And List Of Trainings Available Upon Request.

71
Functional. Shel Horowitz, Northampton, Massachusetts.
A resume with ABC A+B+C structure. Three topics (training, counseling techniques, and management) are stated in the Summary and then elaborated in turn as Skills Areas.

MARLIA L. JAMIESON
400 Hart Lane   Hartland, CA 94000   (000) 999-9999

PROFILE

More than 10 years of progressively responsible achievement in communications, training, and management.
Committed to bringing about positive changes in animal welfare through education.
Enthusiastic, highly motivated, resourceful; can be counted on to get the job done.
Poised and self-confident in dealing with a wide variety of people.
Excellent skills in facilitation and presentation.

PROFESSIONAL EXPERIENCE

Humane Educator (Volunteer)
- Represented Region Five County SPCAs and promoted humane education and community awareness of issues related to animal welfare.
- Developed educational media for preschoolers, elementary, and high school students.
- Researched, prepared, and delivered workshops on responsible pet ownership to:
  - PTAs   - Girl Scouts   - Bible Study Groups
  - Rotary   - Girls' Club   - Students
- Addressed the public and media at community outreach events such as Homeless Animals Day.

Training and Development
- Conducted in-house and off-site training workshops.
- Trained diverse groups: youth and adults, from entry to executive levels.
- Researched, developed, and implemented new training programs to target specialized groups.
- Provided structured training in a high-turnover environment; accomplished departmental goals.
- Reviewed and evaluated employees' performance; recommended developmental courses of action.

Management
- Managed departmental operations in the import of $13 million (cost) of product from Far East sources.
- Directed staff of 7 including hiring, training, supervising, and evaluating.
- Represented company internationally in a variety of capacities including public relations and resolution of legal and banking issues.
- Handled extensive domestic and international correspondence to define contract terms.
- Cut costs by improving and implementing procedures for expediting shipments.
- Negotiated with contract parties to reach mutually acceptable terms and resolve grievances.
- Special Accomplishments: Received "Manager of the Year" and "Department of the Year" awards.

WORK HISTORY

1989-Present	**Trainer**	Civic Social Services, Inc.	Stillerton, NJ
1982-1988	**Imports Manager**	Marsden International Enterprises	New York, NY
1981-1982	**Executive Assistant**	Marsden American Corporation	New York, NY

EDUCATION

1980	B.A., Liberal Arts	Temple University	Philadelphia, PA

- Awarded an Outstanding Achievement Scholarship
- Human Resources Internship Special Projects:
  - Wage/Salary Administration   - EEO   - Benefits
  - Layoffs, bumping, recall   - Seniority System - Turnover Reports

ACTIVITIES AND INTERESTS

Volunteer Humane Educator, Region Five SPCA
Guest Speaker at Lehigh University   •   Biking, Walking, Antiquing, Stained Glass

---

Combination. *Joanne C. Hughes, Ph.D., Bethlehem, Pennsylvania.*
This resume has ABC A+B+C structure too. Three topics (media communications, training, and management) in the first line of the Profile are elaborated in turn in the Experience section.

72

PROFESSIONAL EXPERIENCE
(Name and address on cover)

1978 to Present MERRIMAK CORPORATION   Atlanta, GA

Summary: 15 years experience in positions of progressively increased responsibility in the areas of Quality Control, Direct Marketing, Data Processing, and Production Scheduling. Competent in both technical and managerial areas, with expertise in training and technical consultation, in addition to planning/coordination of data processing projects involving direct mail and credit/collections verification.

Accomplishments

- As **Quality Control Consultant/Trainer**, serve as a liaison between computer programmers and production staff to design and modify extensive direct marketing data base, with responsibility for staff training and supervision of conversion process.

- Selected to participate in qualifying project for highly selective Waldridge Award for Quality.

- As **Manager of Direct Marketing and Scheduling**, planned, scheduled and coordinated multiple marketing projects, directing the activities of a staff of 13.

- Awarded *Manager of the Year* in 1990 for the Direct Marketing area.

- Provided sales support and customer service to major clients such as NationsBank to design and tailor credit prescreening programs.

- Selected as **Team Leader**, with responsibility for coordinating and prioritizing up to 50 projects concurrently and integrating objectives with other departments. Served as liaison to enhance communication and resolve problems.

- Operated KDS System to input and reconcile data and enhance collections.

EMPLOYMENT HISTORY

1978 to Present MERRIMAK CORPORATION   Atlanta, GA

2/93 to Present   *Quality Consultant/Trainer*

1991 to 2/93   *Manager for Quality*
                 Manager of Direct Marketing Scheduling
                 Quality Control Analyst I/II
                 Quality Control Specialist
                 Scheduler - Credit Evaluation

EXCELLENT REFERENCES AVAILABLE UPON REQUEST

CAREER OBJECTIVE

Challenging and rewarding position, utilizing strengths in planning, coordination, and data processing to contribute to organizational goals.

SUMMARY OF QUALIFICATIONS

- Highly competent professional, with 15 years experience for major corporations, encompassing fast-track advancement into management.

- Experience in training and supervising up to 30 employees.

- Extensive computer experience, including data entry, systems analysis, data base management, and collaborative efforts to design and modify programs.

- Project management experience, including designing, planning, scheduling and prioritizing all facets of data processing projects to enhance efficiency and productivity.

- Demonstrated ability to communicate effectively with individuals at all levels of the organization to facilitate teamwork and successful completion of objectives.

SKILLS

- High speed and accuracy on data entry using WordPerfect, Quattro Pro, and Harvard Graphics.

- Detail-oriented, highly organized, record of efficiency and accuracy.

- Communication skills, including writing concise training manuals and developing and conducting formal training classes.

EDUCATION AND TRAINING

B.S. Degree in Marketing
University of Georgia, Athens, GA

73

Combination. *Julianne S. Franke, Lilburn, Georgia.*
The original had a 5 3/8-inch flap, folded vertically on the left, with a title on the outside and a cover letter on the inside. The right column on this page was visible with the flap closed.

Graduating/Graduated Student Resumes at a Glance

Kara G. Wayne

3838 Niblick Drive • Longmont, CO • 80000 • (000) 555-5706

Objective: Teacher.

Highlights of Qualifications

- Tremendous love of children
- Innovative, adaptable and highly organized
- Excellent in working in a team setting
- Proven ability in working in chaotic situations and still maintaining a sense of humor

Education

Student- Senior year (University level)
Major: Elementary Education
Minor: Special Education

Work Experience

1987-93	*Student*	
1992-93	*Day Care Provider*	Madeleine J. Collishaw Center, Santa Clara, CA
1993	*Counselor*	No. California Junior Sports Camp, San Jose, CA
1990-92	*Instructional Aide*	Mary Catherine Marocco Children's Center, Santa Clara, CA
1991-93	*Elementary Aide*	Vine Hill Elementary School, Scotts Valley, CA
1987-88	*Tutor*	College of Notre Dame, Belmont, CA

Professional Experience

DAY CARE: Children 5-18 with physical and mental disabilities
- Taught self-help needs (feeding, dressing, toileting, personal hygiene)
- Distributed medications
- Facilitated communication
- Supervised staff in absence of director
- Kept student progress records
- Scheduled daily activities and field trips
- Monitored and charted seizures

PRESCHOOL: Children 3-5 with learning disabilities
- Supervised class of 8-12 learning disabled preschoolers
- Set-up classroom for daily activities
- Taught fine motor skills
- Kept student progress records
- Trained children to use the restroom

ELEMENTARY SCHOOL: Grades 1-3
- Taught lessons in reading comprehension, spelling and music
- Graded papers
- Assisted with physical education activities
- Worked with teacher in all other areas of teaching responsibilities

COUNSELING: Children 5-16 without physical disabilities-others with spinal cord injuries and multiple amputations
- Supervised children during various athletic activities (tennis, water sports, basketball, racquetball, track and field)
- Assisted with daily living skills (dressing, bathing, toileting)
- Supervised large and small groups on a 24-hour basis

RELATED EXPERIENCE: Tutor – College-age students
- Tutored Spanish
- Tutored English grammar and composition

Combination. *Kathleen Hicks (writer), Sallie Young (designer), San Jose, California.*
Not evident is the arc of a colored rainbow that cut across the upper-left corner of the original version of this resume. Note the distinctive type for the name, address, and headings.

74

Victoria A. Brown

| 3000 Nostrand Avenue, #2B | Brooklyn, N.Y. 10000 | (212) 000-0000 |

DIETARY COUNSELOR

Skilled dietetic seeking a position that will allow me to **offer professional consultation** to meet the nutritional needs, and assist in advancing social needs of individuals and families in a community.

SUMMARY OF QUALIFICATIONS

Dietetic Concentration

Responsible for overseeing the dietetic needs of more than **11,000 patients over 16 years**. Duties included training new employees, individual and family therapy, menu preparation for employees' cafeteria and doctors' dining room, mixing formulas, chef sheets, etc.

- Reported to Chief Dietitian.

- **Saved $10,000** by selecting high-quality, low-cost meals.

- Checked food trucks to ensure proper food selections for over 11,000 patients.

- Visited patients and altered menus whenever possible.

- Planned hospital catering events for **over 500 employees**.

- Planned cafeteria menus.

- Coordinated diabetic patient's diet with doctor's prescription and advised patient and family members of proper nutritional diet.

- Tallied chef sheets.

- Worked all hospital shifts.

Social Work Concentration

Experienced in child welfare, counseling unwed mothers, assisting terminally ill patients, opening day care centers, assisting handicapped children, advising criminal offenders, etc.

- Responsible for <u>opening 10 day care centers</u> for children (ages 3-5) including interaction with City, State, and Federal government officials; complying with Board of Health guidelines to obtain certificates; screening and interviewing prospective employees; planning trips for children and parents; selecting toys and equipment.

- Planned holiday parties and special occasion events for **more than 150 children bound in wheelchairs** and with other disabilities.

- Assisted in **counselling 30-40 male prisoners** on how to live peaceably in society. Inmates completed education, and avoided becoming "repeat offenders."

- Cared for **12 children** so unwed mothers could complete school and find employment. 11 women completed school - were employed by Board of Education, New York University, etc.

- Administered medication to cancer patients; took care of hygienic needs; transported patients to and from hospital.

75

Functional. Margaret Lawson (location withheld by writer's request).
Centered headings and two-column formatting are distinctive features of this effective resume that generated letters of acceptance from seven colleges. Note the shaded box for a header.

Victoria A. Brown

(212) 000-0000

Dietetic Concentration   ### _Social Work Concentration_

- Ordered daily, weekly, and monthly food supply.

- Taught 1st & 2nd cooks, pantry workers, and salad persons to comply with Board of Health guidelines.

- Mixed formulas for ulcer and intravenous patients.

- Written presentations expounding on the functions of Red Cross and the New York Philanthropic League, including organization chart, funding sources, who is serviced, and how choices of service are made.

- **Directed 100 emergency building inspectors** to inspect heat, lack of hot water, and other complaints. Tenants were taught to organize rent strikes by depositing rent in escrow accounts.

WORK HISTORY

New York State Correction Officer
Correction Officer
New York, N.Y.

Project Rescue
Clerk-Supervisor of Shift
Brooklyn, N.Y.

Youth & Action Head Start
Assistant to Bishop's wife
Brooklyn, NY

Interboro General Hospital
Assistant Chief Dietitian
Brooklyn, N.Y.

New York Infirmary Hospital
Dietician
New York, N.Y.

Horace Harding Hospital
Assistant Chief Dietitian
Queens, N.Y.

Jewish Chronic Disease
Dietician
Brooklyn, N.Y.

EDUCATION

Borough of Manhattan Community College
Major: Social Work
Expected date of graduation: June 1992

Institute of Dietetics
Certificate Awarded:
Food and Nutrition

AWARDS

CUNY Coalition of Disabled Students Award   1991
Outstanding Student Award   1989
Women's Forum Educational Award   1988

AFFILIATIONS

CUNY Wide Coalition of Students with Disabilities

The continuation of bullets and two columns tie together the two pages. In the Work History section, centering the seventh job (Dietician) maintains symmetry.

Heather McNamera
1313 W. Nugget Ave.
Butte, Montana 59000
(406) 555-5555

**Job
Objective**

To secure a job which allows for me to save for college while gaining practical knowledge.

Education

***Butte High School**, Butte, Montana - Graduate 1993*
- *College Preparatory Classes*

**Honors
& Awards**

- *Girls State Delegate 1992*
- *National Honor Society 1992*
- *DARE Role Model to Elementary Schools 1991*
- *George Herbert Walker Bush Representative Band, July 4, 1991, Washington, D.C.*
- *Butte High Speech Team - Memorized Public Address*

Experience

*October 1991
to Present*

***Janet Gallsington**, Butte, MT*
- *Housekeeper*

*September 1989
to July 1991*

***United American Presbyterian Church**, Butte, MT*
- *Church Nursery Attendant*

December 1990

***Holder & Associates**, Butte, MT*
- *Substitute Receptionist*

Other Positions Held

- *Nannie*
- *Babysitter*
- *Painter/Laborer*

- *Pet Sitter*
- *Gardener*

• Continued on Reverse Side •

76

***Chronological.** Kathleen Y. McNamee, CPRW, Butte, Montana.*
A resume for a young student prospecting for a job by "cold calling." The original resume had references listed on the reverse side—a format adults might use without a cover letter.

Wendy K. Derrick

8000 South Kennington
Moscow, ID 80003
(206) 555-5555

Objective   *Waitress/cocktail waitress position to supplement college expenses.*

Education   *University of Idaho, Moscow Idaho*
- *Engineering Curriculum*

Butte High School, Butte, Montana - Graduate 1991
- *College Prep Classes; GPA 3.574 (63 out of 337)*

Honors
& Awards
- *National Forensic Qualifier - Extemporaneous Speaking - National Conference, Chicago 1991*
- *Montana Girls' State Delegate - Majority Leader of the House 1990*
- *Model UN - Top Delegate (out of 347) 1991*
- *Hugh O'Brien Youth Delegate - 1990*

Experience

May 1992
to August 1992   **Great Western Plaza Inn**, *Butte, MT*
Cocktail Waitress, Humors Lounge

March 1992
to May 1992   **Paul Revere's Sandwich Shop**, *Butte, MT*
Waitress

September 1991
to December 1991   **J.C. Post Co.**, *Moscow, ID*
Sales Associate
Received Silver Customer Service Award after only 2 months service.

July 1990
to September 1991   **Jace's Restaurant**, *Butte, MT*
Cashier/Hostess/Cocktail Waitress/Prep Cook/Busser

References   *Excellent references furnished upon request.*

Chronological. *Kathleen Y. McNamee, CPRW, Butte, Montana.*
The first of two resumes that show how a resume can expand to reflect a university student's
growth in experience. This resume calls attention to the person's honors and awards.

77

Wendy K. Derrick

8000 South Kennington   *Moscow, ID 80003*   *(206) 555-5555*

Objective

Waitress/cocktail waitress position to supplement college expenses.

Skills and Abilities

CUSTOMER SERVICE:
- *Thorough understanding of "needs satisfaction" selling and service techniques.*
- *Received J.C. Post Silver Customer Service Award after only 2 months service.*

COMMUNICATION:
- *Excellent oral and written communication skills; competed in the National Forensic Conference, Chicago 1991.*
- *Able to relate to people from all walks of life.*
- *Adept at handling confrontational situations, resolving them in a safe and fair manner.*

PERSONAL:
- *Outgoing, enthusiastic personality.*
- *Accepts responsibility; enjoys challenging projects that require creative solution paths.*
- *Dependable, hardworking and efficient.*

Experience

August 1992 to Present
Bambino's Restaurant, *Moscow, ID*
Waitress

May 1992 to August 1992
Great Western Plaza Inn, *Butte, MT*
Cocktail Waitress, Humors Lounge

March 1992 to May 1992
Paul Revere's Sandwich Shop, *Butte, MT*
Waitress

September 1991 to December 1991
J.C. Post Co., *Moscow, ID*
Sales Associate

July 1990 to September 1991
Jace's Restaurant, *Butte, MT*
Cashier/Hostess/Cocktail Waitress/Prep Cook/ Busser

Education

University of Idaho, *Moscow, Idaho*
- *Engineering Curriculum*

Butte High School, *Butte, Montana*
- *Graduate - College Prep Classes; GPA 3.574 (63 out of 337)*

Excellent references furnished upon request.

78

Combination. *Kathleen Y. McNamee, CPRW, Butte, Montana.*
This second resume of the pair—later in time—stresses the same person's skills and abilities. These are categorized for easy viewing.

Terry Lantz
Vandalia High School
16000 Berry Street • Indianapolis, Indiana 00000 • (317) 000-0000

ACADEMIC GOAL

To attend a college or university focusing on Business, Engineering, Math, or Science. Long-term goal is to attain a graduate degree in my chosen field.

ATHLETIC GOAL

To utilize my experience and strong background of 12 years to become a member of a college/university baseball team.

ACADEMIC ACHIEVEMENTS/ACTIVITIES

Vandalia High School, Indianapolis, Indiana
G.P.A.: 3.68   CLASS RANK: 59/727
National Honor Society
Key Club Member

ATHLETIC ACHIEVEMENTS

JUNIOR YEAR, 1991-1992
- **Varsity Baseball** (Marion County Championship Team; Semi-State Finalists)
  * Left Field (Lead-Off Hitter)
  * Second Team All County
- **Varsity Soccer** (State Runner-Up 1991; State Champions, 1992)
  * Defense
  * Academic All-State

SOPHOMORE YEAR, 1990-1991
- **Reserve Baseball**
  * Left Field
  * Indiana Amateur Baseball Association All-Star Selection
- **Reserve Soccer**
  * Defense

FRESHMAN YEAR, 1989-1990
- **Baseball**
  * Left Field
  * Indiana Amateur Baseball Association All-Star Selection
- **Reserve Soccer**
  * Defense
- **Wrestling**
  * Record - 19/3

VARSITY STATISTICS/Junior Year/1992 Season   *Team Leader*

	Avg.	Slg.	OB%	G	AB	Run	H	1B	2B	3B	HR
Spring	.289	.451	.513	30*	85	25*	24	14	6*	3*	1
Summer	.379	.539	.602	16	49	17*	18	11	5*	1	0
	RBI	TB	SC	OE	HP	BB	SO	SB	SA	SB%	
Spring	15	40	4	7	4	31*	20	7*	9*	.779	
Summer	8	26	2	3	0	17*	8	8*	10*	.817*	

Chronological. Gayle Bernstein, CPRW, Indianapolis, Indiana.
A resume for a student applying to college. Dual Goal statements are supported by dual Achievements sections. Sent with a cover letter to coaches, this resume had good response.

79

LESLIE WILEY
80 Johnson Road
Morganville, NJ 07000
(000) 555-3061

EDUCATION: **VILLANOVA UNIVERSITY SCHOOL OF DENTISTRY**

DMD, May 1992

Honors:	Deans List of Academic Achievement
	Stomatognathic Honor Society
	Oral Surgery Honor Society
	Endodontic Honor Society
	Periodontic Honor Society

Activities:	Member of ASDA
	Treasurer of Delta Sigma Delta
	Professional Fraternity

HORACE STAMP CANCER CENTER

Completed course in Oral Cancer Detection In Office Practice, Horace Stamp Cancer Center, Philadelphia, Pennsylvania

YALE UNIVERSITY

Degree: Bachelor of Science and Bachelor of Arts, May, 1988
Major: Chemistry and Psychology

Activities:	Health Career Volunteer at Yale University Hospital and Yale University Eye Center
	Intramural Activities
	Pi Delta Phi Fraternity

EXPERIENCE: **VILLANOVA UNIVERSITY DENTAL SCHOOL CLINIC**

Rendered comprehensive dental care to patients while working in a professional environment. Performed restorative procedures, oral surgery, periodontics and endodontic therapy during the past two years. 1990-1992

Worked under the supervision of Oral and Maxillofacial Surgery Residents at Villanova University Dental School, Villanova Hospital and St. Christopher's Children's Hospital. 1992

Participated in an Anesthesiology Rotation at Villanova University Hospital. 1991

KINGS DOMINION AMUSEMENT PARK
Manager and Supervisor

Responsible for running all aspects of twenty retail stores. Supervise a staff of 70 employees per shift. Train personnel, maintain stock within each store, and order inventory from outside vendors. Spring/Summer 1984-1992

PI DELTA PHI FRATERNITY
President and Treasurer

Responsible for all committees, payment of bills, and collection of dues. Developed annual budget. Appointed Alumni Chairman and Philanthropy Chairman for the Play Units for the Severely Handicapped (national organization - PUSH).

INTERESTS: Snow Skiing, Music, Football, Yale Basketball, Cooking, and Science Fiction.

---

80 *Chronological. Beverly Baskin, CPRW, Marlboro, New Jersey.*
A resume that uses all uppercase letters to call attention to the places where this new dentist has studied and worked. Small type increases white space and gives a neat, uncluttered look.

EDUCATION

Bachelor of Science in **Elementary Education**, concentrations in **Early Childhood Special Education and Computer Science.** State University (SU), Anytown, MN. May 1993. Major GPA 3.80. Overall GPA 3.31.

INTERNATIONAL TEACHING

Student Teacher - Ages 7-9
Anyschool. London, England. Spring 1993 (11 weeks).
- Observed an open classroom setting.
- Planned and implemented lessons with the team teacher based on the terms theme.
- Participated in and planned a Book Week.
- Instituted an international pen-pal program.
- Traveled Europe during school breaks to gain understanding of culture and history.
- Prepared an all-school assembly in which the class presented term projects.
- Adapted lessons and worked with individuals labeled Learning Disabled.

TEACHING EXPERIENCE

Substitute Teaching
ISD #00001. Anytown, MN. September 1993-present.

Practicum - Sixth Grade Students
ISD #00002. Anytown, MN. Winter 1993 (2 weeks).
- Planned and executed hands-on Math lessons on temperature, volume, and weight.
- Participated in Book Week activities and all-school final presentation.

In-School Experience - Third Grade Students
ISD #00003. Anytown, MN. Winter 1992-1993.
- Team developed instruction using an integrative approach.
- Taught theme lessons on famous African-Americans and biography structure.

Practicum - Third Grade Students
ISD #00004. Anytown, ND. Fall 1992 (3 weeks).
- Developed Math instruction with Dienies blocks.
- Developed Whole-Language instruction involving science, art, writing, and reading.

Multicultural Internship - Texas
ISD #00005. Anytown, TX. Spring 1991 (10 weeks).
- Teacher Aide in a second and fifth grade classroom (Five weeks each).
- Traveled into Mexico and observed elementary schools, Hispanic culture, and history.

RELATED EXPERIENCE

Personal Care Attendant
ABC Alternatives. Anytown, MN. Summer 1993.
- Provided personal care for 14-year-old boy with MD.
- Directed therapy - Range of Motion and Respiratory exercises.
- Maintained daily records.

RELATED SKILLS AND ORGANIZATIONS

Professional Organizations:
- MEA/SMEA Member.
- Association for Supervision and Curriculum Development (ASCD).

Music Background:
- Flute, 6 yrs; marching band, 4 yrs; guitar instruction, 2 yrs; organ lessons, 18 mo.
- John Philip Sousa Award recipient for Outstanding Senior.

Combination. *Elizabeth A. Meyer, Willmar, Minnesota.*
The name and address appeared on a cover page not included in this Gallery. Horizontal lines separate the sections, making them easy to identify. Again, small type increases white space.

81

RELATED SKILLS AND ORGANIZATIONS (CONT.)

Foreign Language:
- Completed 2 years of high school **German** instruction.

UNIVERSITY ACTIVITIES

Campus Activities Board - Advertising and Entertainment Committees. 1991-1992.
- Planned and organized various campus activities and their advertising campaigns.
- Supervised and ensured security at events.

Emerging Leadership Program. 1989-1990.
- 20 hours of training in group dynamics, stress management, leadership, learning styles, interpersonal communications, and conflict mediation.

Children's Theater. 1989-1990.

Athletic Activities
- Varsity Level Track. Spring 1992.
- Intramural Competition. (Football, Wiffleball) 1991-1993.

COMMUNITY ACTIVITIES

Adult-Teen Church Camp Seminar. 1987-1989.
- Counseled and prepared activities for campers, ages 13-adult.

4-H Club. 1982-1989.
- Offices Held: Secretary, 1987-1988; Treasurer, 1986-1987.
- Awarded State Fair trip for project accomplishment.

Sunday School Teacher - Volunteer. 1988-1989.

County Princess. 1988-1989.
- Extensive public presentation and product promotion.

Anytown High School Drama. 1988-1989.

HONORS

- Dean's List.
- Honorable Mention, Spring Honors Convocation, 1993.

WORK EXPERIENCE

DELI
XYZ Deli. Anytown, MN. Summer 1993-present.
- Food preparation - salads, sandwiches, party trays, deli meats, and hot food.
- Closing duties.
- Operated and reconciled cash registers.

WAITRESS
XYZ Restaurant. Anytown, MN. Summer 1991-1992.
- Setting attracted customers throughout the United States.
- Gained understanding of regional differences.

REFERENCES

Available upon request from State University Career and Placement Services. Anytown, MN 00001. (516) 555-2131.

Because work experience was limited to summers and directly unrelated to teaching, this section is put next to last and just before the References statement.

STEVEN PAUL

40 Candy Lane	**100 Study Street**
Happydaze, Georgia 30000	**Carrollton, GA 30000**
(404) 000-0000 - Home	**(404) 000-0000 - School**

EDUCATION

WEST GEORGIA COLLEGE, Carrollton, Georgia
B.S. Geography, Major: Regional, State and Local Planning, 1993

Internship, 1993
    CITY OF HAPPYDAZE, Planning and Zoning Department
    Ensure proper licenses are held by local businesses through research and
    follow-up activities. Created filing system to correlate plats, building plans, and
    other related records. Designed database to effectively track and integrate
    records pertinent to annexations, zoning, and all active and completed projects.

Special Projects
- 20-Year Comprehensive Plan for Suburban Community of 10,000 Residents
  to include evaluation and strategical planning for population, housing,
  economic development, natural and historic resources, community facilities,
  land use, and implementation of strategies.
- Prepared Land-Use Map for City of Carrollton, charting and recording detailed
  changes and growth through use of transparent overlays for years between
  1963 and 1992.

Related Course Work
    Regional Planning, Planning Seminar, Aerial Photography, Cartography Lab, Land
    Use Methods, Soils and Waters, and Urban Geography.

HAPPYDAZE HIGH SCHOOL, Happydaze, Georgia
    Graduated 1987

WORK EXPERIENCE

SHARP LANDSCAPING, Happydaze, Georgia	1992 to Present
	Part-Time
CITY OF HAPPYDAZE, Happydaze, Georgia	1984 to 1991
City Maintenance Department, 1988 to 1991	Summers
Park and Recreation Maintenance, 1984 to 1986	

REFERENCES AVAILABLE UPON REQUEST

Chronological. Carol Lawrence, CPRW, Snellville, Georgia.
Education is emphasized for this recent graduate with only summer and part-time work
experience. A symmetrical format is used for addresses and phone numbers.

Lynette C. Rochester

620 Parkview Court
Edwardsville, Illinois 62000
(618) 555-5555

EDUCATION

B.S. in Elementary Education   expected June 1993
SOUTHERN ILLINOIS UNIVERSITY at EDWARDSVILLE, Edwardsville, Illinois

A.A. in Arts & Sciences   June 1990
ILLINOIS CENTRAL COLLEGE, East Peoria, Illinois

EXPERIENCE

Teaching

Student Teacher (4th grade)   January 1993-Present
Clark & Thomas Elementary, River Falls, Illinois
- Wrote lesson plans and taught 24 students in self-contained classroom.
- Assisted with quarterly grading and project assignments.

Student Teacher (5th grade)   September-December 1992
Augusta Elementary, River Falls, Illinois
- Assisted Social Studies Department prepare and teach lessons for 80+ students.
- Arranged numerous field/study trips for entire 5th grade.

Coaching

Assistant Softball Coach   1990-1992
North Oaks Community College, North Oaks, Illinois
- Planned and executed daily practices, fund-raising events, trips, game preparation.
- Assisted with budget planning.

Graduate Assistant Coach   1992
Southern Illinois University at Edwardville, Edwardville, Illinois
- Assisted Head Coach with recruitment player instruction, team practices, and game preparation.
- Helped coordiate the Cougar Classic tournament, including All-Tournament team preparation.

Softball Coach   Summer 1990
Peoria, Illinois
- Coordinated summer softball program for players 16 and under.
- Conducted daily practices, prepared for games, and instructed players.

Volleyball Coach   Winter 1989, 1990
St. Pat's Elementary, Peoria, Illinois
- Coached 6th and 8th grade teams to regional championships in first season.
- Instructed team in basic and advanced skills and strategies.

Playing

SOUTHERN ILLINOIS UNIVERSITY AT EDWARDSVILLE   1990-1992
Edwardsville, Illinois
- Volleyball captain
- Softball: First Team Regional, All-American Select, MVP

ILLINOIS CENTRAL COLLEGE   1989-1990
Peoria, Illinois
- Softball: ranked 2nd and 3rd in nation, 1989, 1990
- Volleyball: ranked 18th in nation, 1990

---

83 *Chronological. Carla L. Culp, CPRW, Edwardsville, Illinois.*
The experiences of this prospective graduate are grouped according to several categories.
She wanted to use this resume for any occasion.

Lynette C. Rochester   2

EXPERIENCE
continued

Related   ***ASA Official***   June 1990—Oct. 1991
                 St. Louis, Missouri
                 · Officiated men and women's league & tournament softball games.
                 · Participated in clinics discussing regulations.

                 Footwear Salesperson (full-time)   June 1991—Dec. 1992
                 THE SPORTS AUTHORITY, Fairview Heights, Illinois
                 · Sell athletic footwear and accessories.
                 · Assist the department manager with various weekly reports.
                 · Assume departmental responsibility when manager is unavailable.

OTHER EMPLOYMENT

                 Kelly Girl   December 1992-Present
                 MASTERCARD, St. Louis, Missouri

                 Maintenance   May 1990—Sept. 1990
                 DRURY INN at Westport, St. Louis, Missouri

                 OREO Assistant   Oct. 1988—Dec. 1988
                 CITICORP MORTGAGE INCORPORATED, St. Louis, Missouri

                 Assistant Production Planner   Jan. 1988—Oct. 1988
                 LINCOLN, A PINTAIR COMPANY, St. Louis, Missouri

HONORS

                 Dean's List, Winter 1991, Fall 1992
                 MVP Golden Glove Award, North Oaks High School, 1987-1988
                 All-Conference, 1985-1989
                 Also enjoy biking, painting, jogging, and gymnastics

REFERENCES

                 References and transcripts furnished upon request.

The person's experiences as a player were just as important to her as her experiences as a student teacher and coach. Therefore, her participation in sports in indicated in detail.

Betty A. Callahan

(Temporary Address)
40000 Wayne Way
Kalamazoo, MI 49000
(616) 000-0000

(Permanent Address)
800 Cole Drive
Canton, MI 48000
(313) 555-5555

CAREER OBJECTIVE

A challenging position in Social Work where my ability to organize and stimulate will promote an opportunity for personal development and professional growth.

EDUCATION

Bachelor of Arts in Social Work
Western Michigan University, Kalamazoo, MI, June 1993
Minor: Psychology

Associate's Degree in Liberal Arts
Frankenmuth College, Frankenmuth, MI, December 1991
GPA: 3.8/4.0

Financed 100% of collegiate and living expenses

EMPLOYMENT

Assistant Manager
Wendy's, Kalamazoo, MI, November 1990 - Present
- Supervise, delegate responsibilities, and monitor the performance of support staff
- Train incoming employees to perform tasks at their potential
- Manage large sums of cash transactions
- Interact extensive with patrons to create positive rapport and repetitive business

Supervisor
Holiday Inn, Benton Harbor, MI, December 1989 - December 1990
- Supervised closing responsibilities of the establishment
- Executed cash management in verifying closing sales transaction totals
- Assisted patrons in the placement within the establishment in an orderly fashion
- Enhanced interpersonal communication skills through direct contact with patrons

VOLUNTEER EXPERIENCE

Big Brother/Big Sister Volunteer
Fundraiser for Helping the Homeless
Tutor to Grade School Students
London Child Care Center
Helping the Children Annual Drive

REFERENCES

Available Upon Request

84

Chronological. Betty A. Callahan, Kalamazoo, Michigan.
This still-at-school student's resume has dual vertical lines at the left margin and typical symmetrical addresses and phone numbers. The Objective statement promotes the person.

RUTH L. BRYANT

3000 Smith Creek Road, Suite 100
Hardwick, Texas 00000
(000) 000-0000

OBJECTIVE: Obtain a challenging entry-level position in Broadcast Journalism, with a special interest in reporting, anchoring and producing with a commercial television station.

EDUCATION: **Bachelor of Liberal Arts**, May 19XX
Famous Texas University, Some City, Mississippi
Major: Broadcast Journalism   Minors: History and Spanish
• Dean's Honor Roll

RELATED BROADCAST EXPERIENCE:

Intern
• WXXX, Channel ##, Some City, Mississippi
July 19XX - October 19XX

Reporting
• XXTV Channel ## News, Famous University
- Developed contacts and stories; responsible for covering stories on a regional and local level
- Developed and researched feature stories reflecting community interest
- Interviewed educational and business leaders concerning newsworthy events
- Developed ability to work under pressure and meet deadlines

• News Anchor, XXTV Channel ## News, Famous University
- Monitored Associated Press releases and wrote news scripts for station
- Produced and managed technical staff for newscast
- Covered fast-breaking news stories

• Weather Director, XXTV Channel ## News, Famous University
- Create local and regional map generation for nightly newscast
- Interpreted weather information from field communications
- Working knowledge of AT&T FC5 weather computer

Producing
• *News Magazine*, Famous University
- Produced and directed a monthly news magazine featuring both hard and soft news
- Supervised all aspects of project including story developments, creative style of magazine and development of script introduction to all magazine stories

Technical Experience
• Developed a working knowledge of videotape editing equipment, videotape camera equipment, videotape recording equipment, studio camera, character generation machine, and audio mixing board

HONORS & ACTIVITIES
• Radio and Television News Directors Association
• Society of Professional Journalists
• Campus Political Organization
• Habitat for Humanity
• Editor of *XXXXX*, Famous University Greek Publication
• Member of a Famous Sorority
  - Publications Chairman and Editor, 19XX-19XX
  - Panhellenic Representative, 19XX-19XX

REFERENCES: Well-known person, WXXX City Bureau Chief, (000) 000-0000
Known scholar, Professor of Journalism, Some City, Mississippi (000) 000-0000
Respected citizen, Owner, local store, Some City, Mississippi (000) 000-0000

Combination. *Leo J. Lazarus, Oxford, Mississippi.*
A divided horizontal line enclosing the name is a distinctive touch for this resume of a graduate whose experience is grouped according to four categories.

85

SYLVIA RODRIGUES

CAMPUS ADDRESS
7000 Wildwood Drive
West Lafayette, IN 47000
(317) 555-5555

PERMANENT ADDRESS
6000 Oakwood Lane
Olympia Fields, IL 60000
(708) 555-5555

PROFILE

Seeking an **entry-level accounting** position. Career committed with an effective combination of analytical, organizational, and communication skills. Able to learn new procedures and material quickly. Work well as part of a team as demonstrated by committee experience. Proficient with Lotus 1-2-3 and Word for Windows.

EDUCATION

B.S. Accounting, December 1993
Purdue University, West Lafayette, IN
Dean's List 1990 - 91

Courses in rhetoric and moral issues in philosophy, 1988
Yale University Summer Programs, New Haven, CT

EXPERIENCE

BOILERMAKER STUDENT FEDERAL CREDIT UNION, West Lafayette, IN

Closing Accountant • 1992 - 1993
Balanced daily transactions; checked balance on computer. Closed out the day's transactions on VERSYSS computer software. Audited teller transactions.

Member - Budget Committee • 1992 - 1993
Worked with other members to revamp and streamline computerized budget system.

Reorganized budget system to meet National Credit Union Association guidelines.

Co-wrote comprehensive Budget Committee handbook to document the budget process and facilitate training.

Member - Investment Committee • 1992 - 1993
Worked with electronic funds transfer; recorded balances. Utilized Lotus 1-2-3 for ratio analysis.

Teller • 1990 - 1991
Developed strong communication and interpersonal skills. Handled stressful situations with diplomacy. Managed heavy work load.

Gained diverse knowledge of credit union operations and financial controls.

References will be provided upon request.

86

Combination. *Jennie R. Dowden, Flossmoor, Illinois.*
Symmetrical addresses and dual horizontal lines create a solid first impression. This is sustained by paragraph style for the Profile section and the Experience statements.

CANDACE A. SMALLWOOD

5008 Cedarwalk Parkway
Tucker, Georgia 50000
(000) 000-0000

OBJECTIVE   I am seeking a challenging career position where I can utilize proven abilities as a *Travel Agent.*

EDUCATION   Tennessee School of Travel, Knoxville, Tennessee
Certificate of Completion in *Travel and Tourism,* May 1993

East Tennessee State University, Johnson City, Tennessee
80 credit hours towards a degree in *Marketing & Advertising.*

Walters State Community College, Morristown, Tennessee
56 credit hours in *Business Management.*

Barbizon School of Beauty, Knoxville, Tennessee

SPECIAL ABILITIES

- Strong organizational skills to effectively prioritize tasks.
- Trained and experienced using DATA'S II computer.
- Ability to establish and maintain trust relationships.
- A self-starter and motivator.
- Reliable, dependable and loyal.

EMPLOYMENT HISTORY

1991 to Present   CEDAR BROOKS APARTMENTS, Morristown, Tennessee
Owner/Manager

1993   UNITED WORLD TRAVEL, Morristown, Tennessee
Leisure and Corporate Travel Consultant

1987 to 1988   BARBIZON SCHOOL OF BEAUTY, Johnson City, Tennessee
Instructor/Model

SIR SPEEDY PRINTING CENTER, Bristol, Tennessee
Spokes Model

1986 to 1987   FINES JEWELRY, Johnson City, Tennessee
Sales Representative

1984 to 1986   WINN DIXIE, Morristown, Tennessee
Cashier

REFERENCES   Excellent references available upon request.

Combination. *Julianne S. Franke, Lilburn, Georgia.*
Side headings, the career goal, fields of study, and various jobs held are all in italic, unifying the resume visually. Filled square bullets call attention to this person's skills and abilities.

87

RECENT GRADUATE, Ms.T.
Accurate Writing & More
P.O. Box 1164
Northampton, MA 01061-1164
(413) 586-2388/(800) 683-WORD

OBJECTIVE: Staff massage therapist in a situation that allows close consultation
                and interaction with other health care practitioners.

EDUCATION: **Ms.T.**, June 1993
                STILLPOINT CENTER FOR MASSAGE, Hatfield, MA
                • Program included 1027 hours of coursework, as well as hands-
                  on clinics

                Coursework:
                Massage Theory and Techniques
                • Swedish Massage
                • Therapeutic Techniques
                • Sports Massage
                • Shiatsu
                • Feldenkrais/Body Mechanics

                Bodywork Sciences
                • Anatomy and Physiology
                • Myology I & II
                • Kinesiology
                • Neurology

                Additional Modalities
                • Holistic Health
                • Visualization and Imagery
                • First Aid/CPR
                • Communication Skills

                Equine Massage Therapy Certification (40 hours)

                Additional Education:
                • International exchange student, Lismore, Australia, 7 months
                • Baccalaureate courses at University of Rochester and University
                  of Massachusetts

PROFESSIONAL   **Massage Therapist**
EXPERIENCE: Canyon Ranch, Lenox, MA, 1993–present.
                • Provide massage therapy for clients at renowned health spa.
                  Mix of Swedish, sports and other techniques, depending on
                  client preferences and needs.

                Massage Therapy Intern
                Farren Center, Turners Falls, MA, Spring 1993.
                • Massage therapy for patients with psychiatric and physical
                  disabilities, including extensive work with geriatric patients.

                Volunteer Massage Therapist
                Boston Marathon, Boston MA, April 1993.
                • Post-event sports massage.

REFERENCES: Available upon request.

---

88   ***Combination. Shel Horowitz, Northampton, Massachusetts.***
          Although the overall design of this resume is chronological, the Coursework section, display-
          ing some learned skills, makes this resume seem more like a combination resume.

RENE CHRISTIAN   *2900 Lindstrom Drive*
(000) 000-0000   *Charlotte, NC 28000*

PROFESSIONAL QUALIFICATIONS

Experience in event coordination, promotions, operations supervision, and customer relations. Commended for initiative, trustworthiness, resourcefulness, and zeal.

EDUCATION

Studying *marketing communications* at University of North Carolina, Charlotte. Hold junior standing in 1993.

Studied marketing/retailing, English, theater arts, sociology, and economics at Central Piedmont Community College. *Cumulative GPA: 3.80.* Invited to join honor fraternity.

Special Project at CPCC: Analyzed compensation options and ethics within the NCAA concerning college athletes (all sports). Also researched the history of college football and how it has developed into a major revenue producer. Received "A" grades in oral and written presentations.

MARKETING EXPERIENCE

Coordinated two benefit screenings at NorthPark Cinema, one for ReadUp Charlotte and one for the Notre Dame Touchdown Club. Arranged catering; managed floor staff and activity during prescreening parties; served as liaison to organizers.

In charge of in-theater promotions at NorthPark, including studio- and company-sponsored contests and displays. Created a "Summer Movie Circus" display that the chain incorporated into its advertising and used nationally.

Designed and had printed a coupon for a theater/video store promotional tie-in. Developed and coordinated cross-promotional efforts between restaurants and nightclubs.

WORK HISTORY

Assistant to Manager, Spelman Cinemas (NorthPark), Charlotte, NC *(1991 - Present)*

Manage theater (with a staff of up to eight) in absence of manager or assistant manager. Work sometimes with company's film office. Have received all possible merit increases.

*****

Employed in the restaurant industry, 1989-91, as *assistant manager* (Bubba's Deli and Fifties Burgers and Shakes; directed up to 10 employees) and *cook/server* (Island Bar & Grill).

Combination. *Barry Wohl, Charlotte, North Carolina.*
This resume was created for someone who was still in school, had little experience, and wanted a position in sports marketing.

89

A. MAERIE JOSEPH
713 Pine Street
Alexandria, Louisiana   70000
(000) 000-0000

CAREER OBJECTIVE:
To obtain a position in apparel merchandising.
Major fields of interest are buying, management, and marketing.

EDUCATION:
B.A. in Apparel and Textile Merchandising
Minor in Marketing
Louisiana Tech University, Ruston, LA
August 1993
GPA: 3.77/4.0

SIGNIFICANT COURSEWORK:

- Fashion Buying
- Textiles
- Apparel Promotion
- Apparel Evaluation
- Retailing Management
- Business Advertising
- Salesmanship
- Accounting

WORK EXPERIENCE:
Internship
Macy's, New Orleans, LA
Assisted sales, received merchandise,
worked with visual merchandising.
6/93 to 8/93

Internship
The Gazebo, Ruston, LA
Assisted sales, designed window displays,
received merchandise.
3/93 to 5/93

Sales Assistant
The Gap, Kenner, LA
Assisted sales, received merchandise.
11/90 to 1/91

ACTIVITIES & HONORS:
President, Fashion Merchandising Club.
Awarded, Honor Senior: College of Human Ecology.
Member, Delta Zeta Sorority.
Awarded, Ruth Hatfield Makar Scholarship.
Member, Gamma Beta Phi Honor Society.
Recruiter, Liaison Team.
Board Member, Organization of Human Ecology.

REFERENCES:
Available upon request from:
Career Planning & Placement Center
Louisiana Tech University
P.O. Box 3153, T.S.
Ruston, LA 71272

90

Chronological. Michael Robertson, Alexandria, Louisiana.
The unique graphic represents the person's qualifications and makes the resume (and its
matching envelope) stand out. Center-aligned, the resume itself looks like a hanging dress.

RÉSUMÉ

HANNA SMITHERS

201 S.E. Cantrell Loop ■ Portland, Oregon 97000 ■ 503 / 555-0000

PROFILE

- Highly motivated with strong interest in establishing career in international business.
- Academic background includes course work in international studies, business administration, accounting and marketing.
- Enthusiastic, resourceful and trainable; able to adapt easily to new environments and successfully handle a wide range of responsibilities and special projects.
- Speak and write fluent French.

EDUCATION

UNIVERSITY OF PORTLAND – Portland, Oregon
BACHELOR OF ARTS, INTERNATIONAL BUSINESS (1993)

NYON LANGUAGE SCHOOL – Nyon, Switzerland
FRENCH LANGUAGE STUDIES (22 months)

APPRENTICESHIP

HEALTH TEC PLUS – Nyon, Switzerland
ACCOUNTING CLERK (6/89-6/90)
Performed various accounting functions for medical supply firm based in Switzerland. Entered invoices and payments into computer system and created invoices for the Order Processing Department. Set up spreadsheets on Lotus 1-2-3. Also provided back-up for the receptionist and assisted the firm's marketing manager; assembled promotional packets and serviced international accounts.

EMPLOYMENT

K-MART – Portland, Oregon
SERVICE CLERK (8/88-6/89)
Provided customer service and maintained all merchandising standards. Worked as evening supervisor and assisted with employee training, discipline and scheduling. Ordered products and supplies. Successfully completed management training program.

REFERENCES

Work references and letters of recommendation provided upon request.

Combination. Pat Kendall, CPRW, Aloha, Oregon.
Like Resume 15, this resume was done in Ventura Publisher. The thickened parts of the horizontal lines draw attention to the headings in different locations for variety.

91

George A. Munroe

Campus : 121 Harper Hall West Lafayette, IN 47000 (317) 555-1212	*Permanent :* 700 Lafayette Road Rossville, IN 47000 (317) 555-1212

Career Focus

Manufacturing/production. Current areas of interest for entry-level opportunities include quality control for polymer processing.

Education

Bachelor of Applied Science in Industrial Technology, May 1994
Purdue University School of Technology
- Focus on Quality Assurance and Polymer Materials Processing
- Major GPA: 5.5/6.0

Areas of Emphasis

- Industrial and Manufacturing Quality Control, Statistics, SPC
- Plastics -- Injection Molding, Blow Molding, Extrusion, Thermoforming, etc.
- Manufacturing Processes
- Materials Handling and Distribution -- JIT
- Facilities Planning -- Designed a manufacturing process for a new product.
- Production Management, Safety and Health, Technical Communications

Computer Skills: VanDorn Molder, Excel, Lotus 1-2-3, VersaCAD, AutoCAD, MacBRAVO, BASIC, Pascal

Manufacturing Experience

Royal Die Casting, South Bend, IN
A leading manufacturer of transmission and a/c casings for the automotive industry.
Machinist, Summers 1993 and 1992
- Assisted in quality assurance and analysis. Helped train new employees and demonstrate proper techniques. Proficient on a variety of industrial machines.
- Personally initiated a study of misfiled parts. Submitted a 25-page analysis to management, recommending systems and training solutions.

Cool-Comp Incorporated, Rossville, IN
A manufacturer of coolant compressors for refrigeration and air conditioning.
Machinist and Laborer, Summers 1991 and 1990
- Acquired assembly line, packaging, and machining techniques.
- Coordinated parts schedules for distribution and storage.
- Helped implement a computerized inventory control system.

Leadership Experience

Purdue University Residence Halls
Student Office Manager, August 1992 - present
- Self-supervised position providing services for 850 residents. Requires decision-making, flexibility, and communication through personal service skills.
- One of 16 selected (from 100 candidates) to staff a new residence hall.

Professional Affiliations

American Society for Quality Control   Society of Industrial Technology
National Society of Professional Engineers

92
***Combination.** Alan D. Ferrell, Lafayette, Indiana.*
A resume for a student's specialized job objective. Manufacturing experience is distinguished from leadership experience. Areas of Emphasis is used instead of Coursework.

Jessica Borders

9000 Allegheny Avenue
Indianapolis, Indiana 46000

(317) 123-4567

TARGET   A position as an *Elementary School Teacher* utilizing my proven abilities to create a motivational and stimulating learning environment. Believe in fostering problem-solving techniques and intellectual growth into positive life-long skills.

THE ABC'S OF MY TEACHING STRENGTHS

✪ *Ability* to *achieve* total educational involvement by developing rapport with students, parents, and peers; *adapt* and *assist* individual learning capabilities encouraging interest and participation. *Actively* participate in making a constructive difference by being an effective teacher.

✪ "Be the *best* I can be" by continually striving to *brainstorm* for educational procedures to *benefit* my students; set *boundaries* by creating democratic, guided, and fair environment. *Believe* students should be accountable for their actions; provide exceptional classroom management.

✪ *Committed* to creating *challenging*, flexible approach methods; always searching for new and stimulating *cooperative* learning activities. Sincere and equal *caring* about each and every student, dedicated to making learning more meaningful and exciting. Utilize basic yet innovative curriculum; active participant *communicating* with parents during conferences.

EDUCATION

INDIANA UNIVERSITY, Bloomington, Indiana
Bachelor of Science/Elementary Education, 6/92
Endorsement in Mathematics   Professional GPA: 3.9/4.0   GPA: 3.15/4.0
- Dean's List, 1989 - 1992
- Computer Literate (Macintosh; Apple IIe; WordPerfect; Lotus 1-2-3)
Special Studies:
- Elementary Methods for Reading/Social Studies/Art/Science/Language Arts/Math
- Calculus   • Analytical Geometry

SEMINARS/WORKSHOPS

Conflict Mediation, Atherton Middle School, 11/92
Performance-Based Accreditation Committee Member, Atherton Middle School, 10/92
Optical In-Service, Warren Township, Windows on Science, 9/92
Classroom Management, Dr. Allison Carlson, Indiana University, 1992

STUDENT TEACHING AND FIELD EXPERIENCE

11/92- Present   **Atherton Middle School**, Warren Township, Indianapolis, IN
- Assist in teaching 155 7th grade students. Established creative educational atmosphere by utilizing manipulatives and various learning styles. Developed vocabulary cards, visual and audio games. Initiated hands-on cooperative learning activities.

8/92 - 11/92   **Westfield Elementary School**, Westfield Township, Westfield, IN
- Developed successful "Our Feelings Are So Delightful" program; designed own tests for student's individual needs; assisted students in taking ownership by setting short- and long-term learning goals. Integrated in-service seminar into science curriculum. Established learning center utilizing strategies to increase math and reading abilities.

1/92 - 5/92   **Blaker Elementary School**, Barrington County Community Schools, French Lick, IN
- Team taught twelve-week Endangered Animal Social Studies unit to Grade 1. Established classroom library; incorporated children's literature and various resources into curriculum.

8/89 - 6/91   **Wilmington County Community School Corporation**, Martinsville, Indiana
4/92 - 6/92
- Assistant Supervisor in Extended Day Program responsible for well-being of 40+ children. Planned and coordinated daily activities.

COMMUNITY SERVICE

1/92 - 5/92   **Madison Elementary School**, Madison County Community Schools, Ellersville, Indiana
- Eagerly worked as a volunteer with children of all ages in a school publishing center. Assisted students in editing and publishing their own stories.

1988 - 1989   **Valpo Elementary School**, Versailles, Indiana
- Volunteer tutor for Grades K-6 students in all subjects.

Combination. Gayle Bernstein, CPRW, Indianapolis, Indiana.
To help this graduating senior enter the competitive field of teaching, the writer created THE ABC'S OF MY TEACHING STRENGTHS and used unusual bullets to call attention to them.

93

John Doe

Permanent   Address

123 Anywhere Court
Montgomery Alabama
36000
Telephone (205)555-5555

Career   Objective

Immediate :   An entry level Programmer / Analyst position

Long term :   Progression to System Annalist responsible for
creation and maintenance of information systems.

Education ;   Auburn University , Auburn Alabama
Bachelor of Science in Business Administration
Major : Management Information Systems
G.P.A. in major - 2.75 / 4.0
Date Graduated March 19 , 1993

M.I.S. Classes :   Analysis and Design of Computer - based Systems
Telecommunications Management
Information Resource Management
Survey of Current Technologies in M.I.S.
Business Computer Applications

Experience :   Installed hardware and software on P. C.-
compatible computers ; am familiar with several
Word Processors ,Database programs , CASE tools ,
COBOL , and Windows. Group leader for three
project teams.

94

Combination (Before). *Don Orlando, MBA, CPRW, Montgomery, Alabama.*
A student's stab at resume writing. Evident weaknesses are extra character spaces, a misspelling
in the long-term objective, and a lack of development throughout.

John Doe

123 Anywhere Court
Montgomery, Alabama 36000   ℘ [205] 555-5555

Objective:	To add to the profitability of XYZ Manufacturing Company by improving or designing customers' computer systems and offering topnotch training for their employees.
Strengths:	• The ability to *listen* • Natural grasp of how information is organized and processes work • Knack for turning irate consumers into understanding clients
Education:	Central University, Central, Alabama
degree	Bachelor of Science in Business Administration (Management Information Systems) – 1993
courses	• Analysis and Design of Computer-Based Systems • Telecommunications Management • Information Resource Management • Survey of Current Management Information Systems Technologies • Business Computer Applications
Experience:	• Installed variety of PC hardware and software. • Convinced businessman to hire me. Reworked his computer system. In only three months, updated his inventory control by entering 10,000 records in my spare time. • Analyzed independent company, found key problems, designed solutions and persuaded tough audience to approve my plan. • Led a team of four to complete 10-week software project despite tight schedule. Turned general guidelines into specific solutions that worked.
Special Qualifications:	• Know DOS 6.0, Windows, BASIC, COBOL, C, word processing, data base and CASE • Widely traveled in European Economic Community countries • Fluent in French; speak Spanish • Hands-on experience with mainframes, VAX, PCs and Ethernet

---

Combination (After). *Don Orlando, MBA, CPRW, Montgomery, Alabama.*
The resume after development. This resume, accompanied by a cover letter and followed up within 24 hours by a thank-you note, helped the student acquire a hard-to-get job.

95

Gavin D. Derrick

800 Hawthorne Drive #120   Moscow, ID 80000   (208) 555-5555

OBJECTIVE

To obtain a full-time position in Development with the ABC Bread Company of Dalton, Montana.

SKILLS AND ABILITIES

MANAGEMENT

- Experienced in supervision of employees. Served as training supervisor.
- Coordinated and accompanied 10-15 newsboys on cold-call selling trips to neighboring communities to initiate new subscriptions.
- Responsible for closing of the tills and daily reports.
- Performed closing procedures, making sure all security measures were followed.

CUSTOMER RELATIONS

- Excellent communication and people skills.
- Thorough understanding of "needs satisfaction" and other selling techniques.
- Adept at handling customer complaints; able to defuse the most complicated of situations.

PERSONAL

- Enthusiastic, energetic and goal-oriented.
- Works well on individual and team projects.
- Enjoys challenging tasks; quick learner.

EDUCATION

UNIVERSITY OF ULSTER, Jordanstown, N. Ireland
BACHELOR OF ARTS - HONORS (1993)

UNIVERSITY OF IDAHO, Moscow, ID
Exchange Student (1991-1992)

EMPLOYMENT HISTORY

1993 - Present

CAMBRIDGE MORNING TRIBUNE, Moscow, Idaho
ASSISTANT DISTRICT MANAGER

1992 - 1993
1989 - 1991

GENERAL'S FRIED CHICKEN, Ballyhackamore, Belfast, N. Ireland
TRAINING SUPERVISOR/ NIGHT AUDITOR/ COUNTER SERVICE/ COOK

1986 - 1989

RON'S FOODS - BAKERY DEPT., Bloomfield, Belfast, N. Ireland
FOOD PREPARATIONS/ BAKER/ COUNTER SERVICE/ NIGHT CLOSE

References Furnished Upon Request

96

Combination. Kathleen Y. McNamee, CPRW, Butte, Montana.
Skills and abilities are grouped according to three categories (management, customer relations, and personal). Key words are underlined. The original was on designer paper.

ANN H. TAYLOR

<u>Campus Address:</u>
Post Office Box 1
University, Mississippi 38000
(601) 555-5555

<u>Permanent Address:</u>
555 Philp Drive
Tupelo, Mississippi 38000
(601) 555-5555

OBJECTIVE: Obtain a challenging entry-level accounting internship which will enhance my education and experience.

PROFILE:
- Above-average mathematical aptitude
- Effective communication skills
- Manage time efficiently
- Ability to work effectively with minimum supervision

EDUCATION: **BACHELOR OF ACCOUNTANCY**, May 1994
University of Mississippi, Oxford, Mississippi
- Cumulative GPA: 3.8 (A=4.0)
- Chancellor's Honor Roll

Campus Honors & Activities:

- Phi Kappa Phi
- Omicron Delta Kappa
- Beta Alpha Psi, Vice President
- Phi Eta Sigma
- Golden Key National Honor Society
- Gamma Beta Phi
- **Sorority Member**
  - Treasurer, 1992
  - Executive Board
  - Chapter Programming Board

- Mortar Board
- Order of Omega
- Alpha Lambda Delta
- Beta Gamma Sigma
- Reformed University Fellowship
- Student Alumni Council
- **Associated Student Body**
  - Wellness Committee
  - Race Relations Committee
  - Miss. Governmental Affairs Committee

Special Project: **Sorority Treasurer.** Corrected bookkeeping problems during first three months of service and implemented a system to convert the manual billing system to a computerized system. Effectively managed an annual budget of $500,000.

Mississippi College, Clinton, Mississippi
August 1990 - December 1990
- Awarded $12,000 Presidential Scholarship for 4 years of study
- Dean's List

WORK EXPERIENCE:

Summer 1993

<u>Hostess</u>
Harvey's, Tupelo, Mississippi

May 1987 - August 1990

<u>Receptionist</u>
Sunsational Tans, Tupelo, Mississippi
- Maintained 3.95 GPA while working 18 hours per week

REFERENCES: Available upon request

Combination. *Leo J. Lazarus, Oxford, Mississippi.*
The Profile indicates chief abilities and skills. Two-column format is then used to list all the student organizations and honor societies this four-year Presidential Scholar belongs to.

97

Kristy M. Smith

<u>Permanent Address</u>
71 Morrowfield Street
Pittsford, New York 14000
716-000-0000

<u>College Address</u>
30 Perspective Hill Rd., Apt. 7
Cortland, New York 13000
607-000-0000

Profile

Creative individual with a diverse background.
Strong organizational, leadership, communication, business, and artistic skills.

Summary of Qualifications

Business Environment
- Effectively managed the organization, storage and retrieval of over 5,000 consumer loan files.
- Determined and computer entered codes for accounts payable processing and distribution.
- Knowledgeable in general office procedures and equipment operation.
- Received payments and balanced cash drawer in a retail setting.

Leadership Roles
- Planned, coordinated, and presented activities for dorm housing primarily foreign exchange students. Worked closely with college administration in fund-raising endeavors.
- Co-founder and advocate for student group organized to provide public awareness of impact of budget cuts on school programs. Encouraged voter participation with resultant turnout that effectively defeated proposal.
- Served as secretary for philanthropic organization which raised funds for community service.
- Facilitated meetings and implemented programs for youth organization.
- Actively involved in local political campaign providing input into and assisting with public relations.
- Ensured the safety and well-being of individuals in the pool area of an apartment complex.
- Selected as captain for varsity sport teams.
- Assumed administrative responsibilities for various school organizations.

Customer Service/Communications
- Enhanced ability to interact effectively with a wide range of individuals through direct interaction with the general public in customer service/sales capacities.
- Volunteered at area senior citizen home providing companionship to the residents and encouraging their participation in activities and programs. Assisted the program director in the design and implementation of events.

Education

State University of New York College at Cortland, Cortland, New York
B.A. - Art; Concentration: **Sculpture**, May 1994
- Sculpture selected for gallery showing.
- Dean's List
- Major Curriculum: Sculpture; Drawing; Design; Painting; Weaving & Fabric Design (computer applications); Ceramics; Printmaking; Photography
- **President:** Haskin Hall Dorm Council

Utica High School, Utica, New York
Regent's Diploma, June 1990
- Tennis & Volleyball (**Captain**); Track; Student Council (**Secretary**); Year Book; Ecology Club; Student Advocacy Group (**Co-Founder/Spokesperson**); Beta Tau (**Secretary**)

Combination. *Lynda C. Grier, Elmira, New York.*
The Education and Experience sections have chronological arrangement, but the Summary of Qualifications has functional format, displaying three categories of achievements and skills.

Kristy M. Smith

Experience

Office Clerk

Chase Manhattan Bank (Consumer Loan Department), Rochester, NY, Summer 1992
Metropolitan Life Insurance (Check Writing Department), Rome, NY, Summer 1991

Waitress

Pierrio's Restaurant, Cortland, NY, September 1993 to present
Perry Hills & Chuckies Restaurants, Rochester, NY, Summer 1992

Head Life Guard

Hill View Apartments, Utica, NY, Summer 1990

Cashier/Sales Associate

Agway, Rome, NY, Summer 1989

Volunteer

New Hartford Senior Citizen Home
Active in *political campaign and youth organizations.*

Additional Information

Interests

Art; Skiing; Tennis; Jogging/Running (Completed 1993 15K "Boilermaker" in Utica).

References

Portfolio furnished upon request

This student majored in art but had a business background and good leadership and
communication skills. The Summary made her marketable in these areas as well as in art.

CAROL OLDHAM

55 Browertown Road, Little Falls, NJ 07000
(201) 555-5555

OBJECTIVE

Internship with a human services organization centering on alcohol rehabilitative counseling in a community, residential or institutional setting.

RELEVANT QUALIFICATIONS

- Served as both participant and advisor in alcohol and drug abuse recovery process including an Alcoholics Anonymous 12-Step Program.
- Keen sensitivity to peoples' feelings and needs to enable joining with clients in early stages of interaction. Direct experience with the maladjusted and mentally ill.
- Trained to uncover key factors that contribute to an individual's problem situation.
- Confident facilitator; relate comfortably with diverse cultural and socio-economic populations, individually or in groups.
- Fully capable of handling assignments involving detailed recordkeeping, analysis and reporting. Efficiently follow through to completion.

EDUCATION

B.A. in Psychology, May 1992. GPA 3.3
Montclair State College, Upper Montclair, NJ
Curriculum focus included: Introduction to Community Psychology; Psychology of Adjustment; Social Psychology; Racial and Ethnic Relations; Quantitative Methods in Psychology; Facilitating Interaction Process I; Peer Counseling; Group Dynamics.

PROFESSIONAL EXPERIENCE

Internship as Assistant to Intake Coordinator at Hope House, a psycho-social rehabilitative agency in Easthaven, NJ (January - May 1992).

- Co-led several groups of mentally ill chemical abusers (MICA), focusing on their recovery.
- Assisted in assessing and prioritizing service requirements for new clients.
- Oriented prospective clients to the rehabilitative setting and the programs available to them.
- Facilitated the adjustment of introductory groups on a daily basis, providing them with support and encouragement to stay with the program.
- Scheduled clients for activities and coordinated community-based services for their welfare.
- Helped mentally ill clients to master the practical aspects of everyday living through a 10-week program which utilized a patient, personally attentive approach.
- Implemented a major project for the institution, involving the collection and analysis of data on the intake process obtained from responses by 92 psycho-social agencies. Conclusions drawn from this material were presented at a professional conference.

OTHER EMPLOYMENT

Office Manager/Ophthalmic Apprentice, Artistic Eyewear, Clifton, NJ (1978-1981)
Hairdresser, International Salon, Clifton, NJ (1977-1978)

SPECIAL TRAINING/CREDENTIALS

Certified in CPR and First Aid
NJ Licensed Beautician (current cosmetology license)

VOLUNTEER ACTIVITIES

Member of St. Paul's parochial school board in Wayne, NJ. Serve as tuition officer and participate in fund-raising events.

99

Combination. *Melanie Noonan, CPS, Little Falls, New Jersey.*
This resume writer believes that bulleted items should be substantial and say what the reader wants to know. With narrow margins and small type, this resume contains much information.

——— MITCHEL R. HANBRIDGE ———
3311 Walter Road   Yorktown Hgts, NY   10000
(914) 000-0000

OBJECTIVE

A position as an Assistant Account Executive which will utilize my background in Advertising and Promotion.

PROFILE

- Organized, detail-oriented professional with demonstrated ability to take a project from the concept stage to successful implementation.
- Ability to identify with the target market and deliver an appropriate message.
- People-oriented; able to work well with individuals on all levels; team player.
- Demonstrated ability to develop and maintain sound relationships with clients anticipating client needs; Demonstrated problem-resolution abilities.
- Effective communicator; experienced presenter.

SIGNIFICANT ACHIEVEMENTS

- Played integral role in conceptualizing total marketing plan and creative strategy for major financial services organization.
- Analyzed market research pertaining to target market's media habits in order to develop an effective and synergistic campaign.
- Utilized Telmar Information Services and analyzed market research pertaining to target market's media habits. Planned gross rating points for both broadcast and print media leading to development of flow charts for the optimal media plan.
- Produced appropriate strategies and main ideas for copy and layout of all advertising for each medium.
- Successfully defended strategy position from potential client while under heavily detailed questioning.
- Received national recognition in American Advertising Federation sponsored National Student Advertising Competition.

EDUCATION

PACE UNIVERSITY, Pleasantville, NY
Bachelor of Business Administration, June 1992
Major: Marketing   Concentration: Advertising/Promotion
Overall Q.P.A.: 3.15   Marketing Q.P.A.: 3.6

HONORS

Recipient of the Creative Marketing Award
Dean's List ; Pace University Trustee Scholarship.
Selected for Pace University Advertising Team
- Head of Planning/Strategy Department
- Selected as one of five to present for PACE's Advertising team.
- Received the *Creative Campaign Award* by the Advertising Club of Westchester.

EXPERIENCE

Finance 50% of college expenses.

June 1986 - Present

McDONALD'S, Yorktown, NY
Shift Assistant Manager
- Received promotion due to ability to improve productivity and teamwork.
- Recommended change in procedure which resulted in cutting waste by 97%.
- Commended for leadership abilities; due to personal initiative in staff training, grill operation received an "A" rating on recent corporate Full Field Inspection.
- Order raw product; maintain equipment.
- Accurately complete paperwork and bank deposits; oversee contents of safe.
- Provide orientation and training for new hires.
- Instituted measures to expedite customer service.
- Served as liaison between crew and management.

May 1991 -
August 1991

FREIDMAN MARKETING, Jefferson Valley, NY
Interviewer
- Screened potential clients and recorded responses
- Administered surveys and taste tests.
- Presented video tapes, new products and concepts.

COMPUTER SKILLS

Significant expertise on IBM PC's: Harvard Graphics, Professional Write, Lotus 1-2-3.
Extensive hands-on experience on Macintosh: Microsoft Word, MacWrite II.

PROFESSIONAL AFFILIATIONS

Pace University Marketing Association
Pace University Advertising Team, VISA Account - Account Executive.
Advertising Club of Westchester

REFERENCES

Available upon request.

Combination. *Mark D. Berkowitz, N.C.C.C., Yorktown Heights, New York.*
For those who think that a one-page resume cannot say enough, this resume shows other-wise. Space is gained by narrower margins, smaller type, and reduced line spacing.

100

RICHARD S. PETERSON
8046 Turman Ave. Apt #620
Papillion, NE 68000
(402) 000-0000

JOB OBJECTIVE:

A position as Protocol Officer where I can utilize my skills and ability to execute a variety of projects simultaneously.

HIGHLIGHTS OF QUALIFICATIONS:

* Personable and persuasive; able to build instant rapport.
* Aggressive, enthusiastic and energetic self starter.
* Effective working both independently and as a team member.
* Ability to relate easily with all kinds of people.
* Practical talent for seeing what needs to be done and doing it.

RELEVANT EXPERIENCE & SKILLS

PUBLIC RELATIONS
Assembled customed marketing packets used in presentation for special projects. I also developed cooperative relationship with the Base Newspaper and other advertising agencies, resulting in successful coverage of events.

PROJECT ORGANIZING
Organized conferences and workshops for special functions involving requesting transportation, making arrangements for conference rooms, advertising, soliciting speakers, making invitations, and providing visual aids.

WRITING
Excellent writing and communications skills. Wrote and edited base operational plan to include base readiness and noncombat evacuation.

SUPERVISION AND TRAINING
Supervised daily activities of staff, quickly shifting priorities as requested by upper management.
Managed the Air Force Aid Society account involving $135,000 in disbursements a year.

WORK HISTORY

1992-Present	Chief, Customer Support	Offutt Air Force Base, Nebraska
1991-1992	Chief, Personnel Utilizations	Offutt Air Force Base, Nebraska
1990-1991	Chief, Personnel Readiness	Clark Air Base, Philippines
1989-1990	Chief, Customer Assistance	Offutt Air Force Base, Nebraska
1988-1989	Chief, Quality Force	Castle Air Force Base, California

EDUCATION

9 college credits towards a Masters Degree in Public Administration with the Golden Gate University in California.
Bachelor's degree in Communication with Southeast Missouri State University.
Completed S.O.S in residence July 1992.

ACHIEVEMENTS

Offutt Air Force Base Outstanding Personnel Junior Manager of the Year for 1992.

AWARDS

Joint Service Commendation Medal
Air Force Achievement Medal (with 1 Oak Leaf Cluster)

101 **Combination.** *Rafael Santiago, Papillion, Nebraska.*
A resume for a person looking for a public administrative position at another Air Force base. The Highlights section lists skills and abilities; the Experience section shows achievements.

JEFFREY D. ACTOR
(000) 555-1234   *1234 Any Street • Anytown, State 12345*

OBJECTIVE

A full-time position in TV that will offer opportunities to develop well-rounded knowledge in all aspects of television production, augmenting my education and experience in broadcasting.

PROFILE

- Excellent **on-camera and behind-camera experience**
- Hands-on training and operation of **video cameras, video editing** equipment, sound equipment and lighting
- **Radio announcer** for 4 years
- Professional background in live theatre including **writing, directing, performing,** set construction and lighting
- Highly professional; work well under pressure
- Strong communication skills

PROFESSIONAL EXPERIENCE

Host, *TV Show* (May 1993-Present)
LOCAL CABLEVISION, Anytown, State
Research and write material for one-hour live production. Interview a wide variety of guests on camera and elicit audience participation. Requires ability to control flow of conversation and "think on my feet."

Announcer (October xxxx-August xxxx)
AUDIO READER, Anytown, State
Provided both live and taped announcing at radio station for the visually impaired. Ran sound board and monitored taped material.

Actor (Summer xxxx)
THE FARM PLAYERS, Resort Area, State
Performed 3 shows weekly in melodramas, playing different role in each play. Wrote radio advertising promoting shows.

Carpenter/Properties Assistant (May xxxx-May xxxx)
UNIVERSITY THEATRE, University of State, Anytown
Built scenery for all University Theatre productions, as well as purchasing and creating stage props.

ADDITIONAL EXPERIENCE

Sales Associate (xxxx-Present)
SPORTSWEAR STORE, Anytown, State

EDUCATION

B.G.S. Theater and Film (May xxxx), *University of State*, Anytown
- Responsible for *100%* of college finances
- Performed in 30 productions, directed 10
- Author of play chosen for production at Inge Theatre...directed and produced play

---

Combination. *Linda Morton, CPRW, Lawrence, Kansas.*
A pair of "thick and thin" horizontal lines encloses the name, address, and phone number. Distinctive "reel" bullets call attention to items in the Profile and Education sections.

102

Insurance/Real Estate Resumes at a Glance

ROBERT SMITH

3003 Rolldown Terrace	Atlanta, Georgia 30000	(404) 000-0000

SUMMARY OF QUALIFICATIONS

Comprehensive knowledge of Sales, Management, and Transportation Operations. Record of consistent achievement, proven P/L management skills, personal commitment, and positive corporate growth. Ability to execute multiple projects simultaneously, communicate ideas to others, and bring functional groups together to achieve a common goal. Dedicated to professionalism; determined to succeed. Excellent organizational skills, well developed sales techniques, and detail-oriented.

Management
- Supervised 80 employees, established training programs, instituted efficient procedures, and coordinated daily operations.
- Directed development of new business and implemented effective methods of account management.
- Total P/L responsibility; negotiated leases, materials, and contracts in various work environments to ensure cost-effectiveness.

Sales
- Skilled at recognizing buying patterns, designing market strategies, and developing geographic sales territories; knowledge of highway networks and major cities throughout the Eastern United States.
- Directed all aspects of sales transactions from initial implication of interest, through all negotiations to consummation of sale; effectively assessed and verified financial documentation of potential customers.
- Developed and implemented canvassing techniques to build client base.

Received Numerous Sales Awards
from the National Association of Home Builders
and the National Board of Realtors

Completed Tom Hopkins Sales Seminar

Transportation
- Administered fleet of 26 trucks for both short and long-distance hauling.
- Generated sales and coordinated movement of fleet to transport diverse materials efficiently.
- Full knowledge of DOT regulations, truck maintenance, and industry requirements.

CAREER HISTORY

Broker / Residential Sales, ROBERT SMITH REALTY
Salesperson, ANOTHER REALTY SALES
Associate Broker, NATIONAL HOMES, INC.
Manager of Housekeeping, ST. JOSEPH'S HOSPITAL
Office Manager, FIDELITY ACCEPTANCE CORPORATION OF AMERICA
Transportation Manager, SMITH TRUCKING

EDUCATION

ANYTOWN COLLEGE, Anytown, Pennsylvania   *Bachelor of Science*

Functional. Carol Lawrence, CPRW, Snellville, Georgia.
Notice the design of this resume. It is mostly a Summary of Qualifications with a brief Career History (without dates) and an Education line. Notice also the centered awards information.

DOUGLAS S. MITCHELL
4000 Cypress Tree Court
Brandon, Florida 33000
000-000-0000

OBJECTIVE

Seeking a **Marketing/Sales** position where I can utilize my related experience and management background to contribute to the expansion of business development and productivity, increase revenues, and achieve career enhancement.

SUMMARY OF QUALIFICATIONS

- Proven performance record in progressively responsible positions; skilled in both **service and product-related sales.** Consistently increase productivity and sales revenues. Grew business approximately 125%.

- Design and implement creative marketing and sales techniques responsible for generating new business accounts. Achieved **Top Salesperson** recognition.

- Well-developed analytical and organizational skills; goal-directed and results-oriented; able to assimilate goals in conjunction with profit objectives, cost-effectiveness, and budget awareness. Decreased marketing expenses while simultaneously increasing profits.

- Excellent written and verbal communications . . . strong "people" skills. Successfully manage and motivate employees, stimulate maximum levels of sales achievement, and provide high standards of service to customer/clients resulting in repeat business that expanded profit margins.

- "Team Player" with the self-motivation, initiative, and business savvy necessary to meet the challenges of today's competitive marketplace.

PROFESSIONAL EMPLOYMENT HISTORY

PRUDENTIAL INSURANCE AND FINANCIAL SERVICES, Tampa, FL   1989-Present
District Agent

- Market and sell a full range of financial products including life insurance, property and casualty insurance, mutual funds, and annuities.

- Successfully developed a detailed bulk mail system and referral network resulting in effective expansion of client base by 100%.

- Provide assistance to businesses and individuals seeking to supplement existing benefit plans; coordinate financial planning focussed on comfortable retirement programs.

- Consistently maintain a high-standard performance record via exceptional service, follow-through, and specific attention to detail which resulted in higher sales.

<u>Accomplishments</u>:

- Consistently rank in the top 10% of sales for the Company.

- Created a book of business exceeding premiums of $490,000 annually.

- Recipient of **Quality Service Award** and **National Sales Achievement Award.**

---

104 ***Combination.*** *Diane McGoldrick, Tampa, Florida.*
The Objective statement is supported by statements in the Summary of Qualifications and by comments about the two work experiences. Special accomplishments are listed separately.

DOUGLAS S. MITCHELL   **Page Two**

EXECUTIVE PHONE SYSTEMS, Tampa, FL   **1987-1989**
Sales Representative

- Initiated and designed strategic marketing plan which included telemarketing and referral systems to generate new business.

- Directly oversaw customer's installation requirements.

- Provided customer service follow-up and promoted sales of additional equipment.

<u>Accomplishments:</u>

- **Top Salesperson for 2 quarter periods.**

- Increased productivity 150% in the first year.

EDUCATION

MISSISSIPPI UNIVERSITY, Columbus, MS   **Graduated 1986**
B.S. Degree - Business Administration

   Worked full time to earn 100% of college tuition/expenses and support my family.

PROFESSIONAL TRAINING/SEMINARS

Participated in several Seminar Training Programs relative to the following topics:

- Internal Sales and Servicing
- Financial Planning
- Tom Hopkins Sales Seminars
- Keystone Selling Skills

- Time Management
- Effective Progressive Discipline
- Discovering Your Management Style
- Fast Track Sales Techniques

LICENSURE

Licenses held in the State of Florida

- Health Insurance
- Variable Annuity
- NASD - Series 6

- Life Insurance
- Property Insurance
- Casualty Insurance

MILITARY

AIR NATIONAL GUARD (Honorable Discharge)   **1979-1985**
Photo Intelligence

AFFILIATIONS/MEMBERSHIPS

Tampa Association of Life Underwriters
National Association of Life Underwriters
Masonic Lodge
Shriners

REFERENCES AVAILABLE UPON REQUEST

The inclusion of professional training/seminars, licenses, military experience, and affiliations justifies the use of a second page. Notice the use of two columns for short bulleted items.

Michael A. McNamera, Jr.   RESUME OF QUALIFICATIONS
9701 West Nugget Ave.
Butte, Montana 59000   Telephone: (406) 555-5555

SUMMARY OF QUALIFICATIONS

MANAGEMENT
Served as Adjuster-In-Charge of the Butte, Montana ABC Adjusting Company office for the past 13 years. Supervised clerical support and adjusters. Last year produced $110,000 billable hours.

MARKETING
Contacted area insurance agencies and national companies on a regular basis to promote ABC Adjusting Company. Developed strong, loyal client base through top-quality, timely service. Took over office in 1980 with 5 claims per month; now average 50 claims per month. (An experienced adjuster normally handles 35 claims per month.)

EDUCATOR
Taught photography classes to bachelor degree candidates at Warren Air Force Base through Los Angeles Community College.

Currently developing a photography course for adjusters to be published by ABC Adjusting Company for world-wide distribution.

Instructed photography adult classes for the Arts Chalet. Conducted numerous seminars for area 4-H groups. Judged local and area 4-H fairs. Facilitated parliamentary procedure workshops for local service clubs and 4-H clubs.

COMMUNICATION
Demonstrated oral and written communication skills. Ability to be personable, yet remain succinct. Experience in commercial photography and public relations including public speaking and media appearances.

COORDINATION
Numerous commendations for the efficient and professional coordination of contractors, consultants and employers on complex projects.

ACADEMIC GROWTH
Continually pursued postgraduate and technical courses to maintain personal standards of excellence. Received Chartered Property and Casualty Underwriter designation 10/92.

ORGANIZATION
Adept at handling complicated cases, keeping focused despite interruptions and distractions.

PROMOTION OF EXCELLENCE
Served as a technical adviser to other ABC Adjusting Company adjusters to assure quality service to clients.

REPUTATION
Business community reports satisfaction over honest and fair dealings.

COMMUNITY
Dedicated to the growth and enhancement of Butte through local service clubs, boards and church.

105 **Combination.** *Kathleen Y. McNamee, CPRW, Butte, Montana.*
A Summary of Qualifications taking up a whole page is impressive. Categories in the left column make it easy for the reader to find quickly qualifications of particular interest.

EXPERIENCE

November 1977
to Present

ABC Adjusting Company, Butte, Montana
Adjuster-In-Charge   (October, 1980 - Present)

- <u>Licensed</u> and <u>bonded</u> as an independent adjuster in the State of Montana.
- <u>Experienced</u> in multiline property and casualty insurance adjusting.
- <u>Analyze</u> complex coverage issues.
- <u>Interpret</u> financial statements for business interruption losses.
- <u>Coordinate</u> independent experts, such as arson investigators or accident reconstruction experts.
- <u>Communicate</u> with policyholders or claimants who have suffered a loss and are therefore anxious, angry, and otherwise stressed.
- <u>Negotiate</u> settlements with attorneys, including structured settlements.
- <u>Mediate</u> disputes between policyholders and their insurers.
- <u>Report</u> succinctly, factually and timely to insurance companies.
- <u>Estimate</u> the cost of repairs for damaged vehicles or buildings.
- <u>Receive</u> and <u>disperse</u> settlement funds--millions of dollars per year.
- <u>Advise</u> self-insured clients regarding liability claims handling, risk management and loss control.
- <u>Travel</u> to other locations to handle specific, complex losses, i.e., railroad explosion in Helena (1989).
- <u>Decide</u> complex issues within settlement authority provided by principals, many times under adverse conditions, e.g., scene of a truck wreck involving perishable cargo, liability exposure, hazardous spills, and bodily injuries.

Adjuster, Cheyenne, Wyoming   (January 1979 - October 1980)
- Multiline adjuster, including the handling of catastrophic level storms involving hail and tornadoes. Concluded 2,000 vehicle estimates and 50 houses in a two-month period.

Adjuster, Cody, Wyoming   (November 1977 - January 1979)
- Multiline adjuster. Handled a fatality the first day on the job.

January 1979
to January 1980

LOS ANGELES COMMUNITY COLLEGE, Cheyenne, Wyoming
Instructor (part-time) - Warren AFB
- College instructor of photography for bachelor degree candidates.

June 1976
to October 1977

DON DORRS, MASTER PHOTOGRAPHER, Sheridan, Wyoming
Wedding and Portrait Photographer

1971 to June 1976

UNIVERSITY OF WYOMING PHOTO/NEWS SERVICE, Laramie, Wyoming
Photographer/Writer

Underlining of key words is combined with bullets to call attention to work activities.
Dates show continual employment from 1971, as well as work as a part-time instructor.

EDUCATION

Chartered Property and Casualty Underwriter Designation (CPCU) 1992

Five-year, postgraduate degree program. Only two percent of insurance professionals complete all 10 parts of this coursework. Designed to provide a thorough understanding of risk management and insurance. Segments include:

- Principles of Risk Management
- Personal Risk Management and Insurance
- Commercial Property Risk Management and Insurance
- Commercial Liability Risk Management and Insurance
- Legal Environment of Risk Management and Insurance
- Business Management
- Accounting and Finance
- Macro and Micro Economics
- Insurance Company Operations
- Ethics

Montana College of Mineral Science & Technology, Butte, Montana
Real Estate Appraisal

University of Wyoming, Laramie, Wyoming
Bachelor of Science Degree in Public Relations-Journalism
- Emphasis in Advertising, Photography, Layout and Design

Corporate Training

- I-CAR Collision Repair 1991
- Error and Omission Loss Prevention 1988
- Advanced Property Adjusting 1986
- Time Element Coverages 1986
- Accounting Fundamentals 1986

Volunteer Activities

- Butte Junior Achievement, Board Member 1991 - 1994
- Butte Junior Achievement, Treasurer 1991
- Butte Junior Achievement, Company Advisor 1984
- Butte Executive Club (275 members), President 1990
- Butte Exchange Club (250 members), Member 1980 - 1992
- Butte Exchange Club, Program Chairman 1987
- United American Presbyterian Church (300 members), Elder 1983 - 1986, 1993 - 1996
- United American Presbyterian Church, Treasurer 1981 - 1986
- Arts Chalet, Member 1988 - Present
- Arts Chalet, Photography Instructor (200 students) 1984 - 1993
- Montana Adjusters Association, Convention Chairman 1991

The wealth of information in the Education, Corporate Training, and Volunteer Activities sections justifies the use of a third page. Bullets unify the last two pages visually.

Maintenance/Manufacturing Resumes at a Glance

ROBERT McGLAUGHEN
201 Westwood Avenue . Huntingdon, Pennsylvania 17000
(814) 000-0000

OBJECTIVE	Heavy Equipment Operator for Brown Lime and Stone Company.
CERTIFICATION	Certified Heavy Equipment Operator/ Driver Category C Class 4 Certified Welder. CDL License (Pending).
SPECIALIZED TRAINING	Equipment Operator: Cranes, RT 58, RT 400, AT 400, RT 500, RT 600, RT 745, RT 990, Scissor Lift, Manlift, Fork Lift, Overhead Industrial Crane (10 Ton and 20). Completed two "Company sponsored" courses on Hazardous Waste Handling and Removal.
WORK EXPERIENCE	WILTON COMPANY - Huntingdon, PA **Maintenance**. February 1993 to Present Maintain/repair bands of conveyor belt used to transport leather hides for painting. ACE SERVICES - Willow Park, PA **Mechanic Assembler**. March 1989 to February 1993 Assembled cranes from frame to completion. Welded, wired, and lubricated equipment. Started, performed troubleshooting procedure. **Shipping/Receiving** Handled incoming parts for distribution throughout the plant. Computerized inventory utilizing IBM computer. KENTUCKY FREIGHT - Pittsburgh, PA **Dock Worker**. September 1992 to January 1993 (part-time) Loaded and unloaded 8000 lbs. freight per hour. SPRINGFIELD FARM - Huntingdon, PA **Dairy Herd Manager**. June 1980 to March 1989 Milking, feeding, general care of herd. Maintained/repaired equipment and buildings. Operated farm machinery: Farm Tractor, Skid Loader, Dump Truck, Combine, Corn Planter, Grain Drill, Chisel Plow, Post Driver, Hay Baler.
EDUCATION	**Diploma** in Heavy Equipment Operation June 1980 Huntingdon Area Vocational Technical School - Huntingdon, PA Maintenance, repair and operation of construction equipment. Recipient of "Outstanding Senior" Award.
REFERENCES	Available upon request.

Combination. Margaret M. Hilling, Huntingdon, Pennsylvania.
Skills and abilities are evident in certifications and in the kinds of equipment the person can operate (see the Specialized Training section). Boldfacing helps the work positions stand out.

ROB MATTISON

3240 N. 42nd Drive
Phoenix, AZ   85019   **(602) 272-2159**

RESUME

Objective: Position in maintenance and repair.

HIGHLIGHTS OF QUALIFICATIONS

- Enthusiastic, dependable, self-motivated; assumes responsibility necessary to get the job done.
- Work cooperatively with a wide range of personalities.
- Equally effective working alone or as a member of a team.
- Skilled in handling the public with professionalism and diplomacy.
- Strong skills in organizing work flow, ideas, materials, people.
- Hired, trained and supervised work crews.
- Takes pride in achieving the best possible results.

WORK HISTORY

1992-Present **Engineer,** SCOTTSDALE PLAZA RESORT, Scottsdale, AZ

9/91-11/91 **Engineer,** OMNI HOTEL (formerly PHOENIX SHERATON), Phoenix, Arizona

8/90-6/91 **Engineer,** CROWN STERLING SUITES HOTEL (formerly EMBASSY SUITES BILTMORE), Phoenix, Arizona

8/88-8/90 **Chief Engineer,** WOOLLEY'S PETITE SUITES HOTEL, Tempe, Arizona

5/87-8/88 **Owner,** MAINTENANCE AND REPAIR, Phoenix, Arizona

6/85-5/87 **Maintenance Worker,** J.P.H. ENTERPRISES, Indio, California

MAINTENANCE SKILLS

Appliances, Carpentry, Electrical, Fencing, Flooring, Locks, Painting, Plumbing, Pools & Spas, Roofing Irrigation and Sprinklers
Air Conditioning, Refrigeration and Heating

EDUCATION

Air Conditioning & Refrigeration
College of the Desert, Palm Desert, California

Electronics
DeVry Institute of Technology, Phoenix, Arizona

MATTISON

PROFESSIONAL EXPERIENCE

Building Repair
- During a monsoon storm in Phoenix, climbed hotel roof to check drains; upon discovering six inches of water and drains patched over with roofing cement, immediately cut through patches and cleared the drains.
- Within three hours, completely rebuilt apartment complex stairs that collapsed after two heavy tenants moved in; added joist hangers and extra supports underneath to meet legal specs and ensure future stability.
- When a four-inch copper pipe burst and flooded a ground-floor room, removed all furniture, pulled up carpet and dug four feet deep to repair the pipe; after drying, filled in hole, poured concrete, installed carpet and put back furniture.
- Replaced broken windows, made screens, hung doors and jambs, hung and patched drywall, textured and painted walls, installed electrical switches and outlets, moved phone jacks, rewired disconnect and breaker panels, installed and repaired lighting.

Mechanical Repair
- During breakfast rush hour, quickly removed stuck soda dispenser solenoid, which caused Dr. Pepper to flood the entire waitress station; temporarily adjusted unit until Coca-Cola repairman arrived.
- Repaired chillers, boilers, water softeners, ice machines, washers, dryers, motors, pumps and other equipment for various establishments; also troubleshoot elevators and escalators.
- Fixed hotel restaurant equipment, including grills, ovens, refrigerators, dishwashers, etc.

Customer Service
- Regularly earned commendations for diplomacy and courtesy toward hotel guests and apartment tenants during work-related encounters.
- Developed cooperative working relationships with management, staff and contracted help; was left in charge of operations of Woolley's Petite Suites for a week when managers and staff went to Florida to participate in a hostile takeover of three hotels.
- Resolved wide range of customer problems, including patiently and diligently working to pry a broken key from a hotel room lock, earning a letter of commendation from the guest who "appreciated his control in a trying situation."

107 *Combination. Sallie Young, San Jose, California.*
An imaginative design to help a maintenance person stand out. Notice the use of brief stories in the Professional Experience section to show how the person solved problems.

FRED JOBSEARCHER

8500 West Cactus Road # 60
Phoenix, Arizona 85000
(602) 000-0000

OBJECTIVE: Seeking a position in Industrial Maintenance that offers challenge and growth potential with an organization where problems and opportunities are well matched to my abilities, and skills to deliver results.

SUMMARY: Over 9 years experience in the industrial maintenance field including 4 years as a Journeyman Electrician. Additional skills include carpentry, plumbing, heating, air conditioning, roofing, laying floors, and masonry experience.

HIGHLIGHTS OF QUALIFICATIONS

- Detail and profit-oriented, with proven ability to identify, repair, analyze and solve problems.
- Performs effectively despite sudden deadlines and changing priorities.
- Highly reliable self-starter; can be counted on to complete assignments with little or no supervision.
- Strong planning, organizational and estimating skills; keeps a sharp eye on the bottom line.
- Ability to determine the cause and justify the resulting cost overruns of completed projects.
- Possess good communication and interpersonal skills.
- Ability to supervise, motivate, train and increase productivity.

SUMMARY OF EXPERIENCE

- Solid experience maintaining (repair or replace) all electrical apparatus to support a 440,000 square foot office and warehouse facility with a $6,000,000 automated/computer-controlled conveyor system. Additional electrical experience includes 115V, 227V, and 480V lighting systems, 480V 3 Phase Motors, Motor Controllers (manual & computer operated), power control centers, installing new runs for lighting systems and outlets, installing motor operated equipment, and installing power systems for computer equipment.
- Troubleshoot/repair to card/component level.
- Replace integrated circuits utilizing special soldering techniques.
- Utilize troubleshooting publications to solve problems; interpret blueprints, manuals, and specification requirements; read schematic wiring diagrams; calibrate equipment.
- Schedule work to be performed and determine completion time; inspect work after completion.
- Perform preventive maintenance service (PMS) when scheduled or needed.
- Demonstrated abilities in industrial construction, repairs, and office remodeling.
- Proficient in the hanging and finishing of drywalls, and plastering.
- Capabilities in masonry including setting forms, tying steel, cement finishing and setting blocks.
- Perform carpentry, framing, and work with siding.
- Proficiency in laying floors including ceramic and marble.
- Oversee maintenance and repair of equipment including heavy machinery, sound and video systems.
- Organize ordering and delivery of materials.
- Supervise installation of materials.
- Ensure project is *always* within budget and on schedule.
- Schedule work of subcontractors and/or company workers.
- Ability to hire, and train employees; monitor all operations to ensure safe and effective performance of personnel.
- Ensure work meets specified standards and safety codes (OSHA, UBC, NEC, UPC).
- Obtain all necessary permits and licenses.
- Act as liaison between labor and management.

EMPLOYMENT HISTORY

Eastman, Inc. - Signal Hill, CA	8/83 to 5/93
Positions: Facilities Maintenance Supervisor	1991 to 5/93
Journeyman Senior	1989 to 1991
Maintenance Mechanic	1984 to 1989
Warehouse - Stocker, Order Filler, part-time Conveyor Maintenance	1983 to 1984

REFERENCES PROVIDED UPON REQUEST

Combination. Bernard Stopfer, Phoenix, Arizona.
The first Summary is an overview of fields and skills, and the Summary of Experience indicates some specific activities. The first four sections make up almost all of the resume.

108

KENNETH A. AVEREZ, JR.
4001 Walnut Drive
Martinsburg, WV 25000
(304) 000-0000

QUALIFICATIONS

EXPERTISE:

- Comprehensive experience in the management, organizational, electrical and mechanical production and maintenance areas within the manufacturing sector of private industry.
- Utilization of a strong, motivational personality; incorporating leadership training and individual development.
- Application of effective time and personnel management; problem solving.
- The ability to adapt to changing situations and the expertise to make a decision and follow through to an effective solution.
- • **Hold Commercial Pilot's License**

CAPABILITIES:

- Full range of electrical and mechanical productive maintenance administration, negotiations and product knowledge and applicability.
- Exemplary communications skills - both written and verbal incorporating presentations with upper management.
- Effective supervision and training on various skill levels.
- Proficient evaluation, analytical and deductive abilities; maintain high level of production and quality of product.

EDUCATION

Bachelor of Science Degree - 1970
United States Air Force Academy
Colorado Springs, CO

Total Productive Maintenance - 1992
Productivity, Inc.
Pittsburgh, PA

Further Education, Seminars and Workshops Listing Available Upon Request.

EXPERIENCE

CERTAINTEED CORPORATION   1981 to 1993

Williamsport, MD
Manufacturer of building products; extruded vinyl siding and window profiles.

MAINTENANCE COORDINATOR/SENIOR PROJECT ENGINEER (1992 - 1993)
- **Established a five-year Total Productive Maintenance Program for cost-effectiveness and productivity increase.**
- **Researched**, recommended and employed professional consultants to familiarize managers/supervisors with the program; presented program to employees to involve them, to ensure "team" effort and success of program.
- **Managed/supervised** electrical and mechanical projects:
  - Installation of five new extrusion lines;
  - Installation of new extruder on existing line.
  - Installation of new plant transformer.
- **Spearheaded** the establishment and initiation of the drafting department; i.e., computerization, installation of ink-jet printing system.

Wichita Falls, TX
Manufacturer of fiber glass reinforcements.

PRODUCT ENGINEER-CHOPPED PRODUCTS (1991 - 1992)
- **Established, implemented and maintained Quality Assurance Statistical Process Control;** reduced quality control holds to two per month.
- **Assisted** Department Manager in the development of the department budget incorporating two product lines.
- **Maintained** a preventive maintenance program.
- **Initiated** cost-savings projects, efficiency projects, and safety program.
- **Designed** safer layout and installed lifting devices on production line reducing injuries.
- **Designed and installed** new classifying deck to increase productivity and quality.
- **Maintained spending 20% below the budget for product line.**
- **Evaluated** budget; investigated and discovered process loss of approximately $30,000, corrected calculation inaccuracies saving approximately $100,000 per year.

109 *Combination. Barbara A. Adversalo, CPRW, Greencastle, Pennsylvania.*
Small type and minimal line spacing provides room for considerable information. The unusual double bullet, together with initial uppercase letters, calls attention to the pilot's license.

KENNETH A. AVEREZ, JR.
Page Two

CERTAINTEED CORPORATION
Wichita Falls, TX (Continued)

FABRICATION ENGINEER/PRODUCT LINE SUPERINTENDENT (1985 - 1991)
- **Developed** preventive maintenance program for various processes.
- **Established** and maintained process specification for chop strand mat.
- **Prepared** appropriation requests; assisted the Manager in developing and maintaining the department budget.
- **Assisted** in designing and procuring a conveyor system that reduced waste in chopped products.
- **Reduced** the cost of expendable parts for chop strand choppers by over $100,000 the first year.
- **Designed** product storage racks to reduce injuries in chop products and new covers to reduce picker piles in the chop strand mat.
- **Introduced** a statistical process control program in chop strand.

FABRICATION DEPARTMENT AREA SUPERVISOR (1981 - 1985)
- **Supervised** 14 Shift Supervisors; interviewed prospective hires; oversaw departmental personnel matters; reduced personnel turnover; improved productivity with a more stable workforce.
- **Assisted** the Fabrication Engineer; ensured that all production schedules were met.
- **Reduced** cost of manufacturing supplies by finding new and different sources of suppliers.
- **Increased/improved** training for "team" effort in improving quality and efficiency.
- **Designed** product storage rack for roving products.
- **Installed** packing tables to reduce back injuries.

CORNING GLASS CORPORATION   1978 to 1981
Martinsburg, WV
Pyroceramic Manufacturing Plant.

PRODUCTION SHIFT SUPERVISOR - FINISHING DEPARTMENT
- **Supervised** approximately 40 hourly employees.
- **Developed** Staffing Manual for Secondary Finishing and Decal Department and maintenance management system for the department.
- **Ensured** all production schedules were met; produced necessary reports and production logs.
- **Guaranteed** necessary maintenance was performed on equipment in order to maintain on-going production.
- **Set and broke standard production records increasing production 100% within a period of one year.**

MILITARY

Pilot and Instructor Pilot
United States Air Force - 1970 to 1977
Kincheloe Air Force Base, MI

AFFILIATIONS

Total Productive Maintenance
Productivity, Inc.

REFERENCES

Available upon Request

In the Experience section, which shows career movement through four successive positions at the current company, the parallel verbs are in boldfacing to make reading easier.

JOHN SMITH
ANYWHERE STREET – ATHENS, TN 37000   (615) 000-0000 OR 000-0000

JOB OBJECTIVE
FULL-TIME MACHINE OPERATOR – ASSEMBLY DUTIES FOR MAJOR MANUFACTURER.

SKILLS AND EXPERIENCE

MACHINE OPERATIONS
* POWDER PORCELAIN AND WET ENAMEL PROCESSES:
  - POSITION 12 AUTOMATIC SPRAY GUNS FOR ELECTROSTATIC SPRAY BOOTHS
    APPLYING ENAMEL TO PARTS USED IN MASS PRODUCTION OF STOVES.
  - SET AIR PRESSURE, REGULATE AMOUNT OF AIR MIXED WITH POWDER, ADJUST
    VOLTAGE FOR EACH GUN.
  - OPERATE AND MAINTAIN WASHERS IN PREPARING STEEL PARTS FOR PORCELAIN
    PROCESS.
  - WORK WITH CAUSTIC CHEMICALS SUCH AS ALKALINE SOAP USED IN WASHERS,
    FLUSH WASHER HEAT EXCHANGER WITH NITRIC ACID, MAKE TITRATE
    MEASUREMENTS CONTROLLING SOAP SOLUTION IN WATER.
  - SET TEMPERATURE AND MAINTAIN 24-HOUR HIGH INTENSITY (1520) FURNACE.
  - USED SPRAY GUN ON LIQUID AND POWDER LINES TO APPLY COATING TO STOVE
    TOPS AND INTERIORS.
* OPERATE LIQUID FOAM INJECTION MACHINE USED IN THE MANUFACTURE OF AUTOMOBILE
  DOOR PANELS.
* WORK WITH DEBURRING MACHINE, SANDBLASTER AND DEGREASER IN CLEANING AND
  PREPARING METAL PARTS FOR PRODUCTION.
* DRIVE FORK LIFT AND ELECTICAL OR GASOLINE ENGINE UPRIGHT LIFT. OPERATE
  OVERHEAD CRANE. USE PRECISION EQUIPMENT IN Q.C. FUNCTIONS.

TROUBLESHOOTING/JUDGMENT SKILLS
* CONTROL POWDER PORCELAIN LINE SPEED FOR DIFFERENT PARTS.
* FOLLOW VENDOR MANUAL INSTRUCTIONS FOR CORRECT MACHINE OPERATIONS.
* AUTHORITY FOR REJECTION OR REWORK OF PARTS LEAVING FURNACE.
* SOLVED STUCK SOLENOID VALVE PUTTING ON NEW DIAPHRAGM – KEPT LINE MOVING.
* READ SCHEMATICS TRACING AUTOMATED EQUIPMENT AIR LINE PROBLEMS.
* ASSIST IN DIRECTING OTHERS IN ABSENCE OF SUPERVISOR.

EDUCATION   - CLEVELAND STATE COMMUNITY COLLEGE, CLEVELAND, TN
                   STUDIED COMPUTER BASICS 1983/84
                 - GRADUATE POLK COUNTY HIGH SCHOOL, BENTON, TN - 1983
                   ESPECIALLY ENJOYED MATH AND SCIENCE COURSES

WORK HISTORY
9/89 - PRESENT   ABC COMPANY, ATHENS, TN
                  MACHINE OPERATOR
10/86 - 9/89   XYC CORPORATION, ATHENS DIVISION, ATHENS, TN
                  POWDER PORCELAIN OPERATOR PROMOTED FROM SPRAY PAINTER
8/85 - 12/85   EMPLOYERS OVERLOAD ASSIGNED TO NATIONAL SEATING, VONORE, TN
                  SANDBLASTER

PERSONAL   AGE: 25 - EXCELLENT HEALTH - FAVORABLE WORK RECORD - RECEIVED
            COMPLIMENTS ON GOOD WORK HABITS - WORK HARD EACH DAY EVERY DAY

---

110 Combination. Adelia Wyner, Athens, Tennessee.
Most companies require resumes from persons in manufacturing and production, but many
resume books ignore these areas. Here is such a resume indicating operations and skills.

MIGUEL RAMIREZ

70 Browertown Road
Little Falls, NJ 07000
(201) 000-0000

Relocating to Florida

3431 Lakeshore Drive
Boca Raton, FL 33000
(407) 555-1212

OBJECTIVE: **Master Machinist** with supervisory responsibilities to act as liaison between engineering and production.

CAREER SUMMARY:
- Over 20 years experience in hands-on manufacturing environments, specializing in precision instruments and machined parts.
- Proficient in any type of computer numerically controlled (CNC) programming, with and without CAD/CAM software.
- Thorough knowledge of all operating procedures and shop equipment to accomplish tooling quickly and efficiently.
- Understanding of materials, metallurgic components and quality control factors regulating the machining, finishing and inspection of a wide variety of work pieces.
- Strongly cost conscious, with ability to detect design flaws and recommend changes to engineers to facilitate production, prevent errors, save time and eliminate scrap.
- Work well both independently or as part of a team.
- Fluent in Spanish.

WORK EXPERIENCE:

1985 - Present

Accu-Med Machine Company, West New York, NJ
PRODUCTION SUPERVISOR for manufacturer of medical instruments and surgical implants.
- Supervise 10 direct reports in shop that has grown from 5 to 45 employees in 8 years.
- Perform all programming on CNC milling machine, design tooling, establish procedures and inspect parts from start to finish.
- Interact with engineers and designers, solving problems for most cost-efficient production.

1980 - 1985

Universal Machine Company, Garfield, NJ
PART OWNER/MANAGER of job shop building predesigned precision equipment.
- Built sales volume to $400,000 over five-year period before selling business to Universal Machine and continuing employment with them.
- Employed 5 operators and trained them in the use of the CNC mill, manual lathe, grinders, drill presses and buffers.
- Established steady clientele which included manufacturers of industrial sewing machines, lithium batteries, food processing and medical services equipment.
- Worked closely with engineers and production people at client companies to ensure complete understanding of processes and 100% satisfaction.
- Designed an attachment to the Bridgeport milling machine that increased the flexibility of stops for faster and more efficient operation. Awarded U.S. Patent #4436462.

1978 - 1980

First Choice Label Company, Wallington, NJ
PRODUCTION LEAD MAN for company that designed and built a line of 20 machines for producing, cutting and packing clothing labels.
- Programmed CNC machine and furthered electro-mechanical knowledge for advanced applications.
- Had supervision over 3 workers.

1972 - 1978

MACHINIST/JOB SHOPPER
- Learned and practiced trade in 3 different machine shops, manual and automated.

EDUCATION:
- Production Engineering degree from SENA (engineering college) Colombia, South America
- Certificates of completion of 8-week courses at Kean College, Union, NJ
  Basic AutoCAD (5/93), and Advanced AutoCAD (7/93)

Combination. *Melanie Noonan, CPS, Little Falls, New Jersey.*
Notice the symmetrical addresses and the centered note "Relocating to Florida" to indicate
movement from one address to the other. Filled square bullets unify the resume visually.

111

JANE DOE
Anywhere - Any Town, TN 37000
(809) 000-0000 (H) or Lv. Msg. at 000-0000

QUALIFICATION SUMMARY

Extensive experience and practical knowledge of high-volume manufacturing operations with strong Quality Control Inspection (SPC) abilities. IBM P.C. computer training - Lotus 1-2-3 in controlling QC statistical information. Recognized for people skills in positively communicating QC standards to line personnel and supervisory staff.

EXPERIENCE

5/83 - 9/90 The Best Company - Chattanooga, TN
QC Inspector for winding and assembly of hermetic motors used in small and large appliance compressors. On-line checks of people, machines, and product made in Winding, Rotor, and Lamination Departments. Final approval for finished goods before shipment. Perform with minimal supervision - given authority to make independent decisions on 2nd and/or 3rd shifts. Very observant to all conditions and can request supervisors to shut down line preventing costly volume rejects. Understand automated assembly line equipment - ensure robots are not malfunctioning. Research product blueprints, inspect for specification measurements and machine setup accuracy. Collect information ... daily updating of written reports. Use diplomacy in assisting individuals on the line ... communicating with line supervisors, my superiors, QC managers, engineers and mechanics. Troubleshoot special problems such as high lamination concentricity and out-of-spec component parts.

Began as Assembler in Winding Department, upgraded to Rotor Department, then upgraded to Spare Parts Checker, promoted to Rotor Borematic Machine Operator, and then to QC Inspector.

4/80 - 3/83 Cracker Barrel - Chattanooga, TN - Waitress and Cashier

EDUCATION   Area Community College - Anytown, TN - 1988
Computer Science

Completed high school in three years, graduating from Town High School in 1981. Graduated #26 in class of 127 - Achieved Membership in National Honor Society. - Class Officer

PERSONAL   Excellent health - Non-smoker - Drug free -
Proven perfect attendance record - Available any shift - PTA fund raiser and enjoy outdoor activities with my family - Can work easily under pressure and handle many tasks at the same time with competence.

112

Combination. Adelia Wyner, Athens, Tennessee.
Another resume for a person in manufacturing. Notice at the end of the Experience section the statement that traces the person's progression from Assembler to QC Inspector.

JESSIE W. FOLGER

305 Calhoon Drive
Greencastle, Indiana 46000
(317) 000-0000

EXPERTISE: PURCHASING / MATERIALS MANAGER

EXPERIENCE:

<u>Cast Metal Products, Inc.</u>, Greencastle, Indiana   3/88-Present

PURCHASING AGENT: Organize, manage, and supervise purchasing department for $30,000,000 manufacturer of die cast aluminum transmission housings.

ACCOMPLISHMENTS/PRIMARY FUNCTIONS:
- Consistently obtain 3%-5% annual cost reduction from vendors.
- Certified Instructor, "Working" Class; increase productivity/worker efficiency daily.
- Member, National Association of Purchasing Managers.
- Negotiate contracts for major commodities; emphasis in $23,000,000 of aluminum annually.
- Cost analysis for numerous items.
- Quality Circle Team Leader, commitment of team leadership/management philosophy.
- Extensive customer relations experience.
- In-depth knowledge of daily workings in manufacturing operation.

<u>Myers Electric Equipment Company</u>, Martinsville, Indiana   6/87-3/88

OUTSIDE ELECTRICAL SALES ENGINEER: Extensive customer interaction for major electrical distributor with four divisions.

<u>ARCO Electric Products Corporation</u>, Martinsville, Indiana   1/76-5/87

VICE PRESIDENT, CUSTOMER RELATIONS: Designed product compatibility systems for consumer needs. In-house and on-site troubleshooting application and engineering assistance.
VICE PRESIDENT, MARKETING: Administered guidance to 23 field agents. Developed new product literature.
NATIONAL SALES MANAGER: Ensured continuity of policies and practices for nationwide distribution market. Developed and implemented training program for representatives.
PURCHASING AGENT/BUYER: Improved inventory control system. Analyzed bids from different suppliers. Assessed and selected raw materials for use in all aspects of production.

EDUCATION:

Bachelor of Science, Education, Indiana University, Bloomington, Indiana

Continuing Education:
- Advanced Purchasing Strategies, Cast Metal Products, Inc.
- Successfully completed three in-house training programs, Cast Metal Products, Inc.
- Dale Carnegie, Simon D. Yancy Associates, Indianapolis, Indiana
- Accounting I, Indiana Vocational Technical College, Indianapolis, Indiana

CIVIC ACTIVITIES:

- Immediate Past President, Kiwanis Marks Club of Greencastle
- Member, Board of Directors, Brothers, Inc. of Morgan County
- Sub-committee Chairman, Partners-in-Education, Monroe County Chamber of Commerce
- Member, Monroe County Chamber of Commerce

Chronological. Carole Pefley, CPRW, Indianapolis, Indiana.
Uppercase letters make positions and accomplishments appear more important than the companies and localities (even with underlining) where the person worked.

ROBERT L. CARROLL
2789 Orange Grove Avenue
Winter Haven, Florida 32000
(407) 000-0000

OBJECTIVE

Seeking expanded opportunities within selected organizations where I can utilize my expertise to implement profit-oriented results.

PROFESSIONAL PROFILE

Extensive experience at the Senior Executive level in marketing multifaceted services for a NASDAQ publicly-held company consisting of 53 drug store units, 6 home/health care convalescent centers, a drug store distribution center, 125 one-hour dry cleaning stores, a dry cleaning distribution center, and a manufacturing subsidiary of windows for drive-in service. Qualifications include a background in progressively responsible positions initiating from entry-level management to CEO and President/Chairman of the Board. Established a successful history in the development and expansion of a diverse market reach resulting in a significant increase of annual gross revenues from $36 million to $80 million. Company was acquired by a national corporation in 1988.

EMPLOYMENT HISTORY

PHARMACEUTICAL/MANUFACTURING CO., Tampa, FL   1993
Director of Trade Relations / Assistant to the C.E.O.

> Public Relations and Corporate Marketing involving assimilation of conceptual and long-range planning strategies for a small, Bay-area, pharmaceutical/manufacturing company.

MANAGEMENT CONSULTANT, Knoxville, TN   1988 - 1993
Multiple Industries

> Provided consulting services to Retailers, Manufacturers and Distributors in the Southeast and Mid-West Territory of the U.S.

CARROLL ENTERPRISES, Lexington, KY   1962 - 1988
Chairman of the Board/President/CEO   1979-1988
President   1974-1979
Vice President - Advertising/Merchandising/Merchandise Distribution   1972-1974
Vice President - Drug Operations   1968-1972
Director of Merchandise / District Store Supervisor   1967-1968
Elected to Board of Directors   1967
Warehouse Manager / Seasonal & Promotional Buyer   1963-1967
Merchandise Manager   1962-1963

EDUCATION

UNIVERSITY OF CINCINNATI SCHOOL OF PHARMACY

UNIVERSITY OF KENTUCKY

PAST PROFESSIONAL AFFILIATIONS

Vice Chairman of the Board, Executive Committee Member, Board Member, Treasurer, Chairman of Finance Committee, and of Chairman of Government Affairs Committee for the **National Association of Chain Drug Stores (NACDS)**, Washington, D.C.

Chairman of **Kentucky Retail Federation**.

References and Detailed Resume Available upon Request.

Combination. *Diane McGoldrick, Tampa, Florida.*
Small type makes room for all the information. For the third company listed in the Employment History, note the remarkable progression from entry-level manager to CEO.

Management Resumes at a Glance

Richard DeSoto

6032 Whippet Pass
Carmel, IN 46000
(317) 000–0000

Objective	Seeks managing position in production in silkscreen printing.
Profile	• *Shop manager* • *Chromist* • *Production manager* • *Printer* • *Screen department manager*

Experience
11/85–Present   **Production Manager.** Myriad Graphics, Indianapolis, IN
- Four-color process printing
- Fine art printing
- Specialized in printing multicolor blends
- Specialized in printing in ultraviolet inks
- Scheduling production time
- Devise production system
- Organize department functions
- Shipping & receiving
- Research and development of new accounts
- Inventory and ordering of materials
- Customer Service
- Quoting
- Hiring, training, scheduling, supervising employees

Accomplishments:
Developed Screen Department.
Converted department from film to direct emulsions.
Saved company $7,000 per year.
Increased production from 47% on time to 89% on time in 6 months.
Converted to dual-purpose emulsion for solvent based or water-based inks.
Instituted department meetings.
Fabricated equipment instead of purchasing expensive equipment.
Constructed a darkroom facility for horizontal screen storage.
Reduced reprints due to mistakes from 25% of jobs to 5%.
Devised a system for stretching large-format screens.

1979–1982   Delivery. Village Furniture, Springfield, OH
1978–1979   Test Driver. Transportation Research Center, Bellefontaine, OH

Education	Bellefontaine High School, Bellefontaine, OH Graduated 1976 Printing and Graphic Arts
Service	Assistant Coach for Little League Baseball
Interests	Music, landscaping, archery, reading

Combination. Richard L. Schillen, Indianapolis, Indiana.
A clean-looking resume in which certain skills are implied by the Profile positions listed. The
use of italic for these positions and the Accomplishments relate the two sections visually.

115

SANDRA MARIE TUCKER
85 North Main Street
Netcong, New Jersey 07000
(201) 000–0000

PROFILE

A self–motivated professional with a strong background in Inventory Control. Demonstrated skill in managing a busy office. Expert troubleshooter and problem solver with outstanding computer skills. Proven written and oral communication ability. Works well with others; resourceful, well organized, and able to assume responsibility.

EXPERIENCE

DEBOISE SOFTWARE CORPORATION   *1985 – Present*
Randolph, New Jersey

- *Oversee an $8 million inventory: coordinate the flow of purchase orders, discrepancies and delays; process invoices; review acknowledgments and issue change notices concerning price, delivery, terms and conditions.*

- *Maintain file orders and updates on over 15,000 active stock items.*

- *Handle emergency calls from USA Regional Offices. Prioritize calls and refer them to the appropriate departments for resolution.*

- *Provide SAP (Systems Application & Products in Data Processing) training to company personnel. Answer phone inquiries regarding system application.*

AWARDS

1993   Suggestion Award   (changed shiplist filing system which resulted in easier access to corresponding data through SAP)

1992   Suggestion Award   (conducted cost study of overnight air carriers)

1992   Quality Award   (SAP Data Base Team)

EDUCATION

County College of Morris   Extended Education Courses: Business Management

REFERENCES

Excellent Personal and Professional References on Request

---

116   **Combination.** *Shari Favela, Stanhope, New Jersey.*
A resume that is all italic. Underlining is used with italic headings to help them stand out. No date is given in the Education section. Dates for recent awards make a good impression.

SUMMARY OF EXPERIENCE

Produced Market Development Report and Marketing Plan for environmental services group. Designed agricultural chemical programs to assist clients with environmental compliance. Managed agricultural chemical remedial investigations and correction action design projects. Managed hazardous waste and petroleum release, transportation and disposal program for an environmental services company. Four years environmental regulations experience with extremely hazardous chemical category. Nine years marketing experience with major agricultural chemical accounts. Extensive experience in establishment and maintenance of customer accounts and creation of successful Agricultural Chemical Facility Compliance Plans.

PROFESSIONAL EXPERIENCE

ENVIRONMENTAL COMPANY

xxxx - xxxx   **Independent Contractor - Market Development**
- Developed Agricultural Chemical Market Development Report
- Designed Agricultural Chemical Marketing Action Plan
- Focused program on site investigation and remediation

ENVIRONMENT CONSULTANTS

xxxx - xxxx   **Agricultural Chemical Specialist**
- Managed agricultural chemical remedial investigations and corrective action design projects
- Worked with Agricultural Chemical Response and Reimbursement Account (ACRRA)
- Prepared an agricultural chemical section of the corporate marketing plan

ENVIRONMENTAL SERVICES

xxxx - xxxx   **Transportation and Disposal Coordinator**
- Managed 85 plus Hazardous Waste Transportation and Disposal Projects
- Worked on Hazardous Waste and Petroleum LUST sites
- Negotiated contracts with major hazardous waste disposal firms and national transporters
- Interfaced with federal and state environmental regulatory agencies
- Supervised field technician transportation and disposal-related activity

LARGE COMPANY

xxxx - xxxx   **Agrichemical Sales Representative**
- Sold agricultural chemicals and programs to key customers
- Exceeded $1 million territory sales budget
- Maintained control over project budgets
- Completed IBM, Lotus 1-2-3 training

AGRICULTURAL PRODUCTS COMPANY

xxxx - xxxx   **Technical Sales Representative**
- Provided market analysis and recommendations
- Implemented Time and Territory Management Plan
- Negotiated product performance inquiries

EDUCATION

UNIVERSITY OF STATE
College of Agriculture
Bachelor of Science-Agronomy, *xxxx*

GOVERNMENT INSTITUTE, INC.
Environmental Law Course: CERCLA, EPCRA, TSCA, OSHA, SDWA, NEPA, FIFRA, RCRA, UST.

LADY ENGINEER • 1234 Any Street • Anytown, ST 12345 • (000) 555-1234

Combination. Linda Morton, CPRW, Lawrence, Kansas.
A resume for a manager not by title but by responsibility and activity. The resume is different because of the dual vertical lines and personal information along the right margin.

117

JOHN APPLETON

3240 SW 5th Place
Panama City, Florida 32000
(904) 000-0000

BACKGROUND

Over 12 years of broad-based business management experience with a proven record of accomplishment in operations, human resources, merchandise management, construction management, and franchise services.

BUSINESS
MANAGEMENT
EXPERIENCE

THE GAP, INC   November 1981 to present

Initially hired as a **Manager Trainee** at the national headquarters in Tampa, Florida. Promoted to **Manager** of 4,000 square foot store in Raleigh, North Carolina in 1982 where I received Manager-of-the-Year Award. Promoted to **District Manager** in 1983. Promoted to a corporate position at the national headquarters in Tampa, Florida in 1984 with responsibility for directing the following administrative functions:

- **Operations** -- Direct all operational activities for 35 corporate stores with a total annual sales volume of $17 million. Supervise 4 District Managers, 35 Store Managers, 25 Manager Trainees, and 250 Sales Associates. Monitor company-wide expenses and inventory. Implement and enforce operational procedures (e.g., security, point-of-sale, check guarantee, credit cards, employee policies) at the store level. Administer a $2.1 million payroll. Direct all activities associated with new store openings. Accomplishments include development of a company operational manual and a mystery shopper program.

- **Human Resources** -- Recruit, interview, hire, and train company personnel. Coordinate relocation arrangements for manager trainees. Developed a comprehensive employee policy manual. Accomplishments include the creation of an in-store training program and the development and implementation a "recruiting center" program at state universities to identify and recruit promising new graduates for the company's management training program.

118

Combination. Steven M. Burt, CPRW, Gainesville, Florida.
A well-organized resume with ABCDE A+B+C+D+E structure. Five areas of accomplishment are indicated in the Background section. Each is described in turn in the Experience section.

**BUSINESS
MANAGEMENT
EXPERIENCE**
(continued)

■ **Merchandise Management** -- Responsible for coordinating a corporate-wide inventory of $3.9 million. Monitor specific shoe categories to determine best sell-thru vs. worst sell-thru. Coordinate shoe stock rotation among the corporate stores. Determine product mix and inventory stock levels. Oversee and develop the apparel buying programs on a seasonal basis. Accomplishments include the development and implementation of The Gap's college contract printing program. Strong background and practical experience in the operation of IBM computer equipment and Island Pacific Management System software.

■ **Construction Coordination** -- Responsible for store design. Review construction bids and select general contractor. Work closely with the project architect. Oversee store set-up upon completion of construction. Monitor all leasehold improvements and individual store fixture requirements. Negotiate and maintain all vendor contracts (i.e., HVAC, electrical, plumbing, pest control, carpet cleaning, etc.) at the store level as well as for the home office.

■ **Franchise Services Management** -- Serve as company liaison to over 100 franchise stores. Coordinate and negotiate buying programs for the franchisee. Direct all activities associated with the start-up of new franchise stores including preparing the initial purchase orders, setting up merchandise accounts, and personnel training. Contribute to the monthly franchise newsletter. Select the Franchise-of-the-Month. Coordinate the annual franchise meeting and participate in the semi-annual Franchise Advisory Committee meeting.

EDUCATION

Florida State University
Tallahassee, Florida
Bachelor of Science in Physical Education, 1981

**PERSONAL
BACKGROUND**

Available to begin work immediately
Willing to travel
References available on request

Notice that the descriptions of the five areas of responsibility are in block paragraph style and that each paragraph is preceded by a filled square bullet, unifying the two pages.

Dale B. Young

7777 La Jolla Avenue • San Jose, CA • 95000 • (408) 555-7777

Professional Experience

Management/Trouble Shooting
- Designed software that enabled real-time analysis of worker productivity, scheduling, job cost and production.
- Handled all corrective action requests, including trouble-shooting, customer relations, writing corrective actions, developing tools to solve problems and implementing new procedures.
- Engineered software to control specialized printing equipment.
- Developed competency evaluations for new job applicants.

Quality Administration
- Developed quality control manual for large printing company.
- Inspected incoming components and materials per military specifications for defense contractor.
- Wrote procedures for new and current processes.

Technical Expertise
- Troubleshot and repaired various tools and equipment; designed and installed new equipment.
- Developed software for chemical analysis and retail sales applications.
- Oversaw installation of IBM and Macintosh network computer systems and their software applications.
- Supervised and worked with union and non-union crews on theater/film lighting, sound and set construction.

Employment History

Quality Assurance Manager/Bar Code Supervisor
MABI LABELS, San Jose, CA, 1990-Present

Air Conditioning Technician
THERMAL SERVICE, San Jose, CA, 1990

Quality Receiving Inspector
FRONTIER ENGINEERING, Stillwater, OK, 1989

Repair/Service Manager
BLUE RIDGE POOLS, Atlanta, GA, 1986-1989

Shop Foreman
Various theatrical and film productions in California and Utah, 1976-1986

RÉSUMÉ OBJECTIVE
Position as
Quality Control Supervisor
with progressive company.

Qualification Highlights

✓ Wide range of experiences with technical equipment, tools, materials and processes.
✓ Solid background in physics, chemistry, mathematics and material science.
✓ Ability to pinpoint problems and initiate creative solutions.
✓ Able to read specifications and technical drawings.
✓ Resourceful, innovative, quick learner; able to adapt quickly to a challenge.
✓ Remain calm and work well under demanding conditions.
✓ Ability to prioritize, delegate and motivate.

Technical Skills

Equipment: Comparators, reticles, Rockwell hardness tester, tensile strength press, various electrical and electronic meters, calipers, scales.
Processes: Welding (gas and arc), plastic fabrication (thermoplastics and thermosetting plastics), photography (motion and still).
Computers: IBM, Macintosh, Atari
Programming Languages: FORTRAN, C, BASIC
Databases: dBASE IV, FileMaker II, FirstChoice
Spreadsheets: Lotus 1-2-3, SuperCalc, Microsoft Excel, VIP, FirstChoice
CAD: Drafix, Draft Plus

Education

B.A., *Technical Theater - Magna cum Laude,* **1982**
(Minor in Chemistry)
Southern Utah State College

Additional studies in
Engineering
Oklahoma State University, 1989
University of Utah, 1988

---

119 **Combination.** *Sallie Young, San Jose, California.*
The monogram, the shadow text box, and the horizontal and vertical lines are the design features of this imaginative resume. Italic headings match the person's name in italic.

KARA LADINSKI

2000 N. Milwaukee Ave.
Apt. 630
Chicago, IL 60000
(312) 555-1234

PROFILE

Seeking position as a **Concierge**. Articulate, personable
hospitality professional who displays initiative and is well
organized.

EXPERIENCE

Gold Coast Hotel, Chicago, IL   8/90-Present
Front Desk Agent and **Concierge**

- Welcome arriving guests and thank departing ones.
- Coordinate amenities for VIPs.
- Utilize computerized and manual registry systems. Develop
  10-day occupancy forecasts. Write housekeeping reports.
- Order tickets for artistic and sporting events.
- Place and confirm airline reservations. Reserve rental cars
  and limousines. Make restaurant reservations.
- Arrange temporary child-care services.
- Fulfill a wide variety of guest requests.

Northwest Area Head Start (Preschool), Chicago, IL   6/88-6/90
Teacher's Aide and **Interpreter**

- Increased participation of Polish immigrant parents in meet-
  ings and classroom volunteering by 65%.
- Assisted in teaching and evaluating students.
- Helped social workers with special case work.
- Researched and coordinated traditional Polish celebrations.
  These cultural activities were filmed by the Anderson Insti-
  tute, a research organization for advanced study in child
  development.

Self-Employment, Chicago, IL   8/88-12/92
Interpreter and **Translator, Polish**

- Interpreted for U.S. District Court, U.S. Department of Jus-
  tice, Circuit Court of Cook County, and law firms.
- Translated and coached a radio commercial for Pearle Vision
  Center.
- Translated advertisements, pamphlets, magazine articles, and
  business correspondence.
- Interpreted for Berlitz Translation Services.

EDUCATION

B.S. Candidate, Accounting, Ongoing
University of Illinois at Chicago, Chicago, IL

REFERENCES PROVIDED ON REQUEST

Chronological. Gerard Hosek, Chicago, Illinois.
A resume for a front-desk agent/concierge who wants to be concierge full-time. Her current
concierge duties and lingo ("amenities" and "VIPs") are played up with diamond bullets.

120

ANDREW F. ARMSTRONG
300 E. Soames Blvd., Hackensack, NJ 00000   (000) 000-0000

FOCUS: CUSTOMER SERVICE - LOGISTICS - SHIPPING - INVENTORY CONTROL

* * Excellent record of dealing with clients and filling orders of technical products including computer hardware and medical/laboratory supplies.
* * Thorough knowledge of air/land courier services. Experienced in shipping technical products as well as hazardous and magnetic materials.
* * Proven ability to find the fastest and least costly way to ship. Skilled at handling "alert orders."
* * Experienced with computerized inventory and distribution procedures.

CAREER EXPERIENCE:

INTELOGIC TRACE, Hackensack, New Jersey   8/92-Date
Logistics Coordinator

- ▸ Ship computer hardware parts valued at $6,000 daily nationwide. Process priority orders to Customer Engineers. Trace orders as required.
- ▸ Maintain inventory records on mainframe system. Conduct monthly cycle counts and reconcile.

IBM/USCO DISTRIBUTION CENTER, Paramus. New Jersey   9/89-2/92
Customer Service/Inventory Control

- ▸ Took orders of IBM parts valued at $2.5 million daily from Customer Engineers.
- ▸ Turned around "Alert" and "A Alert" orders within 15 minutes, approximately 90% of orders.
- ▸ Researched flight schedules and courier costs to ensure quick and cost-effective delivery. Used Airline Book to make flight arrangements. Shipped internationally.
- ▸ Prepared monthly Quality Control report to establish accuracy of shipping operation.
- ▸ Filled orders and received faulty returns from the GE Medical Parts section. Reentered to system.

INTERNATIONAL AMERICAN COMPANY, West Caldwell, New Jersey   2/84-6/89
Supervisor

- ▸ Responded to customer inquiries regarding storage rental space both by phone and in person.
- ▸ Arranged leases and coordinated moves as per customer specifications.
- ▸ Generated monthly invoices. Recorded A/R on computerized program. Made collection calls.

METPATH INC., Teterboro, New Jersey   3/82-2/84
Shipping/Receiving Clerk

- ▸ Verified Receiving Reports of laboratory equipment/supplies. Assigned 5-digit stock number.
- ▸ Conducted physical inventory monthly. Reviewed and adjusted computer records to reconcile.

EDUCATION:

IBM Seminars in Logistics and Shipping Hazardous Parts
H & R Block - Income Tax Preparation
University of West Indies, Jamaica, West Indies - Accounting Curriculum

SPECIAL SKILLS: Data Entry, Computerized Accounting, Bookkeeping, Billing, Collection

121 *Combination. Vivian P. Belen, CPRW, Fair Lawn, New Jersey.*
Each of the Focus areas of expertise is supported with one or two descriptive phrases preceded by an asterisk. In the Career Experience section, italic helps the positions stand out.

Virginia Faye Matzick

219 North Bolton
Indianapolis, IN 46000
(307) 000–0000

OBJECTIVE	Seeking a growth potential position with an innovative Travel Management Corporation.

EXPERIENCE

4/90–Present — **Corporate Supervisor**. Hoosier Travel Service, Indianapolis, IN
- Domestic & international reservations.
- Meeting & incentive contract negotiations & Corporate group reservations.
- Oversee 6 agents & provide back–up for quality control desk.

Accomplishment: Established area to service university & missionary travelers worldwide.

8/88–2/90 — **General Manager**. Merchant Worldwide Travel, Indianapolis, IN
- Responsible for 3 offices: operations: override agreements with vendors, purchasing, review of personnel.

Accomplishments: Consolidated branch offices to decrease overhead expenses; established international ticket & rate desk, & increased corporate accounts.

5/85–8/88 — **Branch Manager**. Atlas Travel, Inc. Port Lavaca, TX
- Responsible for corporate & leisure reservations.
- Coordination of delivery & dispatch of tickets.
- Personnel evaluations, quality control, training of new agents.

Accomplishments: Opened office with 1 corporate account, added 5 more accounts. Built leisure clientele to gross $1 1/2 million from $500,000.

6/83–5/85 — **General Partner**. Leisure Lawn, Victoria, TX

Accomplishments: Founded small landscaping business, established commercial accounts.

9/81–/83 — **Corporate Manager**. Hoosier Travel, Indianapolis, IN
- Responsible for all phases of corporate reservations .
- Domestic & international ticketing, ordering of supplies and equipment, interfacing with accounting & group departments, hiring of travel counselors & support staff, training.

Accomplishments: Established international ticket & rate desk, quality control department.

11/80–5/81 — **Assistant Manager**. **Travel** Unlimited, Houston TX
- Responsible for group reservations, conventions, incentive travel.
- Worked directly with airlines, hotels & ground operators to secure space & special rates.

Accomplishment: Reworked accounting procedures to better track groups.

9/75–9/80 — **Branch Manager**. Harvey Travel, Houston, TX
- Responsible for accounting procedures including sales reports, refunds, accounts receivables, invoicing, researching client problems.

Accomplishments: Established automatable ticket procedures, promoted to agent, assistant manager, branch manager of large location.

EQUIPMENT YEARS of EXPERIENCE	TWA Pars, (3)	American Airlines ADS, (3)
	United Airlines Apollo, (2)	Texas Instruments' Printers, (20)
	Apollo ATB, (2)	Sabre, ATB, (1 1/2)

EDUCATION	Massey Business College, Houston, TX
	Victoria College, Victoria, TX
	Victoria High School, Victoria, TX
	Durban Girls High School, Durban, South Africa

Chronological. Richard L. Schillen, Indianapolis, Indiana.
Horizontal lines, blending with the design of the special paper, separate the sections and the
various work experiences. Accomplishments in italic for each gives a solid sense of order.

122

CARL L. LEHMAN

73 Treble Street
Leander, NY 17000

Home: (212) 555-1212   Office: (212) 555-1212

CAREER FOCUS

Inventory control, purchasing, sales, and small business management

CURRENT OBJECTIVE

Inventory control analysis / materials management in a small business environment

PROFILE OF EXPERIENCE AND ACCOMPLISHMENTS

- Strong experience in all aspects of materials management, including computer applications.
- Six years experience in materials intensive businesses, progressing from shipping, purchasing, and sales to store management.
- Successfully turned around two losing stores for a large consumer products distributor.
- Track record for increasing sales and profits by 35% to 50%, based on a reputation for intuitive problem-solving, strong customer service, versatility, and integrity.
- Completely flexible to relocate and travel.

EDUCATION

Bachelor of Business Administration, 1987
State University of New York at Buffalo
- Coursework in small business management and information systems

Management Accounting courses, 1989-1991
The Regents College (Corning Community College), Corning, NY

COMPUTER SKILLS

CCI J-Con and Triad Systems (accounting, purchasing, inventory control)

Lotus 1-2-3, Microsoft Word, File Express, Express Calc; BASIC and SPSS programming languages

PROFESSIONAL EXPERIENCE

Reliance Auto Stores, Woodstock, NY, 9/89 to present
A subsidiary of Atlas Automotive, the nation's 6th largest aftermarket automotive parts concern, with over 550 stores and 26 warehouses.

Store Manager, Stockton and Ardley, NY, 3/92 to present
- Arrested the decline of a marginally profitable small store, achieving a 35% increase in sales and a 40% increase in profits in one year.
- Transferred to a larger, money-losing store/service center and halved the losses in 6 months. Managed inventories in excess of $400,000.

Inside Sales, Woodstock, NY, 9/89 to 3/92
- Personally wrote one-third to one-half of sales of a 4-person team, increasing store sales 50%.
- Promoted to Store Manager.

Super-Torque, Materials Manager, Woodstock, NY, 6/89 to 9/89
- Set up purchasing and inventory policy and procedures for a new business venture.
- Established customer base through direct mail advertising and other methods.

T.H. Blough Automotive, Buyer, Woodstock, NY, 5/88 to 6/89
- Coordinated purchasing, receiving, and inventory control. Selected new product lines.

REFERENCES AVAILABLE UPON REQUEST

123

Combination. *Alan D. Ferrell, Lafayette, Indiana.*
A resume for a person who developed an interest in computerized inventory control and wanted a materials management position. Work history—of less importance—appears last.

IRMA M. WELSH
3469 Hampton Court
Sarasota, Florida 34000
813-000-0000

OBJECTIVE

To obtain an enhanced **Real Estate Property Management** position providing a challenging opportunity for the utilization of my expertise within this industry.

SUMMARY OF QUALIFICATIONS

Extensive experience at the Property Management level, maintaining commercial real estate portfolios totaling from 500,000 S.F. to 1 million S.F. of space. Qualifications include a background of progressively responsible positions with a demonstrated performance record, and cost-effective monitoring of budgets over $1 million. Excellent communication, leadership, and motivation skills that effectively interact with staff, clients and executive management. Bilingual - fluent English and Spanish.

PROFESSIONAL EXPERIENCE

HENDERSON PARTNERS, Sarasota, FL   **2/92 - Present**
Property Manager
- Maintain portfolio consisting of 500,000 S.F. in office buildings and industrial service centers; **Increased commercial lease occupancy to 100%.**
- Directly responsible for overseeing annual budget, property accounting, preparation of 5-year forecasts and monthly operating reports; tenant relation programs; and contracted services.
- Coordinate tenant improvements and lease negotiations.
- Instrumental in complying with ADA (American Disabilities Act) renovation requirements.
- Supervise on-site personnel.

CDM COMMERCIAL REAL ESTATE, INC., Sarasota, FL   **1/91 - 2/92**
Real Estate Manager / Special Services
- Performed all management services for 3 shopping centers and 2 industrial parks totaling 500,000 S.F.
- Created annual budgets and quarterly reforecasts.
- Provided consulting services; assisted in special projects.
- Automated property management accounting for 13 properties.

USA GROUP LIMITED, Tampa, FL   **4/86 - 1/91**
Property Manager
- Commercial portfolio included management of an office park, service center and high-rise office building; liaison between brokers and prospective tenants; structured renegotiation of leases.
- Hired and supervised support staff; coordinated operations and maintenance plans for a building containing asbestos.

ACORN DEVELOPMENT CORPORATION, Tampa, FL   **8/81 - 4/86**
Property Management Administrator / Data Control
- Instrumental in the establishment of a Property Management Division responsible for overseeing a real estate portfolio consisting of 8 commercial properties totaling 1 million S.F.
- Selected and implemented a Data Base Management System (hardware and software) facilitating accounting cost controls for Corporate and 13 Regional Offices. Conducted in-house training program.

EDUCATION / SPECIALIZED TRAINING

BUILDING OWNERS & MANAGERS ASSOCIATION (BOMA)   **1988**
Real Property Administrator (RPA)

FLORIDA REAL ESTATE SALESPERSON'S LICENSE   **1988**

NEW YORK UNIVERSITY, New York, NY   **1980**
Bookkeeping Certificate

BRONX COMMUNITY COLLEGE, New York, NY   **1972 - 1974**
Associate Degree - Liberal Arts

Combination. *Diane McGoldrick, Tampa, Florida.*
Another one-page resume accomplished by narrow margins and small type. Wider margins for the Objective statement help it stand out. Centered headings offset the wide lines.

124

SANDRA MASON
(704) 000-0000 or (404) 000-0000

3027 Cumberland Drive
Rex, GA 30000

PROFESSIONAL QUALIFICATIONS

Broad aviation experience, including dispatching, crew scheduling, sales and service (passengers and cargo), and station/flight-operations management. Excel at identifying and obtaining necessary rights for international flights. Strong interpersonal/negotiation skills. Adapt readily to ever-changing situations, and make sound time-critical decisions.

WORK HISTORY

Station Manager, LARSON JET INC., Charlotte, NC *(1992-93)*
This charter/scheduled airline flies domestically and internationally, using MD-80 and B-727 aircraft.

Oversaw and performed all aspects of check-in, boarding, and passenger relations. Coordinated operational activities, including weight-and-balance, weather briefings, catering, liquor reports, fueling, de-icing, and interior/exterior cleaning of aircraft. Performed GSC duties.

Directed and trained contracted United Airlines employees in Larson Jet passenger check-in procedures, sales, and ground services (loading and water service). Also personally handled these functions when necessary.

Also worked as the *regional sales manager* for VEGAS SPORTOURS INC., a Larson Jet subsidiary. Sold tours to NC/SC travel agencies; ensured all agency special requests for travelers were met. Coordinated advertising and public relations. Trained and directed sales agents in three cities. Sales efforts led to a 300% rise in total bookings.

Flight Operations Manager, RS ACQUISITION CORP., Baltimore, MD *(1990-92)*

Directed flight routing and dispatch, and crew scheduling and movement, for corporate aircraft test-flying domestically and internationally. Managed 2,500+ aircraft revenue hours a year. Administered a $4 million annual budget. Serviced customer accounts.

Designed and created company's first global operations/sales/service manual. This manual had tremendous impact: 1) it reduced price-quoting errors; 2) it decreased duplicative work; and 3) established FAA/company preferred routings and technical stops (including seasonal data), which led to a $1+ million savings in fuel, crew, and ground-handling costs over one year.

Aircraft Dispatcher, AMERICAN AIRLINES, Dallas, TX *(1989-90)*

Authorized, regulated, and controlled 80+ domestic/international commercial flights a day. Duties included flight planning, weather briefing, and monitoring the progress of flights. Had authority to select fuel stops and delay, divert, or cancel flights. Jointly responsible with captains for the safe release and completion of flights.

(continued)

125 **Combination.** *Barry Wohl, Charlotte, North Carolina.*
This resume and Resume 177 are two different resumes for the same person. This resume is directed toward a position in aviation. Paragraph style is used to present relevant material.

SANDRA MASON   2

ARROW AIR (freight/passenger carrier), Miami, FL *(1985-89)*

    Manager of Flight Operations and Charter/Cargo Sales and Service (1986-89). In charge of 45 crew members, three crew schedulers, and six dispatchers, who were responsible for domestic/international flights. Negotiated pricing for fuel, catering, airport fees, security, and crew transportation and lodging. Negotiated/obtained diplomatic rights (landing, uplift, overflight).

Generated cargo contracts worth $3 million annually. Ensured airline profitability by meeting a quota of 20,000 revenue hours yearly for eight DC-8 aircraft.

    Dispatcher (1985-86). Quickly promoted (over five others) to senior dispatcher. Instructed new dispatchers, and conducted FAA recurrent training for dispatcher staff.

EDUCATION

FAA Aircraft Dispatch License, <u>Sheffield School of Aeronautics</u> -- 1985
Also received **Certificate in Airline Operations**.

Certified as a **Ground Security Coordinator**, American Trans Air school -- 1983

Three years' study toward a ***bachelor's degree***. Courses in *aviation management*, *travel and tourism*, and *marketing* at <u>Georgia State University</u> and <u>Embry-Riddle Aeronautical University</u>.

Graduated <u>Cal Simmons Travel Agency School</u> -- 1992.

The Education section can be shaped to match a specific career goal. Compare the Education section here with that in Resume 177 and note the omission and rearrangement of material.

KAREN SMITH

951 Northlake Dr., No. 51 ◆ San Jose, CA 95000 ◆ (408) 000-0000

OBJECTIVE:

To gain personal and professional growth as a team member performing vital services that contribute to the profitability of a company.

QUALIFICATIONS:

Twelve years of solid experience in the planning servicing and manufacturing industries. Readily accepts new challenges, performing them in a capable and professional way. Highly conscientious of quality, customer service and inventory levels, while consistently meeting tight deadlines.

CAREER SUMMARY:

1984 - present
VARIAN, Sunnyvale, California
Product Support Specialist   1991 - present
  ◆ Maintains spec control drawings.
  ◆ Communicates with factory on ECO when it affects service.
  ◆ Responsible for pricing and adding part numbers to database.
  ◆ Interfaces effectively between customer and service support groups, to procure parts and resolve product part problems in field.
  ◆ Reliably reports problems to purchasing, technical support group, field engineers and customers.
  ◆ Solves internal problems, database inconsistencies, lack of pricing, and invalid information on computer system.
  ◆ MRB PCB field returns.

Senior Production Control Planner/Scheduler   1984 - present
  ◆ Planned, ordered and scheduled parts and supplies from internal divisions and outside sources to accommodate customer demands.
  ◆ Consistently maintains inventory of 1,000 parts at economical levels, while keeping customers satisfied.
  ◆ Coordinates returned boards for repairs at the appropriate place, either factory or vendor.
  ◆ Involved in two computer switch overs involving hardware and software conversions.
  ◆ Wrote procedures as a team member of ISO9001.
  ◆ Developed solutions as part of quality management team for field servicing, drop shipments and order processing.
  ◆ Coordinated final product phase outs.

1979 - 1984
EATON CORPORATION Addington Labs., Sunnyvale, California
Marketing Clerk-Typist, Quote Processor   1983 - 1984
  Handled quote entries, processing, secretarial duties, customer service on returns and expedites.

Senior Material Planner   1981 - 1982
  Responsible for the planning, scheduling and monitoring the movement of materials through the procurement cycle. Coordinated with engineering, purchasing, stockroom and production control.

126 *Combination. Gary Watkins, San Jose, California.*
Boldfacing is used effectively to call attention to the person's various positions. Diamond-shaped bullets indicate the resume's center of gravity—the dual current positions.

Karen Smith
page two

Junior Production Material Planner, Scheduler   1981
Material planner per contractual production schedule for all product lines, maintaining accurate reorder points and lead times.

Inventory Control Coordinator   1980
Coordinated material planning and scheduling of main product line.

EDUCATION:

Homestead High School, Sunnyvale, CA

TRAINING:

Trained in a variety of classes including: Material Planning, Scheduling, Purchasing, Inventory Function, Inventory Control, ECO, ISO, and Lotus 1-2-3.

Dates of employment show a steady increase of responsibility at the preceding place of employment. High school education and training through a mix of classes are put last.

TERRANCE HAUSHOLT
600 Bayview • New Town, MS 70000
(555) 555-5555

EXECUTIVE MANAGEMENT PROFESSIONAL

PROFILE

A seasoned professional with broad experience in both new operational start-ups and "turn-arounds" of manufacturing businesses. A competent and technically sound executive with a proven track record in General Management, Operations and Sales.

EDUCATION

Bachelor of Science Degree in Accounting, with a Minor in Business Administration
The University of Mississippi, New Town, MS
Associates Degree in Accounting
Anyone's College, New Town, MS
Graduate Studies in Business Administration
The University of Mississippi, New Town, MS
Chemical and Mechanical Engineering Studies
The Engineering School, New Town, MS

SPECIAL TRAINING AND DEVELOPMENT

Chemistry and Engineering Courses
Conducted by the XYZ Chemical Company, Anytown, LA
Basic Chemistry and Advanced Polymer Chemistry Courses
Conducted by the XYZ Chemical Company, Anytown, LA
Various Professional Seminars
Conducted by the American Management Association and other Professional Organizations

MILITARY

U.S. Army
Finance Corp - July 1954 to June 1956; Honorable Discharge - 1962

PROFESSIONAL EXPERIENCE

Director of Operations
Major Metals Corporation, Anytown, LA
May 1989 to September 1992

Recruited by this manufacturer of construction metals to reorganize existing two plant operation and to build a multiplant operations team that would oversee operations for the entire company. Assumed responsibility for all aspects of enhancement and growth of a department with an employment level that ranged from 300 to 500 employees.

Vice President of Sales and Marketing
Packaging Company, Inc., Anytown, LA
May 1988 to May 1989

Recruited to reorganize and rebuild the sales force, and to expand and diversify the product lines, markets, and distribution system for this manufacturer of custom flexible packaging products.

127 **Combination.** *Diane Y. Chapman, Aliso Viejo, California.*
Dates of education and special training are omitted in this resume for a "seasoned professional." Dates of employment show continual work since February, 1957.

TERRANCE HAUSHOLT (Continued)

Professional Experience

President
CHYRO Enterprises, Inc., Skyblue, LA
December 1986 to May 1988

Started and operated a manufacturer's representative and consulting company to promote and sell products manufactured by a group of plastic packaging firms.

President
HiTech, Inc., Skyblue, LA
January 1982 to December 1986

Recruited to redirect and restructure this manufacturer and regional distributor of polyethylene products. Transformed the company from a substantial loss position to a profitable and leading principal in the industry, after acquiring the executive position. The first profit was realized in the tenth month. The sales volume was increased from 29,000,000 pounds in 1982 to 51,000,000 pounds in 1985, recording a pre-tax profit of $1,800,000.00.

Vice-President and General Manager
Mega Containers and Sturdy Plastics, Inc., Archer, TX And Clinton, KS
December 1970 to December 1981

Initially recruited to expedite the product line development, marketing direction and growth of these plastics manufacturing companies which were a part of a four-company operation. Became General Manager and Chief Operating Officer for these facilities in 1971.

Sales Manager
R&D Products, Archer, TX
August 1969 to November 1970

Maximized sales development for this manufacturer of custom flexible packaging products.

Technical Sales Representative
Plastics and Metals, Inc., Archer, TX
January 1966 to August 1969

Generated sales for all of Plastic and Metals, Inc.'s thermoplastic resins in the states of Texas, Oklahoma and New Mexico. Increased sales from approximately $1,150,000.00 to over $5,500,000.00 within the first fourteen months.

Operations Manager
UltraCorp, Inc., New Town, MS
February 1957 to January 1966

Joined the company during the Engineering, Construction and Start-up phases of the Mississippi division. After becoming Operations Manager of the Light Hydrocarbons Plant in 1960, responsibilities included operations, maintenance, expansion/upgrade projects and new construction. Also assumed the role of plant liaison to the Engineering departments in both Mississippi and Texas.

Another resume in which center-justified information (position held, name of employer, location, and dates of employment) contrasts well visually with wide paragraphs

JAMES B. SELLERS
4300 Shier Rings Road
Amlin, OH 43000

(614) 000-0000

PROFILE

Versatile quality control professional with 20 years of production management/supervisory experience including problem solving, staff development, logistic sensitivity, in-depth knowledge of production systems and long-standing record in creative resolution of customer needs. Ability to develop staff will contribute to the productivity and profitability of an organization. **Areas of expertise: Production Supervisor . . .Quality Control . . . Shipping (national and international).**

HIGHLIGHTS OF QUALIFICATIONS

- Implemented Quality Control programs updating manuals to conform to spec
- Oversaw production planning, scheduling, and expediting
- Supervised the assembling and packing of precision instruments
- Hired, trained, and evaluated personnel
- Restructured Cork, Ireland, shipping department, reducing cost by half-million dollars
- Certified in welding, heating & cooling, and refrigeration
- Established and maintained operations from ground-floor level

EMPLOYMENT HISTORY

ADVANCE INDUSTRIAL MFG., Columbus, OH   June 1992 - December 1992
Quality Assurance Manager
Managed Quality Control in all four divisions (Fabrication, Machine Shop, Attachment Division, Ramp Division). Supervised 62 employees. Initiated calibration of precision instruments program within acceptable federal tolerance. Re-wrote company Quality Assurance manual to conform with current specs and be aerospace qualified. Designed all quality assurance documents.

STOVER INDUSTRIES INC., Delaware, OH   December 1990 - June 1992
Quality Assurance Manager
Supervised 50 employees generating over $5M during an 18 month period. Customers included Honda, McDonald Douglas, Tosoh SMD Limited, and Nestles. Initiated calibration system reducing cost and eliminating scrape and wastes. Re-wrote company's Quality Assurance manual to conform with current specs resulting in Stover Industries being awarded contract from McDonald Douglas. Designed all quality assurance documentation. Utilized computer to generate reports on quality control and test schedules.

LIEBERT CORPORATION, Columbus, OH   1976-1990
International Shipping Coordinator
Managed shipping and packaging of Cork, Ireland, division. Determined most economic assembly techniques to meet master schedule delivery requirements with high emphasis on cost reduction. Two years documented as saving Liebert 1/2 million dollars in shipping. Dealt with letters of credit, customs, Operation Exodus (shipping technology out of the US). Managed the shipping of air condition units, computers, CPC, parts, and household goods of employees shipping out of Columbus, Ohio, to all international Liebert customer locations.

Supervisor
Supervised up to 32 employees. Assigned to various departments: Electronics, Pantronics, Final Line, Paint Room, Paneling, and Shipping. Managed production schedule and budget responsibilities. Implemented production line in Pantronics to increase production by 25%. Coordinated with Research and Development department to develop required schematics classes for employees. Recipient of several suggestion awards.

Quality Control Inspector
Supervised the flow of material through the production process: Challengers, Chillers, Deluxe Units, FSC Boxes, Condensers, Final Finish inspections on Paint, Welding inspections, Leak Check inspections, Receiving inspections to ensure all parts received were up to spec. In charge of U.S. Air Force inspection of 26 conditioned power units with Federal spec to withstand a 5' drop test and nuclear fallout. Documented all quality control defective parts and stamped approved parts.

128
Combination. *Susan Higgins, Amlin, Ohio.*
A resume which shows that a person doesn't have to go to college to have a good work record. Horizontal lines enclosing Highlights of Qualifications call attention to them.

JAMES B. SELLERS **Page 2**

CARL E. DAVIDSON INC., Columbus, OH — 1973-1976
   Machinist — Operated milling machine, drill press, and turrett lathe
   Welder — Work included cranes, hoist conveyors, material handling systems. Certified on structural steel welding. Involved with productions and installations such as the conveyor system (monorail) for Hobart Kitchenaid, Florence, KY, and two 2-ton bridge cranes for Worthington Industries, Worthington, OH.

STANDARD OIL CO., Columbus, OH — 1972-1973
   Service Station Management
   Managed/supervised entire day-to-day operation.

EMPLOYER OVERLOAD, Columbus, OH — 1970-1972
   Service Station Management
   Area Supervisor responsible for 11 stations, turning them from unprofitable into profitable. Increased profits by a minimum of 300% allowing the stations to be franchised. Prepared profit and loss statements each month for each station. Negotiated with oil companies. Managed all aspects of day-to-day operations including interviewing prospective employees, hiring needed personnel, and evaluating performance. Distributed weekly payroll.

NORTH AMERICAN ROCKWELL, Columbus, OH — 1968-1970
   Turrett Lathe Operator

DEFENSE CONSTRUCTION SUPPLY CENTER, Columbus, OH — 1966-1968
   Shipping, Salvage, & Warehouse

MANAGEMENT DEVELOPMENT PROGRAMS

   Standard Oil Company Management Course, 60 hours
   Liebert Corporation, Leadership and Management Course, 108 hours
   International Trade Institute, Document Preparation, 16 hours
   World Trade Institute, Imports and Exports, 40 hours
   Capital University, Frontline Supervision, 16 hours
   George Washington University, Seminars via Satellite, 4 hours
   Juran Institute, Total Quality Management
   Teamwork in the Quality Era, Peter R. Scholtes
   The New Economics, Dr. Edwards Deming
   Completeness: Managing for the 21st Century, Phillip B. Crosby
   Business and Management, Dr. Peter F. Drucker

TECHNICAL EDUCATION

   North American Rockwell Corporation, 80 hours classroom, 40 hours OJT
      Blueprint reading, precision instruments, and shop drawings

   Columbus Public Schools Adult Education, 2-year, 72-hour Certificate
      Heating, Air Conditioning, and Refrigeration

   Federal Products, Providence, Rhode Island, Model 350 CMM, 40 hours

---

The lower line on this page separates the work record from the person's education.
The development programs attended nevertheless display a commitment to learning.

JANE WEBSTER
857 Westchester Avenue
Old Bridge, New Jersey 08000
(908) 000-0000

OBJECTIVE

To continue my career in Real Estate, specializing in Property and Sales Management.

SUMMARY OF QUALIFICATIONS

Over 10 years of experience working with the public in various capacities:

Corporate Positions:

- Vice President, New Homes Division Huntington Realty, Regional Site Manager, U.S. Builders New Homes Division, Sales Associate.

Political Positions:

- Councilwoman, Old Bridge Township, Council Planning Board Representative, Council Welfare Board Representative, and Spokesperson, Burnt Fly Bog Citizens Committee and the New Jersey Environmental Federation.

- Experienced in all facets of real estate and real estate documentation relating to project development, project management, and set-up of sales forces and marketing plans.

- Familiar with mortgage documentation, public offering statements, master deeds, and bylaws.

- Hold Real Estate Broker's License and a member of M.I.R.M. (the elite Institute of Residential Marketing.)

EXPERIENCE

11/93-Present
EGAN PROPERTY MANAGEMENT, Neptune, New Jersey
<u>Senior Accounts Manager</u>

Work with bank representatives, attorneys, and individuals handling REO and OREO. Purchase bank-owned properties; provide property management and maintenance services for residential, commercial and industrial properties. The properties are revitalized and renovated into affordable housing units.

5/91-9/93
TALL OAKS AT LAKEWOOD, INC., Lakewood, New Jersey
WARREN REALTY, Sole Proprietor
<u>Director of Sales and Rentals</u>

Implemented advertising plans and marketing strategies for project development of new homes and rental properties. Responsible for all sales and rentals. Helped clients to obtain affordable financing including FHA, VA, and FANNIE MAE mortgages for new home sales. Served as a liaison between clients and mortgage companies.

129 **Combination.** *Beverly Baskin, CPRW, Marlboro, New Jersey.*
The Summary of Qualifications indicates the dual concerns of the person, who wanted to combine corporate and political interests in a job with a U.S. Gov't. or state housing agency.

JANE WEBSTER Page 2

5/88-4/90
SUPERIOR REALTY, INC., Freehold, New Jersey
<u>Vice President, New Homes Division</u>

Responsible for setting up real estate projects statewide. Procured listings from new developers. Hired on-site sales personnel. Set up marketing plans and sales office strategies; provided continuing education for on-site salespeople. Trained employees to work with customers from the time that they enter into a contract until closing and follow-up procedures. Handled all administrative and legal forms relating to procurement of on-site sales.

6/85-5/88
U.S. HOMES NEW HOME AND LANDS DIVISION, Morristown, New Jersey
<u>Regional Site Manager of New Home Sites</u>

On-site salesperson. Promoted in 1986 to Regional Site Manager of New Homes Division. Managed the sales of single-family homes, town homes, condominiums, conversions, and revitalizations from $70,000 to $500,000. Achieved U.S. Homes Million Dollar Club.

1983-1987
COUNCILWOMAN, Old Bridge Township, Old Bridge, New Jersey

Adopted and approved all budgets; involved in the daily activities of adopting and approving legislation for the betterment of Old Bridge Township and its citizens. Worked with other council members in writing legislation for Mt. Laurel Affordable Housing to approve zoning for Affordable Housing Legislation in Old Bridge Township.

1984-1986
OLD BRIDGE TOWNSHIP PLANNING BOARD, Old Bridge Township, Old Bridge, New Jersey
<u>Council Representative to Planning Board</u>

Adopted and approved new master plan for Old Bridge Township to allow proper zoning for commercial and residential projects and zoning for Mt. Laurel Affordable Housing.

1985-1986
OLD BRIDGE TOWNSHIP WELFARE BOARD
<u>Council Representative</u>

1987-1989
NEW JERSEY ENVIRONMENTAL FEDERATION, New Brunswick, New Jersey
<u>Spokesperson for Clean Water Action</u>

Spearheaded campaigns for toxic waste clean-up statewide and nationally. Testified before U.S. Senate and U.S. Congress Committees in Washington D.C., New York City, and New Jersey. Also testified before New Jersey DEP Committees. Articles about my environmental projects appeared in the *New York Times, TIME Magazine, Business Week,* and all the local and state newspapers. Appeared on Senator Bill Bradley's weekly television show. CBS produced a 15 minute spot on their Sunday Morning Show on my environmental clean-up work. Guest speaker at numerous environmental and political functions. Woman of the Year Award presented by Senator Bill Bradley for the New Jersey Women's Network.

EDUCATION

N.J. Real Estate School - Broker's Course...N.J. Real Estate School - Sales Person's Course. Attended Brookdale Community College...Member of Institute of Residential Marketing.

References and copies of Trade Publications available upon request.

Dual tracks—one in real estate property and sales management and the other as a Council Representative and Councilwoman—are treated in turn with positions underlined.

Jane E. Doe

OBJECTIVE: To secure a challenging position in **Customer Relations** within your organization that will utilize my education, experience, and unique abilities to further my career opportunities.

SUMMARY OF QUALIFICATIONS:

- ◆ Over five years successful experience in sales, marketing, promotions, and customer service - ability to persuasively relate new concepts and ideas.

- ◆ Outstanding **Communication** skills - proficiently utilizes interpersonal skills in relating with others. Effectively handles difficult situations, negotiates, as well as develops and implements solutions.

- ◆ Excellent **Management** skills - the ability to coordinate multifaceted activities within an unsupervised environment. Effective problem solver/decision maker.

- ◆ Effective **Planning and Organization** skills - accurately performs record keeping, scheduling, inventory control, and related acts to ensure productive operations.

- ◆ Exceptional **Supervisor** - motivates personnel to increase efficiency, quality of service, and increase productivity. Fair with everyone; likes to get things done properly.

- ◆ Hard-working, goal-oriented, perfectionist, and a team player.

EXPERIENCE:

1988 to Present

BOB'S FASHIONS, Hokey, Illinois
Fashions Manager   **(10/90-Present)**
Productively manages the overall operations of seven major departments within the store; i.e., Ladieswear, Menswear, Infants, Fashion Accessories, Hosiery, Domestics, and Jewelry. Maintains $3.6 million annual sales. Accurately administers a $210,000.00 annual payroll budget. Responsible for bookkeeping, scheduling, inventory control, ordering merchandise, sales, and customer service. Effectively hires, trains, supervises and evaluates personnel. Currently responsible for 15 subordinates. Effective in all areas of sales and marketing; i.e., creating promotional impact, display and presentation, price integrity, competitive pricing, open communication, and demanding superior customer service from all employees.
- • Successfully increased sales from $2.9 million to $3.6 million in under three years.
- • Annual sales volume, 1992 - $3.4 million and projected 1993 - $3.6 million.

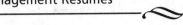

123 Lois Lane • Chatham, Illinois 62000 • (217) 555-0000

Manager (10/89-10/90)

Responsibly managed the daily activities in the Belleville, Illinois, location; i.e., establishing and implementing store goals, inventory and waste control, stockroom management, merchandising displays, customer service, bookkeeping, cash control, collections, and sales. Administered various personnel functions; i.e., hiring, training, scheduling, supervising, evaluating, and occasionally terminating employees.
- Annual sales volume, 1989 - $2.7 million.
- Promoted to Fashions Manager, Hokey, Illinois, in October, 1990.

Assistant Manager (06/88-10/89)

Effectively trained and assisted in managing the retail operations in Kansas City, Kansas. Charged with supervision of the sales floor, monitored inventory and fitting rooms, ensured employees adhered to all policies and procedures, administered the completion of annual reviews and conducted review sessions.
- Promoted to Manager October, 1989.

September 1987
to May 1988

JOE'S MATERIAL MART, Hokey, Illinois
Part-time Sales Associate

Responsible for customer assistance, sales, inventory, merchandise display, and operating the cash register.

September 1985
to May 1988

COOL UNIVERSITY, Cool, Illinois
Part-time Office Assistant

Efficiently performed typing, filing, scheduling, and updating records.

EDUCATION:

COOL UNIVERSITY, Cool, Illinois
Bachelor of Science in Clothing and Textile
Minor: Marketing

CREW SENIOR HIGH, Crew, Illinois
Diploma

PERSONAL:

Hobbies/Interests: Golf, sewing, travel, reading, and aerobic dancing.

Willing to travel.

REFERENCES: Available upon request.

The use of two pages makes it possible to give more information about each of the jobs the person has had—in this instance, by promotion within the same company.

LEANNA BOYD

990 E Campbell   Seattle, WA 00000   [206] 000-0000

SUMMARY OF QUALIFICATIONS:

- ◆ Over 10 years experience in Human Resources/customer service....

- ◆ Regional Vice-President/Branch Manager for permanent/temporary placement service....

- ◆ Successfully brought new businesses on-line/profitable....

- ◆ Increased commercial account base 20%....

- ◆ Extensive background in interviewing/testing/placements....

- ◆ Became temporary placement service pilot office for nationwide agency....

- ◆ Comprehensive knowledge of long-distance communication services....

- ◆ Provided training to long-distance agents....supervised 23 agents....

- ◆ Maintained lowest employee turnover rate in two different businesses....retained valuable employees....

- ◆ Reorganized business/brought from negative to profitable basis....

- ◆ Achieved highest volume of business for one quarter in history of company in Arizona....

- ◆ Established strong/loyal client base....

- ◆ Excellent communications skills....seek challenges....able to establish rapport with executive-level clients....dedicated....maintain highest personal/business integrity....

TRAINING: US SPRINT - Train the Trainer & Agent Training
SNELLING & SNELLING - Management, Sales, Operations
SEATTLE COMMUNITY COLLEGE - Seattle, WA
  Major: Business

131 *Combination. Fran Holsinger, Tempe, Arizona.*
Brochure style was used for this resume also. Double-spacing the qualifications in the Summary of Qualifications creates an impressive first page. Notice the distinctive bullets.

---

personal profile

PROFESSIONAL HIGHLIGHTS:

HUMAN RESOURCES/PLACEMENT

Supervised 18 - 25 employees/3 branch offices....reorganized offices....hired/fired/trained staff....developed record-keeping procedures still being utilized....worked closely with corporate Vice-President in developing new services....increased business by 125% in one year....opened new branches....set record of 29 new in-takes in one day....billed over 1000 hr/week within short period of time....devised award system to recognize staff members: Office/Sales Rep/Employee of the Quarter....

Major Clients:
- American Express (2 Div) - US Sprint   - APS
- Resolution Trust Corp   - CalComp   - Pepsi Cola - West

OPERATIONS SUPERVISOR

Initially hired as contract Human Resources Consultant to assist in interviewing/hiring for new facilities....offered permanent operation position after 3 weeks....interviewed 4000 for 400 agent openings/staff positions....oversaw start-up of Long Distance Operator Services Facilities....agent group had lowest turn-over/absenteeism rate/#1 in production....devised motivational contests/awards....

EMPLOYERS: AppleOne Employment Services - Seattle, WA
  Regional Vice President/Branch Manager: 1990 - 1992
 US Sprint - Seattle, WA
  Operations Supervisor: 1989 - 1990
 Snelling Temporary Services - Everett, WA
  Manager/Owner: 1983 - 1989
 Career Path - Snohomish, WA
  Supervisor: 1981 - 1983

COMMUNITY AFFILILATIONS:

Snohomish C of C - Past President/Interim Executive Director
Zonta International

AWARDS: ● Snelling & Snelling Manager of the Year - 1986 ● Quick Start Award

---

A different touch is to use ellipses (....) to separate items in the two Professional Highlights subsections. Underlining emphasizes positions rather than employers in the Employers section.

M A R Y   A.
RAYMOND

*2095 California
Street
Apt. 555
San Francisco, CA
94109*

(415) 555-5905

OBJECTIVE:

Position as a

Portfolio Manager

or Securities Analyst.

Certification:

Chartered

Financial

Analyst

HIGHLIGHTS OF QUALIFICATIONS

✔ In-depth knowledge of technological fields.
✔ Strategic thinker; able to synthesize information quickly.
✔ Thorough researcher who tests hypotheses in the field.
✔ Strong communication skills; proven ability to simplify advanced concepts for "user-friendly" comprehension.
✔ Experience as a technology analyst, both as an industry consultant and as a securities analyst.
✔ Strong record in software market and securities analysis.

PROFESSIONAL EXPERIENCE

Securities Analysis & Portfolio Management

■ Managed $20 million for high net worth investors, whose customized accounts ranged from conservatively to aggressively managed; most aggressively managed account had annual return of 45 percent in 1993.
■ Conducted proprietary research on companies such as CompuWare, Xilinx, First Financial Management and Newbridge Networks, which formed the core of more aggressively managed portfolios.
■ Provided research ideas for $200 million managed account base.
■ As securities analyst, emphasized finding values others failed to recognize.

Market Analysis

■ Analyze U.S. software products and services markets, providing written and oral reports to companies such as IBM, Hewlett-Packard, EDS, Andersen Consulting and Unisys.
■ Directed Vendor Analysis Program for market research firm, studying individual companies in a number of information technology industry segments.
■ Provided investment banking consulting for clients in the information technology industry.

EMPLOYMENT HISTORY

1993-*Present*	*Principal Consultant*	INPUT, Mountain View, CA
1992-93	*Portfolio Manager*	PORTSMOUTH FINANCIAL, San Francisco, CA
1991-92	*Director of Research*	ROSENBLUM, SILVERMAN, SUTTON INVESTMENT COUNSELING FIRM, San Francisco, CA
1988-91	*Program Manager*	INPUT, Mountain View, CA
1986-88	*Senior Securities Analyst*	DAVIS SKAGGS DIVISION, SHEARSON LEHMAN BROTHERS, San Francisco, CA
1977-86	*Senior Securities Analyst*	WEDBUSH MORGAN SECURITIES; HENRY SWIFT; and BIRR WILSON, San Francisco, CA
1976-77	*Research Assistant to Director of Research*	HAMBRECHT AND QUIST, San Francisco, CA

EDUCATION

M.B.A., GOLDEN GATE UNIVERSITY, San Francisco — Finance (3.75 GPA)

M.S., UNIVERSITY OF MINNESOTA, Minneapolis — History and Philosophy of Education
Teaching Assistant to Department Director

B.S., University of MINNESOTA, Minneapolis — Social Sciences Major, English Minor
Phi Lambda Theta Women's Honorary Society

References furnished upon establishment of mutual interest.

132

Combination. *Sallie Young, San Jose, California.*
Note the various formats. The left column is right-justified; Highlights and Experience are full-justified; Education is center-justified; and the History has three columns.

Mark T. Bradley, B.S.

4833 Catalpa ● New Holland, Michigan 48000
(612) 555-5555

PROFILE:

Background of proven success in *Hospitality Management* including food and beverage control in various hotel and resort establishments. Experience features involvement with fine dining facilities in a 4-star, 4-diamond hotel, banquet facilities, and corporate fast-food operations. Customer service a priority.

EDUCATION:

College of Business, B.S. Hospitality Management, A.A.S. Diversified Business
Ferris State University, Big Rapids, Michigan

SUMMARY OF SKILLS AND TRAINING:

- Hire, train, schedule, and supervise up to 25 employees
- Develop advertising/marketing strategies
- Assist in determining menu selections stressing variety and utilizing seasonal foods
- Handle cost controls (food and labor), inventory controls, pricing, and purchasing
- Ensure all sanitation standards are being met including city, state, and federal codes
- Prepare and submit forecasting for financial and management matters
- Define goals for day-to-day operations
- Assist guests with room registration providing personalized service maximizing revenue and customer satisfaction
- Perform room service operations
- Set up and served banquets to 600 people
- Utilize computer for audits, reports, scheduling, etc.

PROFESSIONAL EXPERIENCE:

Manager
Pizza Hut, South Haven, Michigan

Internship
Amway Grand Plaza Hotel, Grand Rapids, Michigan (Front Desk)
Marriott's Marco Island Resort, Marco Island, Florida (Room Service and Banquets)

Bellhop/Room Service
Clarion Hotel & Conference Center, Big Rapids, Michigan

RELATED PROFESSIONAL ACTIVITIES:

- Purchasing Committee Chairman 1994 Annual Gala
- Training Intervention Procedures by Servers of Alcohol (TIPS)
- Front Office Procedures Certificate
- SYSCO Frost Pack Food Show, New Holland, Michigan

Functional. Patricia L. Nieboer, CPS, CPRW, Fremont, Michigan.
Except for a gala event, no date is given in this resume for a person who has progressed from bellhop to hospitality manager. The graphic makes the resume distinctive.

133

M. BRANDON YORK

700 Granite Drive   •   Lilburn, Georgia 30000   •   (404) 000-0000

SUMMARY OF QUALIFICATIONS

Comprehensive knowledge of Sales Management and Financial Operations.   Ability to effectively communicate ideas to others. Well organized, highly motivated, and results-oriented.

Management

- Diagnosed problem areas of operation, established training programs, and instituted new procedures to increase productivity.
- Supervised Finance and Sales Departments with a total of 20 staff members.
- Trained dealer personnel to cultivate lease business.

Finance

- Effectively assessed and verified financial documentation; negotiated with lenders to attain funding for customers.
- Emphasized and demonstrated the advantages of short-term leasing to customers and staff.

Increased Leasing from 3% to 31% within one year.

Sales

- Skilled at recognizing buying patterns and designing marketing strategies to expand business.
- Record of consistent achievement and positive organizational growth through development of new business and successful execution of existing accounts.

Received Numerous Sales Awards.

CAREER HISTORY

Finance Manager, 1993
   MAJOR CAR DEALERSHIP, Lawrenceville, Georgia
Finance Director, 1991-1992
   MINOR CAR DEALERSHIP, Lilburn, Georgia
Finance Director, 1989-1990 *Finance Manager,* 1988 *Sales Associate,* 1987
   BEST CARS, Stone Mountain, Georgia
Sales Associate, 1986-1987
   GOOD CARS, Duluth, Georgia
Owner/Manager, 1983-1986
   YORK ENTERPRISE, Muscle Shoals, Alabama

REFERENCES AVAILABLE UPON REQUEST

134 **Combination.** *Carol Lawrence, CPRW, Snellville, Georgia.*
The centered personal information at the top of the page calls attention to the centered achievement statements about increased leasing and the receipt of numerous awards.

John Doe
Route 5, Box 123
Fernandina Beach, Florida 32000
(555) 555-5555

OBJECTIVE:
A position in Operations, Maintenance or Quality Assurance in the Power Generation Industry with opportunity for professional growth.

EDUCATION:
<u>**AEET - Electronic Technology Institute**</u>

Naval Nuclear Prototype Training	Nuclear Field ET "A" School
Naval Nuclear Power School	Reactor Theory School

QUALIFICATIONS ACHIEVED:

Reactor Technician	Nuclear Quality Control Inspector
Reactor Operator	Controlled/Hazardous Material Petty Officer
Shutdown Reactor Operator	Qualification Petty Officer
Electrical Operator	Primary Valve Operator
Shutdown Electrical Operator	Radiological Control Point Access Watch
Secondary Control Watch	Auxiliary Electrician

EMPLOYMENT HIGHLIGHTS:

* 2 Years as Reactor Plant Work Center Supervisor, responsible for the scheduling, supervision, and completion of routine, preventive, and corrective maintenance of reactor C&I systems.

* 2 Years as Reactor Technician providing technical support for complex refueling overhaul. Coordinated initial alignments of upgraded reactor protection and control instrumentations.

* 1 Year Nuclear Quality Control Inspector ensured Grade 'A' specification requirements are met on primary/secondary systems.

* 1 Year Qualification Petty Officer and Senior Drill Team Member responsible for training personnel on primary/secondary systems and operations. As senior drill team member, coordinated primary/secondary casualty scenarios while ensuring reactor safety is observed.

* 4 Years operational experience on pressurized water reactor plant and its related systems during critical, start-up, and shutdown operations. Primary Reactor Operator for physics acceptance testing.

* 6 Months as Electronic Lab Assistant. Duties included conveying electrical fundamentals while maintaining electrical safety in a laboratory environment.

* 1 Year as Top Direct Sales Representative for Warner Cable Incorporated. Selected for special assignments in collections and customer relations in cable system upgrade conversion project.

Functional. Rose Montgomery, Fernandina, Florida.
No dates are given in this resume whose sections are separated by horizontal lines. Two-column format is appropriate for short statements about training and qualifications.

135

Resume of

John Mark Pauling

0000 E. Shore   Hometown, CA 00000
(000) 000-0000 Home   Work (000) 000-0000

WORK EXPERIENCE: KZZZ Television, Channel 6
                              NBC Affiliate
                              Hometown, California

1987 - Present   Director and Technical Director for commercial production and station
                              promotions productions.

1983 - 1987   Director and Technical Director for station's Evening News

1982 - 1983   Studio Crew (part-time)

1981 - 1982   KBBB Radio
                              3000 Bay View Drive
                              Shoals, California

                              Disc Jockey

MILITARY SERVICE: United States Navy
1974 - 1978   Photographer's Mate 3rd Class. Honorable Discharge

EDUCATION: 1973 Graduate Mountain View High School, Mountain View, California;
                              Completed 93 units of Broadcasting Major, University of San Francisco

ABILITIES: Director and graphics production for station, including newscasts and
                              station promotions. Voice over work for station promotions and sponsor
                              billboards, commercial productions and PSAs.

                              Equipment used: Chyron iNFiNiT!, Chyron IV with font compose and
                              auto display; Grass Valley and Bosch production switchers with effects
                              memories; Adda ESP II Still Store; NEC DVE System 10 digital effects
                              with curve/linear effects; 1", 3/4" and Beta video tape editing.

REFERENCES: Available upon request.

136

Combination (Before). *Susan B. Whitcomb, CPRW, Fresno, California.*
An undeveloped resume from a Creative Services person in the television industry. Small type
for a short resume makes the resume seem too short. It's the wrong kind of white space.

JOHN
MARK
PAULING

CAREER EMPHASIS

Over 10 years experience in Creative Services, including:

- Direction - Special Programs, News
- Production Management
- Pre- and Post-Production
- Station Promotions
- Electronic Graphic Design
- Voice-Over Work

PROFESSIONAL QUALIFICATIONS

- Extensive experience producing, directing, and editing, with an excellent record for on-time and on-budget.

- Leading creative talent in the market; implemented changes which subsequently became new standard for the area.

- Noted for ability to produce quality work with limited resources ... skilled at making videotape emulate film.

- Good communicator with writers, talent, crew, production, and post-production techs.

- Station resource for mastering new equipment and training studio crew.

EXPERIENCE SUMMARY

KZZZ Television, Channel 6 (NBC Affiliate)   1982-Present
Director/Technical Director -- commercial production and
    station promotions production (1987-Present)
Director/Technical Director -- Evening News (1983-1987)
Studio Crew (1982-1983)

KBBB Radio, Disc Jockey   1981-1982

PERSONAL PROFILE

- Solid work history ... frequently go above and beyond the call of duty in creativity and commitment.

- Complimented by station management for independently producing work volume normally accomplished by 1½-2 people.

- Popular with station's sales and promotions departments for ability to meet client demands and produce under pressure.

- Maintain composure under crisis ... timely sense of humor.

EDUCATION

Degree Program: BROADCASTING
University of San Francisco

EQUIPMENT

Chyron iNFiNiT!, Chyron IV with font compose and auto display; Grass Valley production switchers with effects memories; Beta video tape editing; much, much more.

CONTACT

(000) 000-0000 • 0000 E. Shore, Hometown, California 00000

Combination (After). Susan B. Whitcomb, CPRW, Fresno, California.
After development, the same resume displays better use of white space. Note that the size
of type is the same. The dual thick-and-thin vertical lines make the resume distinctive.

137

KENNETH BARLOW, Ph.D.

OBJECTIVE

A position requiring acute business insight, strong conceptual and people skills, within a rapidly expanding international business organization.

EXPERIENCE

MANAGEMENT

- Plan, develop and coordinate business strategic directions to maximize growth, profit, and return on investment for international markets.
- Manage and conduct product development activities of all hypoallergenic products.
- Ensure adherence to schedules in development projects.
- Develop, review and implement business plans.
- Manage and develop staff under MBO and Project Managing Systems.
- Direct major cost-reduction projects.

MARKETING

- Review and generate product features and differentiations to enhance business growth potentials.
- Conduct field trips to identify business/marketing deviations for individual markets and develop practical solutions.
- Review and approve advertising and promotional materials to comply with Corporate Policies and Guidelines.
- Design and develop product handbook and product sales training manuals to achieve marketing and sales objectives.
- Consolidate resources from operational and functional units in pursuit of new product launches, promotional campaigns to enhance competitive edge.
- Coordinate functional groups in launching new products.

TECHNOLOGY MANAGEMENT

- Act as liaison between Product Development and key worldwide flavor and suppliers.
- Establish technical alliances to maximize product development efficiencies for all professionals.
- Provide advice and consultation to all professionals in Product Development area.
- Involved in inspecting, qualifying and recommending contract manufacturers.
- Evaluate project requests to assess technical feasibility, manpower and time requirements.
- Develop nutritional products for global markets.
- Develop consumer food products for U. S. market.
- Coordinate product development activities with marketing and sensory evaluation personnel.
- Assist in setup of quality assurance programs.
- Provide technical assistance in pilot plant scale-ups and production start-ups.

138 **Combination. Teresa Collins, CPRW, Evansville, Indiana.**
Almost a full page is devoted to a list of activities grouped by three categories. With white space between the groups and in the left column, the page is visually balanced.

KENNETH BARLOW, Ph.D.

EMPLOYMENT MOUNT VERNON PRODUCTS, Evansville, Indiana
Senior Principal Investigator
    Product Development 4/90 - 12/91
Senior Manager
    International Business & Technology Development 7/88 - 3/90
Senior Research Scientist/Manager/Section Manager
    Product Development 5/71 - 6/88

HUNTINGTON, INC., Long Beach, California
Technologist 3/70 - 4/71

JOHNSON SEAFORTH, INC., Lexington, Kentucky
Research Scientist 10/68 - 3/70

EDUCATION LAVAL UNIVERSITY, Quebec, Canada
Ph.D. Food Science & Technology (Magna cum Laude) 1968
M.S. Food Science & Technology (Cum Laude) 1965

PURDUE UNIVERSITY, West Lafayette, Indiana
B.S. Chemistry 1961

SELECTED MANAGEMENT WORKSHOPS

Strategic Planning (AMA)
Effective Decision Making and Analytical Problem Solving (Kepner-Tregoe)
Managing Interpersonal Relationships (Wilson Learning)
Transfer Technologies from R&D to Manufacture (AMA)
Negotiation Skills
Time Management
Speechcraft
Boomerang - EEO
Delegation
Managing Personal Diversity

Fluent in **German** and **French**

PATENTS, PUBLICATIONS AND REFERENCES AVAILABLE UPON REQUEST

**7700 Clayton Court
Evansville, Indiana 47000
(812) 555-1212**

This page shows the extent of this person's work in product development. Notice that patents and publications are included in the references statement.

VIRGINIA C. MORRISON
4502 Belleville Place
Tampa, FL 00000
(000) 000-0000

CAREER OBJECTIVE

HEALTH CARE MANAGEMENT/ADMINISTRATOR

AREAS OF SPECIALIZATION

- Health Care Management
- Managed Patient Care
- Quality Assurance
- Protocols/Standard of Care
- Home Infusion Therapy
- Marketing/Sales Health Care Products and Services

- Neonatal Nursing
- Pediatric Nursing
- HIV/AIDS
- JCAHO Accreditation
- Home Health: Pediatric & Adult
- Neonatal/Pediatric Emergency Transport

EDUCATION

UNIVERSITY OF SOUTH FLORIDA, Tampa, Florida   1988
   MPH

UNIVERSITY OF TAMPA, Tampa, Florida   1986
   BSN

UNIVERSITY OF TAMPA, Tampa, Florida   1985-1986
   MBA Candidate

UNIVERSITY OF SOUTH FLORIDA, Tampa, Florida   1984
   BS

HILLSBOROUGH COMMUNITY COLLEGE, Tampa, Florida   1982
   A.A.

HILLSBOROUGH COMMUNITY COLLEGE, Tampa, Florida   1976
   A.S. Nursing

CONTINUING EDUCATION PROGRAMS

- AIDS Update • HIV Counseling • Drugs & Alcohol in the Workplace: Managing the Problem
- PICC Line Overview • PICC Lines: Principles, Insertion & Maintenance • Chemotherapy
- ECMO: Nursing Issues in Ecmology • Pediatric Case Management • Clotting Central Lines
- Managed Care and Case Management • Rehab Case Management • Pediatric IV Therapy
- Framework for Nursing Standards • Nursing Child Assessment Satellite Training • Pediatric Home Care

PROFESSIONAL NURSING LICENSURE/CERTIFICATIONS

- Florida: #0000000   • Georgia: #R100000

Chemotherapy Certification
PICC and Midline Catheter Insertion
NAACOG Certification - Neonatal Intensive Care
Pediatric Advanced Cardiac Life Support Certification
Neonatal Advanced Life Support - Instructor Certified
Neonatal Emergency Transport Certification
American Heart Association - Advanced Cardiac Life Support Certification

AWARDS

Who's Who In American Nursing
Nurse of the Year - Tampa General Hospital

139 ***Combination.** Diane McGoldrick, Tampa, Florida.*
Various formats break up this page into clusters. The Education section separates the two
sections with bullets. The centered material at the bottom matches the centered headings.

VIRGINIA C. MORRISON   **Page Two**

EXPERIENCE SUMMARY

Clinical: INTERIM HEALTHCARE, INC., Tampa, Florida   **1990-Present**
(Formerly Medical Personnel Pool)
    Branch Manager; Administrator   (1992-Present)
    Director of Health Care Services   (1990-1992)

PRESCRIBED PEDIATRIC EXTENDED CARE FACILITY, Tampa, Florida   **1989-1990**
    Per-Diem Staff Nurse

THE TAMPA GENERAL HOSPITAL, Tampa, Florida   **1976-1991**
    HIV Counselor   (1989-Present)
    Per-Diem Staff Nurse: PICU, Pediatrics and Newborn Nursery   (1989-1991)
    Relief House Supervisor   (1985-1990)
    Head Nurse: Neonatal Intensive Care, Intermediate Nursery and
                Newborn Nursery   (1979-1990)
    Coordinator: Neonatal/Pediatric Transport Program   (1980-1990)
    Neonatal Transport Nurse   (1977-1980)
    Charge Nurse: Neonatal Intensive Care Unit   (1978-1979)
    Staff Nurse: Neonatal Intensive Care Unit   (1976-1978)

Consultant
Services: Provided Consultant Services to various organizations (i.e., Critikon, Johnson & Johnson Company; Gesco, Inc.) on IV Infusion Devices; Pulse Oximetry, Non-Invasive Blood Pressure Monitoring; Neonatal/Pediatric Central Venous Access Devices. In conjunction with Herman Smith Associates (Hinsdale, Illinois), established a "Center for Excellence for Family Centered Care" and coordinated the "Design and Development of a 42-bed Neonatal Intensive Care Unit and 65-bed Newborn Nursery." Instrumental in implementing the "Design and Development of Infant Care Products" for Ohmeda Inc. (Columbia, Maryland) and the "Neonatal/Newborn Patient Classification Tool" for Chi Systems Inc. (Ann Arbor, Michigan).

Teaching: Conducted Educational Programs/Seminars involving subject matters such as: JCAHO Accreditation in Home Care; Enteral and Parenteral Nutrition in the Neonatal/Pediatric Patient; The Ventilated Patient in the Home; Universal Precautions and the Home Care Nurse; Neonatal Advanced Life Support; Improving Perinatal Outcomes; Managers of NICU's; and others.

Research
Involvement: Participated in research projects exploring "Noise Levels in NICU and its Effect on Weight Gain"; "Clinical Evaluation of the Createch Infant Apnea Monitor"; "Clinical Trials EXOSURF"; "Clinical Trials of the Jelco Catheter" and "Clinical Trials Dinamap Thermometry Study."

Publications: Coauthor of: *Pediatric TPN: Standard Techniques*, (1986) - Protocols of TPN Administration and CVC Maintenance. Collaborated the research and implementation of several other publicized Creative Works and Program Developments.

PROFESSIONAL ORGANIZATIONS

NAACOG	American Nurses Association
The National Association of Neonatal Nurses	COECHA
The Association for the Care of Children's Health	Case Management Society of Tampa Bay
IV Nurses Society (National & Gulfcoast Chapters)	Sun Coast Aids Network
Florida West Coast Case Management Study	Bay Area Pediatric Society
Local Interagency Community Collaboration Project	National Pediatric Society
Tampa AIDS Network (T.A.N.)	March of Dimes

References and Curriculum Vitae Available upon Request.

The information in the Experience Summary is easily accessed through the categories in the left column. Two columns accommodate all of the professional organizations listed.

MELANIE B. SIMON
447 Dodge Street
Riverside, Illinois 60006
(708) 000-0000

CAREER OBJECTIVE

To contribute to the effective management of the human resources department of a progressive organization.

EDUCATION

Bachelor of Arts degree in **Communication Studies** with an emphasis in **Business**, The University of Iowa, Iowa City, Iowa. May, 1991

Study Abroad Program, Tufts University, Boston, Massachusetts. Summer, 1990
　　Studied Anthropology and French at Le Prieurie, Annecy, France.

PROFESSIONAL EXPERIENCE

NEW ARCHERY PRODUCTS, INC., Berwyn, Illinois. Employee-oriented manufacturer of specialized archery accessories with sales in excess of $5,000,000.

Management Trainee - Summers and University breaks, 1981 to Present

Management
-- Cross-trained on all aspects of product assembly to ensure maximum product quality.
-- Brainstormed with management to develop ideas to increase employee productivity by reducing "task burnout."
-- Observed employee performance review process.

Customer Service
-- Resolved customer concerns to mutual satisfaction.
-- Verified credit history and references for prospective dealers/distributors.
-- Ensured accurate completion of shipping and receiving forms.

Marketing
-- Manned company booths during industry-wide international expositions.
-- Participated in decision-making process for new-product advertising campaign.

Administrative
-- Computed payroll for 40 employees using a commercial accounting ledger program.
-- Monitored A/R and A/P to avoid delinquent accounts or late charges.
-- Entered Lotus 1-2-3 data for "budget versus actual" reports.

WORK EXPERIENCE

Acquisitions Processor - Binding Department, Main Library, The University of Iowa, Iowa City, Iowa. January to May, 1990
 -- Prepared materials for shelving with identification markings and theft-prevention sensors.

Temporary Secretary - Manpower, Inc., Berwyn, Illinois. Summer, 1988
 -- Verified accuracy of purchase requisitions for Westlake Community Hospital.

ACTIVITIES

ALPHA DELTA PI SORORITY, Iowa City, Iowa. 1988 to 1991
 -- Volunteered time during various philanthropic activities including Ronald McDonald House and March of Dimes Association.

140 *Chronological. Elizabeth J. Axnix, CPRW, Iowa City, Iowa.*
This resume distinguishes between Professional Experience and Work Experience, with Professional Experience featured in four categories of activities.

4501 Bruenno Avenue   Alameda, CA 94000   415-000-0000   **LYNDE A. HARRIS**

PROFILE

A results-oriented self-starter with highly developed management skills, encompassing expertise in the following significant areas:

Food Service Management - Manage $1 million budget. Experienced in all aspects of providing nutritionally balanced menus.   Write innovative menus, plan and implement promotional events. Cater special functions. Open new accounts and facilities. Monitor balance between stock availability and need. Creative use of government commodities for school lunch program.

Human Resources Development/Management - Supervise 55 employees. Screen, hire, and train all personnel. Plan and conduct in-service training programs. Write performance objectives. Assess skill levels. Ensure conformity to company policies, established practices, and safety standards.

Facilities/Operations Management - Operate well in wide span of control, directing a variety of line/staff managers, personnel, and production facilities. Monitor expenditures and maintain pertinent inventory and payroll records. Assess needs and establish priorities. Control inventory, purchase equipment and supplies.

Personal Strengths - Strong communications skills. Interrelate well with people at all levels. Highly creative and adaptable to a variety of people and situations. Ability to motivate personnel to perform at top efficiency levels; to exercise prudent judgment in decision-making areas. Public Relations activities. Consulting.

PROFESSIONAL EXPERIENCE

SERVICE AMERICA CORPORATION   1984 to Present
A food service management company, contracts with businesses, schools, health care facilities, and hospitality industries to provide food service.

Mountain School District ,   Mountain Run, PA,   1990 to Present   **Food Service Director**
   Manage $1 million budget, providing food service for 8 schools, managing 55 employees, and delivering 3250 Type A meals a day. Oversee operations of 6 on-site kitchens and 2 satellite kitchens.
Litton County Community College,   Litton, PA, 1986 to 1990   **Food Service Director**
   Opened new account, establishing Cafeteria with staff of 8 permanent employees.
   • Increased catering services by 300%.
Falls Church Area School District,   Falls Church, PA, 1984 to 1986   **Food Service Director**
   Opened new account: 5 on-site kitchens, 4 satellite kitchens, staff of 45, enrollment 4,500.

CORNELL UNIVERSITY, FOOD SCIENCE, Ithaca, NY, 1982 to 1984   **Grad. Teaching/Research Asst.**

NORTHWESTERN UNIVERSITY, Evanston, IL 1979 to 1982   **Food Administrator I**

EDUCATION

CORNELL UNIVERSITY   Ithaca, NY   **Food Science graduate study; Nutrition minor**   1982 to 1984

INDIANA UNIVERSITY OF PENNSYLVANIA   Indiana, PA   1979
Bachelor of Science in Dietetics.   Second major: English.
• Summa cum laude   • Certificate for Outstanding Scholarship   • President of English Club

---

Martine Sommersby

3000 E. Pleasant Run Parkway
Indianapolis, IN 46000
(317) 000-0000

OBJECTIVE	A supervisory position with broad public contact with active participation in the planning and implementation of departmental policies and strategies.
SUMMARY of CAPABILITIES	Project management. Conduct thorough research to obtain data. Motivation of personnel to ensure work as scheduled. Preparation of conceptual & budgetary proposals. Generation of new source of revenues for the company. Negotiation of contracts. Coordination of correspondence & communication with foreign manufacturers. Marketing strategies and promotional techniques. Research of targeted markets. Creation of products that will broaden market appeal. Improvement of communications within and between departments. Hiring, training, managing, and assessment of staff. Bookkeeping, payroll, & general administrative duties. Supervision of a volunteer work force. Product research. Development a solid base of customers.
EXPERIENCE	**Project Supervisor.** Q.C. Inc., of Indianapolis, IN **Administrative Assistant.** Indiana Clinton/Gore Campaign, Indianapolis, IN **Business Administrator.** Tropicolors North America, Inc., Memphis, TN **Project Manager.** Stanton J. Groulnick Architect Associates, Springfield, IL **Project Manager.** Planit Studio, Springfield, IL **Interior Designer/Sales.** Jerry's Finishing Touch, St. Paul, MN **Interior Designer/Sales.** Skandia Interiors, Tallahassee, FL **Textile Designer/Business Assistant.** Bloomcraft Incorporated, New York, NY
EDUCATION	*Master of Science.* Florida State University, Tallahassee, FL *Bachelor of Arts.* Wesleyan University, Middletown, CT
SEMINARS in FIELD	International Trade Seminars, 1991 Marketing Strategies for Small Business, 1987 Finance for Women in Business, 1987 Small Business Start–up, 1987 Marketing, 1977
AFFILIATIONS	Woman in Management, Member American Association of University Women, Member International Student Association, Board Member
COMMUNITY SERVICE	Habitat for Humanity, Volunteer; Interpreter for Old State Capitol Building; Ronald McDonald House, Volunteer.

142 **Combination.** *Richard L. Schillen, Indianapolis, Indiana.*
Horizontal lines make the sections easy to recognize. The top horizontal line accentuates the inverted pyramid style for the name, address, and phone number. Original on elegant paper.

6014 N. 36th Drive • Phoenix, AZ • 85019
(602) 973-1744

WILLIAM F. MATTISON

OBJECTIVE: Management position in accounting field.

HIGHLIGHTS OF QUALIFICATIONS

- Creative in cutting costs and solving problems.
- Ability to prioritize, delegate and motivate.
- Confident and decisive under stressful conditions.
- Talent for picking the right people for the job.
- Highly effective in motivating and supervising employees.
- Firsthand experience with worldwide range of cultures.

PROFESSIONAL EXPERIENCE

Management
- Designed and implemented credit disbursement and recovery system for international office.
- Strengthened and improved acceptable policies and procedures for international agricultural firm in cooperation with headquarter officials, Bangladesh Bank and American private sector.
- Formulated credit policies and standards, and administered all company credit operations, domestically and abroad.
- Increased efficiency for accounting operations of 2,000-acre farming corporation and packing shed.

Supervision/Training
- Supervised, trained and developed Afghans and Bangladeshis in private enterprise system.
- Recruited and oversaw staffs of up to 50 people.
- Initiated and maintained relationships with customers, financial institutions, service agencies, credit organizations, attorneys and accountants.
- Maximized effectiveness and morale of staff by assigning tasks related to their interests and promoting teamwork rather than competitiveness.

Organizing/Record Keeping
- Forecasted cash flow, budgeted capital expenditures, audited computer reports and accounts receivables, submitted supporting income tax forms annually.
- Installed and operated IBM 36 computer and bridge software that streamlined accounting procedures and increased efficiency.
- Completely analyzed all balance sheet accounts on a monthly basis.
- Evaluated and reported on utilization of $55 million in project credit funds.

WORK HISTORY

1991-Present	**Accountant**	SMITTY'S MARKETS, Phoenix, AZ
1989-91	**Consultant**	TEMPORARY EMPLOYMENT AGENCIES, Phoenix, AZ
1987-89	**Credit Consultant**	BANGLADESH AGRICULTURAL DEVELOPMENT CORP., (BADC), Dhaka, Bangladesh
1986-87	**Credit Manager**	ARIZONA MILLWORK, Phoenix, AZ
1983-86	**Controller**	EL DORADO PACKING COMPANY, Indio, CA
1979-83	**Division Controller**	COACHELLA VALLEY TELEVISION, Palm Desert, CA
1978-79	**Controller**	CY MOURADICK AND SONS, INC., Thermal, CA
1976-77	**Controller**	WESTERN FARM SERVICE, Yuma, AZ
1975-76	**Credit Manager**	RELIANCE STEEL, Phoenix, AZ
1972-75	**Office Manager/ Personnel Director**	AFGHAN FERTILIZER COMPANY, Kabul, Afghanistan

EDUCATION

Business Administration
ARIZONA STATE UNIVERSITY, Tempe, Arizona

© THE WORDSMITH, Sallie Young, 1991

Combination. *Sallie Young, San Jose, California.*
Slanted shadow boxes are distinctive graphics in this resume. Notice, too, the small caps in the Work History. Categories for Professional Experience show major areas for an overview.

JOHN T. SMITH
8705 Shrank Drive
Independence, MO 64000
(816) 000-0000

OBJECTIVE

A challenging upper-management position with an organization that has philosophies centered around quality, customer-service and the belief that the people within the organization contribute to the success of the company.

ACCOMPLISHMENTS

❏ Developed an effective five-year plan in 1986 including justification of capital expenses of $750,000 and presented to senior management for approval. Several years later, these decisions have been the benchmark for the successful operation now in existence.

❏ Developed and implemented a "Quality Awareness Plan" which included: team concepts, empowerment, statistical process control, and continuous improvement. The success of the Department/Quality Plan was measured by pre-determined goals set at the beginning of each calendar year. Individual performance was duly noted; however, final rating for all associates was based on department performance.

❏ Successfully motivate and empower associates to make efficient decision-making skills.

❏ Utilized "Quality Action Team" concepts to determine appropriate software for supply unit of printing services.

WORK HISTORY

Manager Printing Services   Byer & Associates
January 1985 to Present   Kansas City, Kansas
- Initially was hired in a capacity to evaluate and assess the current printing department's effectiveness and made recommendations and necessary steps to achieve company goals—was then promoted to manager of printing services after three months.
- Implementation of profit/loss system in an effort to better focus the department printing direction.
- Oversee the total operation of the printing department.
- Manage four supervisors directly and 18 associates indirectly.
- Authorize all purchasing and vendor negotiating decisions made by supervisors.

Production Manager   ACD Corporation
September 1981 to January 1985   Kansas City, Missouri
Promoted from Pressman after two years.
- Billing
- Schedule production process
- Hiring and training
- Purchasing raw materials
- Bulk mailings United States Postal Service
- Operated two-color offset presses, multi-color stripping, platemaking, black and white line and half-tone photography, and bindery activities.

144 **Combination.** *Teresa Duey, Independence, Missouri.*
Shadow squares—used as bullets—direct attention to accomplishments. Narrow left and right margins are offset by considerable white space in the left column for the side headings.

JOHN T. SMITH

8705 Shrank Drive
Independence, MO 64000
(816) 000-0000

WORK HISTORY (Cont.)

Pressman/Bindery   BCR Services
September 1979 to August 1981   Kansas City, Missouri
• Operated two-color offset press and bindery work.

Pressman/Bindery   Quick Press
April 1978 to September 1979   Kansas City, Kansas
• Operated two-color offset press and bindery work.

EDUCATION

B.S. in Business Management
University of Missouri-Kansas City, 1977

Kansas City Vocational Technical Center
Graphic Arts Certificate

SEMINARS

NAPL Top Management Conference, 1992 & 1993
1991 Graph Expo/Desktop Publishing

PERSONAL SUMMARY

Believing in team concepts; one-on-one coaching with direct and indirect associates—the developing of potential leadership candidates; utilization of the empowerment process and the willingness to live with all end results; managing all financial resources to ensure the operation provides customers with a quality, timely, cost-effective end product that align with the company business needs.

In the Work History, placing company names at the right margin gives prominence to the person's positions and shows the progress from pressman to manager of printing services.

MARY SMITH
1212 Easy Street
Some City, California 91212
777/555-1212

Profile: Presenting 10+ years of diversified *Advertising/Public Relations* experience:

Demonstrating award-winning skills in:

- Print, electronic & direct marketing

- Local, regional, national & international publicity campaigns

- Producing events, themed promotions & convention exhibits

For clients* in the following fields/industries:

- Entertainment

- Retail - Corporate - Professional - Healthcare

- Restaurants - Hotels - Nightclubs

Career History:

Owner/Manager - **Mary Smith & Associates, Some City, CA (1980 to present)**

Develop and implement detailed marketing plans including target markets, budgets ($50,000 to $1.5 million), and timelines.

Utilize extensive local, national and international media contacts to ensure mass market exposure.   Generate specialized mailing lists for direct-mail campaigns.

Create logos, copy and collateral materials to support advertising and marketing campaigns.   Source and monitor vendors for costs, quality and adherence to deadlines.

Research and screen special events and national conferences for best participation opportunities.   Handle staffing and logistical arrangements for each event.

Awards: Award of Excellence - Some Big Corporation Identity Package.

Maxi Award - Marketing Package - Some City Mall.

National Marketing Award - Consumer Market Network package.

Other: *Client list, references and extensive portfolio available at interview.

145

Combination. *Nita Busby, CPRW, Placentia, California.*
The first of two resumes that are identical except for the middle section. The Career History of this "40 hours per week" resume shows what the person does from 9 to 5 for a living.

MARY SMITH
1212 Easy Street
Some City, California 91212
777/555-1212

Profile: Presenting 10+ years of diversified *Advertising/Public Relations* experience:

Demonstrating award-winning skills in:

For clients* in the following fields/industries:

- Print, electronic & direct marketing
- Local, regional, national & international publicity campaigns
- Producing events, themed promotions & convention exhibits

- Entertainment
- Retail - Corporate - Professional - Healthcare
- Restaurants - Hotels - Nightclubs

Career History:

    Owner/Manager - **Mary Smith & Associates, Some City, CA (1980 to present)**

Achievements:

Center for Gynecology Problems - patient numbers increased by 300 in two years.

Consumer Market Network - increased revenues 10% in first year.

Some Hospital - reduced *Yellow Pages* advertising by $120,00 per year.

Emergency Service Office   - in 12 weeks increased weekly patient registration by 100%.

Big Performer - conducted international promotional activities for his #1 hit, "The Something of My Life."

American Performance Awards - handled complete public relations activities for foundation benefit and celebrity auction.

Awards: Award of Excellence - Some Big Corporation Identity Package.

Maxi Award - Marketing Package - Some City Mall.

National Marketing Award - Consumer Market Network package.

Other: *Client list, references and extensive portfolio available at interview.

Combination. *Nita Busby, CPRW, Placentia, California.*
The second of the two nearly identical resumes. The Achievements section of this "20 hours per week" resume shows the results of certain efforts during the work week.

146

Sally Larce
8978 Sunset Drive, #978
San Jose, CA 95000
(408) 000-0000

OBJECTIVE:

Report, analyze and preserve medical records information using health information technology.

SUMMARY OF QUALIFICATIONS:

- Four years experience in software quality assurance configuration management.
- Eight years experience with relational database management using INGRES.
- Ability to complete multiple projects on schedule.
- Detail-oriented and adaptive to new systems.
- Excellent analytical and organizational skills.

RELEVANT EXPERIENCE AND ACCOMPLISHMENTS:

TECHNICAL

- Compiled, linked and assembled 20 software configurations in C, JOVIAL and FORTRAN to facilitate development and testing.
- Assisted 40 software engineers with debugging software configurations.
- Oversaw installation of network software between a subcontractor and prime contractor. Estimated savings for company $100,000+.
- Set up a database system to track global software configuration items.
- Developed graphics for configuration control board requirements presentations.
- Trained various staff members to use VAX computer system.

ADMINISTRATIVE

- Received, released, controlled and closed 20 software configurations using both manual and automated methods.
- Performed audits of magnetic media, procedures, computer accounts and baselined configurations to ensure government compliance.
- Wrote contract letters and procedures for software configuration functions.
- Prioritized and delegated configuration management work to three analysts.
- Total quality management team member that studied improvement of software turnover process between Software Engineering and Software Quality Assurance.

EMPLOYMENT HISTORY:

1982 - present	**General Space,** Sunnyvale, CA *Software Configuration Management Analyst*
1979 - 1982	**Dynamic Systems,** San Diego, CA *Administrative Assistant*
1976 - 1979	**Saddle Park,** Washington, DC *Secretary*

147

Combination. *Gary Watkins, San Jose, California.*
A resume that shows the value of boldfacing for directing the eye. It moves from the name at the top of the page, down the major side headings to the company names at the bottom.

Sally Larce
page two

COMPUTER PROFICIENCY:

VAX/VMS, IBM, Macintosh, UNIX, INGRES

AFFILIATIONS:

IEEE Computer Society, New York, NY
Career Action Center, Palo Alto, CA
The Commonwealth Club, San Francisco, CA

EDUCATION AND RELEVANT TRAINING:

Certificate, Project Management, ECD, UC Santa Cruz Extension, Santa Cruz, CA   1993
- System Engineering
- Risk Management
- Software Development Process

Certificate, First Line Supervisor Program (two-year program), LMSC Mgmt. Assoc.   1987
       Sunnyvale, CA

AA, Office Administration, Strayer College, Washington, DC   1979

Additional Courses: Medical Terminology
                         ICD-9-CM and CPT
                         Systems Analysis and Design
                         Database Management
                         Data Communications
                         Introduction to Statistical Analysis System (SAS)

The subheadings for Relevant Experience and Accomplishments provide an important focus for grouping achievements. Although it is short, page 2 is indispensable for a full picture.

DIANA MOSS

908 Crestview Court • Freehold, New Jersey 07000 • (908) 000-0000

OBJECTIVE

An administrative position in the area of rehabilitation/geriatric health care utilizing my knowledge of clinical, community, and patient services.

SUMMARY OF QUALIFICATIONS

Increasing responsibilities in areas including:

- Medical Rehabilitative Services
- Speech and Language Pathology
- Contract Sales

- Rehabilitative Marketing Services
- Treatment Coordinator and Liaison
- Public Relations

PROFESSIONAL ACCOMPLISHMENTS

Administration

- Supervised treatment programs at numerous skilled nursing facilities throughout the states of New Jersey and Pennsylvania.

- As Clinical Coordinator for PermaCare, responsible for direct patient care, planning, patient and family counseling.

- In charge of Medicare documentation lending to reimbursement for each facility. Assist in budgeting for rehabilitative services.

- Plan restorative nursing programs and provide consultation to appropriate agencies.

- Write program goals.

- CFY supervision.

Speech and Language Pathology

- Responsible for patient identification, evaluation, case consultations, goal setting, and direct care.

- Receive referrals from within the facility and from outside referring agencies.

- Conduct public and private speech-language, and hearing screenings. Involved in public education of communication disorders; knowledge of OBRA regulations.

Sales/Marketing/Public Relations

- Work with patients, families, and community agencies. Communicate facility's services; advertise availability and quality of services.

- Perform public relations functions in both corporate and hospital environments.

148

Combination. Beverly Baskin, CPRW, Marlboro, New Jersey.
An administrative position is the objective, so administrative accomplishments are put first, and administrative experiences are indicated first on page 2.

DIANA MOSS

Page 2

ADMINISTRATIVE EXPERIENCE

PERMACARE, INC., *Corporate Headquarters* King of Prussia, PA

Clinical Coordinator, Speech Language Pathology 1992-Present

CENTRAL JERSEY REHABILITATION AND HEALTH CARE CENTER, Lakewood, NJ

Director, Speech Language Pathology 1992

SPEECH AND LANGUAGE PATHOLOGY SERVICES

AUDIOTECH ASSOCIATES, Freehold, NJ 1985-1992

MCOSS, Edison, NJ 1984-1985

WOODBRIDGE CONVACENTER, Woodbridge, NJ 1980-1985

MONROE PUBLIC SCHOOL, Monroe, NJ 1982-1984

ABERDEEN PUBLIC SCHOOL, Aberdeen, NJ 1982-1984

OLD BRIDGE MEDICAL CENTER, Old Bridge, NJ 1973-1982

LICENSES AND CERTIFICATIONS

CCC, American Speech and Hearing Association

License, Speech-Language Pathology, State of New Jersey

License, Speech and Hearing Handicapped, State of New York

License, Speech Correction, State of Pennsylvania

Affiliated with National and State Professional Associations

EDUCATION

HOFSTRA UNIVERSITY, Hemstead, New York

Master of Arts, Speech Pathology

Bachelor of Arts, Speech and Hearing Handicapped

Excellent References Furnished upon Request

A set of dual lines, part of a pair enclosing the address and phone number at the top of page 1, is used as part of a header on page 2. Note the use of uppercase on page 2.

Johanna Breitmorgan

6110 Sneckner Court
Morro Bay, California 90000
Telephone (213) 000-0000

Experience and education have provided detailed working knowledge of these key areas:

Financial Services	**Business Strategies**
Organization Development	**Customer Service**
Program Development	**Staffing & Training**
New Product Introductions	**Employee-Community Relations**

Highly motivated, results-oriented business professional with sixteen years of progressive accomplishments. Highly effective leadership skills, with an established track record of achievements. Fluent in French, German and English.

CRÉDITE INTERNATIONALE   Morro Bay, California   1977 - Present
Have played key roles in managing change, building organizations, and working with senior management throughout this financial services organization that has 300 million cardholders in 240 countries and sales of $500 billion.

Director - Management Communications 1989 - Present
Partnering with the president and senior management of this 2,500-employee organization, created and launched programs for an executive speaker's bureau, employee communications, and community relations.

- Aggressively capitalized on opportunities and doubled the first year's number of speeches given by executive management; grew the total fourfold within three years.
- Developed and introduced a successful speech-merchandising program that, through press releases, op-ed articles, and reprints, delivered a strengthened image of Crédite as an industry leader.
- Developed a community relations program that made grant money available to nonprofit organizations in which Crédite employees were working as volunteers.
- Recruited and worked closely with some 10 external speech writers.
- Planned and directed a complete redesign of the employee newsletter from improved graphics to an editorial planning calendar to meet the needs of multiple levels of management and staff.

Executive Assistant to the COO 1988 - 89
Proactively identified several significant corporate issues and, working with senior managers, developed plans to effect improvement.

- Resolved a growing problem of compliance between merchants and banks issuing the Crédite card.
- Revamped an outmoded mailing system to ensure prompt delivery of important communications to banks.
- Prepared new policy and guidelines for employees to communicate with customers.

Director - Member Services 1985 - 88
Called in to manage a troubled, 35-employee unit that had an operating budget of $2 million and supported 80 major data centers, representing 1,500 banks, in the Western U.S. and Asia-Pacific.

- Restored high level of morale to the unit and reduced turnover to near zero.
- Managed and oversaw two complete changeovers in system software that enhanced productivity.

Earlier in member services (1981-85), presented trainings and seminars in the U.S. and Asia to enhance effectiveness and profitability of Crédite's computer systems.

Operations Coordinator 1979 - 81
Championed the development of an Fast-Pay Refund System when Crédite introduced travelers checks in 1982 and played a vital part in the worldwide implementation as liaison between the business unit and operations center.

Joined the company in Strasbourg, France, in 1977.

BA Degree - Psychology
STANFORD UNIVERSITY   California

149
***Combination.** Ted Bache, Palo Alto, California.*
A resume that displays the progressive 16-year rise of an individual within the same company. Activities move from revamping company systems to improving corporate communications.

555•123•4567

JON Q. PUBLIC
123 Main Street
Anytown, USA 12345

OBJECTIVE
*To work for a well-established construction firm in the South Bay
to Monterey area as Construction Foreman/Project Manager.*

SUMMARY OF QUALIFICATIONS

- Self-employed nine years in construction industry
- Fifteen years experience in construction-related fields
- Demonstrated record of customer commitment
- Continually reading to stay on cutting edge of industry
- Responsible for the training and supervision of personnel for two years

RELEVANT SKILLS

- Plan take-off and cost estimating
- Extensive knowledge in reading blueprints
- Experience dealing with permits and inspections
- Construct and remodel residential wood structures
- Foundation and form work
- Spec home completion
- Tile-setting, glass block and custom cabinetry

EMPLOYMENT HISTORY

Self-Employed, 1983-present
Tile Setter/General Contractor

Many of the bids I secure require multiple skills to accomplish. I've dealt with subcontractors, coordinating schedules for the completion of a task. I am highly organized and have worked extensively with estimating and ordering various materials to the jobsite for an efficient operation.

- Willing to relocate, temporary or permanent, for job or company requirements
- Willing to work weekends and overtime as needed
- Wages negotiable
- References available upon request

Combination. Elaine Jackson, Boulder Creek, California.
An unusual border arrangement makes this resume unique. Notice the placement of the
phone number and the oblique left-alignment of the name and address.

150

Peter W. Canfield

30000 Lyndale Road • St. Louis, Missouri 63000 • (315) 555-5555

Summary

Experienced, degreed Construction Project Manager with 14 years experience in maintenance, building, and manufacturing construction seeks continued employment as **Construction Project Manager**. Technical expertise in all phases of project management from preparation of contruction documents to completion of construction. Competent, reliable, and committed professional, with proven record of success in assuming increasing levels of responsibility.

Highlights of Qualifications

- Excellent presentation and communication skills; demonstrate clear and professional manner with crew, contractors, management, and clients.
- Skilled at maintaining a balanced, objective viewpoint during contract negotiations and in addressing problems.
- Maintain 95% or higher success rate for completing construction projects within budget and on time.
- Enjoy challenge of new projects and handling several priorities at once.

Experience & Selected Accomplishments

Project Management

- Supervise various trades on direct hire projects at different project phases, including slab on grade, asphalt, foundations, underground piping/electrical, structural steel, roofing, process piping, fire protection, and HVAC.
- Manage mechanical quality control of $60 million medium-security federal correctional institution and a minimum security prison camp consisting of 25 buildings on a 208-acre site for U.S. Department of Justice.
- Oversee mechanical contract administration, cost estimating, change order negotiation, CPM scheduling review, and coordination and resolution of field problems between contractors and architect/engineer.
- Managed multiple projects at different stages of completion to upgrade facilities or install production equipment.
- Review design and constructability of projects, including preparation of construction documents, contractor selection, bidding, budget and cost, scheduling, invoicing, coordination, change order approval and negotiation, daily project administration throughout substantial completion, punch list, start-up and turnover for numerous construction projects.
- Provided electrical and mechanical designs for installation in office, manufacturing, and industrial facilities.

Combination. *Carla L. Culp, CPRW, Edwardsville, Illinois.*
A substantial resume. The Summary includes an objective statement, and the Highlights of Qualifications section displays enthusiasm—a component often missing in resumes.

Peter W. Canfield 2

Employment History

Mechanical Inspector • 1992-Present
ABC Construction, Chicago, Illinois

Project Manager Construction • 1986-1992
ACME Construction, St. Louis, Missouri

Maintenance Design Engineer • 1979-1986
ACME Construction Corporation, St. Louis, Missouri

Education

B.S. Industrial Technology
Southern Illinois University at Carbondale, Carbondale, Illinois

A.S. Construction Management Technology
Belleville Area College, Belleville, Illinois

References

Personal and professional references available upon request.

The thick-and-thin dual lines at the top of page 1 are part of the header for pages 2 and 3.
The writer preferred to put this information on page 2 rather than squeeze it on page 1.

Peter W. Canfield

30000 Lyndale Road • St. Louis, Missouri 63000 • (315) 555-5555

PROJECT ADDENDUM

Project	Location	Date	Cost
A-6 Weapon System Trainer	Oceana Naval Air Station Oceana, Virginia	August-October 1992	$100K
• Installation of structures, primary power, HVAC, and equipment.			
F-14 Mission Flight Trainer	Mirimar Naval Station San Diego, California	November 1991- January 1992	$150K
• Installation of primary power, HVAC, and equipment.			
F-14 Weapon System Trainer	Mirimar Naval Air Station San Diego, California	April-August 1991	$1M
• Installation of dual trainers, including primary power, HVAC, structural platforms, projector and cock pit installation, computer rooms, fire protection, and equipment.			
Repair and Replace Aluminum and Titanium Process Line	Building 27 St. Louis, Missouri	October 1990- January 1991	$1.2M
• Removal of entire process line to replace timber tank supports. Process piping, compressed air, steam, exhaust systems, and walkways. All work completed in hazardous environment, i.e., nitric acid, hydrofluoric acid, potassium dichromate, and sulfuric acid.			
Relocate T-45 Goshawk Final Assembly	Palmdale, California to St. Louis Missouri	November 1989- January 1990	$750K
Remove 10,000-ton Forming Press	St. Louis, Missouri	September 1989	$100K
Re-roof Buildings	St. Louis, Missouri	April-July 1989	$800K
• Tear off, build-up, and install 2-ply modified Bitumen.			
Install New Tool Coolant System	St. Louis, Missouri	January 1989	$350K
• Installed approximately 2 miles of PVC piping within one manufacturing building to distribute coolant to several milling machines.			
Repair Steam Room/Asbestos Abatement	St. Louis, Missouri	January 1989	$100K
Align and Repair Overhead Crane System	St. Louis, Missouri	August-December 1988	$100K

The stature of this resume becomes fully evident in this impressive Project Addendum. Although this table is complex, thick horizontal lines make the sections easy to identify.

DONALD A. JONES

2000 Baywatch Boulevard
Treasure Island, FL 30000
(813) 000-0000

SENIOR FACILITIES/PROPERTY MANAGEMENT PROFESSIONAL

SUMMARY OF QUALIFICATIONS

- Innovative, results-oriented **Senior Management Professional** with over 11 years of solid experience in progressively responsible positions, and proven achievements in all aspects of Facilities and Property Management.

- Assimilation of company goals/objectives involving the analysis and administration of operational procedures, annual budgets, and future projections.

- Extremely focused on identifying potential problem areas, minimizing issues, formulating and executing competent solutions.

- Demonstrated expertise in strategic planning, organizational development, team building, and staff enhancement.

- Excellent communication, leadership, negotiation, troubleshooting and motivation skills that effectively interact with staff, internal clients, community leaders, and executive management.

- Team Player with the ability to consistently provide high-level, systematic standards of performance.

PROFESSIONAL EXPERIENCE

DATA SERVICES, Tampa, FL   **4/85 - Present**
Facilities Manager
Responsibilities:

- Directly accountable for the administration of an annual capital budget ($3M to $15M) and annual expense budget ($15.5M) for all Corporate Headquarters and South Area properties, combined with overseeing physical assets of buildings ($100M+) and the environmental protection of computer hardware ($200M+).

- Efficiently and economically maintain all owned and leased buildings and ensure compliance with all applicable local, state, and federal regulations, including OSHA requirements. Analyze expansion, renovation and move plans, together with proposed changes in city or county ordinances that impact operational costs.

- Manage and direct an in-house staff of 28 personnel, 25 full-time outside contractors, and more than 100 outside contracted service vendors.

- Coordinate and establish the development of policies, procedures and standards consistent with providing optimum service to a customer group of 3,500+ employees. Routinely monitor all safety policies, and research and evaluate effectiveness of any required changes.

- Oversee preventive maintenance activities for all support facilities, review established schedules, and reinforce presence of competent supervision for each activity.

Achievements:

- Coordinated opening of new data center/office complex totalling over 1 million sq. ft. Data Center consists of 100,000+ sq. ft. of raised floor computer space.

- Gained extensive benchmarking experience with companies in similar industries. Travelled to multiple sites conducting interviews and establishing a network of industry peers to create on-going exchange of information. Authored summary report distributed to Executive Management.

- Initiated training procedures for upgrading customer service standards. Devised "pro-active" approach enforced by frequent customer visits to verify quality assurance. Originated survey forms to obtain customers' comments and monitor efficiency levels.

Combination. *Diane McGoldrick, Tampa, Florida.*
Extra attention is given to the current position by distinguishing between Responsibilities and Achievements and providing paragraphs for each category. Square bullets have extra weight.

DONALD A. JONES   **Page Two**

- Defined need for automated work order system. Conducted screening selection of vendors for software development to institute a tailored work order/request system for the entire department.

- Developed 24-hour emergency response service for all facilities and related service activities.

- Instrumental in structuring implementation of several programs in support of OSHA standards (e.g. Lock-Out/Tag-Out, Hazardous Communications, etc.) and overseeing compliance with the ADA (Americans with Disabilities Act).

PARADOX CORPORATION, Largo, Florida   **1/83 - 3/85**
Facilities Engineering Project Manager

As Facilities Planning Engineer, responsibilities included design and layout of office space for on-site and field office. Promoted to Project Manager – accountable for all phases of office construction and moves including preliminary research and design, cost estimating, project approval, scheduling, bidding, and supervision of all contractors from conception to completion. Structured the implementation of a Computer-Aided Design and Drafting System (CADD) including instructional training on use of system.

BOAT CRAFT CORP., Sarasota, Florida   **3/82 - 11/82**
Industrial Engineer

Managed all industrial engineering functions, together with four production facilities in Florida. Reported directly to Vice President of Manufacturing Services. Conducted: Cost Studies, Cost Reduction Projects, Plant/Office Layout, Process Analyses, Determination of Standard Hour Assignments per Department. Directly supervised and coordinated $3.5 million expansion of Sarasota facilities.

PEARSON COMPANY, Cincinnati, Ohio   **6/79 - 3/82**
Industrial Engineer Coordinator

Began as co-op student engineer. Upon completion of co-op program, hired as full-time Industrial Engineer. Promoted to Industrial Engineer Coordinator. Interacted with Product Development, Manufacturing Engineering, Quality Assurance and Marketing Communications Departments. Functions included: Time Studies, Cost Studies, Methods Analyses, Plant/Office Layout, Package Design, Supervision of three Shop Technicians.

EDUCATION

UNIVERSITY OF TAMPA, Tampa, Florida
Master's Degree Courses - Business Administration

UNIVERSITY OF CINCINNATI, Cincinnati, Ohio
College of Design, Architecture and Art - Graduated June, 1981
Bachelor of Science Degree - Industrial Design
(Five-Year Professional Practice Program)

PROFESSIONAL EDUCATION/SEMINARS

- Achieving Results in a Changing Environment
- Managing Innovation and Change
- Advanced Management Education
- Computer-Aided Design Operation
- Indoor Air Quality for Facility Managers
- Data Center Management
- Organizational Leadership I & II

AFFILIATIONS/MEMBERSHIPS

BOMA - Building Owners & Managers Association
IFMA - International Facilities Managers Association
AIPE - American Institute of Plant Engineers

Uppercase is used consistently for company names, and positions are in boldface. Center-justification in the Education and Affiliations sections provides visual relief from paragraphs.

Professional Service Resumes at a Glance

G. MATHEW COLLINS

Height	5'11"
Weight	160
Hair	Red
Eyes	Blue

Present:
123 W. 30th
New York, NY 10000
(212) 555-5555

Permanent:
2001 Bridger Rd
Evansville, IN 47000
(812) 555-5555

TRAINING

BFA-Musical Theatre
University of Concord College-Conservatory of Music

Acting: Diane Kvapil, Alan Arkin
      Jeff Corey, Meisner Technique
Voice: Mary Henderson, Phillip Ewart

Vocal Coaching: Terry LaBolt, Phil Kern,
      Jeff Saver
Dance: James Truitte - Modern
      Diane Lala - Jazz

PROFESSIONAL THEATRE

• Evita	Che	New Monterey Theatre, New Monterey, MA
• Man of La Mancha	Don Quixote	Long Winter Nights, Concord, OH
• Forum	Marcus Lycus	HSN
• Gail Warnings	Joseph	Cape Park/Columbia Playhouse
• Pirates of Penzance	Samuel	Southwest Montana Opera

UNIVERSITY MUSICAL THEATRE

• Company	Bobby	University of Concord College Conservatory of Music
• Chess	American	UC, CCM
• Carousel	Jigger	UC, CCM
• Working	Mason, Gas Man, Hippie, Executive	UC, CCM
• Kiss Me Kate	Harrison Howell	UC, CCM
• Two Gents. of Verona	Eglamour	UC, CCM
• Candide	Voltaire, Pengloss, Governor	Indiana University

UNIVERSITY THEATRE

• Crucible	Governor Danforth	UC, CCM
• One For The Road	Nicolas	UC, CCM
• Zoo Story	Jerry	ISU
• Romeo and Juliet	Mercutio	ISU

SPECIAL SKILLS: Guitar • Football and Baseball • Historian • Cabaret • Studio Vocalist

Functional. Teresa Collins, CPRW, Evansville, Indiana.
Height, weight, and color of hair and eyes—important for casting a play, musical, or opera—
are put first. Information about training and experience are visually united in the shaded box.

153

Madd Maxx Hammer

7777 Greenville Avenue
Dallas, Texas 75231   (214) 555-3143

Professional Experience

Air Talent
KEGL, Dallas, Texas   1993 to Present
• Air talent, personal appearances and production.
Afternoon Drive Personality/Music Director
Satellite Music Network, Z-Rock, Dallas, Texas 1986 to 1993
• Broadcast via satellite to markets such as New York City, Phoenix, Chicago, Dallas, Houston, Miami, New Orleans, Denver, Portland, Cleveland, Seattle, Providence, Kansas City, Honolulu and San Diego.
• Host the world's only weekly live syndicated hard rock countdown show, THE Z-ROCK 50, heard in 23 major markets in the United States, as well as in England on Beacon Radio and GWR Radio, and in Russia, in Leningrad and Moscow, on Europa Radio.
• Conduct live on-air in-studio interviews with performing artists such as Poison, Motley Crüe, Metallica, Anthrax, Ozzy Osbourne, Alice Cooper Band, Megadeth, David Coverdale, Guns'n'Roses, Iggy Pop, Skid Row and Slaughter.
• Travelled to Z-Rock affiliate cities for personal appearances and live remote broadcasts.
• Hosted the Metallica Album Listening Party in Madison Square Garden in 1991.
• Broadcasted live from Foundation Forum '91 and the R&R Convention 1990 in Los Angeles, and the 1989 NAB Convention in New Orleans.
• MC major concerts, including Metallica, Queensryche, and the Kiss-Winger-Slaughter concert at Madison Square Garden in November 1990.
• Hosted live remote concert broadcasts featuring major rock acts; conducted pre- and post-concert interviews with performing artists.
• Select new music; introduce new artists; supervise music research; and organize weekly playlist.

CHR Music Director/Afternoon Drive Personality
Buck Owens Production Co., Inc., KKXX, Bakersfield, CA 1983 to 1986
• Rotated new music; broke new artists; reviewed music research; put together weekly playlist.
• Three-time R&R CHR PM Drive Dominator under the name Dave Kamper.

Career Highlights

• Awarded seven platinum records in appreciation for recognizing talents before their time: Motley Crüe/*Shout at the Devil*; Ratt/*Out of the Cellar*; Twisted Sister/*Stay Hungry*; Poison/*Look What the Cat Dragged In*; Guns'n'Roses/*Appetite for Destruction*; Skid Row/*Skid Row*; and Extreme/*Porno Graffitti*.
• Also awarded four gold records: Anthrax/*I'm the Man*; Britany Fox/*Britany Fox*; Megadeth/*Rust in Peace*; and Pantera/*Vulgar Display of Power*.
• Founder and editor of Heavy Metal Radio Newsletter, a publication years before its time.
• Performed live on stage with major acts such as Warrant, Firehouse, Trixter, L.A. Guns and Pantera.
• Hosted the Metallica Album Listening Party in Madison Square Garden, New York City, in 1991.

Other Related Experience

• Hosted video music shows on Dallas Music Video.
• Developed extensive background in news, sports and talk radio as news director, sports reporter and live talk show host.

• • • • • • • • • • • • •

Intangible Qualities

• Proven ability to consistently achieve high ratings.
• Knack for recognizing hit bands, artists and music before their time.
• Ability to communicate easily with a wide range of people.
• Reliable, timely, innovative.
• 18 years' broadcast experience.

154 ***Combination.*** *Sallie Young, San Jose, California.*
Four overlapping 3-D boxes, extended visually to four different vanishing points on three different horizons explains the wild design of this personality-matching resume. Truly unique.

Arlene C. Smith

MAKEUP ARTISTRY
CONCEPT THROUGH DESIGN

1(800) 000-0000

Coast-to-Coast Coverage!
California, Florida, North Carolina

FILMS AND TELEVISION

Where the Dead Are
Twilight Zone Movie
Stars: Patrick Bergin, Jack Palance

In My Daughter's Name
Overruled Productions
Stars: Donna Mills, Lee Grant

Race Day
TNN Motor Sports
5 TV Episodes

Tom Smith Interviews
Capitol Satellite & FLTV

Country Hitkickers
Halloween Special
Fox Television

Candlelight
Sound Rep Group

Callia
Steele Films, Inc.

Bikini Summer II
PM Entertainment
Stars: Jessica Hahn, Jeff Conaway

Outside
Panoptikon Films
Stars: Alex Courtney, Bill Dunlevy

Sunset Strip
PM Entertainment
Starring: Jeff Conaway

Unbecoming Age
Ringlevision
Stars: Diane Salinger, Colleen Camp

**Free Aspirin and
Tender Sympathies**
Lopes Productions
Starring: Efrain Figueroa

COMMERCIALS AND INFOMERCIALS

WESTERN AUTO
4 Commercials
Avatar Group Int.

FOOD LION
24 Commercials
Avartar Group Int.

BRENDLE'S
3 Commercials
Avatar Group Int.

VLASIC PICKLES
Commercial
MC Group

OSCAR MAYER
Commercial
MC Group

TWILIGHT ZONE
Commercial
Steele Films, Inc.

LEVIS
Commercial
Burton Pierce Co.

DALIPRINTS
Commercial
2M Productions

CHARLOTTE AD CLUB
2 PSA's
Doggett Advertising

CUB FOODS
8 Commercials
Avatar Group Int.

JOHNSON & JOHNSON
Commercial
Avatar Group Int.

LEGGETT'S
3 Commercials
Archdale Advertising

WHEELS RACING
Commercial
Avatar Group Int.

BELK
9 Commercials
Wildwood Prod.

LA Z BOY
3 Commercials
Peter Corbett & Company

ALL DATA
Commercial
2M Productions

METROLINA EXPO
3 Commercials
Avatar Group Int.

FOOD LION RESPONSE
Infomercial
FLTV

BURGER KING
6 Commercials
Even the Bigger
Picture Prod.

SOMINEX
5 Commercials
Whitewater Productions

WATSON INSURANCE CO.
Commercial
Avatar Group Int.

LEGAL BRIEFS
2 Commercials
Avatar Group Int.

COMMUNITY CASH
5 Commercials
Avatar Group Int.

NBA AUTHENTICS
Commercial
NBA Entertainment

HAVOLINE OIL
2 Commercials
Crash Films, Inc.

LEGGETT'S
4 Commercials
Tularosa Film Co.

GRAND PIANO & FURNITURE CO.
4 Commercials
Boulevard Films

SOMINEX
2 Infomercials
Whitewater Prod.

REFUND AMERICA
Commercial
Avatar Group Int.

INSTRUCTION, INDUSTRIAL and PROMOTIONAL VIDEOS

Refund America
Promotional
Avatar Group Int.

General Motors
Promotional
Parallel Productions

Wix-Dana Corporation
Corporate / Promotional
Thirty's Film & Tape

Club Armageddon
Promotional Video
Marlis Seefe
Productions

The Hampton Zone II
Industrial Video
SBL Vision Merchants

TRAINING AND REFERENCES
The Institute of Studio Makeup, Ltd.
James Brown, President (555) 555-5555

Tim Brown	Panoptikon Films	(555) 555-4444
Jim Ross	Makeup Artist	(555) 555-5553
Victor Long	Avatar Group Int.	(555) 555-2222

Motion Picture ★ Video ★ Television ★ Prosthetics ★ Beauty ★ Horror ★ Special Effects

---

Functional. Rose Montgomery, Fernandina, Florida.
A resume that looks like an ad for this experienced makeup artist. Experience is not only grouped by categories but also placed in boxes.

155

PERSONAL

Sarah Smith
1212 Easy Street
Some City, CA 90000
(123) 444-1212

WORK EXPERIENCE

INTERIOR DESIGN

Independent - 1988
Accomplishments:
Converted 10,000 sq. ft. print
shop into executive offices

Independent - 1985
Accomplishments:
Redesigned a kitchen, family
room, and laundry room. Space
planned, selected, and purchased
cabinets, appliances, counter-
tops, flooring, etc.

OFFICE EXPERIENCE

Some Furniture Mfg. Co. 1984
Accomplishments:
Created, organized, and expe-
dited bookkeeping procedures.
Ordered all equipment and
supplies for plant and offices.

South County Bell Telephone Co.
1959-60
Accomplishments:
Tabulated all monies and
expedited billing.

RETAIL SALES

Big City Jewelers 1983
Accomplishments:
"Diamond Counselor," Designed
case displays, increased sales.

Large City Jewelers 1981-83
Accomplishments:
Increased sales, negotiated
collections, court representative, designed window
and case displays.

Bigger City Jewelers 1980-81
Accomplishments:
Manager's Assistant, increased
sales, ordered from reps.

BUSINESS EXPERIENCE

Best Cleaners 1978-79
Accomplishments:
Owner - Expedited all
phases of the business,
increased customers, did alter-
ations, and doubled initial
investment.

156 *Combination. Nita Busby, CPRW, Placentia, California.*
Underlined display type for variously placed headings is an evident feature of this different
resume. Accomplishments are indicated for each position in the Work Experience section.

Sarah Smith -2-

EDUCATION

Certificate, Interior Design 1989
A.A. Degree, Interior Design 1988
New College. Emphasis:
Office Space Planning, Space
Planning, Drafting, Visual
Design, Graphics, Floor Plans
and Elevations, Kitchen
Design, Color Boards, and
Professional Practices

VOLUNTEERISM

Major City Hospital 1975
Public Relations Desk

Girl Scouts 1970
Calendar Chairwoman

MEMBERSHIPS/AWARDS

Interior Design Club
President 1989-90
Vice President 1988-89
Hospitality Chairwoman
1987-88, New College

I.S.I.D.
Student Scholarship 1989
Student Member 1987-90
New College
I.S.I.D. Student Night
Juried project displayed
1987

President's Honor Roll - 1988
New College

Women of Distinction
Nominee-1988
New College

Gordon J. Thompson Jr.

Combination. *Patricia L. Nieboer, CPS, CPRW, Fremont, Michigan.*
This resume was in brochure style, so this first page with its PGA logo was an outside cover.
Notice the abundance of white space for an expansive look.

Gordon J. Thompson Jr.
P.O. Box 90 ● Fairfield, Michigan 49000-0000
(616) 555-5555

PROFESSIONAL STANDING

A-1 PGA Professional
Elected to Membership January 1992

PLAYING ABILITY

Qualified Great Lakes Open 1993
Winner Calidonia Pro-Am Best Ball 1987
Fifth Place State Tournament 1982
Kellogg Community College 1981-1982

QUALIFICATIONS

Sixteen years experience in golfing industry, eight as **Head Golf Professional**. Knowledgeable in all aspects of club operations. Developed valuable communication skills, strong public relations abilities, and excellent rapport with people.

CAREER OBJECTIVE

As a PGA Professional, my goals are to work for an upscale golf club, develop and maintain a long-term working relationship, develop and promote one of the best teaching programs in the area, and have the golf shop of the club be picked as one of the 100 best in operations.

A professional golfer's standing and playing ability are important, so these are put first and centered to stand out. Block paragraph style is used for Qualifications and Career Objective.

PROFESSIONAL EXPERIENCE

Head Golf Professional   April 1988 - present
Fairfield Country Club, Fairfield, Michigan
- **Increased gross sales since 1988 to present by 55% while membership increased by 5½%.**
- Responsible for creating a pleasant golfing atmosphere for members and guests.
- Direct, coordinate, and supervise all golf activities, such as club tournaments, outside groups, private outings, and fund raisers.
- Provide membership with quality golf instruction in beginner, intermediate, and advanced levels.
- Initiated Junior and Women's golf camps, which resulted in excellent levels of participation.
- Own and operate fully computerized golf shop and professional shop services, which include handicapping and gas golf cart fleet.
- Financially responsible for all of the above areas and staffing for the golf operation.
- Familiar with all budgeting and accounting procedures.

Head Golf Professional   April 1986 - November 1987
Riverside Country Club, Riverside, Michigan
- Promote, plan, and coordinate golf operations.
- Create an enjoyable golfing atmosphere for membership.
- Render services to members: i.e. teaching, operations of golf shop, club storage, driving range, and gas golf cart fleet.
- Manage and supervise personnel.
- Direct and coordinate tournaments and golf outings.
- Order, display, and maintain adequate inventory of golf merchandise to meet membership needs.

Assistant Golf Professional   April 1983 - November 1984
Riverside Country Club, Riverside, Michigan
- Teaching, club repair, inventory control, supervision over club storage personnel.
- Assist with club tournaments.
- In charge of coordinating junior golf programs.

The first list of duties and responsibilities begins with an important accomplishment in bold-face. Bullets visually tie together the different work experiences.

Golf Club Assistant   April 1977 - October 1982
  Riverbend Golf Course, Riverbend, Michigan
  • Experienced all aspects of golf operations, with emphasis in ground
    maintenance for 27-hole public golf club.

EDUCATION

PGA Customer Service Workshop 1993
PGA Golf Shop Software Workshop 1993
PGA Merchandising Workshop 1993
PGA Psychology of Golf 1992
PGA Wage and Hour Workshop 1992
PGA Business School II 1991
PGA Business School I 1987

REFERENCES

Available upon request.

The PGA training events are centered, echoing the formatting at the beginning.

HENRY W. SMITH
88 Evans Ridge Road
Salem Bay, Massachusetts 02000
(508) 000-0000h   (508) 000-0000w
CLASS A PGA PROFESSIONAL

SUMMARY: A college-educated Professional with over ten years experience in a variety of golf environments. Specific strengths include excellent teaching skills, a profit-and-results-oriented business sense, a flair for current merchandising trends, strong tournament organizational abilities and solid playing experience.

PROFILE: "Henry has a strong commitment to excellence and is extremely knowledgeable in his field...His superior organizational skills and leadership ability have helped to build a strong program...He is exceptionally reliable, honest, well liked and respected by members and his peers." **Letter of recommendation, Golf Director**

EDUCATION: ADAMS UNIVERSITY   Big Rapids, MT
Bachelor of Science, 1985   Major: Professional Golf Management
Specialized coursework included: Turf Grass Management, Horticulture, Kinesiology, Educational Psychology, Golf Instruction Methods, Golf Car Management, Rules of Golf & Golf Club Design and Fitting.

**PROFESSIONAL
EXPERIENCE:**   OCEANSIDE COUNTRY CLUB   Truro, MA
1990 - Present   **Head Golf Professional**
Hired originally as a member relationship specialist for this large Cape Cod ocean-side development. Instrumental in reworking the entire golf program to better serve all member categories.
Selected accomplishments:
• Achieved a measurable increase in member participation through new ladies programs and group clinics.
• Developed a new Junior Golf program including weekly clinics and a very successful Junior Club Championship.
• Turned an unprofitable golf shop operation into a success by utilizing selective buying, creative merchandising and solid credit accountability.
• Placed in charge of the cart operation including leasing supervision and daily safety / maintenance checks.
• Instituted a consistent and equitable tournament program designed to satisfy all membership categories and to promote a private club atmosphere.
• Utilizing course management and horticultural background, provide daily assistance in the areas of course conditions and playability.
• Maintain total cost control and accountability for entire golf program.

1986-1990   WELLINGTON CLUB   Wellington, MO
Assistant Golf Director
Supervised and coordinated the golf operation of this prestigious private club with an 18-hole championship course and new executive course.
Selected accomplishments:
• Conducted two-day minischools with LPGA Tour player Donna Black.
• Organized Junior Golf Clinics with 60-70 participants.
• Co-hosted PGA Tour Professionals in the Chrysler Team Championship.
• Consulted with Johnny Milton on the redesign of holes 14-18.
• Managed the daily golf operation during multimillion dollar clubhouse and Carl Lappen-designed executive course construction.

1985   WINSTON COUNTRY CLUB   Bangor, ME
(Internship)   **Second Assistant Golf Professional**

REFERENCES: Professional and personal references available upon request.

158 ***Combination.*** *Joe Roper, Hingham, Massachusetts.*
The rank of the person is put first—just below the phone numbers. Note the use of a testimonial for the Profile statement. Accomplishments are featured as important experiences.

SHE T. JOBFINDER

6000 Hammond Drive G-3000, Atlanta, GA 30000 **(404) 000-0000**

LEGAL CAREER HIGHLIGHTS

- Researched legal real estate issues and documented findings.
- Conducted title searches, executed foreclosure sales, and aided with residential closing preparations.
- Provided assistance to the foreclosure, bankruptcy, and litigation departments.
- Assisted with depositions and interacted with clients.
- Participated in witness interviews, researched precedent cases, and assisted with trial preparation.

Other Highlights:

- Labor Law Society
- International Law Society - *Vanderbilt International*
- Vanderbilt Bar Association
- First-round winner in the King and Spalding Moot Court Competition

EDUCATION

J.D. Degree, Vanderbilt University School of Law, Nashville, TN, May 1993
Bachelor of Arts – Psychology, Duke University, Durham, NC, December 1989

PERSONAL PROFILE

- Dedicated and detail-oriented individual with strong interpersonal abilities
- Excellent communication and writing skills

EMPLOYMENT HISTORY

Associate
TOGETHER & FOREVER, Charlotte, NC 6/93-Present
Intern
NOTRE DAME LONDON LAW PROGRAM, London, England, 1992
Intern
STATE ATTORNEY'S OFFICE, 4TH JUDICIAL CIRCUIT, Jacksonville, FL, 1991

Previous Employment:
Human Resources (summer)
BARNETT BANK, Jacksonville, FL, 1988
Assistant to Director (summer)
DEPARTMENT OF HOUSING AND URBAN DEVELOPMENT, Jacksonville, FL, 1986-1987
Assistant
DUKE UNIVERSITY PRESS, Durham, NC, 1985-1987

Combination. *Terek A. Jabali, CPC, Atlanta, Georgia.*
Highlights, Education, and a Personal Profile are put first for this new attorney with relatively little career experience. Work History, with dates, includes internships and summer jobs.

159

Brad A. Brand

12345 Duross Avenue
Cleveland, Ohio 44000
(216) 000-0000

CAREER OBJECTIVE Responsible position in Human Resources with emphasis on employee relations and labor relations.

PROFILE

- Results-oriented professional with over nine years of progressive experience in labor relations and employee relations.
- Superior negotiation skills especially in arbitration and collective bargaining agreements.
- Well versed in employment law, such as Title VII and Age Discrimination in Employment Act (ADEA).
- Excellent written and oral communication skills.
- Proven leader, manager and teamplayer.
- Outstanding academic credentials from top-tier institutions.

PROFESSIONAL ACHIEVEMENTS

Employment Relations and Labor Relations

- Operate law practice that emphasizes labor law, collective bargaining agreements, and arbitration cases for small-to-large businesses and corporate clients. Provide internal grievance and arbitration representation to client-base at both offices.

- Orchestrated successful campaign to prevent United Auto Workers from organizing a union at Kingston Toyota dealership (*Kingston, New York*).

- Represented 16 Fortune 500 clients before the National Labor Relations Board, state and federal court proceedings with a less than 15% lost-case rate.

- Negotiated personal services and player contracts for NBA and NFL professional athletes.

- Represented Booth Memorial Medical Center of Queens New York and received favorable rulings from American Arbitration Association hearings.

- Provided legal counsel and represented United Parcel Services, General Motors Corporation, Federated Department Stores and Time, Inc. Handled E.E.O.C. charges, unjust dismissal, Title VII, federal and state regulatory issues and collective bargaining.

- Negotiated labor agreement with the City of East Cleveland Board Department of Education.

- Drafted and directed the implementation of 15 Affirmative Action Plans for Board of Directors for 10 small-to-mid-sized businesses and corporations.

Management

- Manage 23 employees including associates, paralegals and support staff. Principal contact for recruitment, hiring, performance review and termination.

- Control budgeting, administration and operations for two law offices in Ohio and New York.

160 **Combination.** *Loretta J. Barr, Dallas, Texas.*
A polished professional presentation. Filled square bullets unify the page. The first Professional Achievements category echoes the Career Objective. The second adds another dimension.

Brad A. Brand   page 2

EMPLOYMENT HISTORY

1987 - present   *Brand & Associates - Cleveland, Ohio & Rye Brook, New York*
                        Attorney/Principal
1986 - 1987   *Finley, Kumble, Wagner, Heine, Underberg, Manley Meyerson & Casey -*
                        New York, New York
                        Attorney
1984 - 1986   *Proskauer Rose Goetz & Mendelsohn - New York, New York*
                        Labor Associate

Internships

Fall 1983   *Proskauer Rose Goetz & Mendelsohn - New York, New York*
                        Labor Legal Assistant
Summer 1983   *Donovan, Leisure, Newton & Irvine - New York, New York*
                        Summer Associate
Fall 1982   *Office of the Corporation Counsel - New York, New York*
                        Legal Intern
Summer 1982   *Hahn, Loeser, Freedhiem, Dean & Wellman - Cleveland, Ohio*
                        Summer Associate

BAR MEMBERSHIPS

                        New York State, United States District Court for the Southern and Eastern Districts of New
                             York; United States Court of Appeals, Sixth Circuit.

                        Association of the Bar of the City of New York,
                             Westchester County, National, Metropolitan Black and American Bar Associations.

EDUCATION

                        Columbia University School of Law - New York, New York
                        Juris Doctor

                        Brown University - Providence, Rhode Island
                        Bachelor of Science

                        University School - Chagrin Falls, Ohio
                        Graduated 11 in class of 73

HONORS/
AFFILIATIONS

                        Selected as 1 of 30 *Future Leaders of America* by Ebony Magazine, June 1988
                        Recognized as *Top 10 Future Executives* by Money Magazine, December 1988
                        Awarded *Outstanding Young Men of America* distinction by United States Jaycees, 1987
                        Charles Evan Hughes Fellow
                        Harlan Fiske Stone Moot Court Competition - Semifinalist
                        Minority Recruitment and Admissions - Member
                        Black American Law Students Association - President
                        Dean's List - 5 semesters *(Brown University)*
                        Who's Who Among American Law Students
                        Omega Psi Phi Fraternity, Inc.

In the Employment History, using italic for the firms and boldface for the positions helps to
distinguish the two. The same strategy in the Education section maintains consistency.

Thomas J. Allen, Ph.D., M.C.C.

6584 Pine Cove
Jefferson, Michigan 46000
(526) 000-0000

● *Professional Objective:*

Seeking a challenging position as a <u>psychological counselor / therapist</u> utilizing my education and life experience most successfully, and where there is *"opportunity to serve others in need."*

● *Summary of Qualifications:*

- 11 years experience in counseling others on a variety of human issues and emotions
- **Areas of counseling include:** marriage, pre-marriage, depression, anxiety, grief work, co-dependency, divorce, single parenting, victimization, adultery, anger, self-control, self-esteem, rejection, fear, inter/intro personal conflict, jealousy, guilt, loneliness, thought life, and habits.
- Experienced utilizing a variety of psychological test / profiles
- Ability to counsel well, one-on-one or in group sessions
- Compassionate, good listener, and very supportive in client recovery
- Ability to work with individuals from a variety of backgrounds and social sectors

● *Education:*

<u>Evers University, Dixon, MO</u>
Ph.D. - Doctorate in Counseling (Psychology), May 1993

<u>Christian College, Santa Mesa, New Mexico</u>
M.C.C. - Master's in Christian Counseling, December 1991

<u>Christian College, Santa Mesa, New Mexico</u>
Bachelor of Theology, December 1989

● *Certifications / Licenses:*

Licensed Pastoral Counselor - Lic. No. A0000000
DSM 111-R Clinical Procedures - April 1993
Candidate For: Adolescent Therapy - June 1993
Crisis and Grief Specialists - June 1993
Clinical Counselors License - January 1994

● *Internship:*

Worked under the direction of Dr. Richard Ontorio, Ph.D., (the executive director of the Psychologist Counseling Association). Duties included counseling on a variety of human issues. Obtained a total of 3000 counseling hours. Traveled extensively including trips to Bilice, Mexico and the Philippines (1986-1988). Researched and wrote master's thesis 1989-1991.

See following page for additional counseling experience

161 ***Combination.*** *P. J. Margraf, New Braunfels, Texas.*
Large bullets direct attention to section headings throughout the resume, unifying the two pages. Small bullets in the Summary of Qualifications call attention to skills in one section.

Resume Continued

═══ *Thomas J. Allen, Ph.D., M.C.C.* ═══

● <u>*Work Experience:*</u>

<u>Life Center, Jefferson, Michigan</u>   1984 to Present
Counselor / Therapist
Work with individuals counseling in areas of marriage, pre-marriage, relationships, depression, anxiety, and victimization. Conduct group counseling (26 session per week) teaching self-image concepts and principles to an enriched life. Provide one-on-one consultation at any hour, if needed. Additionally, offer a variety of assessment test: TAP - Temperament Analysis Profile,   Mate - Premarital and Marriage Perception Analysis, Family Relations Inventory, Slossen Intelligence Test (I.Q.), and Occupational Interest Test.

<u>Marriage Retreat, Mexico City, Mexico</u>   1984 - 1986
Counselor
Provided marriage counseling first week of each month.

● <u>*Professional Organizations / Achievements:*</u>

Member: National Counselors Associations - July 1992
<u>Achievements as a Member of the National Counselors Association</u>:
Licensed Pastoral Counselor -Sept. 1992
Professional Clinical Member - Jan. 1993
Diplomat - April 1993
Member: Michigan Christian Counselors Association - May 1993

● <u>*Personal / Hobbies:*</u>

Single, non-smoker. Enjoy fishing, camping and children.
Also enjoy flying an airplane and travel in general.

References Available upon Request

Dual lines are top and bottom borders on both pages, further unifying the resume. The recurrence of the person's name within border segments is a third unifying device.

SAMUEL ROSENBERG
          509 W. Jersey Street, Elizabeth, N.J. 07000   (201) 000-0000

          Professional Social Worker/Therapist skilled in
          helping others develop a greater sense of self-
          determination leading to quality of life enhance-
          ment. Integrate flexible and appropriate approaches.

RELATED QUALIFICATIONS/ACHIEVEMENTS... M.S.W. focusing on case management
          and clinical skills with utilization of use of "self." Proven
          effectiveness in assisting clients to identify weaknesses and reframe
          them into strengths.

Assessment and Diagnosis
- Conduct psycho-social evaluations and in-depth individual/family intake interviews.

- Assess needs of clients on diverse issues such as:
  - Crisis Intervention
  - Family Role Disruption
  - Child Abuse
  - Loss and Grief Counseling
  - Acceptance of Aging
  - Depression
  - Adolescent Acting Out
  - Destructive Relationships
  - Divorce, Family/Child Adjustment
  - Adjustment to Chronic Illness
  - "Empty Nest" Syndrome
  - Remarriage Adaptation

Treatment
- Counsel individuals/families during times of major family crises.

- Assess personal strengths and coping mechanisms.

- Develop and implement treatment plans consistent with the needs and resources of individuals and families. Set and focus on priorities.

- Mediate marital disputes as well as disputes between individuals and groups concerning individual needs, relationships, divorce agreements and contractual conflicts.

Group Counseling
- Co-led long-term psychotherapy groups for mixed panic group, sex offenders group, and adolescents with suicidal tendencies.

- Designed and co-led a unique time-limited Second Generation Holocaust Survivors Group.

                                        Continued.....

---

162   *Combination. Adelia Wyner, Athens, Tennessee.*
A resume which shows that two-page resumes are appropriate for some people, particularly
when there is no access to laser printing and the advantages of smaller type.

SAMUEL ROSENBERG   Page Two

ADDITIONAL RELATED EXPERIENCE
*   Counseling in a pastoral setting for ten years.

*   Conduct and lead successful lectures and group discussions with
    emphasis on effective parenting and marital/relationship intimacy.

*   Organized committees for in-house as well as outreach projects.

*   Organized a committee on community needs assessment for the elderly.

PROFESSIONAL AFFILIATIONS

1989 to Present	Sr. Clinician –	COMMUNITY MENTAL HEALTH SERVICES OF PASSAIC COUNTY – Paterson, N.J.
1988/1989	Internship –	JEWISH FAMILY SERVICE OF MIDDLESEX COUNTY
1987/1988	Internship –	IRVINGTON COMMUNITY MENTAL HEALTH CENTER
1977/1979	Executive Director –	LINCOLN SQUARE SYNAGOGUE – New York City
1970/1977	Product Manager –	MARLENE INDUSTRIES – New York City

EDUCATION/AWARDS/ASSOCIATIONS

– Family Training Institute of N.J. (Monica McGoldrick) – Currently attending
   3/4 completion of studies toward Family Therapist Certification

– Wurzweiler School of Social Work, Yeshiva University, N. Y. M.S.W. 1989
– Baruch College of C.U.N.Y., New York, Toward M.B.A. – A.B.T.
– Baruch College of C.U.N.Y., New York, B.B.A. 1970
– Torah Vodaath Talmudical Seminary – Ordination 1969

– Recipient of National Science Graduate Fellowship 1970
– Member of National Association of Social Workers
– Participant in Seminar on Family Dynamics Conducted by Peggy Papp

OTHER FACTS   Enjoy the challenge of assisting others. Combine humor and
                     perseverance in times of crises showing genuine concern for
                     and sensitivity to client needs.

Various groups of qualifications and achievements indicated on the first page offset silence
about seven years (1980-1986) for which no information seems given.

Joseph A. DiGiorgio
3912 Boardwalk East
Erie, Pennsylvania 16506
Residence (814) 838-9690
Office (814) 868-4620

Career Objective:
Seeking an opportunity to utilize my training, communication, and leadership abilities to enhance the success of your organization.

Education:
Bachelor of Science in Business Education, 1960
Bachelor Science in Business Administration, 1957
Gannon University
Erie, Pennsylvania

Certified Career Transition Specialist
Pennsylvania Teacher Certification No. 2 16656. Social Studies, Commercial Law, Commercial Math, Salesmanship, Economics and Retail Selling.

Summary of Experience: Broad base of teaching, counseling, advising, and leadership expertise within a horizontally integrated work environment. Thirty years of diversified experience with an established record of accomplishments in career transition training, professional employment recruiting, public education, and radio & television journalism.

Skills and Abilities

Organization
Analytical
Problem Solving:
Create, design, and deliver effective career programs.
Implement strategies for personal growth and development.
Utilize "empowerment" to meet organizational objectives.
Assess, analyze, and develop workable solutions.

Training:
Teach, tutor and counsel adolescent and adult students.
Inspire a strong focused team spirit; consult with business, industry, school districts and social service agencies; Conduct training seminars, workshops, and review sessions.

Communication:
Stimulate creative thought; utilize effective listening techniques.
Interact with various personalities and skill levels.
Prepared and copyrighted the "HRS Career Discovery Process."

Leadership:
Coordinate a team of outsource specialists.
Stimulate positive "quality oriented" attitudes.
Open to taking risks; goal-oriented and motivated.
Establish trust and cooperation; build relationships.
Served as Evening Administrator and Academic Advisor for CE unit.

Personal Qualities: Knowledgeable and personable, a task-oriented individual who views obstacles as challenges and gets things done; an honest, confident, hardworking leader - a person of keen judgment who senses the proper course of action, determines the appropriate resources, implements and achieves.

---

163 **Combination.** *Joseph A. DiGiorgio, Erie, Pennsylvania.*
The writer's own resume in all italic. Education is placed first because it indicates important credentials up front. Skills and Abilities are grouped by four categories.

Employment History of Joseph A. DiGiorgio   *Page 2*

Human Resource Services, *June 1980 to Present*
Erie, Pennsylvania
A resume and career transition company that offers services on a fee-for-service basis.

Certified Career Transition Specialist, Owner
Responsible for creating, designing, and delivering a full range of career services: resume writing, career counseling, interview coaching, career change guidance, creative networking, targeted job search programs, weekly "job hunt" group sessions, workshops and seminars.

- *Developed a multi-dimensional personal development and career discovery process.*

- *Produced a 140-page career guide workbook which was copyrighted in 1987.*

- *Served as Evening Administrator and Academic Advisor for the Division of Continuing Education at Penn State-Behrend between May 1991 and June 1993.*

Management Recruiters of Northwestern Pennsylvania, *April 1970 to May 1980*
Erie, Pennsylvania
A national franchise contingency search and recruiting company.

General Manager & Principal Partner
Responsible for coordinating and supervising a staff of 14 placement and recruiting specialists in finance, sales, administration, technical, engineering, manufacturing management, and executive search.

- *Served as a recruiting specialist concentrating in the plastics industry.*

School District of the City of Erie, *January 1961 to April 1970*

Coordinator of Educational Television and Radio, *January 1967 to April 1970*
Responsible for researching, designing, and constructing a closed-circuit communication network linking the Erie City elementary and secondary schools to a central studio facility.

Classroom Teacher, *January 1961 to January 1967*
Taught all subjects at Diehl and Jones Elementary Schools, American History at Roosevelt Junior High School, Commercial Math at Strong Vincent High School, and English at Columbus Night School for the foreign born. During my tenure as a teacher, I worked concurrently in commercial radio and television as a staff announcer, producer, and director of news and public affairs; also worked for the Erie Dispatch as a newspaper reporter assigned to city hall and the county courthouse. Wrote an "Around-the-Town" feature column under the pen name of Jay Andre'.

Upon graduation, I joined the management training program at General Telephone Company. I also worked as an advertising account-executive for the Lake Shore Visitor. I obtained my teacher certification from Gannon University in January of 1961 and received my permanent certification on March 2, 1964.

References Available upon Request

The unity of the Employment History would have been disrupted if the Education section had been put on this page—another reason for putting the Education section where it is.

Resume of

CLYDE THOMAS

200 Lipton
New Haven, Texas 98000

Home: (563) 000-0000
Pager: (563) 000-0000

SEEKING A POSITION AS A NARCOTIC AGENT UTILIZING MY EXPERIENCE AND
EDUCATION EFFECTIVELY

● **SUMMARY OF QUALIFICATIONS:**

- Case agent in over 40 felony deliveries *(in one year)*
- Case agent in over 15 search warrants *(in one year)*
- Participated in numerous buy / bust operations
- Work well under cover as "buyer" utilizing innovative approaches
- Experienced with local and government enforcement agencies:
- (FBI, TABC, DEA, Customs, Button County, Casper County)
- Utilize job-related equipment (Surveillance, Kale, Night Vision, TCIC, NCIC)
- 470 hr's basic law enforcement, intermediate, and advanced courses *(See Education)*
- Dedicated, reliable, responsible - Can be counted on to support fellow officers in need

● **LAW ENFORCEMENT EXPERIENCE:**

Atlas Area Narcotic Task Force
Narcotic Agent Assigned from CCSO (Casper County Sheriffs' Office)   2/92 - 2/93

Atlas Area Narcotic Task Force
Narcotic Agent Assigned from CCSO (Casper County Sheriffs' Office)   6/91 - 12/91

Atlas Area Narcotic Task Force
Narcotic Agent Assigned from CCSO (Casper County Sheriffs' Office)   7/89 - 11/89

Casper County Sheriffs' Office
Narcotic Investigator   7/89 - 2/93

Casper County Sheriffs' Office
Deputy Sheriff   5/86 - 2/93

Casper County Sheriffs' Office
Deputy Reserve   6/84 - 5/86

See following page for Education and Honors

164 **Combination. P. J. Margraf, New Braunfels, Texas.**
Personal information is placed symmetrically at the top of the page, and horizontal lines
enclose the goal statement. Note again the use of large bullets with headings.

Resume Continued

CLYDE THOMAS

● EDUCATION:

<u>Advanced Courses Sponsored by:</u>

> Atlas Area Law Enforcement Academy - Instit. of Criminal Justice Studies - U.S. Dept. of Justice
> Federal Highways Administration - Texas Dept. of Public Safety - National Sheriffs' Association

Commercial Vehicle Drug Interdiction Techniques 10/20-22/92
Commercial Motor Vehicle Drug Interdiction Techniques 10/22/92
NCIC/TCIC Training 9/25/91 - Sexual Assault, Dom. Violence and Child Abuse 9/18/91
Firearms Stress Training 9/12/91 - Texas Prison Gangs & Jamaican Posses   91
Juvenile Law for Street Officers   9/10/91 - ASP Tactical Baton Training 5/17/91
Clanstine Drug Laboratories 4/17-19/91 - Community Mobilization for Juvenile Justice 4/91
Advanced Narcotics Investigation   7/20/90 - "Drug Investigation for Patrol Officers" 5/3/90
Narcotic Case Preparation   4/6/90 - Narcotic Investigators' Course 4/4-7/89

<u>Basic Courses Sponsored by:</u>

> Atlas Area Law Enforcement Academy - Dectar Electronic, Inc.
> Region Law Enforcement Academy - Texas Commission on Law Enforcement

<u>Intermediate Proficiency Certificate</u>   5/91
Tactical Handcuffing Course 8/9-10/88 - Basic PR-24 Baton Course 11/16-18/87
Police Speed Radar 7/16/87 and 7/15/86 - Police Driving School 3/11/87
<u>Basic Proficiency Certificate - Peace Officer</u>   3/86
Atlas Area Law Enforcement Academy, Basic Course - Reserve Office 6/21/84
High School Education: Riverside High School, New Haven, Texas - Graduated 1979

● HONORS / ORGANIZATIONS / PERSONAL:

Certificate of Appreciation, "5 Years Dedicated Service to Casper County" 10/24/91
Award of Appreciation, "Outstanding Contribution to the Texas War on Drugs" -
Texas Narcotics Control Program - Atlas Area Task Force - 4/12/90
Certificate of Appreciation, "Exemplary Special Duty" 3/1/90
<u>Member</u>: TNOA (Texas Narcotic Officer's Association)
<u>Personal</u>: Married, Non-Smoker, Born: 3/21/54, Excellent Health. Hobbies: Hunting, Fishing

Professional and Personal References Available upon Request

Two wide shadow boxes, containing the names of various educational institutions and sponsors, add visual interest to this page, devoted mostly to Education and certification.

Yvette Winhauser, LCSW, LPC

314 Tilden Court
Creve Coeur, Missouri 63000
(314) 555-5555

SPECIALTIES & QUALIFICATIONS

- Licensed clinical social worker; nationally licensed counselor.
- Dedicated to establishing cooperative family relationships, building self-esteem and providing effective parenting information and support.
- Accomplished speaker, trainer and consultant for hospitals, schools, corporations, professional and community service organizations.
- Frequent featured guest in major newspapers, magazines and on nationally syndicated talk shows.
- Coauthor of internationally acclaimed books addressing fresh and positive approaches to parenting.

PROFESSIONAL EXPERIENCE

12/89 - Present
- Manage clinical counseling services for individuals, married couples and families in crisis.

1/77 - Present
- Develop and cultivate time-limited parent education groups for metropolitan community organizations.

9/87 - 11/89
- Licensed counselor for Comprehensive Clinical and Consulting Services, providing individual, marriage and family counseling.

11/81 - 12/83
- Parent Educator and Family Counselor, providing professional individual, family and marriage counseling to patients in a pediatric practice.

1981 - 1982
- Adjunct Professor at Maryville College, Webster University, and University of Missouri at St. Louis. Taught "Building Self-Esteem in Children."

EDUCATION

- **M.A., Counseling Psychology,** Alfred Adler Institute of Chicago, IL
- **M.A.T.,** Webster University, St. Louis, MO
- **B.A., Elementary Education,** Washington University, St. Louis, MO

PUBLICATIONS

- Winhauser, Y., & Friedman, K. (1991). Stop Struggling with Your Child. Harper Collins.
- Winhauser, Y., & Friedman, K. (1988). Stop Struggling with Your Teen. Viking Penguin, Inc.
- Winhauser, Y. (1978). A practical guide to family meetings.
- Collaborated with writing and production of ABC News week-long series, "The Parent Test," St. Louis, MO
- Collaborated with writing and production of six-week parenting news special on WCPO-TV, Cincinnnati, OH sponsored by St. Elizabeth Hospital.

PROFESSIONAL ORGANIZATIONS

- North America Society of Individual Psychology
- American Counseling Association
- National Speaker Association
- National Committee for Prevention of Child Abuse

165 **Combination.** *John A. Suarez, CPRW, St. Louis, Missouri.*
The shaded left column, containing headings and dates. balances visually text on the right.
The bullets are useful because the text is single-spaced and some items occupy two lines.

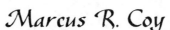

Marcus R. Coy

Objective: Master cake decorator in search of leadership position with company catering to clientele in demand of high-quality bakery products.

Specialties

Marzipan florals • characters • coverings
Poured and rolled fondant
Gum paste florals • ornaments • figurines
Royal icing flowers • Pulled and spun sugar
Portfolio available upon establishment of mutual interest

Highlights of Qualifications

- Able to handle a multitude of details at once, meeting deadlines under pressure.
- Sharp, innovative, quick learner; proven ability to adapt quickly to a challenge.
- Capable of speed and organization in a highly productive setting.
- Committed to harmonious working environment.
- Work cooperatively with a wide range of personalities.

Work History

1988-Present	*Cake Decorator*	DRAEGER'S GOURMET MARKET, Menlo Park, CA
1986-88	*Cake Decorator*	KELLY'S FRENCH PASTRY, Santa Cruz, CA
1986 (3 mos.)	*Apprentice Pastry Chef*	HANSEL AND GRETEL'S, Los Gatos, CA
1980-86	*Cake Decorator*	BAKER'S SUPERMARKETS, Omaha, NB
1978-80	*Cake Decorator*	EMMINGER BAKERY, Omaha, NB
1978-80	*Apprentice*	THE CAKERY, INC., Omaha, NB
1976-78	*Cleanup Crew*	ROTELLA'S ITALIAN BAKERY, Omaha, NB

Professional Experience

Design & Decorating

- Designed centerpiece cake for Mutual of Omaha benefit attended by the Ambassador to Great Britain, which included baking and extensively detailed cake decoration.
- Baked, decorated and assembled wedding cakes of all sizes and complexities.
- Fashioned variety of gum paste flowers for stunning visual effects, including cake tops and floral arrangements of violets, tulips, lilies, orchids, fresia, and roses.
- Devised gum paste figurines in designer fashions made of gum paste for cake tops or as individual gifts, including four "dolls" presented to Bill Blass "wearing" his designs.
- Operated Kopy Kake machine, emblazoning company logos, photos and other designs on cake surfaces; also used airbrush to enhance color, shadows and other artistic details.

Instruction

- Successfully trained apprentices in the art of cake decorating, teaching how to construct and ice cakes, create marzipan roses and other basic skills.
- Instructed series of gum paste flower classes at various cake supply shops in San Jose area.
- Demonstrated creation of marzipan animals at Menlo Park street fair.

Customer Relations

- Identify customer's desires concerning cake design, recommending cake flavors and decorations.
- Resolve wide range of customer problems, including dissatisfaction with taste and texture of cakes and frostings, design discrepancies, occasional misplaced orders and other miscommunication problems.

Education

Advanced and Lambeth Continental courses,
WILTEN SCHOOL OF CAKE DECORATING AND CONFECTIONARY ART
Woodridge, IL — 1985

1307 Burrows Road • Campbell, CA • 95008 • (408) 555-0913

© The Wordsmith, Sallie Young, 1992

Combination. *Sallie Young, San Jose, California.*
The background screen for this resume was done in Aldus Freehand and imported along with text into PageMaker. The original was printed on colored Decadry Print birthday cake paper.

GARY D. RIETER
4650 Shore Lane, Elkhart, ID 46000
Phone (000) 000-0000

JOB OBJECTIVE: *Pilot position*

RATINGS/CERTIFICATES

Airline Transport Pilot - Multiengine
Commercial - Single Engine Land
Commercial - Single Engine Sea
Certified Flight Instructor
Certified Flight Instructor (Instrument)
Medical Certificate: FAA Class I - No Restrictions

FLIGHT TIME:

Total Flight Time	2683	Total Alaska Time	1000
Pilot in Command	1800	Instrument	250
Multiengine Land	412	Instrument Simulator	50
Single Engine Land	600	Military Flight Engineer	829
Single Engine Sea	810		

QUALIFICATIONS

Owner-Operator Line Pilot, Chief Flight Instructor and Company Safety Supervisor, Seahawk Air, Kodiak, Alaska, 1992-1993

Flight Engineer HC130H, U.S. Coast Guard, Florida & Alaska, 1989-1992. Safely logged 829 hours flight time. Member of Total Quality Management Team and Civil Rights Committee

Chief Flight Instructor, U.S. Coast Guard Flying Club, Kodiak, Alaska, 1990-1992. Implemented and monitored training and safety procedures

Flight Instructor, Keys Air Flight Training, Florida, 1989

SPECIALIZED TRAINING AND EDUCATION

Cockpit Resource Management, U.S. Air Force, completed annually 1987-1992
HC130H Advanced Electrical System, Dyess AFB, Texas, 1990
Basic & Advanced Flight Engineer, Little Rock AFB, Arkansas, 1989. Graduated top 10% of class. Course topics: turbine engine theory; systems - pressurization, bleed air, electrical, hydraulic, fuel, anti-ice, de-ice; and emergency procedures
University of Montana, Missoula, MT, 1982-1984

COMMUNITY AFFILIATIONS

Kodiak Civil Air Patrol, 1990-1992
Kodiak People for Pets (Humane Society)

References available upon request

167 **Combination.** *Jacqueline K. Herter, CPS, Kodiak, Alaska.*
One of the resume writer's favorite resumes. The airplane graphic was also placed on a large gray envelope having a preprinted return address.

VENNIE VENTURE
777 Perils Avenue
This Town, USA   12345
(888) 888-8888

OBJECTIVE: Position in International Relations utilizing education and experience gained while traveling and studying abroad.

HIGHLIGHTS:

- Majored in International Relations with emphasis in Western European Studies
- Fluent in Italian and possess reading and speaking skills in French, German, and Swedish
- Traveled and studied abroad (including Europe and Canada)
- Attended diplomatic and international social functions while studying abroad
- Lived, worked, and studied in Washington, DC, and attended numerous Embassy functions
- Worked closely with executive-level personnel of major international corporations

EDUCATION:

Bachelor of Arts, The Best University Around, Any City, USA   1991
Studied at University of Montreal, Canada and University of Lund, Sweden

- GPA: 3.52 on 4.0 scale
- Coursework: studies included 12 hours of graduate-level courses
- Awards: Italian National Honor Society, International Relations National Honor Society
- Offices Held: 2nd Vice-President, Student Government Association, and Treasurer for Sorority
- Volunteer Work: Special Olympics, Convalescent Homes, Heart Fund and Cancer Research Fund Raisers, International Philanthropy, and Homeless March/Fund Raiser

PROFESSIONAL EXPERIENCE:

Assistant Account Executive   1993 - present
Wonderful Public Relations Firm, My Town, USA

As company representative, work directly with Vice-Presidents and high-level officials of major corporations in developing public relations and advertising programs. Responsible for contacting media to inform them of major up-coming events, introducing them to new products by major manufacturers, and preparing announcements concerning new public safety products which are being introduced by manufacturers. Train interns.

Restaurant Manager   1991 - 1992
Best Food Cafe, My Town, USA

Responsible for day-to-day operations of restaurant and catering of special events. Handled personnel/staffing needs, sales projections, purchasing, and daily bookkeeping. Ensured licensing requirements were being met. Served as liaison between corporate office/owners and restaurant staff. Maintained excellent customer relations.

ADDITIONAL EMPLOYMENT:

Waitress, Eat 'em Up Restaurant, This City, USA   1990 - 1991
Waitress/Hostess, Let's Eat Restaurant, This City, USA   1989 - 1990
Front Desk Clerk, Best Hotel in Town, Any City, USA   1987 - 1988

REFERENCES:

Excellent professional and personal references available upon request.

Combination. Susie Brady, CPRW, Virginia Beach, Virginia.
The degree and university, as well as the Professional Experience positions, are emphasized through boldfacing and underlining. Good use of spacing throughout.

168

JANE MAEYERS
123 Alexandria Drive
Alexandria, Louisiana   71000
(318) 000-0000

JOB OBJECTIVE   Position as Director of Recreational Programming, Leisure Services, Social Services, or related position which offers broad participation, immediate challenges and a career opportunity.

SUMMARY

Offering 10 years of extensive and diversified experience as a Recreation Specialist: Providing strong experience in recreation, sports, outdoor adventure; capable of organizing programs tailored to organization's needs/budget; full knowledge of equipment, activities/games, health/safety skills.

PROFILE

Self-starter ready for a "take-charge" position requiring an individual who can make decisions, handle own responsibilities, adapt to any job/situation. A people-oriented individual with the ability to contribute significantly to the rapport between staff/administrators and the community.

Personal qualities include the ability to recognize and resolve problems, inspire organizational cooperation, and develop the means to achieve organizational goals on a prompt and efficient basis.

HIGHLIGHTS OF QUALIFICATIONS

- Bachelor of Arts Degree in Education, Recreation Management.
- 7 years successful recreational supervisory experience with Department of Defense, United States Air Force and 3 years in the private sector.
- Certified Leisure Professional-National Recreation and Park Association.
- Developed, organized and implemented numerous recreation programs for preteens, junior teens and senior teens.
- Responsible for annual budget of $350,000.
- Experienced fund-raiser; successfully raised thousands of dollars through the United Way Campaign, corporate sponsorships and special grants.
- Hired, trained, and monitored personnel (15 staff members).
- Selected, trained and monitored volunteers (400 volunteer members).
- Supervised maintenance of recreational facilities: gymnasium, swimming pool, softball/baseball/soccer fields, etc., and related equipment.
- Effective and knowledgeable in working with cultural/social differences.
- Commitment to work which promotes social interaction, development of recreational skills, and physical and emotional growth of youth of all ages.

EMPLOYMENT HISTORY

Recreation Specialist	1984 to 1992
Department of Defense, United States Air Force	
Director, Youth Activities Center	3/91 to 2/92
England Air Force Base, Alexandria, LA	
Director, Youth Activities Center	10/89-3/91
Royal Air Force Upper Heyford, United Kingdom	
Director, Youth Activities Center	3/89-10/89
Royal Air Force Fairford, United Kingdom	
Director, Youth Activities Center	8/87-3/89
McConnell Air Force Base, Wichita, KS	
Program Director, Youth Activities Center	12/84-8/87
McConnell Air Force Base, Wichita, KS	
After School Program Coordinator	9/84-12/84
Little Pal's Day Care Center, Wichita, KS	
Horse Program Director, Camp Wiedemann	Summer 83/84
Wichita Area Girl Scout Council, Wichita, KS	

169

Combination. Michael Robertson, Alexandria, Louisiana.
Boxed symbols under most of the headings are distinctive features of this resume. Most of the symbols are sports- or education-related.

JANE MAEYERS
Page 2

EDUCATION & **SPECIALIZED** **TRAINING** 	Bachelor of Arts Degree in Education Major: Recreation Management **WICHITA STATE UNIVERSITY,** Wichita, KS Honors: • Graduated <u>Cum Laude</u>. • Dean's Honor Roll • Cumulative GPA: 3.26	1985

Associate of Arts Degree in Education   1982
FORT SCOTT COMMUNITY COLLEGE, Fort Scott, KS
      Honors: • Graduated <u>Cum Laude</u>.
               • Dean's Honor Roll
               • Cumulative GPA: 3.65

Continuing Education Units   1985
"Volunteerism: Skills for the 80's"   9 CEU's
WICHITA STATE UNIVERSITY, Wichita, KS

Master Level Course Work in Management   88/89 term
WEBSTER UNIVERSITY, St. Louis, MO   6 credit hours GPA: 4.0

Master Level Course Work in Recreation   88/89 term
FLORIDA STATE UNIVERSITY, Tallahassee, FL 2 credit hours GPA: 4.0

• United States Air Force **Child Abuse,**   1985
  Child Sexual Abuse & Child Neglect Training Program
  McConnell Air Force Base, Wichita, KS   40-hour training course

• United States Air Force in Europe   1985
  Teen Outdoor Adventure Training Program
  Berchtesgaden, Germany   64-hour training course

• United States Air Force in Europe   1990
  Youth Directors' Training Conference
  Ramstein Air Base, Germany   40-hour training course

• United States Air Force **Morale, Welfare**   *1990 Honor Graduate*
  and Recreation Managers Training Course
  Keesler Air Force Base, Biloxi, MS   260-hour training course

CERTIFICATIONS

• Certified Leisure Professional-National Recreation & Park Association
• National Certified Softball Umpire-Amateur Softball Association
• High School Softball Official-National High School Scholastic Association
• High School Basketball Official-National High School Scholastic Association
• Lifetime Coach and Certified Clinition-National Youth Sports
  Coaches Association

MEMBERSHIPS

• National Recreation and Park Association

HONORS &
AWARDS

• Certificate of Achievement for Excellent Leadership and Management of
  Morale, Welfare & Recreation Programs for the United States Air Force 1986
• Program Excellence Award for Outstanding Programming of Morale, Welfare
  & Recreation Activities, United States Air Force   1986 and 1991
• Letter of Appreciation from Youth Activities Director, McConnell Air Force
  Base, KS, for superior program planning/management assistance; led to
  <u>Outstanding</u> rating from Military Inspection General Rating Team   1985

REFERENCES   Available upon request.

Uppercase letters help the universities and community college stand out. Bullets in the
Education section help the United States Air Force training courses stand out also.

JANE MAEYERS
Additional Achievements

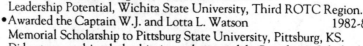

<table>
<tr><td>

**WORK
RELATED
HONORS**

</td><td>

• Nominated as Non Appropriated Funds Employee of the Quarter
McConnell Air Force Base, KS.   1986
• Nominated as Non Appropriated Funds Employee of the Quarter
McConnell Air Force Base, KS.   1985

</td></tr>
<tr><td>

**EDUCATION
RELATED
HONORS &
AWARDS**

</td><td>

• Awarded the President's Scholarship   1982-83 and 1983-84
of Wichita State University, Wichita, KS.
• Awarded the Veteran of Foreign Wars Award   1983
for the most outstanding Cadet who shows excellent
Leadership Potential, Wichita State University, Third ROTC Region.
• Awarded the Captain W.J. and Lotta L. Watson   1982-83
Memorial Scholarship to Pittsburg State University, Pittsburg, KS.
Did not accept this scholarship, instead accepted the President's Scholarship
to Wichita State University.
• Applicant to Martor Board   Fall 1983/Spring 1984/Spring 1985
National Honor Society of Wichita State University, KS.
• Awarded the Board of Trustees Academic   1980-81 and 1981-82
Scholarship to Fort Scott Community College, Fort Scott, KS.

</td></tr>
<tr><td>

**SPORTS &
RECREATION
HONORS &
AWARDS**

</td><td>

• Voted "YOUTH COACH OF THE YEAR"   1986
by fellow coaches of the Bel Aire Heights Baseball and Softball League.
• Head Coach of the "WICHITA SPIRITS ALL STAR TEAM" Girls
Softball age 9-10, summer 1986. Finished 1st in league and in division,
record 16 wins, 2 loses.
• Certificate of Appreciation from the   1985-86 season
Wichita United Soccer Association for being an outstanding volunteer.
• Head Coach of the Sunnyside Baseball League "ASTROS" boys baseball
age 8-9, summer 1985. Finished 2nd in league, record 17 wins, 3 losses.
• Certificate of Appreciation from Earhart Environmental Complex for
Volunteer Service during the 1985-86 school year.
• Certificate of Appreciation from AYSO Region #49, Wichita, KS
for serving as CHIEF GIRLS COACH for the 1983-84 season.
• Co-Captain of Fort Scott Community College Women's Softball Team of
1982, and Senior Letterman of 1981 and 1982 season.
• Most Valuable Player of the Circle "E" Lions Softball Team of 1980, and
Senior Letterman in 1977, 78, 79 and 80.

</td></tr>
</table>

Note that this resume contains almost a full page of honors and awards from the military,
universities, and leagues.

Sales/Marketing
Resumes at a Glance

LADY S. LOOKING

1234 Any Street • Anytown, State 66000 • (913) 000-0000

PROFILE

Marketing/Customer Relations professional with management experience in the tour and travel industry; demonstrated organization and planning skills.
+ Accomplished facilitator; able to coordinate multiple/complex projects
+ Skilled at problem mediation and resolution while successfully upholding company objectives
+ Highly adaptable to rapidly changing requirements and situations
+ Task-oriented and precise, with high performance standards
+ Well-developed awareness and understanding of different cultures
+ Excellent mass communicator...experienced with people from East and West Coasts, Midwest and Europe

EDUCATION

B.S. Communication Studies (xxxx), *University*, Anytown
+ Emphasis: Organizational and Interpersonal Communication
+ *100%* financial responsibility for education

EXPERIENCE

Travel Company, Anytown, State (xxxx-Present)
Supervisor, Reservations Department
Market over 150 tour packages to international and domestic travel agencies. Oversee 10 reservation clerks. Interact with individuals from clerks to top management. Create and maintain professional rapport with travel industry vendors. Perform site inspections to ensure customer satisfaction.
ACHIEVEMENTS
+ Instrumental in developing international markets for tour packages. **Increased bookings from 10 to 100** in first year.
+ Created and produced procedures/training manual for reservation clerks
+ Established training process; implemented manual and trained new employees
+ Visited hotels, museums, and restaurants in 30 international and domestic locations *on my own time* to evaluate quality and suitability for consumers

Bar and Grill, Anytown, State (xxxx-xxxx)
Assistant Bar Manager
Organized and controlled liquor inventories. Served a diverse clientele.

Day Care Center, Anytown, State (xxxx-xxxx)
Home Care Assistance Provider
Prepared meals; transported students from school to day care center.

University Motor Pool, Anytown, State (xxxx-xxxx)
Office Assistant
Scheduled and reserved university automobiles and lift van rides for handicapped students. Managed accounts payable and receivable.

EXCELLENT REFERENCES AVAILABLE UPON REQUEST

Combination. *Linda Morton, CPRW, Lawrence, Kansas.*
Distinctive bullets (variants of plus signs) tie together visually the three sections of this resume. Italic and boldfacing are used to call attention to names, positions, and key ideas.

170

PRINCE CHARMING

6500 Shier Rings Road   Amlin, OH 43000   (614) 000-0000

Sales/Marketing

Dedicated to providing a high-quality sales performance
for a high-quality product and/or service.

PROFESSIONAL SKILLS/KNOWLEDGE

- Over 8 years sales/marketing experience
- Consultative sales
- Negotiation of sales/leasing contracts
- Sales/motivational training
- Sales lead generation
- New business development
- Quality customer service

- Long-term account loyalty
- Competitive strategies
- Market penetration
- Advertising and promotions
- Financing
- International sales
- Fluent in German and English

PROFESSIONAL EXPERIENCE

ABC AUTO GROUP, Anytown, OH, 05/87 - Present
Sales/Leasing Representative. Represent and sell automobiles for six European high group manufacturers. Certified representative for Porsche, Audi, and Range Rover. Develop advertising and marketing strategies for use in the local market.

Selected Achievements:

- Expanded market penetration 20% in past three years; continually exceed sales targets
- Attained outstanding sales record resulting in ABC becoming a Premier Porsche Dealer
- Top Sales Representative with highest sales volume of over $2.4 million; recognized with numerous awards for excellent salesmanship
- Primary contributor in new BMW franchise becoming #1 in zone and #6 in sales nationwide
- Sold the most expensive new car ($745,000) in Ohio (1990)

MERCEDES-BENZ CORPORATION, Bonn Germany, 01/85-12/86
Sales Representative. Selected through extensive screening process to represent one of the world's best automobile and truck manufacturers.

Selected Achievements

- Consistently averaged 20%-30% above sales quota
- Awarded corporate privileges well before peers thanks to exemplary sales record

Continuing Education

- Sales Techniques
- Customer Oriented Marketing

- Psychology of Sales
- Service Strategies

MILITARY   Fulfilled mandatory obligation of 15 months in Territorial Army, Rheinbach, Germany

EDUCATION   B. A. in Business Administration, Administrative College, Bonn, Germany, 1983

Excellent personal and professional references
are available, and will be furnished upon request.

171 *Combination. Susan Higgins, Amlin, Ohio.*
Another resume with different bullets. The resume begins and ends with centered text.
Achievements are listed for each job held. Note the price of Ohio's most expensive 1990 car!

LLOYD N. PARKER

8000 Timber Lane • Snellville, Georgia 30000 • (404) 000-0000

SUMMARY OF EXPERIENCE:

Successfully administered Sales, Marketing, and Management responsibilities on regional, national, and international levels. Expertise in developing sales and marketing management plans; recruiting, hiring, training, and directing employees; sales forecasting; budgeting, accounting, and financial/compensation planning; advertising; order development; implementing systems and procedures. Record of consistent achievement and positive corporate growth through increased profitability and specific analysis and development of geographical sales territories.

CAREER HISTORY:

MARKETING CONCEPTS, Pittsburgh, Pennsylvania   1992 to Present
Southeast Senior Account Manager, Advertising & Public Relations
Developed new client base extending to the medical, hardware, travel and leisure, outdoor activity/entertainment industries. Provide strategic planning, budgeting, and scheduling guidelines. Analyze needs, submit recommendations, and implement cost-effective programs encompassing market research, public relations, target relationship marketing, strategic alliances, sales support materials, sales promotions, telemarketing, training, marketing, and advertising.

MYSHOW, Atlanta, Georgia   1990 to 1992
Partner and Director of Sales
Established a marketing communication agency to serve the medical and legal fields. Assumed full responsibility for daily operations, long-range planning, staff and client development, and all financial aspects of the business. Sold partnership.

PRINTING CORPORATION, Annapolis, Maryland   1985 to 1990
Formerly Hasbeen Printers, St. Petersburg, Florida
Southeast Vice President, Sales and Marketing
International Sales and Marketing Manager, Modern Graphic Arts Division
Developed Southeast U.S. and Caribbean region for this international printer of publications and catalogs. Accountability included staff management, sales marketing plans, and financial growth.

GROWING ATLANTA CORPORATION, Atlanta, Georgia   1982 to 1985
Vice President of Sales, Commercial Division
Completely restructured sales force and territories to effect improved representation, increased sales, and enhanced image.

References and prior employment history available upon request.

EDUCATION:

BOSTON UNIVERSITY, Boston, Massachusetts
Bachelor of Business Administration, Marketing

Combination. *Carol Lawrence, CPRW, Snellville, Georgia.*
The year of graduation from a university and information about employment before 1982 are
omitted for this Senior Account Manager. This silence helps to prevent rejection due to age.

172

David M. Allison

2202 Western Avenue
Indianapolis, Indiana 46000

Telephone:
(317) 000-0000

SALES / CUSTOMER RELATIONS

Expertise in . . . Servicing Existing Accounts / New Account Development / "Closing the Deal"

HIGHLIGHTS

☑ Competitive spirit; strong ability to set short- and long-term goals. "People person" with the "*will to win*" and achieve professional success.

☑ Personnel and account management skills; effective motivator who "learned by doing" and increased company revenue by more than doubling sales within first year of employment in a highly competitive market.

☑ Strong presentation, negotiation, and sales closing skills. Utilize verbal comunication and listening abilities to identify client needs and/or problems.

EDUCATION

HANOVER COLLEGE, Hanover, Indiana
Bachelor of Arts/Business Administration, 5/92
Area of Concentration: **Economics**
Activities:
Varsity Football Team Member
• Most Valuable Linebacker Award • Most Improved Player Award • All Conference Team Member
Beta Theta Pi Fraternity Member

PROFESSIONAL EXPERIENCE

MCI TELECOMMUNICATIONS, Indianapolis, Indiana
Territory Sales Representative, 1992 - Present
• Promoted to higher level of sales within eight months of hire. Increased client base by approximately 230% in 12-month period through referrals, cold calls, telemarketing, and direct mail. Succeeded in position without the benefit of a specialized training program.
• Team member of #5 branch in the country. Achieved 117% of average yearly sales quota. Consistently achieve monthly sales quotas.
• Established and developed program to execute cooperative sales with outside vendor in order to increase individual company profits. Perform total sales process from inception to completion.
• Successful and proven ability to "cold call close" sales. Provide continual follow-up to potential clients in order to ensure future sale.
• Implement sales marketing plans, perform analysis of individual client billings, and evaluate needs for potential clients in order to promote, enhance value, and sell product and services.

LIBERTY NATIONAL BANK AND TRUST COMPANY, Louisville, Kentucky
Intern/Teller Program, 5/90-8/90; 5/91-8/91 (Summer student position)
• Full teller responsibilities handling transaction volumes of up to $50,000 each.
• Trained on NCR off-line machines; on-line computers and audio phone lines.
• Processed sales of savings bonds and official checks.
• Operated drive-through window; selected for bank teller pool.

M & M VALET PARKING SERVICE, Louisville, Kentucky
Manager, 1986 - 1992 (Part-time student position)
• Established and managed an exclusive country club valet service; expanded to servicing private contracts throughout the city. Conducted price negotiations for services.
• Hired, trained, and managed staff of up to 10 employees. Coordinated scheduling of entire operations. Handled payroll, provided excellent customer service and utilized problem-solving skills.

COMMUNITY SERVICE

United Way Youth Basketball League Coach/St. Thomas Aquinas Church
• Coach weekly inner city youth basketball team instilling discipline, self confidence, teamwork and leadership skills.

References Available upon Request

173 **Combination.** *Gayle Bernstein, CPRW, Indianapolis, Indiana.*
Parallel lines enclose the Expertise statement. Checked boxes are a nice touch for a
Highlights section. A resume for a graduate looking for his second job since graduation.

MIXED FORMAT, SHOWING PROMOTIONS
Accurate Writing & More
P.O. Box 1164
Northampton, MA 01061-1164
(413) 586-2388/(800) 683-WORD

SUMMARY:
- Eight years, with several promotions, at same company
- Extensive experience in all back-end retail operations
- Supervisory, customer service, and vendor contact experience
- Knowledge of point-of-purchase merchandising
- Computer-literate
- Strong desire for professional advancement and opportunity

EXPERIENCE:

7/85–present   *A Growing Manufacturing Co.*   South Peru, MA
    7/89–present   **Processing Specialist/Liaison to Sales and Service**
Provide customer service to retail outlets on all questions
concerning merchandise displays. Audit and tabulate (daily,
weekly, and monthly) shipping totals, employee
hours/productivity, etc. Implement retroactive order changes
from sales and service departments.
- Implemented successful order tracking system that reduced average "hold and search" time by 93%
- Working with MIS manager to computerize all departmental functions
- Elected representative to OSHA steering committee

    7/88–7/89   **Day Supervisor—Wholesale Distribution**
Maintained active contact with other departments to ensure
appropriate stocking levels of all products. Resolved all
departmental employee and temporary worker questions and
grievances.
- Developed and implemented new merchandising display for remarketed product line

    7/87–7/88   **Assistant to Traffic Manager/Warehouse Supervisor**
Received all raw goods shipments; stored and distributed
materials within plant. Determined cost- and speed-effective
carriers and routes for each shipment; placed pick-up orders;
monitored freight fees and discounts.

    7/85–7/87   **Shipping Clerk**
- Selected to serve as liaison with sole Canadian distributor (average order $150,000+ when most wholesale orders were less than $2,000): coordinated shipments to exacting schedule; extensive contact with distributor and broker personnel; coordinated international export paperwork

6/91–4/93   **Part-time Bartender**, freelance, licensed.

1984–85   *Rice Oil*   Greenfield, MA
    1985   **Weekend Manager**
- Promoted from sales clerk at age 17, after seven months

EDUCATION: **Marketing Program**, Center for Degree Studies   PA

Combination. Shel Horowitz, Northampton, Massachusetts.
Education is put last in this resume for a person who has been promoted three times, with
increased responsibilities, within the one company.

174

A S P I R I N G   J O B S E E K E R

123 Main Street, Any Town, New Jersey 07000   (201) 000-0000

PROFESSIONAL OBJECTIVE

SALES / SERVICE OPERATIONS SUPPORT POSITION REQUIRING FIRST-HAND EXPERIENCE IN PRODUCT DISPLAY & MERCHANDISING - INVENTORY CONTROL - CUSTOMER SERVICE

---

* 13 + years experience with retail-consumer product merchandising, including sales, production support, customer service, marketing, and quality control.

* Skill in constructing eye-catching product displays, working with inventory and order processing systems, and wholesale and retail distribution systems.

* Receptive to the needs and concerns of customers, co-workers and management; demonstrated ability for assuming responsibility without direct supervision.

* Have the requisite industry and trade knowledge, work ethic, and enthusiasm.

Bilingual (English / Italian) - Willing to Travel

CAREER SUMMARY

RETAIL / FOOD INDUSTRY EXPERIENCE (1987 - Date)

GROCERY SUPERCENTER, West Orange, NJ
As Dairy Clerk for this fast-paced 24-hour, 75-employee superstore, ensuring the proper stocking, pricing, and rotation of all dairy products. Displaying all sale signs. Inform managers of shortages or special orders. Received many commendations for sustaining the lowest levels of food spoilage. (1988 - Date)

NEIGHBORHOOD SUPERMARKET, West Orange, NJ
Hired as the Frozen Food Clerk, often filled in for Dairy Clerk. Restocked shelves, ensured that product displays were clean and organized. (4/87 - 8/87)

DEPARTMENT STORE / GENERAL MERCHANDISING EXPERIENCE

LARGER RETAILER, East Hanover, NJ
Served in both a Sales and Stock capacity within the sporting goods, toys, and seasonal departments. Made sure that there were adequate quantities of items on display.   Repackaged damaged items for return to the warehouse or manufacturer. Assisted customers with product selection. (1983 - 1984)

SEARS, Livingston Mall, Livingston, NJ
Responsible for assembling and arranging various displays throughout the store (floor and window displays), for seasonal and special sales. (1981 - 1982)

KORVETTE'S, West Orange, NJ
Was one of this store's Display Crew up until company's closing. (1979 - 1980)

EDUCATION

Graduate, Scholastic High School, Any Town, NJ   June 1979

Complete references and details of all jobs provided at interview.

---

175   *Combination. Robert H. Markman, Cedar Grove, New Jersey.*
Horizontal lines enclose skills listed with asterisks under the Professional Objective statement. Experienced in paragraphs is grouped under centered subheadings in the Career Summary.

JAMES R. DUNN
28 Mountain Road
Mason, Georgia 30000
(404) 000-0000 Home / (404) 000-0000 Work

SENIOR SALES / SALES MANAGEMENT EXECUTIVE
Capital Equipment for the Medical, Industrial and Manufacturing Industries

Top-Producing Sales Executive with 10 years professional experience building and leading high-caliber sales, marketing and account management organizations. Consistently successful in outselling market competition through development of long-term, high-profit client relationships. Outstanding communication, presentation, negotiation and leadership qualifications.

PROFESSIONAL EXPERIENCE:

LINCOLN MEDICAL, Lincoln, Illinois   1988 to Present
(Specialized Medical Facilities Manufacturer)

REGIONAL SALES REPRESENTATIVE

Sell/market state-of-the-art medical facilities that house MRI diagnostic testing and cardiac catheterization laboratories, operating rooms, clinical treatment areas and other specialized health care environments for cardiology, urology and radiology practice. Customer base includes national hospital chains (e.g., HCA, Humana, Health Trust), private hospitals, physicians and paramedical businesses (including remarketers) in a 12-state region in the Eastern and Southeastern U.S.

- Increased regional sales from $4 million to $12+ million within 30 months.
- Ranked as one of the top revenue producers in the corporation for the past five years.
- Championed new product development and led market introduction of specialized mammography and health clinic units to penetrate "lower end" market, and directed roll-out of refurbished units. Generated over $1 million in first-year sales.
- Negotiated profitable strategic alliances with medical equipment and leasing companies nationwide for joint sales/marketing efforts.
- Consistently outsold major market competition despite higher cost (and higher quality) of Lincoln equipment.

U.S. ALLA LTD., Buena Park, California   1984 to 1988
(Computer-Controlled Metal Fabrication Equipment Manufacturer)

REGIONAL SALES MANAGER (1987 to 1988)
PRODUCT SPECIALIST (1985 to 1987)
SALES REPRESENTATIVE (1984 to 1985)

Fast-track promotion through a series of increasingly responsible sales/sales management positions to final promotion directing a multistate sales region with seven field representatives. Clientele included a diversity of corporate and industrial companies, from small job shops to Fortune 500s. Held full P&L responsibility for sales region. Recruited/trained sales professionals, developed strategic marketing and account development plans, innovated selling solutions to meet customer needs, and personally managed key account presentations, negotiations and closings.

- Named **"Top Producing Regional Manager"** in 1987 (150% of quota).
- Named **"Top Producing Product Specialist"** in 1986 (170% of quota).
- Consistently ranked in the Top 10 within a large national sales team.
- Designed and implemented company-wide voice mail system. Facilitated introduction of regional time management system and in-house training program.

EDUCATION: **Master of Arts in Theology,** Fuller Theology Seminary, Pasadena, California, 1982
                         Bachelor of Science in Communications, Trinity College, Miami, Florida, 1979

Combination. *Wendy S. Enelow, CPRW, Forest, Virginia.*
A pair of dual lines encloses a summary of the person's career and qualifications. Notice after each firm a capsule description in italic and within parentheses. Achievements are bulleted.

176

SANDRA MASON
(704) 000-0000 or (404) 000-0000

3027 Cumberland Drive
Rex, GA 30000

PROFESSIONAL QUALIFICATIONS

Broad leisure/corporate travel-industry experience. Skilled at arranging transportation lodging, meeting space, tours, catered functions, and support services for individuals and groups. Adept at negotiating, selling, and planning transportation for a wide variety of people and commodities. Excel at identifying and meeting customers' needs.

WORK HISTORY

Regional Sales Manager, Vegas Sportours Inc., Charlotte, NC *(1993)*
ASI arranged and sold travel packages to Las Vegas and other destinations.

Sold company's tours to NC/SC travel agencies. Oversaw passenger relations, including check-ins, special requests, and troubleshooting. Coordinated regional print advertising (selected media) and public relations (sweepstakes and special events). Trained and directed sales agents in three cities. Sales efforts led to a 300% rise in total bookings.

Operations Manager, Advantage Adventures, Greenville, SC *(1992)*
Vantage wholesaled and retailed deluxe tours and ecotourism in Europe, Asia, and Costa Rica.

Oversaw daily activity at company's only U.S. office. Sold and booked high-ticket, customized packages. Handled domestic and international money transfers/exchanges and accounting. Helped build Advantage into the second-largest tour operator in Costa Rica.

Manager/In-House Travel Agency, RS Acquisition Corp., Baltimore, MD *(1990-92)*

Hired to create this department and eliminate commissions to outside travel agencies. Booked air/ground transportation, lodging, and meeting space, globally, for employees.

Manager/Charter Sales and Service, Arrow Air Inc. (freight carrier), Miami, FL *(1985-89)*

Solely managed charter flights worldwide. Sold flight time and space to freight forwarders, government agencies, and other airlines. Provided support to flights by negotiating and coordinating diplomatic rights, fuel, catering, security, and crew lodging/ground transportation.

Managed contract sales of $3 million annually. Met a quota of 20,000 revenue hours yearly to ensure airline profitability.

EDUCATION

Graduated Cal Simmons Travel Agency School, Alexandria, VA -- 1992.

Three years' study toward a **bachelor's degree**. Courses in *travel and tourism*, *marketing*, and *aviation management* at Georgia State University and Embry-Riddle Aeronautical University.

177 **Combination. Barry Wohl, Charlotte, North Carolina.**
Another resume for the same person as in resume 125. This one-page resume is directed toward the travel industry. Notice the selection of information for this industry.

JESSICA L. JOHNSON
148 Washington Street
Lombard, Illinois 60000
(708) 000-0000

OBJECTIVE
To secure a Sales / Sales Support position.

EXPERIENCE
Lemitz Manufacturing   Addison, Illinois   February 1991 - June 1993

MARKETING COORDINATOR
- Company business line: manufacturer of hardware used in utility industry.

- Set prices for hardware and fiberglass specialty products using advanced knowledge of geographic markets.

- Coordinated hardware requirements for transmission power line projects with engineering/construction firms, utility companies, and various company departments. Demonstrated technical knowledge and outstanding communication skills.

- Prepared sales proposals presented to customers. Formulated the proposal used to secure a $1 million order—the company's third largest order in history. Detected a discrepancy between this order and the original sales contract, which resulted in $25,000 in revenue; detail-oriented and profit-minded.

- Investigated and resolved debits and credits; exhibited problem-solving ability. Authorized returns and negotiated applicable terms and conditions. Devised and implemented an order review system which reduced debits and credits by approximately 25%.

- Organized storm emergency shipments and prioritized shipments delayed because of storms.

Craige Manufacturing (hardware for utility industry)   Elmhurst, Illinois   February 1984 - January 1991

ACCOUNT REPRESENTATIVE
- Operational responsibilities included: editing orders and entering into computer system, scheduling shipping dates, quoting prices, generating invoices, and inputting debits and credits. Responsibilities increased from 28 specialty accounts to 58 general and specialty accounts over the seven-year period.

- Managed Original Equipment Manufacturer (O.E.M) accounts: set prices, identified product specifications, coordinated customer requests with internal departments, and determined terms and conditions.

- Forecasted yearly and quarterly sales figures based on blanket purchase orders and market conditions.

- Recommended order entry/billing programs which reduced delivery time by 50%.

- Created two sales brochures which introduced new products into the marketplace.

EDUCATION
Northern Illinois University   DeKalb, Illinois
Bachelor of Science   **Major:** Business Administration   Graduated May 1983

Software Knowledge: Quattro Pro, Lotus 1-2-3, and WordPerfect

---

Functional. Georgia Veith, Elmhurst, Illinois.
Instead of being a laundry list of responsibilities, the bulleted items integrate skills and accomplishments, illustrating the contributions this person can make to a company.

178

RESUME

Robert Biscay
7000 East Feldon Way
Phoenix, AZ 00000

EDUCATION

Attended Flagstaff City College 1980-1983, General
Education W. Smith High School   Graduated 1980

EMPLOYMENT HISTORY

1986-Present
ROUTE SALESMAN - Colorado Waters Co., Phoenix, AZ
Duties include servicing existing accounts,
soliciting new accounts, billing and collections
of all accounts

1985-1986
MACHINIST - Arizona Equipment, Phoenix, AZ
Rebuilt old drivelines and made new drivelines

1984-1985
ROUTE DRIVER - Watersoft, Flagstaff, AZ
Route included exchanging the water softening
tanks

1980-1984
DRIVER/REPAIRMAN - Business Machines, Inc.,
Flagstaff, AZ
Made all necessary deliveries, I also made minor
repairs and cleaned the calculators

1978-1980
CASHIER/ASSISTANT NIGHT MANAGER - McDonald's,
Flagstaff, AZ
Worked as a cashier and balanced money drawer at
closing

PERSONAL STRENGTHS

I am very strong in math skills, work well with my co-
workers as well with clients. I am a very loyal and
responsible employee

SALARY REQUIREMENT

Minimum of $30,000.00 per year

REFERENCES FURNISHED UPON REQUEST

---

179 *Chronological (Before). Susan B. Whitcomb, CPRW, Fresno, California.*
The person's original resume. It begins with an Education statement that shows graduation
only from high school and ends with the Salary Requirement, which invites rejection.

ROBERT BISCAY

2222 East Feldon Way
Phoenix, Arizona 90000
(222) 222-2222

OBJECTIVE

Outside Sales ▪ Route Sales position with a company that will benefit from my proven ability to generate new business, service and develop existing accounts, and earn bottom-line profits.

PROFESSIONAL EXPERIENCE

COLORADO WATERS COMPANY, Phoenix, Arizona   1986-Present

Route Salesman, Bottled Water Division: Over six years' commission sales experience, managing business growth, account retention, and deliveries to Phoenix-area customers. Developed new business through prospecting and referrals. Serviced over 800 commercial and residential accounts. Prepared daily activity reports to track sales, inventory, collections, and cash receipts. Accustomed to heavy work load and long hours. (1986-1992)

- Increased territory volume approx. 155% despite influx of new competition.
- Continually exceeded goals, generating sales to warrant territory division into three separate routes.
- Selected for Hall of Fame two years (top 10% for sales, add-on sales, and new customers).
- Collected cash on 37% of accounts, well above the company norm.
- Trained 10 new salesmen over tenure, many of whom are now top producers.

Route Salesman, Coffee Division: Presently managing coffee route for two territories, covering some 100 miles daily. Perform sales, sales recordkeeping, and training responsibilities similar to those listed above. (1992-Present)

- Built number of accounts from 90 to 150 in just one year.
- Demonstrated company loyalty and longevity throughout seven-year tenure (average employee turnover for industry is two years).

ARIZONA EQUIPMENT, Phoenix, Arizona   1985-1986

Machinist: Built drivelines for diesel trucks and automobiles using high-technology equipment.

WATERSOFT, Flagstaff, Arizona   1984-1985

Route Driver: Scheduled and made deliveries of water softening tanks throughout the Central Valley.

BUSINESS MACHINES, INC., Flagstaff, Arizona   1980-1984

Driver/Repairman: Part-time employment concurrent with college.

EDUCATION

Accounting/General Education -- Flagstaff City College, Flagstaff, Arizona

References Upon Request

Chronological (After). Susan B. Whitcomb, CPRW, Fresno, California.
The preceding resume developed into a resume that got an excellent response. Notice the expanded description of the current position. Education now appears last.

180

Andrew D. Britton

Current Address:
500 Maple Lane
Oakland, CA 00000
(000) 000-0000

Permanent Address:
1000 Green
Tacoma, WA 00000
(000) 000-0000

OBJECTIVE: To acquire a position in an aggressive, people-oriented organization with opportunity for professional growth where advancement in management is based upon my professional skills and contributions.

EDUCATION: CALIFORNIA STATE UNIVERSITY, LONG BEACH
B.S., Business Administration - 1989
Emphasis: Marketing/Sales
Strong background in Biological Sciences
GPA in Major: 3.38

EXPERIENCE: *Provided 90% of educational and support expenses during college.*

Marketing Representative, Pension & Employee Benefits Department
JONES, BARBARICH & RICHARDS, Attorneys at Law, Barlow, California

Conduct group presentations for sales of financial services to company principals and individually to their employees: describe benefits; forecast return on investment; secure employee's execution of documents; close transactions. Developed new and effective marketing strategies for prospective clients. Set up and administer various types of pension plans. Held primary responsibility for establishing the firm's new Cafeteria Benefits Plan. Calculate and determine benefits for client proposals. Position requires proficiency in operation of various computer software.

Actuarial Assistant
American Eagle Pension Plan, Santa Barbara, California

Position required critical thinking and accuracy, working daily with Defined Benefit and Defined Contribution Plans. Responsible for performing actuarial calculations and generating planned proposals using Datair System.

Marketing Representative
North Star Sales, Minneapolis, Minnesota

Marketing responsibilities included calling on clients, writing sales orders, determining profit margins, and maintaining good customer relations. Prepared scheduling and management reports.

Salesman
Evans Automotive Supply, Inc., Van Nuys, California

Utilized sales and interpersonal skills in working with the public.

ACTIVITIES and AWARDS:
- Dean's List, Spring 1987, Fall 1987
- Active Member, Inter-Business Council
- Student Representative, Scholarship & Awards Committee, School of Business
- Secretary, Commons Hall Government
- Intramural Sportsmanship Award
- Social Chairman and Activities Director, CSULB Atkinson Hall
- Active Member and Founding Father, Alpha Gamma Pi Fraternity
- Elementary Wrestling and Football Coach

181 *Functional (Earlier). Susan B. Whitcomb, CPRW, Fresno, California.*
The resume prepared by the writer five years earlier. Compare it with the following resume for the same person.

ANDREW D. BRITTON

1111 Green • Tacoma, WA 92222
(111) 111-1111

STRENGTHS

Sales ▪ Territory Management ▪ New Business Development ▪ Customer Retention

PROFESSIONAL EXPERIENCE

BOSTON PHARMACEUTICALS   6/89-Present

Professional Medical Sales Representative, Tacoma, WA (1991-Present)

Manage western Washington sales territory, generating approximately $1.6 million in annual volume. Develop business among general practitioners, specialists, hospitals, and pharmacies. Work with Hospital Formulary Committee physicians for approval of cardiovascular and upper respiratory products. Train new sales representatives; coordinate Regional Speaker Programs; manage territory budget; and order marketing materials, forms, and physician samples for territory.

- Earned "Distinguished Salesman of the Year" award among 70 in 6-state region (1992).
- Won "Most Improved in Region" for turnaround of territory from last (18th) to first place.
- Three-time national sales club winner for annually exceeding 100% of quota.
- Rank #1 for three of four products in districtwide sales.
- Honored as Founding Member of national sales club.
- Gained hospital formulary approval for all new products.
- Led district in physician speaker programs for 1992.

Sales Representative, Portland, OR (1989-1991)

- Achieved highest Amacillin index in history of territory.
- Advanced territory from 11th to 2nd place for overall weighted performance.
- Secured business with previously "no see" physicians.
- Selected as 1991 District Product Manager.

JONES, BARBARICH & RICHARDS, Attorneys at Law   1988-1989
Pension & Employee Benefits Department

Marketed and administered pension plans. Prepared proposals with ROI analysis and presented to company principals. Met with employees to explain benefits. Administered plans.

- Held primary responsibility for establishing the firm's new Cafeteria Benefits Plan.
- Assisted in developing marketing strategies to target new market segments.

EDUCATION

CALIFORNIA STATE UNIVERSITY, LONG BEACH

Degree:	**B.S., Business Administration** (1989)
Emphasis:	**Marketing/Sales**
Honors and Activities:	Financed 100% of education; Dean's List; Inter-Business Council; School of Business Scholarship & Awards Committee; Secretary, Commons Hall Government; Intramural Sportsmanship Award; Founding Member, Alpha Gamma Pi Fraternity

▪ ▪ ▪

Combination (Later). *Susan B. Whitcomb, CPRW, Fresno, California.*
Strengths are put first, and the Education section is put last. Achievements are listed as
bulleted items, and previous, unrelated job positions are not mentioned. Laser printed.

LYNN E. HIGGINS
104 Benner Road
Allentown, PA 18000
(213) 555-5555

OBJECTIVE

Seeking a challenging position as an Advertising Copywriter utilizing proficient research, sales and writing skills.

SKILL AREAS

Writing
- Sales call scripts
- Presentation guidelines
- Procedure manuals
- Sales training programs
- Monthly reports
- Client correspondence

Research/Analytical
- Customer Surveys
- Individual business profiles
- Sales campaign planning
- Competitive market analysis
- Sales training research

Program Management
- Interviewing and hiring
- Establishing program goals
- Counseling/Advising
- Sales training

Sales
- Customer needs analysis
- Sales presentations
- Overcoming objections
- Post-sale follow-up

PROFESSIONAL EXPERIENCE

MATRIXX MARKETING, INC., Cincinnati, OH   1978-1992
Subsidiary of Cincinnati Bell, Inc.
Sales Program Manager, 1981-1992
- Directly supervised inside sales representatives assigned to client programs.
- Analyzed market information and developed program objectives with clients.
- Researched cross-section of sales training materials; designed and wrote two company training programs.
- Planned and conducted sales strategy meetings with sales representatives.
- Analyzed sales calls; adapted presentations for increased effectiveness.
- Planned and executed sales incentive programs.

Inside Sales Representative, 1978-1981
- Maintained on-going sales coverage of business customers generated from MATRIXX clients.
- Developed individual business profiles involving products used, buying patterns, deciding factors, business size, etc.
- Signed new products, upgrades and line extensions; switched customers from competitors.
- Provided quality customer service coverage.
- Earned two "Outstanding Sales Performance" awards.

EDUCATION

B.A., **Political Science** (Cum Laude), Miami University, Oxford, OH

REFERENCES AVAILABLE UPON REQUEST

---

183 *Combination. John A. Suarez, CPRW, St. Louis, Missouri.*
The clustering of skills into four areas in two columns is a distinctive feature of this resume. Bullets in the Professional Experience section indicate both duties and achievements.

Sᴇʟʟ M. Mᴏᴏʀᴇ

1515 Gogetem Crescent
Any City, USA   22222

Home: (808) 666-6666
Business: (808) 444-4444

RETAIL SALES / MANAGEMENT

Seeking position in retail sales where extensive experience can be utilized. Capabilities include:

- Operations Management
- Leasing Negotiations
- Budget Control
- Customer Relations

- Store Design/Setup
- Cash Management
- Personnel Management
- Personnel Training

- Inventory Control
- Advertising / Media Buying
- Forecasting
- Merchandising

RETAIL EXPERIENCE

Owner / Manager, The Great Store, Any City, VA   1986 - present

Developed and built business from ground floor level. Generated annual sales to a high of $2,100,000. Actively involved in all operations.

- Negotiated contracts for leasing of space and pricing from suppliers.
- Designed store lay-out and merchandise display.
- Supervised staff of 9 full-time employees and 8 - 12 part-time/seasonal employees.
- Handled all aspects of advertising including media buying, writing ad copy, and co-op advertising with suppliers.
- Full responsibility for sales projections, budgeting, and inventory control.

Vice President, The Best Possible Company, Any City, VA   1979 - 1985

Began as manager of one store with annual sales of $1.5 million. Within 3 years, advanced to supervisor of six stores. In 1983, promoted to Vice President with responsibility for twelve stores.

- Developed leases to open new stores.
- Coordinated store design with architects and contractors.
- Actively involved in setup and opening of all new stores.
- Monitored expense budgets/sales projections for each store.
- Supervised store managers. Wrote training manuals for use by managers.
- Handled all advertising including media buying, writing ad copy, generating co-op advertising dollars from suppliers.

Manager Trainee, World's Best Company, This City, VA   1977 - 1978

Completed 1-year management training program.

EDUCATION

Bachelor's Degree, The Greatest University, Any Town, USA

Combination. Susie Brady, CPRW, Virginia Beach, Virginia.
A symmetrical resume that opens with a scan list of abilities enclosed within a pair of horizontal lines. In the Retail Experience section, paragraphs indicate achievements.

184

Helen K. Lewis

3000 Blue Field Road
East St. Louis, Illinois 62000
(618) 000-0000

*"...energetic, willing, and
enthusiastic worker."*
—E. Pepperidge, Customer

*"...makes customers feel warm
and appreciated..."*
—Capt. Paul Jamison
Department of the Air Force
Lackland AFB, TX

*"...genuinely dedicated and
professional individual..."*
—Jerry M. Wallace
Branch Brigade Exchange
Fort Sam Houston, TX

*"...an exceptional employee
with outstanding job knowledge, desire to excel, and
willingness to satisfy
customers."*
—Robert Matthews, General Manager
Scott Main Exchange, SAFB, IL

*"...sales driven and an excellent
merchandiser..."*
—Cherry Kamen, Retail Manager
Scott Main Exchange, SAFB, IL

*"...unbridled energy and
passion for her duties..."*
—Georgia McLeod, Retail Manager
Fort Leavenworth Exchange
Fort Leavenworth, KS

*"...a joy to customers and very
knowledgeable in all product
areas...personally ensures that
all patrons receive the best
possible service."*
—Kevin Roberts, Exchange Manager
Four Seasons/Toyland
Lackland AFB, San Antonio, TX

Profile

Experienced **Sales Manager** with retail sales and management career spanning 20+ years in increasingly responsible positions with military exchange service. Bottom-line-oriented with consistent record of exceeding standards and expectations. Aggressive and organized, with exceptional ability to motivate and train team workers and subordinates. Demonstrated drive and skills needed for successful progression in field.

Professional Experience

Sales & Merchandise Manager   1992-1993
ARMY & AIR FORCE EXCHANGE SVC, Scott Air Force Base, IL

Planned, coordinated, and directed selling, reordering, and merchandising activities for all store selling departments for on-base military retail store with average monthly sales of $2.3 million. Trained and supervised four department managers.

Accomplishments:

- Employed aggressive sales management techniques to increase sales by over 10% over previous year.
- Motivated department managers and workers resulting in 13% increase in productivity over 1-year period.

Sales & Merchandise Manager   1991-1992
ARMY & AIR FORCE EXCHANGE SVC, Ft. Leavenworth, KS

Supervised store operations for $1.9 million/month retail sales operation. Managed 3 department supervisors.

Accomplishments:

- Maintained planned turn rates and established sales goals—despite decreased activity—during and after major renovation of store.
- Supervised in-store merchandising programs and maintained inventory variance well above tolerance.

Operations Manager   1990-1991
ARMY & AIR FORCE EXCHANGE SVC, Scott Air Force Base, IL

Managed administrative, customer support, and sales and expenditures activities in 4 major areas: stock room, accounting office, customer support, and central checkout/cashier's cage. Also supervised RPOS computer operations and related support activities.

Accomplishments:

- Instituted expense controls resulting in net decrease in overall expenditures of 1.2% over prior year.
- Mastered schedules and MSO program for drop in personnel costs and measurable increase in productivity.
- Contributed to increase in sales of over 10% above previous year.

185 **Combination.** *Carla L. Culp, CPRW, Edwardsville, Illinois.*
A stellar resume for a person whose work experiences were all from the military and relatively similar. Several letters of recommendation became the source of the testimonials.

Helen K. Lewis   2

Store Manager   1989-1990
FOUR SEASONS/TOYLAND STORE, Ft. Sam Houston, TX

Managed outdoor recreation, lawn and garden, furniture, live plant, and toy merchandise with monthly sales averaging over $260,000.

Accomplishments:
- Increased monthly sales activity 62% during one-year period.
- Closely supervised accountability controls resulting in improved variance figures for year.
- Developed extensive product knowledge of outdoor merchandise.

Store Manager   1986-1989
FOUR SEASONS/TOYLAND STORE, Lackland AFB, TX

Managed outdoor recreation, lawn and garden, furniture, live plant, and toy merchandise with monthly sales averaging over $215,000.

Accomplishments:
- Decreased bloated inventory levels and excess damaged merchandise resulting in financial improvement in all areas.
- Aggressive leadership style resulted in new products, new services, and customers brought into facility.

Retail Manager   1984-1986
BRANCH EXCHANGE, Ft. Sam Houston, TX

Managed all areas of small retail operation on base.

Accomplishment:
- Contributed to high growth rate in sales and productivity of installation's retail activities with personal leadership ability, management skills, and experience.

Special Training

Numerous specialized supervisory, management, and retail sales training courses:

"Professional Retail Management Seminar" (1 week, 1992)
     University of Arkansas, Fayetteville
"Challenge of Retailing"
"Retailing for Manager"
"Retail Accounting Procedures"
"Retail Management Review"
Toy, Jewelry and Outdoor Living Seminars
Retail Branch Store Operations
Shoppette Seminars and Workshops
Audio, Photographic, Camera & Electronics Products Seminars

Personal and professional references provided upon request

More testimonials on this page would have been overkill. Accomplishments at the end of each experience make a strong marketing tool.

6000 Belleton Way   **William C. Burton**   **(000) 000-0000**

San Jose, CA 00000

OBJECTIVE: Position utilizing my skills in sales and management of high-end products and graduate degree with emphasis in telecommunications in a major telecommunications company in the Bay area.

EDUCATION: UNIVERSITY OF CALIFORNIA, Los Angeles (UCLA)
M.B.A. Telecommunications, May '91; Courses in Telecommunications Applications & Management, Systems Planning and International Telecommunications.
UNIVERSITY OF CALIFORNIA, Santa Barbara
B.S. Business Administration, 1980

EMPLOYMENT HISTORY:

'91-Present   Territory Manager   MIS-ADVANCEMENT, INC., San Jose, CA
Sold hardware, software and factory communication solutions to auto dealerships throughout Central San Joaquin Valley.   Achieved 126% of gross sales in first year and President's Club in second year. Recognized at the 1992 Western Division Strategy Convention as having "increased territory by 100%."

1989   General Sales Manager   PACIFIC LINCOLN-MERCURY/MAZDA, Sacramento, CA
Responsible for profits of both new and used car divisions.   Trained and supervised sales staff of 12. Succeeded in closing deals on sales and leases which were previously considered lost sales, increasing sales beyond established goals.

'87-'89   General Sales Manager   HARLY LINCOLN-MERCURY, Oakland, CA
Coordinated the finance and insurance department of Harly Motor Sales.   Achieved over $100,000 in finance income with less than 100 cars delivered.   Promoted to G.S.M. one month after hire.   Recruited, trained and motivated sales staff of 12, emphasizing professional sales approaches.   Doubled per car gross income within sixty days.   Maintained consistently high closing ratio and achieved store record sales volume in September '88.   At the same time, supervised extensive customer follow-up, advancing from 17th to top 3 in customer satisfaction of all northern California Lincoln-Mercury dealers.

'86-'87   Finance & Insurance Coordinator/Sales Manager   BELLEVIEW TOYOTA, Chatsworth, CA
Recruited, trained and supervised eight business managers at flagship store.   Introduced a new computer system organization-wide (eight dealerships) and a step sell and package sell concept approaches to Finance and Insurance Department.   Consistently top sales producer from my sales crew.   Improved faltering sales at new Toyota franchise.   Increased sales from 7 to 47 units in the first month, making it the top retail Toyota dealership in the Southwestern United States for October '86.

'82-'85   Branch Manager   AMERICAN FINANCE, A Bank of New York Co., Aristo, CA
Joined growing division of a leading financial services corporation to enhance management skills. Responsible for the 1983 Eastern Region Office of the Year Award with a quarter of a million dollar budget and a staff of five.   Conducted sales presentations to clients, bankers and brokers and enlarged dealer portfolio tenfold.   Introduced new financial service products to spur future investments.

EDUCATIONAL RECOGNITION:
National Communications Association (NCA) Telecommunications Scholarship Recipient '92-'93.
Dean's List '79;   Edward Bennett Award for Outstanding Athletic and Scholastic Ability '79.

ADDITIONAL TRAINING:
IBM Strategic Sales Training, Chicago, Illinois
Tom Hopkins International Advanced Sales Training, Los Angeles, California
Total Quality Management Training, Phase I and II, San Francisco, California
Bank of New York, Effective Leadership Program, San Francisco, California
Dale Carnegie Sales Course, Anaheim, California

Additional work experience at various auto dealerships in sales, sales management and business operations.

186   *Chronological (Before). Susan B. Whitcomb, CPRW, Fresno, California.*
Narrow margins make room for a wealth of information, but it worked against the person because most of it drew attention to his "car salesman" experience.

WILLIAM C. BURTON

6000 Belleton Way
San Jose, California 00000
Voice Mail: (800) 222-2222, ext. 2222

EXPERTISE

Sales ▪ Sales Management ▪ Business Development ▪ Account Retention

PROFESSIONAL EXPERIENCE

MIS-Advancement, Inc., San Jose, California   6/90 - Present

TERRITORY MANAGER

Manage $1.6 million sales territory, generating new business and maximizing existing account sales for largest international supplier of data processing technology. Make sales presentations for capital expenditures which exceed $100,000 per sale; present ROI analysis and schematic configurations; obtain buy-in from multiple departments. As technical specialist, consult management on applications for XENIX-based operating system with new technology for multiuser groups of up to 90 including system configuration and interface for 20 software applications.

- Doubled territory volume, generating increase from $800,000 to $1,600,000.
- Produced 126% of quota in just nine months of FY 1991/92.
- Earned membership in President's Club, exceeding corporate directives in FY 1992/93.
- Achieved 100% of quota to date for FY 1993/94.
- Selected among nine Territory Managers as representative to attend customer trade show in New York.

EDUCATION

M.B.A., Telecommunications, University of California, Los Angeles (UCLA)
- Partial list of coursework includes Telecommunications Applications and Management, Systems Planning, and International Telecommunications.
- International Communications Association Telecommunications Scholarship Recipient.

B.S., Business Administration, University of California, Santa Barbara

SPECIALIZING TRAINING

IBM Strategic Sales Training, Chicago, Illinois
Tom Hopkins International Advanced Sales Training, Los Angeles, California
Total Quality Management Training, Phase I and II, San Francisco, California
Bank of America, Effective Leadership Program, San Francisco, California
Dale Carnegie Sales Course, Anaheim, California

PRIOR EXPERIENCE

Financed M.B.A. coursework through concurrent full-time employment in Sales/Management. Prior career highlights include:

- Three years in branch management for American Finance, a Bank of New York Company, earning Eastern Region Office of the Year Award for profits and growth;
- Achieved record sales volume, won regional customer satisfaction award, and ranked as top producing unit in various retail sales management responsibilities.

Combination (After). Susan B. Whitcomb, CPRW, Fresno, California.
An example in which "less is more." The writer cut much of the material, focused on the person's current experience and M.B.A., and delivered a far more marketable resume.

187

FRANK SMITH
123 Main Street • La Costa, California • 92000
(619) 000-0000

OBJECTIVE

To secure a sales management position in an established business

QUALIFICATIONS

- Extremely motivated and focused
- Proven successful sales leader, trainer, and motivator
- Performance-driven -- only satisfied with being #1
- Excellent speaking and presentation skills

EMPLOYMENT HISTORY

District Sales Manager

Dun & Bradstreet/Donnelley Information Publishing - San Diego, California - *January 1989 to present*
Responsibilities include internal and external sales training, campaign strategies, sales meetings, interviews, credit and collection follow-up, sales projections, and overall supervision of account executives and managers.
Accomplishments:

- President's Club
- Distinguished Sales Achievement Award
- Rookie of the Year
- Outstanding Sales Trainer Award
- #1 Sales Rep in the company
- Currently #1 District Sales Manager in the company
- Offered promotion to Area Sales Manager Position

Director of Marketing/Sales

N. T. Corin Company, Lubbock, Texas - *March 1988 - December 1988*
Responsibilities included sales, recruiting, and training, developing sales visuals and marketing tools, advertising, and raising money through investors. Established customer base.

Regional Sales Manager

Network Direct, Inc., Lubbock, Texas - *October 1984 - March 1988*
Responsibilities included recruiting, training, and supervision of 9 District Sales Managers and 67 Sales Representatives throughout Texas and Oklahoma.
Accomplishments:

- #1 District Sales Manager in the Nation
- #1 Regional Sales Manager in the Nation
- #1 Recruiting and Training Award
- Established most of the Texas and Oklahoma offices

Director of Purchasing/Sales

Canco Equipment, Inc., Levelland, Texas - *March 1982 - July 1984*
Responsible for sales recruiting and training, located and purchased inventory throughout Texas and Oklahoma, developed marketing tools, established pricing guidelines, and set up transportation and delivery of materials in a four-state area.
Accomplishments:

- Built company from the ground up
- Created a large customer base that generated over seven million dollars in sales

EDUCATION

Southwest Texas State University
Texas Tech University - Architecture

188 **Combination.** *Ruth L. Binder, CPRW, San Diego, California.*
Shading (original) and a border make this resume distinctive. Bullets guide the eye downward to qualifications and accomplishments. Positions are emphasized through boldfacing.

BACKGROUND SUMMARY: Over fifteen years experience in the RV industry, with emphasis on sales, sales management and general management.

SUMMARY OF QUALIFICATIONS:

* Experience with all phases of smooth business operation and profitability
* Maintain all departments within operating budgets, set sales projections
* Purchase new and used inventory, manage floor planning and curtailments
* Handle finance and insurance including contracts and warranties
* Select and train sales and administrative staff, conduct staff meetings
* Establish inventory levels, determine value on trade-ins
* Handle advertising campaigns, co-op advertising, display merchandise
* Supervise parts, service and warranty departments, schedule deliveries
* Plan, set up and work RV trade shows, including travel nationwide
* Self-motivated, effective, proven ability to close retail sales
* Professional attitude and appearance, excellent communication skills

==

DANIEL DAUGHERTY

600 No. Huber Drive
Casper, Wyoming 82000
(307) 000-0000

==

SPECIAL TRAINING:

Recreational Vehicle Selling - Fleetwood Enterprises
Sheehan Training Systems
Grayson Schwepfingers Recreational Vehicles
Recreational Vehicle Management Workshop - Spader and Associates

PROFESSIONAL HISTORY:

Max's Motor and Marine, Inc., Casper, WY
3/91 to present   **RV Manager**
1/90 to 3/91   **Salesman**

Foss Motors, Marine and RV, Casper, WY
4/88 to 12/89   **RV Manager**

Ingram's RV Center
10/85 to 1/88   **Co-Owner/General Manager**
10/82 to 10/85   **General Manager**
5/80 to 10/82   **Sales Manager**

Western RV's, Casper, WY (later known as Ingram's RV)
2/77 to 5/80   **Salesman**

REFERENCES: Available upon Request

Combination. *Valerie Kulhavy, Mills, Wyoming.*
When you don't have access to a laser printer, you must take other steps to make a resume look different. Here, enclosing and lowering the name and address alter the appearance.

189

Akram Hamid

2200 Gateshead Lane, Apt. 80
Indianapolis, IN 46000
(317) 000–0000

OBJECTIVE	Sales Position.
AREAS of EXPERTISE	• Sales Management • Public Relations • Administration • Marketing • Advertising • Accounting
EXPERIENCE 4/92—7/1993	**Vice President**. Shared Equities, Inc., Indianapolis, IN • Start-up of operations: Sales & Marketing. • Traveled world-wide to generate business. • Generated many major business accounts with international firms, still producing profits for company. • Advised companies on trade with the Middle East. • Developed successful outside sales techniques.
1991—1992	**Sales Manager**. L.S. Carr and Company, Inc., Indianapolis, IN • Successfully renewed every account assigned. • Increased net new sales over 50%. • Consistently met or exceeded sales goals established by the company. • Selected as I.F.T. after 3 months with L.S. Carr. • Developed highly successful outside sales techniques.
1987—2/1991	**International Trade Manager/Partner**. Silver Tower Trading Establishment, Doha, Qatar • Planned & implemented Sales & Marketing Strategies for start-up of operation. • Generated major accounts with international firms still profiting company. • Organized & managed all administrative work at offices. • Traveled to generate business in over 100 countries. • Advised foreign companies on trade with the Middle East. • Represented company in trade shows and exhibitions (local & international).
1986–1987	**Public Relations Manager**. Almeer Travel Agencies, Doha, Qatar • Directed all public relations & advertising activities. • Planned & implemented campaigns resulting in larger business volume.
EDUCATION & ADDITIONAL TRAINING	**Bachelor of Arts**, Business Administration, 1986, Damascus University, Syria Course in Marketing, Asem Corporation, Genoa, Italy, 1987 Course in Sales Management, Commerce Corporation, Lupuliana, Yugoslavia, 1987 Course in Corporation Management, Smelt, Lupuliana, Yugoslavia, 1989 3 Courses in Advertising, Alvak LTD, London, England, 1988–1990 Business & related Seminars, Qatar Chamber of Commerce & other organizations in Qatar
INTERESTS	3-time Squash National Champion in Qatar, marathon running.
REFERENCES	Available upon request.

190 **Combination.** *Richard L. Schillen, Indianapolis, Indiana.*
A sharp-looking resume, especially on its original "decorator" paper. Notice that the section headings are centered within the left column (originally textured). This prevents a boxy look.

KATHY A. STUPP
123 Hamming Drive
Worcester, Massachusetts 01000
(508) 000-0000

JOB OBJECTIVE
Seeking employment as a support worker in Marketing/ Public Relations or Sales.

CUSTOMER SERVICE SKILLS
* Serve as a resource to community for school policy issues.
* Ability to relate to and converse with diverse populations.
* Answer customers' questions regarding Retirement Planning Seminars.
* Design orders according to customers' instructions.
* Interviewed applicants for Pife Paper Company.

SALES SKILLS
* Demonstrated sales skills in Financial Group, Stupp Creations, and Mary Kay Cosmetics.
* Identified in civic and church groups as a successful fund-raiser.
* Increased sales of Stupp Creations by 300% in 3 years.
* Presentation of Mary Kay product line in home demonstrations.

COORDINATION SKILLS
* Ability to organize work environment and time to efficiently carry out work responsibilities.
* Wrote and compiled first Employee's Handbook for Pife Paper.
* Coordinate design and creation of projects for Stupp Creations.
* Served as contractor for new residential construction.

WORK EXPERIENCE

1992	Telemarketing Representative	Financial Group Worcester, Massachusetts
1989 to present	Kindergarten Volunteer/ Art Consultant	Holden Public School/ Dawson & Jefferson Schools
1987 to present	Owner/ Designer	Stupp Creations Worcester, Massachusetts
1982 to 1984	Sales Representative	Mary Kay Cosmetics Co. Worcester, Massachusetts
1978 to 1982	Personnel Coordinator/ Order Expeditor	Pife Paper Company Worcester, Massachusetts

EDUCATION
B.A. 1978   Assumption College, Worcester, Massachusetts

REFERENCES SUPPLIED UPON REQUEST

Combination. *Myla Clark, Oxford, Massachusetts.*
The three groups of skills under centered headings are the most notable feature of this resume. Notice also the three-column formatting of the Work Experience section.

191

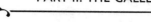

KENNETH POLANSKY
16 WHITEWOOD DRIVE
EDISON, NEW JERSEY 08837
(908) 225-5510

SUMMARY

Experienced manager with excellent team abilities; strong leadership and presentation skills. Ability to recruit, motivate, and develop long-term employees. Accomplished in repositioning product markets and developing alternative distribution channels.

STRENGTHS AND ABILITIES

- Operations Management
- Merchandising
- New Program Development

- Sales and Marketing
- Strategic Planning
- Field Supervision

WORK HISTORY with RELEVANT EXPERIENCE

MEINEKE INTERNATIONAL, Pittsburgh, Pennsylvania   1992-Present

MARKET MANAGER, Central New Jersey

- Maximize the markets' profit contribution to Meineke International by increasing sales and controlling expenses. Manage $5.5 million in sales; contribute approximately $600,000 to Midas International in operating income. In charge of unit managers, assistant managers, technicians, and an administrative assistant.

- Administer a $5.5 million sales budget and a $1.4 million payroll budget. Manage a $387,000 advertising budget and a $600,000 controllable expense budget; handle a $650,000 fixed expense budget.

- Responsible for sales and profit, asset management, consumer relations management, safety management, human resource management, and systems management.

- Interface with various internal vice presidents, external vendors including consumer research groups, advertising agencies, and media buying services.

- Assisted in the development and implementation of a shop manager/technician compensation plan designed to reward consumer satisfaction, adhere to a specific sales processes and increase sales.

- Selected as part of the team to develop and implement a new marketing positioning strategy. Involved in the development and implementation of a phone survey designed to measure customer satisfaction.

DENNYS CORPORATION, Hartford, Connecticut   1990-1992

DISTRICT MANAGER

- Oversaw a territory consisting of 76 locations generating in excess of $18.5 million in annual sales.

- Reversed a 10-year negative sales trend. This was achieved by evaluating the strategies, strengths and weaknesses of direct and indirect competition; determining the market's characteristics and studying opportunities for increased profitability. Created a back-to-basics business plan, which guided the territory and led to a 5.3% increase over the previous year.

- Expanded Dennys operations into supermarkets, stadiums, and arenas; developed alternative distribution channels. Organized financial and accounting information; measured results against plans.

Combination. Beverly Baskin, CPRW, Marlboro, New Jersey.
Horizontal lines enclosing the Summary call attention to it. The person considered the positions and companies of equal importance, so both appear in all uppercase.

PAGE 2...KENNETH POLANSKY

WAWA CORPORATION, Iselin, New Jersey   1987-1990

    FIELD CONSULTANT   (1987-1990)
    MANAGEMENT TRAINEE   (1987)

* Oversaw the turnaround of company owned and operated stores. This was accomplished by putting into place a program which upgraded the facility, improved the stores merchandising efforts and trained the staff in customer service techniques.

* Held responsibility for 10 locations. This included the stores' profitability as well as the locations' physical plant and equipment.

* Administrated a $200,000 promotional budget.

* Named "1988 Rookie of the Year" and "1989 Field Consultant of the Year."

* Managed a Field Group which consistently outpaced the market in both sales and sales increases over the previous period.

* Maintained records and prepared reports to meet corporate financial reporting requirements. The reports were used by store managers in planning and controlling the business.

* Established contracts with contractor to provide both routine maintenance and emergency repair services.

* Trained and developed seven management trainees.

* Created inventory control systems which provided greater accuracy and reduced losses by approximately 18%.

MID STATE SUPERMARKET, Metuchen, New Jersey   1979-1983

    FAMILY OWNED/OPERATED BUSINESS

* Turned around a bankrupt company. Within three months the operation was repositioned and generating a return on the investment for the owners of this privately held business.

* Developed creative marketing and advertising promotions which included sponsoring community events, direct mail, and discount programs.

* Negotiated vendor contracts which reduced expenses by 22.5%

* Opened a second location in only one year.

* Developed and oversaw an $855,000 budget.

EDUCATION

Bachelor of Science...Marketing...University of Maryland, College Park, Maryland...1987

PERSONAL

I am married and in excellent health. In addition, I am active within my community and enjoy golf, skiing, camping, and working on home improvement projects.

CONFIDENTIALITY REQUESTED   **WILLING TO TRAVEL**

Throughout the resume, bulleted items indicate achievements more than duties or responsibilities. Note the extra comments in some of the items.

Susan Steinfeld

85 Browertown Road

Little Falls, NJ 07000

(201) 000-0000

Objective

Senior administrative management position with an innovative company, where the professional execution of their special events and various marketing programs will be valued.

Personal Profile

Entrepreneurial, creative manager with strong leadership and motivational skills; extremely service-oriented; unique combination of intuitive and analytical abilities; astute at recognizing areas in need of improvement, with the vision to develop action steps and see them through to a prompt and successful completion, well within budgetary framework; knowledge of conversational French.

Areas of Expertise

Special Event/Meeting Planning

- Eleven years of experience in the start-to-finish management of high-budgeted, multifaceted projects for the hospitality, franchise and other industries.

- Demonstrated exceptional ability to plan and organize a broad range of considerations from site negotiations to finishing details and amenities, with the style and panache befitting events such as grand openings, major conferences, fund-raisers and employee/corporate functions.

- Screen and select agency personnel, freelancers and in-house staff, promoting harmonious working relationships throughout entire event staging process. Scope of involvement includes: coordination of attendees and presentors, travel/accommodations planning, theme-oriented decor, room set-up, food and beverage services, entertainment, audiovisual productions, and more.

Marketing Communications

- Heavy exposure to the entire creative execution of corporate marketing plans, guided only by minimal directives from management.

- Contract for and direct the activities of implementation teams which include: communications consultants, print and audiovisual production houses, photographers, artists, designers and public relations agencies, in addition to internal support staff, to produce creative promotional materials reflective of the corporate image.

- Awarded recognition for multiple print and other corporate communications pieces, such as annual reports, franchise brochures, videos, consumer information bulletins, and company newsletters.

... Continued

193 *Combination. Melanie Noonan, CPS, Little Falls, New Jersey.*
Filled square bullets are used with paragraphs throughout this resume. The Areas of
Expertise section contains two groups of three paragraphs for a balanced look.

Susan Steinfeld   Page 2

Professional Experience

HOST SERVICES INTERNATIONAL, New York, NY   1991-Present

Director of Event Marketing for hotel property franchisor controlling 2500+ Howard Johnson's, Days Inn and Ramada facilities. Report to Executive Vice President of Marketing. Responsible for planning and executing major special events including annual conferences, cause-related marketing, corporate meetings, and creative contributions to marketing plans.

- Within six months, orchestrated two successful major meetings normally requiring two years from inception of plans.
- Utilized economics of scale to produce two corporate functions with similar themes, back-to-back at the same location, saving the company at least $500,000 had they taken place at different times of the year.

BILLY BOB'S CHUCKWAGON, INC., Houston, TX   1981-1991

Director of Marketing Communications Services (1988-91) at Corporate Headquarters of $1.4 billion, 2400+ unit international restaurant chain.

- Reported to the Vice President of Corporate Communications and managed a staff of four in the areas of corporate communications/public relations, special events, publications, audiovisuals, and large scale meetings. Controlled a $1.2MM meeting budget.
- Promoted through the ranks of the marketing organization to director post by proving ability to take charge of problem areas and effect beneficial solutions.
  - ... Initiated marketing information center to answer various inquiries from individual franchise operators; published a quarterly directory listing contacts for available services.
  - ... Facilitated distribution of newly introduced but difficult to obtain marketing items. Traced cause of problem to short-term lack of inventory and developed monitoring system to prevent recurrences.
  - ... Took over meeting planner responsibility upon former incumbent's resignation three months before annual convention. With brand new management, developed and executed plans quickly, smoothly and to their satisfaction.
- Assumed permanent charge of event planning for the next seven years, each year progressively improving it with regard to increased attendance, quality of service and graphic design.
- Received Billy Bob's Outstanding Performance Award (four years) for quality and prompt execution of projects and recognition for award-winning annual reports.

Education

McGill University, Montreal, Canada (1975-77). Major in Marketing and Advertising. Management and Creative Writing seminars while at Billy Bob's.

Memberships

Meeting Planners, Inc.
Women in Communications

References and portfolio available upon request.

The Professional Experience section indicates two places of work. The bullets call attention to achievements, and more information is given about the longer of the two jobs held.

ROBERT P. BUTLER
6000 Homestead Road
East Brunswick, New Jersey 00000
(908) 000-0000

SUMMARY OF QUALIFICATIONS

Broad-based responsibilities within the Petroleum Industry in areas including:

- Supervision
- Sales/Service
- Purchasing
- Financial Management
- Customer Relations
- Product Diversification

Experienced in starting up and managing turnkey operations.

PROFESSIONAL ACCOMPLISHMENTS

Management

- Initially started in outside sales. Gained technical expertise within the industry and promoted to the positions of Senior Sales Person and General Manager.

- Operated a 2M Gallon Storage Terminal. Managed the salespeople and clerical staff; supervised a fleet of trucks and drivers for transport and delivery.

- Provided service and installation; managed a 24-hour Service Department.

- Responsible for daily cash management with regard to purchases and daily payable/receivables. Handled credit with large accounts.

- Performed all banking and loan functions. Established excellent business relationships with savings banks in the area.

Purchasing

- Negotiated yearly contracts with major oil companies and all other vendors. Familiar with state, local, and municipal bid procedures.

- Working knowledge of purchasing on the Mercantile Exchange and Petroleum Futures.

Sales

- Established a new outside sales effort which diversified the company's products and services.

- Increased yearly sales figures enabling the company to offer efficiency testing and installation of central air-conditioning. Carried a line of diesel fuel and lubricant products.

- Sold products and services to local businesses, schools, municipalities, and Fortune 500 corporations.

---

194 **Combination.** *Beverly Baskin, CPRW, Marlboro, New Jersey.*
Note the right-aligned name and address. This person was an entrepreneur with his own company for many years, so the purpose of this page is to market his transferable skills.

Robert P. Butler

Page 2

EXPERIENCE

CENTRAL JERSEY OIL COMPANY, Woodbridge, New Jersey 1990-Present

Sales Manager

REMSEN OIL COMPANY, Edison, New Jersey 1975-1990

President/General Manager

Sales Manager

Salesman

Service Mechanic

Driver (started part-time while attending school)

AFFILIATIONS

Former President, Essex County Oil Heat Association
Member Trustee, New Jersey Merchants Association
Member, Petroleum Marketeers of America
Middlesex County Chamber of Commerce
Active in community, civic, hospital and business affairs on local level.

EDUCATION

Union County College 1977-1979
Degree Program: Business Administration

Graduate, Washington Technical Institute
Program: Heating System Service

PERSONAL

Married: two children
Age: 37   Health: Excellent

Excellent references available upon request

The succinct information on this page does not compete with the preceding page for the reader's attention. The dominant page is the first page, which lists the person's skills.

GUDREN JOHNSEN
20000 North Park Drive
Sunnytown, CA 92000

(555) 555-5555

SALES AND MARKETING PROFESSIONAL

SUMMARY OF QUALIFICATIONS

- Demonstrated track record in increasing revenues in declining markets.
- Extensive contract negotiation skills.
- Special events coordination and planning expertise.
- Strong and accomplished representative of the business community.
- Excellent communicator and motivator.
- Able to project both a positive and professional company image.

PROFESSIONAL EXPERIENCE

SALES / PROMOTION

Hired as the first Outside Sales Representative for a forty-year-old wholesaler, and meat distributor, to the health care industry, specializing in acute care, convalescent and retirement facilities. Maintain established accounts and generate new business through cold calling throughout the Southern California territory.

Developed and implemented Personal Shopper Program "Retail By Appointment" for Major Shopping City Plaza store and men's store. Coordinated special programs to promote sales of merchandise and services. Facilitated corporate as well as personal shopping.

Produced impressive results with initial marketing effort for new luxury apartment community in Southern California County. As Marketing Director in pre-leasing period obtained a 42% occupancy. Upon promotion to Resident Manager exceeded expectations with an overwhelming 120% increase in leases to final lease-up of 98% occupancy in a five-month period.

As an outside salesperson in the building materials industry, called upon retail and wholesale building supply companies. Managed Southern California territory to monitor and maintain inventory levels and facilitate customer service.

SPECIAL EVENTS

Traveled throughout the Western United States to promote hospitality and concession services for major sporting events. Served as on-site coordinator and liaison between city officials and promoters; interacted with planners and ground and tour operators for off-site hospitality for conventions and corporate events. Researched and secured vendor contracts.

Successfully coordinated hospitality and concession efforts for the Sunnytown Open (January 1989, 340,000 spectators) and sports car race (October 1988, 75,000 spectators.) Coordinated the Sunnytown Grand Prix in 1989. Negotiated contracts and coordinated golf tournaments throughout the Western United States. Worked closely with city officials and building, fire, and health department officials on local requirements.

Facilitated negotiations with XYZ Golf Tournament officials and corporate sponsors for all hospitality requirements. Traveled extensively to coordinate all aspects of events. Gained familiarity with each function executed by 70 employees as liaison between tournament and hospitality operations.

195
Combination. *Diane Y. Chapman, Aliso Viejo, California.*
Centered headings offset wide paragraphs in this two-page resume. The Professional Experience section is arranged by three subheadings and extends to page 2.

Gudren Johnsen **Page 2**

SPECIAL EVENTS Professional Experience (continued)

Managed payroll, travel arrangements and accommodations. Direct contact with tournament directors resulted in obtaining six additional golf tournaments in six months.

ENTREPRENEURIAL

Owned and operated a women's professional clothing store. Developed and implemented all open buying, marketing, advertising, and sales efforts. Coordinated both in-store and off-site fashion shows for profit and non-profit events. Served as personal shopper and color/image analyst for professional men and women. Conducted research of competitors and compared reports on market penetration in competitive fields. Served as home office liaison for sales force.

<u>EMPLOYMENT HISTORY</u>

Outside Sales and Marketing Representative
  Meat Products, Inc., Sunnytown, CA 1992 to Present
Personal Shopping Consultant
  Major Store, Sunnytown, CA 1991 to 1992
Resident Manager
  Moon Bluff Apartments, Sunnytown, CA 1989 to 1991
Corporate Events Coordinator
  Exceptional Catering, Sunnytown, CA 1988 to 1989
Corporate Events Executive
  Big Time Catering, Sunnytown, CA 1987 to 1988
Owner
  Lady Time, Sunnytown, CA 1983 to 1987
Administrative Assistant to VP Sales and Marketing
  Research Tech, Sunnytown, CA 1981 to 1983
Multi-line Sales Representative
  Ivy League Marketing, Sunnytown, CA 1979 to 1981

<u>SPECIAL TRAINING AND DEVELOPMENT</u>

Personal Power For Unlimited Success with Anthony Robbins, 1992
Richard Chang Sales Training Seminar, 1990
Personnel Policies and Procedures Training, 1990
Time Management by Time Systems, Inc. 1989

<u>PROFESSIONAL AFFILIATIONS</u>

Sunnytown Chamber of Commerce   Multiple Sclerosis Society
National Association of Female Executives Women in Sales

<u>EDUCATION</u>

Business Studies
  Sunnytown Business College, Sunnytown, CA
  Coast Community College, Sunnytown, CA
  Golden College, Sunnytown, CA

The Employment History displays continual employment from 1979 to the present. All of the dates contrast with the absence of dates in the Education section.

John C. O'Brien

8900 Robinhood Way
Lawrenceville, Georgia 30245
(404) 564-9773

CAREER OBJECTIVE

Challenging opportunity in sales/management/marketing, utilizing proven track record of success to contribute to corporate expansion and profitability.

SUMMARY OF QUALIFICATIONS

Offering over 13 years of successful experience in manufacturing and retail sales environments, encompassing expertise and accomplishments in the following areas:

- **Sales** - Highly persuasive, with excellent negotiation skills. Demonstrated ability to build and maintain effective business relationships based on responsive flexible approach and comprehensive needs assessment.

- **Business Management** - Consistently maintained or exceeded profitability status in all management positions through the identification and implementation of numerous cost saving initiatives. Initiated and set standards in the areas of inventory control, Just-In-Time purchasing/distribution, and merchandising to enhance profitability. Upgraded and streamlined administrative and computer systems.

- **Marketing** - Promoted diversified product lines, with ongoing market analysis to determine optimum product mix sales strategies. Developed and maintained excellent dealer/vendor relations servicing multiple locations. Created responsive advertising campaigns and marketing strategies.

- **Personnel Management/Training** - Developed and conducted formal and on the job training in response to identified needs. Motivated staff and enhanced employee morale which resulted in low turnover and progressive staff development.

- **Personal Strengths** - Record of sound planning and decision-making to effectively resolve problems and enhance productivity. Resourceful, efficient, well organized, and flexible. Solid analytical skills, utilizing computer tools, including Lotus 1-2-3. Excellent communication and interpersonal relations skills, with proven results building and motivating winning teams that exceed objectives and meet the ever-changing needs of the customer. Reputation as an efficient manager of people and resources with a record of integrity, dependability, and exceptional customer service.

EMPLOYMENT HISTORY

1992 to Present	AAA TIRE COMPANY, INC.	Lawrenceville, GA
	General Manager	
1989 to 1992	BRIDGESTONE/FIRESTONE, INC.	Atlanta, GA
	Area Sales Manager	
1988 to 1989	TIRE KINGDOM, INC.	Atlanta, GA
	District Supervisor	
1979 to 1988	BIG 10 TIRES, INC.	Atlanta, GA
	Store Manager/Assistant Manager/Tire Technician	

EDUCATION

Dekalb College, Lawrenceville, Georgia - A.S. Degree in Marketing

Georgia State University, Atlanta, Georgia - Professional Development Course, 1990

---

196 **Combination.** *Julianne S. Franke, Lilburn, Georgia.*
A "power resume" that could end at the bottom of the first page, but page 2 packs a wallop with its Career Accomplishments.

John C. O'Brien

CAREER ACCOMPLISHMENTS

History of fast track advancement into positions of increased responsibility for leading service organizations, in addition to recruitment from one company to another based on reputation within the industry and established business relationships. Track record of success in sales, business management, and personnel management based on solid problem solving skills, astute recognition of talented personnel, efficient utilization of resources, a flexible approach, and the ability to develop and maintain excellent business relationships. Key accomplishments by skill area include:

Sales
- As General Manager at AAA Tire Company, increased sales 19% from 1992 to 1993, with 1993 year end projections of $8,540,050.

- At Bridgestone, successfully maintained the highest sales volume territory which produced $8.2 million in 1991.

- As District Supervisor for Tire Kingdom, successfully opened 6 new locations within a 6 month period and increased sales in existing locations, resulting in a 100 percent monthly sales increase over the period.

- As the youngest Store Manager in Big 10 company history, achieved numerous awards and sales contests over a 9 year period, including **Million Dollar Club (1986, 1987), Highest Volume Sales in One Day, Ten Percent Club (1985, 1986),** and **Manager of the Year (1984, 1987 finalist).**

Profitability
- Streamlined operations at AAA Tire Company which saved the company over $260,000 in annual operating expenses.

- Increased net profits at AAA Tire Company by 6% in 1992-1993 due to reduced costs, enhanced product mix selling, and streamlined inventory and staffing.

- Collaborated with Southern Bell to initiate a cost-saving communications strategy which reduced monthly telephone expenses by 50 percent.

- Contributed to profitability turnarounds at numerous locations through selective staffing, reduced turnover through effective training, the establishment of cost controls to reduce theft, effective problem solving, and analysis/promotion of optimum product mix.

- Through persistent effort to remove bureaucratic obstacles, erected a sign which increased store visibility and resulted in a threefold increase in monthly sales.

Marketing
- At Bridgestone, expanded product markets through the development and maintenance of business relationships with major corporate retail dealers, including NTW, Big 10 Tires, Pep Boys, KMart, and Sears, among others.

- Initiated public relations promotions and targeted advertising campaigns based on identified market needs in response to seasonal demands.

Training
- Developed and conducted formal training sessions for major retail dealers.

- Set district standards for training, reporting, and merchandising.

- Successfully completed numerous corporate sponsored training programs in sales, negotiation, computers, product knowledge, training, and time management.

The grouping of Career Accomplishments by four categories prevents this page from being an imposing wall of information.

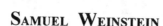

SAMUEL WEINSTEIN

7000 East Shaw Avenue
Fresno, California 93000

Residence: (000) 222-2222
Business: (000) 111-1111

EXPERTISE

Retail Management ▪ Merchandising ▪ Marketing

Seasoned executive with impressive track record with national retailer. Currently provide visionary leadership and management for operation with **$40+ million in sales**. Demonstrated aptitude for regional general merchandise management, as well as store operations, buying, assorting, and merchandising. Special talent for regionalized marketing, advertising, promotions. Career reflects consistent record of corporate recognition for contributions to operations, sales, and profit.

PROFESSIONAL EXPERIENCE

RETAILERS OF AMERICA

Store Manager, Valencia, CA (1988-1993): Full profit-and-loss responsibility for high-volume store staffed with 300. Direct and monitor management team of 25 in buying, assortment, presentation, marketing, advertising, housekeeping, and merchandising functions.

- **Increased volume from $30 to $40 million,** reversing trend from red to black P&L. Led store to rank in top 25 among 800 nationwide.
- Created and introduced innovative domestics line, generating $4+ million in sales; department has subsequently been launched in over 100 stores with profitable results.
- Envisioned regionalized marketing, advertising, and promotional strategies to tap large Hispanic market.
- Made substantial strides in affirmative action, creating staffing mix representative of the community.

Store Manager, Angus, CA (1984-1987): Hands-on management for $30 million unit with 200+ employees.

- **Doubled net profit,** with volume increase from $25 to $30 million.
- Directed $1.9 million remodel project (brought in on time and under budget, using store staff).
- Formed a cohesive staff using skills in recruitment, team building, empowerment, employee relations.

Regional General Merchandise Manager, Los Angeles, CA (1983-1984): Managed total store buying, assortment, and advertising for $400 million region with 27 locations throughout Nevada and California.

- **Boosted national ranking** of region from bottom 40 **to top 15** for profitability.
- Was first in company to implement "flighting" advertising.
- Served as youngest General Merchandise Manager in the company.

Store Manager, Stockton, CA (1982-1983): Was entrusted with large-volume store in first store manager assignment; promoted within six months to Regional General Merchandise Manager.

Prior Experience:

Western States Territorial Staff General Merchandise Manager, Los Angeles, California (1981-1982)
Group Staff Merchandise Manager (Home Fashions/Home Improvement), Los Angeles, CA (1978-1980)
Soft Lines Merchandise Manager, Las Vegas, NV (1976-1977)
Hard Lines Merchandise Manager, Phoenix, AZ (1971-1976)

EDUCATION

B.S., Business Administration, California State University, Fresno

---

197 **Combination.** *Susan B. Whitcomb, CPRW, Fresno, California.*
Information is kept to one page by grouping earlier work experience under the heading Prior Experience near the bottom of the page. Not the subtle use of boldfacing for emphasis.

S U S A N   G.   A L T H O F F ———————— 8888 Pomar Way
Walnut Creek, California 44444
Phone: (415) 555-5555

OBJECTIVE   Heavy responsibility involved with
Sales - Marketing - Training - Credit Control - or related activities

23 years experience in the following

specializing in the FOOD INDUSTRY and COLLECTIONS...

Selling to: - Professional business people, regional associations.
- Medical, Industrial, Wholesale, and Utilities.
- Credit, Collection, Institutional fields.
- Corporate Headquarters, Distributors, Retail Outlets.

Marketing: - New product development; packaging, advertising, sales and
service, and distribution.
- Recruiting, hiring, training, and managing personnel.
- Budgeting and controlling profit/cost ratio.
- Pricing, credit control, coordination of company policies.

Training: - Conducted formal and field training sessions.
- Planned, organized, and implemented sales objectives for
all in-house personnel.
- Worked with employees of clients to maximize the use of
products and services.
- Developed field sales and management personnel to handle
additional responsibilities for growth of the company, as well
as for the growth of the individuals.

EDUCATION   University of San Francisco, San Francisco, California   2 years
Major: Business Administration

Additional Education:

Toastmasters International

Semi-Annual Corporate Seminars

Dale Carnegie Training Course

School of Practical Experience

HOBBIES   Golf, Tennis, Jogging, and Coaching Youngsters

REFERENCES   Personal & Business References are available upon request

---

Functional. Margo Burkhardt, Antioch, California.
A resume without dates. The message is that what matters most is "What" and not
"When." Some indication of "How long" is given in the references to 23 years and 2 years.

198

J E R R Y   C .   C L A R K ————————————— 8000 Glenview Drive
Willing to travel and/or relocate   Pleasant Hill, CA 90000

                                                         Home: (415) 555-5555

OBJECTIVE   S A L E S - with growth potential...

EMPLOYMENT BACKGROUND

1988 – Present	**CADEMATORI TRUCKING**, Oakland, California
1987 – 1988	**DELTA LINES**, Oakland, California
1986 – 1987	**BALKEN CONSOLIDATORS**, Oakland, California
1983 – 1986	**GEM TRANSPORT**, Oakland, California
1978 – 1983	**RHODES & JAMISON**, Pleasanton, California

CAREER HIGHLIGHTS *(Examples of capabilities)*

Problem Solving - Initiative

I organized warehouse floor space and palletizing procedures, enabling the operation to function in a more mechanized and efficient manner. I also laid out and organized a new container storage and repair facility in very limited space - which greatly improved the efficiency of the operation. (Balken)

Customer Relations

Have a proven track record to verify my ability to relate well to the wide variety of people with which I've had to deal, and to the fact that I've had 100% cooperation from route customers, even though I've spent only a minimum amount of time with each one. I've always kept customers up to the minute on the status of their equipment and have handled their repairs. (Gem, Cadematori).

Supervisory Experience

I was Dock Foreman in charge of all dock personnel. My suggestions on hiring and work assignments were always implemented. (Gem, Balken)

As Yard Supervisor in charge of the entire yard operations, my responsibility included hiring outside contractors, purchasing parts, and taking customer orders. (Balken)

I was Yard Supervisor at our home terminal, and as such, was sent to Los Angeles to supervise all operations during the opening of a new terminal there. (Cadematori)

Financial Success

I have always been the highest-paid employee, yet employers would keep me on at overtime rates rather than hire another person at straight time, due to my efficiency of production. I've always been willing to put in the extra hours and travel when necessary, to attain financial success.

EDUCATION   California State University at Hayward 1979 - 1984
                     University of Nevada at Reno   1975 - 1977

199 **Combination.** *Margo Burkhardt, Antioch, California.*
Dates of employment are given up front, but abilities are presented by category and in paragraphs in the Career Highlights section, with the employer(s) indicated in parentheses.

Technology/Engineering/Science Resumes at a Glance

MICHAEL JOHNSON
900 Powers Blvd.
Colorado Springs, CO 80000
(719) 000-0000

CAREER OBJECTIVE: A position with a results-oriented company that requires an ambitious and career-conscious person where acquired skills and education will be utilized toward continued growth and advancement.

EXPERIENCE: •**Motorcycle Technician** - Jurgen Spath Harley Davidson, Nuernberg, Germany

August 1990 to March 1993

Position started part-time cleaning the shop, ordering parts, and maintaining the parts department. After attending the International Correspondence School for motorcycle mechanics, the position led to an apprenticeship. Hands-on training began with working closely with the owner of the shop. Duties performed included frame alignments, clutches, cam gears, kick starters, belt drives, tires, electrical and engine repair, and working on transmissions.

•**Warehouse Worker** - Troop Issue Subsistence Activity, Nuernberg Military

Community, Germany   April 1991 to September 1993

Unloaded bulk food products from delivery trucks by hand, forklift, and pallet jacks. Broke down pallets and stored products in designated areas, making sure items were accounted for, checked for damage, and labeled properly. Maintained proper rotation of stock on hand, rearranged and restacked items as necessary removing all damaged products from area. Informed supervisor of any storage-related problems. Cleaned all equipment to meet safety and sanitation standards. Performed inventory of all items for accountability, reorder, and price-change purposes.

•**Shift Supervisor / Waiter** - Pizza Hut, Owings Mills, Maryland

March 1988 to May 1990

Supervised a staff of ten employees to ensure that all products were continually stocked, food was cooked in a timely manner, and the service was prompt. Responsible for balancing the cash drawer and the hiring and termination of personnel. Maintained a sanitary environment for customers, and made sure the night shift ran smoothly.

EDUCATION: **University of Maryland,** Maryland, Germany, October 1992 to January 1993. Courses Studied: German and Accounting.

International Correspondence School, Scranton, Pennsylvania, January 1991 to January 1993. Courses Studied: Motorcycle Mechanics. GPA 95.6/100.

Arbeitetshandswerk Schule Vor Motorrads, i.e. Working with hands for Motorcycles, 1990 to 1991.

Maryland Bartending Academy, Inc., Glen Burnie, Maryland, January 1, 1986 to January 14, 1986. Mixology and Bar Operations. Approved by the Maryland State Board for higher education.

REFERENCES: Excellent References Available upon Request

Chronological. Gina V. Bump, Colorado Springs, Colorado.
In the Experience section the positions are emphasized with boldfacing and thin underlining; in the Education section the institutions are emphasized with boldfacing.

200

GAYLON DOUGLAS HAMILTON

8000 Sunset Boulevard #90 • Lexington, SC 29000 • (803) 000-0000

OBJECTIVE: To obtain a position in research and development that will allow me to use my knowledge and experience of electronics and the computer mainframe-to-terminal environment. It is my preference to relocate, and I prefer assignment in the Greenville, SC, area.

EMPLOYMENT HISTORY:

NCR, Inc., Columbia, SC   Nov. 1986 - Present
Senior Development Electronics Technician
- Responsible for maintaining operations and troubleshooting NCR Tower family Mini-Mainframe Computer and automation testing of circuit boards.
- Work with research and development engineers to implement PCB modules from design phase to production.
- Install and troubleshoot 3550 start-up LPB and power supply interface modules.
- Provide technical support services for other NCR employees.
- Initiated a plan to start a "team work concept" for the failure analysis group.
- Electrostatic Discharge Certification.

Wackenhut Corporation, Greenville, SC   Nov. 1985 - Nov. 1986
Security Guard
- Maintain security and regulate access to facility.

Libco Mill, Liberty, SC   Oct. 1980 - Aug. 1983
Final Inspection Technician
- Maintained quality assurance for plant productions.

KNOWLEDGE AND EXPERIENCE:

- Intel and Motorola microprocessors
- Intel Multibus II
- Communications circuits (RS-232 & IH DLC)
- C, BASIC and Pascal programming languages
- Tektronix Oscilloscope
- Tektronix 1240/1241 Processor Analyzer
- Motorola Assembler Mnemonics
- UNIX System V & UNIX Shell
- Digital Logic
- MS-DOS 5.0
- ELAN Processor Analyzer
- Reading Schematics

EDUCATION:

Tri County Technical College, Pendleton, SC
Major: Electronics Engineering Technology
Degree: Associate of Science (A.S.)   GPA: 3.54 / 4.0
Graduation Date: 1986

Honors:
- Who's Who Among Students in American Junior Colleges
- National Dean's List

Easley Senior High School, Easley, SC
Graduation Date: 1977

Honors:
- High School Honor Graduate
- Certificate in Industrial Electronics

REFERENCES AVAILABLE UPON REQUEST

201 **Combination.** *Nancy P. Stein, Columbia, South Carolina.*
Horizontal lines separate sections. Notice how items related to computer knowledge and experience are grouped in one section. Education ending in an associate degree is put last.

JOANNE LaRANGE — (formerly Alarcon) ———— 7000 Crest Oaks
Concord, CA 94000

(415) 000-0000

OBJECTIVE   Technical Support Position involved with Computers
...or related responsibility with growth potential

Areas of Knowledge:

- PC Hardware and Software including Lotus, WordStar, MultiMate and Wang V.S. 100 System administration.

- Very complicated building communications wiring schemes and equipment.

- All management phases of AT&T System 75 phone system.

Achievements & Attributes:

- Received commendation for my "significant contribution" during the consolidation of two Homequity business offices.

- My ability to respond to user's needs in an efficient and timely manner exemplifies my service attitude.

- I am a highly motivated individual with a tenacious ability to get the job done correctly — and on time!

BUSINESS EXPERIENCE (Note: Please do not contact employer without permission)

1984-Present   HOMEQUITY RELOCATION, Walnut Creek, California
Information Services Technical Assistant - in Regional Office
Serve as one of a three-member team supporting 180 Personal Computers and software which includes an online system consisting of 200 screens, Wang V.S. 100 System and related equipment, and other communications wiring and equipment. In addition, have sole responsibility for the AT&T System 75 with 200 stations.

Participated in the successful consolidation of the San Mateo and Walnut Creek offices by supporting the San Mateo office for six weeks (with no prior knowledge of their computer hardware or their systems).

1982-1983   SUNWEST PROPERTIES, San Diego, California
Property Management for family-owned business.

1981   STANDARD FEDERAL SAVINGS, Chicago, Illinois
Computer Operator serving Main Office and 10 Branch Offices
Operated Univac 90/60 System under VS/9. Responsible for bringing the online system down, processing scheduled work, and backing up files.

1971-1981   MIDAS INTERNATIONAL CORPORATION, Chicago, Illinois
Coordinator - Data Services (1979-1981)
Lead Operator - Inventory Control Accounting System (1973-1979)
Data Control Clerk (1971-1973)

- 29 -

Combination. Margo Burkhardt, Antioch, California.
This informal resume has remarks in parentheses and first-person statements in the Achievement & Attributes section. Horizontal lines enclose the Objective statement.

202

LUCILLE HALL

500 Holly Hill Road
Enterprise, Alabama 36000

(205) 000-0000

CAREER OBJECTIVE

A career at the leading edge of electronic technology using earned skills in management, design, troubleshooting, and implementation.

EMPLOYMENT BACKGROUND

Field Service Engineer
(1988 - Present)

CAE Link Corporation
Binghamton, New York 13902-1237

Performed maintenance, troubleshooting, repair, and modifications on rotary wing and combat mission flight simulators and their associated motion, linkage, weapon, audio, and visual computers and systems.

Independent Contractor
(1985-1987)

Kansas City, Missouri 64131

Preparing wiring cable for missle guidance systems, for Torotel Electronics.

Meat Processing Foreman
(1980-1984)

Roman Packing Company
Norfolk, Nebraska 68701

Operated and performed preventive maintenance on: electric bandsaw, grinder, hydraulic pumping machine. Trained and oversaw work of 1 to 3 line workers.

Steel Worker
(1979-1980)

Vulcraft
Norfolk, Nebraska 68701

Operated various welders, hydraulic shears, and benders to fabricate steel joists.

Drywall Construction Foreman
(1967-1979)

Eliason and Knuth Drywall Inc.
Lincoln, Nebraska 68507

Operated various power tools. Trained/supervised up to 12 workers. Started branch office in Norfolk, Nebraska. Performed quality control, sales, material ordering/shipping. Interfaced with architects to resolve and troubleshoot building and construction problems.

EDUCATION

Student
(1984-1988)

DeVry Institute of Technology
Kansas City, Missouri 64132

Bachelor of Science, Associate of Science, Electronics Engineering Technology

Computer Languages
- BASIC
- Machine
- Turbo Pascal
- Z80 Assembler

Computer Systems
- IBM PC   • Commodore
- Hewlett-Packard 6400
- Perkin/Elmer 8/32, 3200 Series
- DEC PDP 11/45, 55 Series

SPECIAL TRAINING

- Extensive first aid and CPR training   • Personnel Management seminars -- 1975, 1976
- Architectural Drafting -- Northeast Technical Community College, Norfolk, NE. 1977
- Soldering and Circuit Board Rework Training to Military Specifications
- Department of Defense Security Clearance, 1989 - Present

References Available upon Request

Please keep information confidential.

203 *Chronological. Penny J. Rotolo, Enterprise, Alabama.*
Horizontal lines interrupted by headings is an evident design feature. Note the two-column distinction between Computer Languages and Computer Systems in the Education section.

Thomas B. Newbury   (000) 000-0000

1000 E. Liberty Road, Princeton, NJ 00000

PROFILE: **Architect, Planner** and **Designer** with diversified experience in all phases of client relations, project management and planning/designing.

PROFESSIONAL:

FAMOUS UNIVERSITY, SCHOOL OF ARCHITECTURE, **Bachelor of Architecture**
<u>Registered Architect</u>, New York and New Jersey
National Council of Architectural Registration Boards
Fellow, Society of American Registered Architects
Attended classes to upgrade computer skills - DOS, Word Processing and AutoCAD

ARCHITECTURAL:

Services - Programming; Planning; Designing; Detailing; Engineering Coordination; Construction; Field Observation

Project Highlights

- ▸ Famous University Rare Book Library, Some City, State
- ▸ School of Journalism Building, Some University, State
- ▸ Airport Control Tower - Design
- ▸ Well-Known Apartments, Some City
- ▸ Classroom Building Complex at Famous Institution, Some City, State

INTERIORS:

Services - Contract Negotiations; Programming; Planning; Site Studies; Block Layouts; Stacking Plans; Test Layouts; Space Planning; Designing; Decorating Coordination; Construction Documents; Field Observation; Moving Coordination

Project Highlights

- ▸ Famous Headquarters Office Building, Some Location, Some City
- ▸ Some Firm - Some Office Facilities, Some Place, Some City
- ▸ Some Firm - Some Facility, Some City, Some Region
- ▸ Some Company - Some Facility, Some City, State
- ▸ Some Firm - Some Facility, Some City

CORPORATE FACILITIES MANAGEMENT:

Services - Research; Data Gathering; Programming; Project Reports; Cost Control; Scheduling Control; Contract Negotiation; Planning; Test Layouts; Real Estate Site Selection; Project Design; Construction Coordination; Hazardous Waste/Asbestos Removal

Project Highlights

- ▸ Network Broadcast Center Building Expansion, Some City
- ▸ Network - TV/News Complex, Some City
- ▸ Network City Radio Station, Some City, State
- ▸ Network Radio News Room, Some City
- ▸ Network Division Offices Relocation, Some City

Functional. Vivian P. Belen, CPRW, Fair Lawn, New Jersey.
No dates are given in this functional five-section resume. To gain the reader's interest, emphasis is put on the person's prestigious projects rather than on a long career chronology.

204

JOHN A. DOE

Any Street
Any Town, USA 00000
(000) 000-0000

QUALIFICATION SUMMARY

Acquired 23 years experience in the technology, planning, and monitoring of U.S. South Communications' network facilities in Florida and Mississippi. Overall achievements include development of detailed network configurations for local loop access architecture involving multiple alternatives, end-user customer needs, and overall economics of implementation; provisioning high capacity digital service; and maximizing current utilization and investment of the embedded base. Specific responsibilities include developing strategic network plans to deploy fiber/digital electronics in local loop, calculating capital funds required for construction of infrastructure, participating in market unit sales strategy sessions to position the network to be available for sales, and interfacing with numerous network segments to implement recommendations.

PROFESSIONAL EXPERIENCE

SOUTHEASTERN BELL TELEPHONE/U.S. SOUTH COMMUNICATIONS   1980 - Present

Planning Engineer, Network Facilities
Responsible for western half of Florida (11/92 - Present)
Responsible for western half of Mississippi (1980 - 11/92)

SOUTHWESTERN BELL TELEPHONE COMPANY

Design Engineer, Network Facilities	1978 - 1980
Communications Technician	1974 - 1978

AMERICAN TELEPHONE and TELEGRAPH COMPANY   1970 - 1974

Microwave Radio Technician

UNITED STATES GOVERNMENT   1966 - 1970

Electronics and Radar Technology Technician
Civilian employee with the Department of the Navy (1969 - 1970)
United States Army (1966 - 1969)

RELATED TRAINING   **U. S. SOUTH COMMUNICATIONS**

* Loop Electronics Inventory Module (LEIM) (40 hrs.)   1992
* Loop Planning Economic Computer Module (PLAN) (40 hrs.)   1988
* Economic Selection Module/Loop Engineering Assignment Data (ESM/LEAD) (40 hrs.)   1988
* Integrated Services Digital Networks (40 hrs.)   1987
* Lightwave Design Technology (24 hrs.)   1984
* Digital Communications Technology (32 hrs.)   1983
* Subscriber Carrier Planning (40 hrs.)   1983
* Loop Feeder Administration (40 hrs.)   1982
* Long Range Outside Plant Planning (60 hrs.)   1980
* Engineering Economics (16 hrs.)   1979
* Network Facilities Basic Engineering (40 hrs.)   1978

EDUCATION

Technical Level Education:

Mississippi Institute of Electronics - Tupelo, MS   1970
• Electronics Technology course

Redstone Arsenal - Huntsville, AL   1968
• Electronics Technology course

College Level Education:

Georgia State University - Atlanta, GA   1972
• Completed 16 quarter hour credits in accounting and psychology

University of Florida - West Palm Beach, FL   1969
• Completed 27 semester hour credits in basic college courses

AWARDS/CERTIFICATES

* Received Engineering Merit Awards for Individual Performance (1992, 1987, 1985, 1984, 1982)
* Certified Radio Technician through National Association of Business and Educational Radio
  (1989 - Present)
* Hold Federal Communications Commission First Class License (1970 - Present)

This second page is devoted to related training, education, certification, and licensing. The extensive amount of related training is put first and arranged chronologically.

John A. Anthony
9000 Dewey Lane
Youngstown, Ohio 12000
(216) 000-0000

Career Objective: *Seeking an opportunity to use my skills and abilities to enhance the success of your organization.*

Education: *Bachelor of Science in Mechanical Engineering Technology, 1982*
Bachelor of Arts in History, 1972
Gannon University
Erie, Pennsylvania

Computer Proficient: MathCAD, WordPerfect 5.1, Quattro Pro and TK!Solver

Summary of Experience: *Broad base of design, engineering and manufacturing expertise. Nineteen years of progressive responsibilities with accelerated advancement and a proven record of accomplishments in the areas of Computer-Assisted Design/Computer-Assisted Manufacturing (CAD/CAM). Cellular Manufacturing, and Total Quality Improvement using ISO 9000.*

Skills and Abilities

Organization   *Assessed, analyzed, and developed workable solutions.*
Analytical   *Utilized qualitative and deductive analysis, CAD/CAM, industrial engineering procedures, and other techniques.*
Established positive working relationships, in-house and externally, with all levels and types of individuals.

Design   *Designed products for manufacturability to customer specifications.*
Engineering   *Documented and maintained procedures for ISO 9000 compliance.*
Manufacturing: *Provided technical support to internal and external customers.*
Facilitated implementation of world-class cellular manufacturing.

Communication   *Conducted in-house CAD training sessions.*
Developed strong problem-solving teams.
Prepared, proposed, and executed projects.
Served on EAP program and ISO 9000 steering committees.

Leadership: *Led project design teams of two to six support personnel.*
Utilized "empowerment" to meet company objectives.
Stimulated positive quality-oriented attitudes.
Built effective working relationships; established trust and cooperation.

Personal Qualities: *A decisive, intelligent, task-oriented individual who views obstacles as challenges; an honest, confident and hardworking leader - a person of keen judgment who can sense the proper course of action, determine the appropriate resources, and understand the complexities of today's world marketplace.*

206 **Combination.** *Joseph A. DiGiorgio, Erie, Pennsylvania.*
A resume for a person whose entire career has been four different positions with one company. This first page groups skills and abilities by four categories.

Employment History of John A. Anthony   *Page 2*

Autoclave Engineers, Inc, Erie, Pennsylvania, April 1974 to May 1993
A world leader in advanced technology for high pressure applications for production and research. Manufacturers of high temperature equipment, autoclaves, pressure vessels, valves, and fittings.

Operations Engineer, April 1992 to March 1993
Responsible for facilitating the implementation of world class manufacturing: tooling acquisition, equipment evaluation, process development, operations research, plant layout, line balancing, resource optimization, general problem-solving, supporting and participating in team activities as well as training, directing and assisting other employees.

- *Significantly improved production efficiency of manufacturing cell via time study and line balancing techniques.*

- *Served as an internal auditor for ISO 9000 compliance.*

Design Engineer, May 1982 to April 1992 and March 1993 to May 1993
Responsible for designing products to marketing specifications: completing specifications and drawings to meet customer requirements, writing special instructions and data books, documenting and maintaining procedures for ISO 9000 compliance, contributing ideas to support product cells and teams, facilitating transfer of information, providing technical support to internal and external customers and contributing leadership to cell and teams.

- *Engineered and coordinated $750,000 process system project for a major oil firm.*

- *Co-patent holder for supercritical cleaning process and equipment.*

- *Established design calculation format for pressure vessels to ASME Code Section VIII division 1 criteria.*

- *Engineering department representative to MRP system installation task force.*

Design Checker, January 1980 to May 1982
Responsible for checking layouts and drawings prior to final approval: ensuring that customer specifications are met, reviewing projects for conformance with Autoclave Engineers systems and procedures, resolving existing problems, acting as liaison with other departments and assisting in supervision of drafting/design staff.

- *Completed engineering technology degree while working full-time.*

Drafter, April 1974 to January 1980
Responsible for drawing layouts, sections, schematics, and assemblies: completing math computations, investigating and procuring reference materials, maintaining files and supporting documents, modifying software as required, and checking drawings of other drafters.

I completed a co-op assignment for a manufacturer of heat exchangers while attending high school. Upon graduation, I worked in the finishing room at Hammermill Paper Company.

References Available upon Request

Note that the person's role of Design Engineer was interrupted for an 11-month term as an Operations Engineer.

Charles R. Swanson

00000 Kingway Drive ▪ St. Louis, Missouri 63000 ▪ (314) 000-0000

▪ ▪

■ ## Summary

Twenty years experience as a chemist encompassing many phases of product development in the over-the-counter pharmaceutical field and industrial chemicals area. Fifteen years in pharmaceutical product development with extensive experience in formulations, testing, pilot and scale-up processes, production and formula troubleshooting, process validation, methods development, and data evaluation. Developed emulsions, suspensions, and tablets of major brand name over-the-counter domestic and international product lines. Patents U.S. and foreign. Familiar with good manufacturing and laboratory practices.

Developed surfactant entities for pharmaceutical, cosmetic and industrial use. Familiar with synthesis and production processes for surfactants.

■ ## Major Product Lines

- Oxy Residon't Medicated Face Wash
- Oxy 10 Daily Face Wash
- Oxy Daily Face Wash (Canada)
- Extra Strength and Sensitive Skin Line Extensions
- Liquiprin

- Oxy pads, regular, Low Alcohol, and Sensitive Skin Line Extensions
- Tums Plus Antigas/Antacid with Simethicone
- Natures Remedy
- Orafix/Brace Denture Adhesive

■ ## Selected Accomplishments

Design & Development

- Served as technical liaison between companies during product development and manufacturing.
- Developed innovative emulsion system for encapsulating simethicone.
- Designed new technology for tastemaking of bitter drugs.
- Designed new technology for the controlled release of over-the-counter and prescription drugs.
- Designed new process for controlled release pharmaceutics which significantly releases solvent emissions and process time, and is more operator-independent than most current processes.
- Developed formulations which led to new and unique emulsion system primarily used for delivery of topical skin protectants and active ingredients.
- Designed formulations with unique flow properties which made possible products previously thought to be not manufacturable.
- Modified analytical techniques for determination of substantivity of topical formulations such as protective lotion and sunblocks.
- Supervised pilot and full-scale manufacturing of new products and product line extensions.

207 **Combination.** *Carla L. Culp, CPRW, Edwardsville, Illinois.*
A filled square bullet beside each main heading helps to tie together visually the three pages of this resume. Matching smaller square bullets call attention to products and achievements.

Charles R. Swanson   2

___

■ **Selected Accomplishments (continued)**

Technical Writing & Research

- Have written:
  - product stability protocols.
  - protocols for over-the-counter products and chemical and physical testing of those products.
  - process validation protocols.
  - raw material specifications.
  - product manual describing all phases of the manufacture and packaging of each product.
  - product manual describing the development and testing of each product.
  - patent disclosures.
- Generated questionnaire for consumer studies of topical over-the-counter products, resulting in marketable product.
- Conducted small scale in-house consumer studies of topical products which resulted in new liquid soap product which is sold internationally.

Process Trouble Shooting

- Implemented new manufacturing process which eliminated packaging problem.
- Traced product problems to change in raw material physical and chemical properties not detected by usual quality control testing.
- Set up innovative quality control tests for raw materials, which improved quality and manufacturing of products.

■ **Professional Experience**

Senior Research Chemist   1989-Present
ABC PHARMACEUTICAL, St. Louis, Missouri

- Formulated liquid, semisolid, and solid dosage forms.
- Provide support and supervision of pilot and production scale-up operations.
- Provide technical service to customers.
- Develop new and improved drug delivery systems.

Senior Research Chemist/Project Scientist, Technical Consultant   1982-1989
ACME PHARMACEUTICAL PRODUCTS, St. Louis, Missouri

- Developed pharmaceutical products and unique methods of analysis for major brand product lines.
- Performed process validation and troubleshooting.
- Prepared clinical samples and evaluated raw material.
- Prepared extensive production and data manual for each product.
- Performed stability testing interfacing with marketing and medical personnel, and in-house product studies.

___

Selected Accomplishments in three areas and spread across the first two pages make a strong impression. Notice the use of hyphens as second-level bullets.

Charles R. Swanson   3

■ **Professional Experience (continued)**

Product Development Chemist   1976-1982
ABC PHARMACEUTICAL, St. Louis, Missouri
- Supervised activities of degreed chemist and lab assistant in development of new product formulations.
- Responsible for formulation, in vitro testing, analytical, raw materials appropriation, pilot plant and full-scale production, and packaging of topical health products.

Research Assistant   1978-1980
SOUTHERN ILLINOIS UNIVERSITY AT EDWARDSVILLE, Edwardsville, Illinois
- Conducted research and work activities related to thesis.

Technical Service Chemist   1975-1976
O. K. TOMAKE CHEMICALS, Fall City, Illinois
- Synthesized anionic, cationic, and non-ionic surfactants.
- Provided technical support in the areas of formulation development and process troubleshooting for both Tomake and clients.
- Involved in development of new surfactant entities.

Physical Science Assistant   1973-1974
U.S. ARMY, Aberdeen Proving Ground, Maryland
- Performed instrumental analysis of samples for chemical engineering and organic synthesis group.

■ **Patents**

- Issued U.S. Patent #4,000,000 May 10, 1999; Fire Starters. Inventors: Calvin W. Brown and Charles R. Swanson. Assignee: ABC Pharmaceutical.
- Issued U.S. Patent #4,000,000 May 24, 1999; Stable High Internal Phase Ratio Topical Emulsions. Inventor: Charles R. Swanson. Assignee: ABC Pharmaceutical.
- Issued U.S. Patent #4,000,000 April 7, 1999; Encapsulated Antacid. Inventor: Charles R. Swanson. Assignee: Jaymar Industries, Inc.

Several Patents Currently Pending

■ **Education**

Master of Science in Chemistry   1980
Southern Illinois University at Edwardsville, Edwardsville, Illinois

Bachelor of Arts Degree in Chemistry   1972
Blackburn College, Carlinville, Illinois
Minor: Mathematics

■ **Professional Associations**

American Chemical Society
Society of Cosmetic Chemists: Technical Writer, St. Louis Chapter Newsletter (1989, 1990)

For Professional Experience, six positions spread across the second and third pages perpetuate the stong impression. The list of patents provides a strong note on the last page.

Addendum

MARGO S. BERNS
Executive Account Assistant
Addie Advertising, Inc.

PROMOTION COORDINATOR

Handle promotions in their entirety. Most recent promotion was for Hardee's and Conner Prairie. Responsibilities included producing promotional support items for in-store distribution.

SKILLS ACQUIRED

Team Member - Quick Learner - Coordinator - Able to Meet Deadlines - Creativity - Professional Attitude

ACCOUNT COORDINATOR

During my tenure with Harrington Associates, I worked as an Assistant Account Executive on the Hardee's fast food account. Am familiar with the Indianapolis market and its competitors.

SKILLS ACQUIRED

Analytical Reports - Overseeing Projects - Verbal Communication Skills - Putting Forth Best Effort *At All Times*

FLEXIBLE AND DEDICATED

Take responsibility for getting the job done completely and efficiently. Can work well on all levels - from budgetary needs, product knowledge, demographics, to planning marketing objectives for future quarters. Computer skills include Macintosh, WordPerfect and Microsoft Word.

SKILLS ACQUIRED

Managerial Skills - Being Persistent and Not Giving Up! - Public Relations - Never ending Search for Knowledge and Information

CLIENT AND SERVICE ORIENTED

Experience in the service industry. Assertive personality which allows me to deal with clients and franchisees in a professional manner. Able to think quickly and prioritize needs from corporate to client level. Educational background in Business/Marketing.

SKILLS ACQUIRED

High Energy Level - Ability to Speak in Front of Crowds - Listening Skills - Able to Analyze Client Needs - Negotiating Techniques

---

Addendum. *Gayle Bernstein, CPRW, Indianapolis, Indiana.*
Here is an Addendum than can be included with a thank-you letter after an interview. The Addendum reminds the reader of key areas and skills indicated in the resume.

Part III

Best Cover Letter Tips

Part III

Best Cover Letter Tips

In an active job search, your cover letter and resume should complement one another. Both are tailored to a particular reader you have contacted or to a specific job target. To help you create the "best" cover letters for your resumes, this part of the book mentions some common myths about cover letters and presents 30 tips for polishing the letters you write.

Myths about Cover Letters

1. **Resumes and cover letters are two separate documents that have little relation to each other.** The resume and cover letter work together in presenting you effectively to a prospective employer. The cover letter should mention the resume and call attention to some important aspect of it.

2. **The main purpose of the cover letter is to establish friendly rapport with the reader.** Resumes show that you *can* do the work required. Cover letters express that you *want* to do the work required. But it doesn't hurt to display enthusiasm in your resumes and refer to your abilities in your cover letters.

3. **You can use the same cover letter for each reader of your resume.** Modify your cover letter for each reader so that it sounds fresh rather than canned. Chances are that in an active job search, you have already talked with the person who will interview you. Your cover letter should reflect that conversation and build on it.

4. **In a cover letter, you should mention any negative things about your education, work experience, life experience, or health to prepare the reader in advance of an interview.** This is not the purpose of the cover letter. You might bring up these topics in the first or second interview, but only after the interviewer has shown interest in you or offered you a job. Even then, if you feel that you must mention something negative about your past, present it in a positive way, perhaps by saying how that experience has strengthened your will to work hard at any new job.

5. **It is more important to remove errors from a resume than from a cover letter, because the resume is more important than the cover letter.** Both your resume and your cover letter should be free of errors. The cover letter is usually the first document a prospective employer sees. The first impression is often the most important one. If your cover letter has an embarrassing error in it, the chances are good that the reader may not bother to read your resume or may read it with less interest.

6.   **To make certain that your cover letter has no errors, all you need to do is proofread it or ask a friend to "proof" it.** Trying to proofread your own cover letter is risky, even if you are good at grammar and writing. Once a document is typewritten or printed, it has an aura about it that may make it seem better written than it is. For this reason, you are likely to miss typos or other kinds of errors.

Relying on someone else is risky too. If your friend is not good at grammar and writing, that person may not see any mistakes either. Try to find a proofreader, a professional editor, an English teacher, a professional writer, or an experienced secretary who can point out any errors you may have missed.

7.   **After someone has proofread your letter, you can make a few changes to it and not have it looked at again.** More errors creep into a document this way than you would think possible. The reason is that such changes are often done hastily, and haste can waste an error-free document. If you make *any* change to a document, ask someone to proofread it a final time just to make sure that you haven't introduced an error during the last stage of composition. If you can't find someone to help you, the next section gives you advice on how to eliminate common mistakes in cover letters.

Tips for Polishing Cover Letters

You might spend several days working on your resume, getting it "just right" and free of errors. But if you send it with a cover letter that is written quickly and contains even one conspicuous error, all of your good effort may be wasted. That error could be just the kind of mistake the reader is looking for to screen you out.

You can prevent this kind of tragedy by polishing your cover letter so that it is free of all errors. The following tips can help you avoid or eliminate common errors in cover letters. If you become aware of these kinds of errors and know how to fix them, you can be more confident about the cover letters you send with your resumes. These tips are based on errors found in actual cover letters.

Using Good Strategies for Letters

1.   **Use the postal abbreviation for the state in your mailing address.** See resume writing strategy 1 in Part I.

2.   **Make certain that the letter is addressed to a specific person and that you use this person's name in the salutation.** Avoid using such general salutations as Dear Sir or Madam, To Whom It May Concern, Dear Administrator, Dear Prospective Employer, and Dear Committee. In an active job search, you should do everything possible to send your cover letter and resume to a particular individual, preferably someone you've already talked with in person or by phone, and with whom you have arranged an interview. If you have not been able to make a personal contact, at least do everything possible to find out the name of the person who will read your letter and resume. Then address the letter to that person.

3.   **Adjust the margins for a short letter.** If your cover letter is 300 words or longer, use left, right, top, and bottom margins of one inch. If the letter is shorter, the width of the margins should increase. How much they increase is a matter of personal taste. One way to take care of the width of the top and bottom margins is to center a shorter letter vertically on the page. A maximum width for a short cover letter of 100 words or fewer might be two-inch left and right mar-

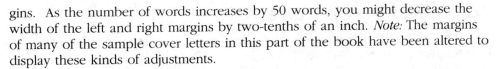

gins. As the number of words increases by 50 words, you might decrease the width of the left and right margins by two-tenths of an inch. *Note:* The margins of many of the sample cover letters in this part of the book have been altered to display these kinds of adjustments.

4. **If you write your letter with word processing or desktop publishing software, use left-justification to ensure that the lines of text are readable with fixed spacing between words.** The letter will have a "ragged right" look along the right margin, but the words will be evenly spaced horizontally. Don't use justification in an attempt to give a letter a printed look. Unless you do other typesetting procedures, like kerning and hyphenating words at the end of some lines, full justification can make your letter look worse with some extra wide spaces between words.

Using Pronouns Correctly

5. **Use *I* and *My* sparingly.** When most of the sentences in a cover letter begin with *I* or *My*, the writer may appear self-absorbed, self-centered, or egotistical. If the reader of the letter is turned off by this kind of impression (even if it is a false one for you), you could be screened out without ever having an interview. Of course, you will need to use these first-person pronouns because most of the information you put in your cover letter will be personal. But try to avoid using *I* and *My* at the beginnings of sentences and paragraphs.

6. **Refer to a business, company, corporation, or organization as "it" rather than "they."** Members of the Board may be referred to as "they," but a company is a singular subject requiring a singular verb. Note this example:

    New Products, Inc., was established in 1980. It grossed over a million dollars in sales during its first year.

7. **If you start a sentence with *This,* be sure that what *This* refers to is clear.** If the reference is not clear, insert some word or phrase to clarify what *This* means. Compare the following lines:

    > My revised application for the new position will be faxed to you by noon on Friday. You indicated by phone that *this* is acceptable to you.

    > My revised application for the new position will be faxed to you by noon on Friday. You indicated by phone that this *method of sending the application* is acceptable to you.

    A reader of the first sentence wouldn't know what *This* refers to. Friday? By noon on Friday? The revised application for the new position? The insertion after *This* in the second sentence, however, tells the reader that *This* refers to the use of faxing (rather than regular mail or Federal Express).

8. **Use *as follows* after a singular subject.** Literally, *as follows* means *as it follows,* so the phrase is illogical after a plural subject. Compare the following lines:

Incorrect:	My plans for the day of the interview are as follows:
Fixed:	My plans for the day of the interview are these:
Correct:	My plan for the day of the interview is as follows:
Better:	Here is my plan for the day of the interview:

    In the second set, the improved version avoids a hidden reference problem—the possible association of the silent "it" with *interview.* Whenever you want to use *as follows,* check to see whether the subject that precedes *as follows* is plural. If it is, don't use this phrase.

Using Verb Forms Correctly

9. **Make certain that subjects and verbs agree in number.** Plural subjects require plural forms of verbs. Singular subjects require singular verb forms. Most writers know these things, but problems arise when subject and verb agreement gets tricky. Compare the following lines:

   Incorrect: My education and experience has prepared me . . . .
   Correct: My education and experience have prepared me . . . .

   Incorrect: Making plans plus scheduling conferences were . . . .
   Correct: Making plans plus scheduling conferences was . . . .

   In the first set, *education* and *experience* are two things (you can have one without the other) and require a plural verb. A hasty writer might lump them together and use a singular verb. When you reread what you have written, look out for this kind of improper agreement between a plural subject and a singular verb.

   In the second set, *making plans* is the subject. It is singular, so the verb must be singular. The misleading part of this sentence is the phrase *plus scheduling conferences*. It may seem to make the subject plural, but it doesn't. In English, phrases that begin with such words as *plus, together with, in addition to, along with,* and *as well as* usually don't make a singular subject plural.

10. **Whenever possible, use active forms of verbs rather than passive forms.** Compare these lines:

    Passive: My report will be sent by my assistant tomorrow.
    Active: My assistant will send my report tomorrow.

    Passive: Your interest is appreciated.
    Active: I appreciate your interest.

    Passive: Your letter was received yesterday.
    Active: I received your letter yesterday.

    Sentences with passive verbs are usually longer and clumsier than sentences with active verbs. Spot passive verbs by looking for some form of the verb *to be* (such as *be, will be, have been, is, was,* and *were*) used with another verb.

    A trade-off in using active verbs is the frequent introduction of the pronouns *I* and *My*. To solve one problem, you might create another (see Tip 5 in this list). The task then becomes one of finding some other way to start a sentence.

11. **Be sure that present and past participles are grammatically parallel in a list.** See resume writing style Tips 82 and 83 in Part I. What is true about parallel forms in resumes is true also in cover letters. Present participles are action words ending in *-ing,* such as *creating, testing,* and *implementing.* Past participles are action words usually ending in *-ed,* such as *created, tested,* and *implemented.* These are called *verbals* because they are derived from verbs but are not strong enough to function as verbs in a sentence. When you use a string of verbals, control them by keeping them parallel.

12. **Use split infinitives only when *not* splitting them is misleading or awkward.** An *infinitive* is a verb preceded by the preposition *to,* as in *to create, to test,* and *to implement.* You split an infinitive when you insert an adverb between the preposition and the verb, as in *to quickly create, to repeatedly test,* and *to slowly implement.* About 50 years ago, split infinitives were considered grammatical errors, but opinion about them has changed. Many grammar handbooks now recommend that you split your infinitives to avoid awkward or misleading sentences. Compare the following lines:

Split infinitive: I plan to periodically send updated reports on my progress in school.

Misleading: I plan periodically to send updated reports on my progress in school.

Misleading: I plan to send periodically updated reports on my progress in school.

The first example is clear enough, but the second and third examples may be misleading. If you are uncomfortable with split infinitives, one solution is to move *periodically* further into the sentence: "I plan to send updated reports periodically on my progress in school."

Most handbooks that allow split infinitives also recommend that they not be split by more than one word, as in *to quickly and easily write.* A gold medal for splitting an infinitive should go to Lowell Schmalz, an Archie Bunker prototype in "The Man Who Knew Coolidge" by Sinclair Lewis. Schmalz, who thought that Coolidge was one of America's greatest presidents, split an infinitive this way: *"to instantly and without the least loss of time or effort find . . . ."*[1]

Using Punctuation Correctly

13. **Punctuate a compound sentence with a comma.** A compound sentence is one that contains two main clauses joined by one of seven conjunctions *(and, but, or, nor, for, yet,* and *so).* In English, a comma is customarily put before the conjunction if the sentence isn't unusually short. Here is an example of a compound sentence punctuated correctly:

    I plan to arrive at O'Hare at 9:35 a.m. on Thursday, and my trip by cab to your office should take no longer than 40 minutes.

    The comma is important because it signals that a new grammatical subject (*trip,* the subject of the second main clause) is about to be expressed. If you use this kind of comma consistently, the reader will rely on your punctuation and be on the lookout for the next subject in a compound sentence.

14. **Be certain not to put a comma between compound verbs.** When a sentence has two verbs joined by the conjunction *and,* these verbs are called *compound verbs.* Usually, they should not be separated by a comma before the conjunction. Note the following examples:

    I *started* the letter last night *and finished* it this morning.

    I *am sending* my resume separately *and would like* you to keep the information confidential.

    Both examples are simple sentences containing compound verbs. Therefore, no comma appears before *and.* In either case, a comma would send a wrong signal that a new subject in another main clause is coming, but no such subject exists.

    Note: In a sentence with a series of three or more verbs, use commas between the verbs. The comma before the last verb is called the *serial comma.* For more information on using the serial comma, see resume writing style Tip 98 in Part I.

---

[1] Sinclair Lewis, "The Man Who Knew Coolidge," *The Man Who Knew Coolidge* (New York: Books for Libraries Press, 1956), p. 29.

15. **Avoid using *as well as* for *and* in a series.** Compare the following lines:

Incorrect: Your company is impressive because it has offices in Canada, Mexico, as well as the United States.

Correct: Your company is impressive because it has offices in Canada and Mexico, as well as in the United States.

Usually, what is considered exceptional precedes *as well as,* and what is considered customary follows it. Note this example:

Your company is impressive because its managerial openings are filled by women as well as men.

16. **Put a comma after the year when it appears after the month. Similarly, put a comma after the state when it appears after the city.** Compare the following pairs of lines:

Incorrect: In January, 1994 I was promoted to senior analyst.
Correct: In January, 1994, I was promoted to senior analyst.

Incorrect: I worked in Chicago, Illinois before moving to Dallas.
Correct: I worked in Chicago, Illinois, before moving to Dallas.

17. **Put a comma after an opening dependent clause. Compare the following lines:**

Incorrect: If you have any questions you may contact me by phone or fax.

Correct: If you have any questions, you may contact me by phone or fax.

Actually, many writers of fiction and nonfiction don't use this kind of comma. The comma is useful, though, because it signals where the main clause begins. If you glance at the example with the comma, you can tell where the main clause is without even reading the opening clause. For a step up in clarity and readability, use this comma. It can give you a "feel" for a sentence even before you begin to read the words.

18. **Use semicolons when they are needed.** See resume writing style Tip 99 in Part I for the use of semicolons between items in a series. Semicolons are used also to separate main clauses when the second clause starts with a *conjunctive adverb* like *however, moreover,* and *therefore.* Compare the following lines:

Incorrect: Your position in sales looks interesting, however, I would like more information about it.

Correct: Your position in sales looks interesting; however, I would like more information about it.

The first example is incorrect because the comma before *however* is a *comma splice,* which is a comma that joins two sentences. It's like putting a comma instead of a period at the end of the first sentence and then starting the second sentence. A comma may be a small punctuation mark, but a comma splice is a huge grammatical mistake. What are your chances for getting hired if your cover letter tells your reader that you don't recognize where a sentence ends, especially if a requirement for the job is good communication skills? Yes, you could be screened out because of one little comma!

19. **Avoid putting a colon after a verb or a preposition to introduce information.** The reason is that the colon interrupts a continuing clause. Compare the following lines:

Incorrect:	My interests in your company *are:* its reputation, the review of salary after six months, and your personal desire to hire handicapped persons.
Correct:	My interests in your company *are these:* its reputation, the review of salary after six months, and your personal desire to hire handicapped persons.
Incorrect:	In my interview with you, I would like *to:* learn how your company was started, get your reaction to my updated portfolio, and discuss your department's plans to move to a new building.
Correct:	In my interview with you, I would like to discuss *these issues:* how your company was started, what you think of my updated portfolio, and when your department may move to a new building.

Although some people may say that it is OK to put a colon after a verb like *include* if the list of information is long, it is better to be consistent and avoid colons after verbs altogether.

20. **Understand colons clearly.** People often associate colons with semicolons because they sound alike, but colons and semicolons have nothing to do with each other. Colons are the opposite of dashes. Dashes look backward (see resume writing style Tip 101 in Part I), and colons usually look forward to information about to be delivered. One common use of the colon does look backward, however. Here are two examples:

> My experience with computers is limited: I have had only one course on programming (Introduction to FORTRAN), and I don't own a computer.

> I must make a decision by Monday: that is the deadline for renewing the lease for my apartment.

In each example, what follows the colon explains what was said before the colon. Using a colon this way in a cover letter can impress a knowledgeable reader who is looking for evidence of writing skills.

21. **Use slashes correctly.** Information about slashes is sometimes hard to find because *slash* often is listed under a different name, such as *virgule* or *solidus*. If you are not familiar with these terms, your hunt for advice on slashes may lead to nothing.

At least know that one important meaning of a slash is *or*. For this reason, you often see a slash in an expression like ON/OFF. This means that a condition or state, like that of electricity activated by a switch, is either ON or OFF but never ON and OFF at the same time. As you saw in resume writing style Tip 96 in Part I, this condition may be one in which a change means going from the current state to the opposite (or alternate) state. If the current state is ON and there is a change, the next state will be OFF, and vice versa. With this understanding, you can recognize the logic behind the following examples:

Incorrect:	ON-OFF switch (on and off at the same time!)
Correct:	ON/OFF switch (on or off at any time)
Correct:	his-her clothes (unisex clothes, worn by both sexes)
Correct:	his/her clothes (each sex had different clothes)

Note: Although the slash is correct in *his/her* and is one way to avoid sexism, many people consider this expression clumsy. Consider some other wording, such as "clothes that both men and women wear" or "unisex clothes."

22. **Think twice about using *and/or.*** This stilted expression is commonly misunderstood to mean *two* alternatives, but it literally means *three.* Look at the following example:

> If you don't hear from me by Friday, please phone and/or fax me the information on Monday.

What is the person at the other end to do? The sentence really states three alternatives: just phone, just fax, or phone *and* fax the information by Monday. For better clarity, use the connectives *and* or *or* whenever possible.

23. **Use punctuation correctly with quotation marks.** A common misconception is that commas and periods should be placed outside closing quotation marks, but the opposite is true. Compare the following lines:

Incorrect:	Your company certainly has the "leading edge", which means that its razor blades are the best on the market.
Correct:	Your company certainly has the "leading edge," which means that its razor blades are the best on the market.
Incorrect:	In the engineering department, my classmates referred to me as "the guru in pigtails". I was the youngest expert in programming languages on campus.
Correct:	In the engineering department, my classmates referred to me as "the guru in pigtails." I was the youngest expert in programming languages on campus.

Unlike commas and periods, colons and semicolons go *outside* double quotation marks.

Using Words Correctly

24. **Avoid using lofty language in your cover letter.** A real turn-off in a cover letter is the use of elevated diction (high-sounding words and phrases) as a bid to seem important. Note the following examples, along with their straight-talk translations:

Elevated:	My background has afforded me experience in. . . .
Better:	In my previous jobs, I. . . .
Elevated:	Prior to that term of employment. . . .
Better:	Before I worked at. . . .
Elevated:	I am someone with a results-driven profit orientation.
Better:	I want to make your company more profitable.
Elevated:	I hope to utilize my qualifications. . . .
Better:	I want to use my skills. . . .

In letter writing, the shortest distance between the writer and the reader is the most direct idea.

25. **Check your sentences for an excessive use of compounds joined by *and.*** A cheap way to make your letters longer is to join words with *and* and do this repeatedly. Note the following wordy sentence:

> Because of my background and preparation for work and advancement with your company and new enterprise, I have a concern and commitment to implement and put into effect my skills and abilities for new solutions and achievements above and beyond your dreams and expectations.
> [44 words]

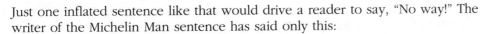

Just one inflated sentence like that would drive a reader to say, "No way!" The writer of the Michelin Man sentence has said only this:

> Because of my background and skills, I want to contribute to your new venture. [14 words]

If, during rereading, you eliminate the wordiness caused by this common writing weakness, your letter will have a better chance of being read completely.

26. **Avoid using abstract nouns excessively.** Look again at the inflated sentence of the preceding tip, but this time with the abstract nouns in italic:

> Because of my *background* and *preparation* for *work* and *advancement* with your *company* and new *enterprise,* I have a *concern* and *commitment* to implement and put into *effect* my skills and *abilities* for new *solutions* and *achievements* above and beyond your *dreams* and *expectations.*

Try picturing in your mind any of the words in italic. You can't because they are *abstract nouns,* which means that they are ideas and not images of things you can see, taste, hear, smell, or touch. One certain way to turn off the reader of your cover letter is to load it with abstract nouns. The following sentence, containing some images, has a better chance of capturing the reader's attention:

> Having created seven multimedia tutorials with my videocamera and Gateway Pentium computer, I now want to create some breakthrough adult-learning packages so that your company, New Century Instructional Technologies, Inc., will exceed $50,000,000 in contracts by 1995.

Compare this sentence with the one loaded with abstract nouns. The one with images is obviously the better attention grabber.

27. **Be sure to put each word in the right location.** In a typical Latin sentence, it makes no difference where the words appear. The meaning of each word and of the sentence is determined by the *inflection,* or particular ending, of each word. English is not an inflected language, so the meaning of a sentence is determined by the order of the words in the sentence. As the location of a word changes, the meaning of the sentence changes. If you accidentally put a word in a wrong location, your sentence can say something you never intended it to say. Compare the follow lines and see how the meaning changes as the location of just one word changes:

> *Only* I have skills for your company.   [No one else does.]
> I *only* have skills for your company.   [But I may not use them.]
> I have *only* skills for your company.   [No interests, just skills.]
> I have skills *only* for your company.   [Never against your company.]
> I have skills for *only* your company.   [And for no one else's.]
> I have skills for your *only* company.   [Who said you had two?]
> I have skills for your company *only.*   [You better believe it!]

The words *only, also, not only . . . but also,* and *too* appear often in the wrong place. When you use these words, look critically at where you put them so that the meanings of your sentences are perfectly clear. Generally, it is best to place these modifiers right before the word or phrase being modified or altered.

28. **Avoid wordy expressions in your cover letters.** Note the following examples:

> at the location of (at)
> for the reason that (because)
> in a short time (soon)
> in a timely manner (on time)
> in spite of everything to the contrary (nevertheless)

in the event of (if)
in the proximity of (near)
now and then (occasionally)
on a daily basis (daily)
on a regular basis (regularly)
on account of (because)
one day from now (tomorrow)
would you be so kind as to (please)

After each of these phrases is a suitable substitute in parentheses. Trim the fat wherever you can, and your reader will appreciate the leanness of your cover letter.

29. **Avoid using well-worn sentences, particularly as the last sentence of the cover letter.** The two most conspicuous sentences of most letters are the first and last sentences. If you make the first sentence interesting but toss in a canned sentence for the last sentence, your letter fizzles out at the end. The following are "stock" last sentences:

    Thank you for your consideration.
    Thank you for your time and consideration.
    I look forward to meeting with you.
    I look forward to hearing from you.
    I look forward to your reply at the earliest convenience.

Find a way to come up with something original. Think of any conversation you had with the person to whom you are sending the letter. Go back and reread a letter the person might have sent to you. Pick up on something the person said that interested you and express your interest in pursuing that matter further. Do anything to make your cover letter end uniquely. Your last sentence may be the kicker that gets the reader's attention.

30. **At the end of your cover letter, don't make a statement that the reader can use to reject you.** For example, suppose that you close your letter with this statement:

    If you wish to discuss this matter further, please call me at
    (555) 555-5555.

This statement gives the reader a chance to think, "I don't wish it, so I don't have to call." Here is another example:

    If you know of the right opportunity for me, please call me at (555) 555-5555.

The reader may think, "I don't know of any such opportunity. How would I know what is right for you?" Avoid questions that prompt yes or no answers, such as, "Do you want to discuss this matter further?" If you ask this kind of a question, you give the reader a chance to say no. Instead, make a closing statement that indicates your optimism about a positive response from the reader. Such a statement might begin as follows:

    I am confident that . . . .
    I look forward to . . . .

In this way, you invite the reader to say yes to further consideration.

Exhibit of Cover Letters

The following Exhibit contains sample cover letters that were prepared by professional resume writers to accompany certain resumes submitted for this book. In almost every instance, the formatting of the letters is different from that of the original letters. For example, typefaces have been changed freely for variety of appearance; margins have been widened according to the length of the letter; and in some cases the names, addresses, and identifiable facts have been changed to ensure the confidentiality of the original sender and receiver of the letter. For each letter, however, the essential substance of the original remains intact.

Below each sample cover letter is a brief comment about the letter. If a cover letter was written for a resume displayed in the Gallery, the resume number is indicated along with the name of the resume writer. If the letter was written for a resume not included in the Gallery, only the name of the writer is given.

The arrangement of the cover letters in the Exhibit is by number of paragraphs—from three-paragraph letters to six-paragraph letters. Many of the comments point out the letter's *pattern,* which consists of the order of the main topic(s) of each paragraph in the letter. By comparing these patterns, you can develop a sense for seeing how certain letters resemble other letters in spite of differences in the number of paragraphs presented.

Use the Exhibit of cover letters as a reference whenever you need to write a cover letter for your resume. If you have trouble starting and ending letters, look at the beginnings and ends of the letters. If you need help on writing about your work experience, describing your abilities and skills, or mentioning some of your best achievements, look at the middle paragraph(s). Search for features that will give you ideas for making your own cover letters more effective. As you examine the Exhibit, consider the following questions:

1. **Does the person show a genuine interest in the reader?** One way to tell is to count the number of times the pronouns *you* or *your* appear in the letter. Then count next the number of times the pronouns *I, me,* and *my* occur in the letter. Although this method is simplistic, it nevertheless helps you see where the writer's interests lie. When you write a cover letter, make your first paragraph *you*-centered rather than *I*-centered. *See also* Tip 5 earlier in Part III.

2. **Where does the cover letter mention the resume specifically?** The purpose of a cover letter is to call attention to the resume. If the letter fails to mention the resume, the letter has not fulfilled its purpose. Besides mentioning the resume, the cover letter might direct the reader's attention to one or more parts of the resume, increasing the chances that the most important part(s) will be seen by the reader. It is not a good idea, however, to put a lot of resume facts in the cover letter. Let each document do its own job. The job of the cover letter is to point to the resume.

3. **How likely is it that the last word of the letter (not including the close) will trigger a reply?** As you look through the Exhibit, notice the last word of the last paragraph. That word sits on one of the choicest spots for emphasis in a letter. It's a dollar location, but if you put a nickel word in that location, you're throwing 95 cents out the window. If you use a word like *meeting, response, reply, call,* or *success,* you not only get your money's worth but also increase your chances for getting a response to your letter. But if you put an anticlimactic or uneventful word in that spot, you might lull the reader into inactivity and never hear from that person. It boils down to putting emphatic words in

emphatic locations. In your cover letter, you want that last word to be a trigger word—that is, a word which triggers the reader into action.

4. **Where and how does the letter express interest in an interview?** The immediate purpose of a cover letter is to call attention to the resume, but the *ultimate* purpose of both the cover letter and the resume is to help you get an interview with the person who can hire you. If the letter doesn't display your interest in getting an interview, the letter has not fulfilled its ultimate purpose.

5. **How decisive is the person's language?** This question is closely related to the preceding question. Is interest in an interview expressed directly or indirectly? Does the person specifically request an interview on a date when the writer will be in the reader's vicinity, or does the person only hint at a desire to "meet" the reader some day? When you write your own cover letters, be sure to be direct and convincing in expressing your interest for an interview. Avoid being timid or wishy-washy.

6. **How does the person display self-confidence?** As you look through the Exhibit, notice the cover letters in which the phrase "I am confident that . . ." (or a similar expression) appears. Self-confidence is a sign of management ability but also of essential job-worthiness. Many of the letters display self-confidence or self-assertiveness in various ways.

7. **How does the letter indicate that the person is a team player?** From an employer's point of view, an employee who is self-assertive but not a team player can spell T-R-O-U-B-L-E. As you look at the cover letters in the Exhibit, notice the many letters in which the word *team* appears.

8. **How does the letter display skills, abilities, and accomplishments?** If the person is looking for a job in the same field as the current line of work, are *job-related* skills evident in the letter? If the person is changing careers (such as leaving the military and returning to civilian life), are *transferable* skills mentioned in the letter? In any case, are any of the person's *adaptive* skills (personality traits) revealed in the letter? A good cover letter discloses the best about the person to help bring about an interview. If the cover letter instead covers up the best about someone by revealing little, a great opportunity may be lost.

9. **How does the letter make the person stand out?** As you read the letters in the Exhibit, do some letters present the person more vividly than other letters? If so, what does the trick? The middle paragraphs or the opening and closing paragraphs? Use what you learn here to help you write distinctive cover letters.

10. **How familiar is the person with the reader?** In a passive job search, the reader will most likely be a total stranger. In an active job search, the chances are good that the writer will have had at least one conversation with the reader by phone or in person. As you look through the cover letters in the Exhibit, see whether you can spot any letter which indicates that the writer has already talked with the reader.

After you have examined and the cover letters in the Exhibit, you will be better able to write an attention-getting letter—one that leads the reader to your resume and to scheduling an interview with you.

S. OLIVIA HANSON
4444 Kitz Road
Evansville, IN 47711
(812) 555-5555

December 3, 1993

Ms. Ruth L Hightower
Excello Corporation
1515 N. Arapaho Road
Phoenix, AZ 85000

Dear Ms. Hightower:

I am an experienced Executive Secretary whose knowledge can make a major contribution to your organization. I enjoyed a progressive career for five years with Pioneer Corporation where, through hard work and promotions, I was secretary for the Director of Engineering. During this time, I assisted in the start-up of two company branches, one of which is located in Brazil, South America. Arranging all aspects of international and domestic travel, plus communicating with Spanish-speaking professionals, was a challenging yet motivating learning experience. Unfortunately, because of downsizing, my position was eliminated.

My record is one of increased responsibility, variety in job assignments, and solid accomplishments. I am accustomed to a fast-paced environment where deadlines are priority and handling multiple jobs simultaneously is the norm. Constant negotiations with all levels of management and union employees have strengthened my interpersonal skills.

I would appreciate having the opportunity to meet with you to discuss my qualifications for the Administrative Assistant position available with Excello Corporation. My resume is enclosed for your review. I will be in the Phoenix area during the month of January, 1994, and will call you to schedule a mutually convenient interview time. If you wish to contact me before January, you may call me at (812) 555-5555. Thank you for your time and consideration. I look forward to our meeting.

Sincerely,

S. Olivia Hanson

Enclosure

For Resume 30. Teresa Collins, CPRW, Evansville, Indiana.
A three-paragraph letter with an experience–accomplishments–arrangements pattern.
The 1st paragraph indicates the reason for termination; the 3rd refers to an interview.

1

JASON DEAN

(209) 222-2222 • 5000 West Blue • Athens, CA 93000

December 14, 1993

Mr. Bryan Harbison, Sales Manager
ABC Company
1234 Sunshine Way
City of Hope, TX 12345

Dear Mr. Harbison:

Your need of an **Experienced Sales Professional** caught my interest, as the notice calls for skills and training that closely match my background. The enclosed resume will provide you with a brief outline of my experience and accomplishments; in summary, they include these achievements:

- Top sales producer status with my current employer, a Fortune 1,000 company specializing in automated data processing systems.

- Over 14 years of experience in sales and sales management positions, consistently making contributions to corporate sales, profit, and growth.

- Well versed in the technical arena, with expertise in tele-communications and automated data processing systems.

- Strong academic preparation, including an M.B.A. with emphasis in Telecommunications, a B.A. in Business Administration, and ongoing professional development seminars.

Given the combination of these factors, I am confident I would quickly be valued as a contributing and vital member of your team. Your consideration of my qualifications is appreciated. Should you require additional information before a personal interview, I would be happy to accommodate you.

To ensure your receipt of my material, I will follow up by telephone during the upcoming week and look forward to speaking with you at that time.

Sincerely,

Jason Dean

Enclosure

2

***For Resume 4.** Susan B. Whitcomb, CPRW, Fresno, California.*
A three-paragraph letter in which the 1st paragraph introduces a list of bulleted achievements. Though short, the 2nd paragraph is a strong focus; the 3rd promises a follow-up.

KIRSTEN MARYA SÖDERBLUM
1010 Lane Allen Drive
Somerville, NJ 00000
(000) 000-0000

April 27, 1994

RE: International Sales/Management/Technical Consulting

Ms. Veronica S. Blakely
General Manager, Foreign Sales
ViaTEL
5001 Sound View Drive
Seattle, WA 00000

Dear Ms. Blakely:

Enclosed is my resume for your review. I am confident that my broad-based experience in the areas of international sales and consulting will serve as an asset to your organization. As Technical Sales Manager for the South Pacific Expansion (SPE) Group since 1985, I developed the Austro-Asian markets and sold technical packages to the United States, Canadian, and European markets.

I received two promotions: one to work in Australia, and the other to my present position as Technical Sales Manager in the United States for Whitney, Inc. (a subsidiary of the South Pacific Expansion Group). The following are recent accomplishments:

- Successfully developed the South Pacific market, increasing sales from $300,000 in 1987 to $7.5 million in 1993.

- Consistently obtained a 15% share of new accounts each year. Known in the United States, European, and South Pacific markets as an excellent troubleshooter and technical consultant. Established vendor relations for new international markets.

- Trained personnel in the areas of sales, engineering, and quality control. Wrote policies and procedures. Developed modifications in new territories.

- Coordinated and closed the first sale of the innovative fragrance pump to D'Arginé. D'Arginé is the parent company to major cosmetic sales organizations in the United States and France.

I look forward to speaking with you personally so that we may discuss my qualifications in greater detail. In the interim, thank you for your consideration, attention, and forthcoming response.

Very truly yours,

Kirsten Marya Söderblum

Enclosure

Beverly Baskin, CPRW, Marlboro, New Jersey.
A three-paragraph letter with an experience–accomplishments–arrangements pattern. The 2nd paragraph introduces a list of bulleted achievements. Note the RE: focus after the date.

3

LOOKING FOR A HUMAN RESOURCE MANAGER?
ONE WITH A HIGHLY SUCCESSFUL TRACK RECORD?

If you are, please take a look at me . . .

- Twenty-four years experience in the United States Air Force . . . from vehicle operator and dispatcher . . . to Vehicle Operations Manager in seven U.S. and foreign locations.

- A proven track record in training and development . . . as a driver's school instructor successfully training 90 students per month . . . initiated in-house training programs for dispatchers, improving customer service and self-motivation in the trainees.

- Innovative and creative . . . likes challenges and enjoys bringing order from chaos and improving techniques.

- A skilled manager . . . over a 24-year period have managed six 60-personnel operations . . . excellent job of handling yearly budgets averaging $800,000+.

- Ideas that work . . . with documented results showing successful accomplishments of varied operational projects.

- An established reputation . . . known for being a highly motivated achiever of even the most difficult operations and management tasks.

My personal characteristics include . . . a high level of dedication to work . . . strong personal values of honesty and integrity . . . excellent professional training . . . professional appearance and manner . . . even temper and an ability to handle stress well.

Want to hear more? I've enclosed my resume and would like the opportunity to discuss further how I can be a successful member of your team. I look forward to your call.

Sincerely,

Eric B. Throckmorton

Enclosure

ERIC B. THROCKMORTON
245 North Range Line Road
Willow, NE 00000
(000) 000-0000

4 *Rafael Santiago, Papillion, Nebraska.*
An informal letter with a number of original features: a monogram at the top in the original version, dual opening questions, ellipses (. . .) throughout, and name and address at the end.

RONALD C. PLOTH
6105 S. Oak Terrace, Apt. #210
Lincoln, NE 00000
(000) 000-0000

January 8, 1994

Major Marjorie T. Landau
2010 Grand Ave.
Unit 23EC
Kinross Air Force Base, IL 00000-0000

Dear Major Landau:

The purpose of this cornmunication is to introduce myself and then to meet with you about joining your organization.

My experience has acquainted me with numerous facets of public administration, including problem solving, conference setup, and quality assurance. I am confident that my expertise in these areas will prove to be an asset to your organization.

As you can see from the enclosed resume and the performance reports, I have a record of consistently producing results in managing personnel and services. I enjoy the challenge of investigating and solving administrative problems.

I would very much like to discuss opportunities with your organization. I will be calling you within the next few days to see if you have received this package. In the meantime, if you have any questions, I may be reached at the number above. Thank you for your consideration.

Sincerely,

Ronald C. Ploth

Rafael Santiago, Papillion, Nebraska.
The 1st of a number of four-paragraph letters. Although this letter is concise, you or your is mentioned 10 times! The pattern is purpose–experience–record–plan (arrangements).

5

Dear Mr. Jamison:

I am interested in exploring employment opportunities with your organization. Enclosed is my resume with details of my qualifications, experience, and accomplishments for your review and consideration.

My background includes 15 years of diverse experience for Merrimak Corporation in the areas of marketing, database management, data processing, and quality control. In these positions, which included hands-on and managerial roles, I have developed excellent skills in project coordination and the design and development of computer databases to access and retrieve information. I would like to utilize these qualifications, in addition to my excellent oral and written communication skills, to enhance your organization's goals and objectives.

I would appreciate an opportunity to meet with you in person to discuss your needs and my potential to contribute as a member of your team.

Thank you for your time and consideration. I look forward to your reply at the earliest convenience.

Sincerely,

Carolyn T. Madison

6

For Resume 73. Julianne S. Franke, Lilburn, Georgia.
The original appeared on page 2 of a four-page, brochure-style resume. The pattern is purpose–experience/skills–interest in meeting–thanks. You or your appears nine times.

JOHN MARK PAULING
0000 E. Shore
Hometown, CA 00000
(000) 000-0000

December 8, 1993

William J. Sherrow
Director of Operations
WXXX - TV
0000 North Michigan
Chicago, IL 00000

Dear Mr. Sherrow:

Please accept this letter in response to your need for a **Creative Services** professional. The enclosed resume outlines my qualifications, which closely parallel your requirements for the position.

With over 10 years of experience in television, I have a background that encompasses all phases of producing and directing, with an emphasis in creative services. Among Operations Managers in our market, I am well known for my creative and technical talents; my work has become the standard against which other stations are measured. Balancing my creative talents are a stable work history and a personal commitment to being the best in my field.

As a native of Chicago, I plan to relocate to the area in early 1994. I will be visiting in January and would appreciate a brief opportunity to meet with you during this time. I will be in touch regarding an appointment time. Should you have questions before that time, I can be reached at (000) 000-0000 or 000-0000.

In advance, thank you for your time.

Sincerely,

John Mark Pauling

Enclosure

For Resume 137. Susan B. Whitcomb, CPRW, Fresno, California.
A letter with a similar pattern: purpose of letter–experience/skills (talents)–interest in meeting–thanks. Second paragraph focuses on the need for a creative person.

7

CHARLES F. NOTTINGHAM
2300 New Farmers Road
Hillsville, NJ 00000
(000) 000-0000 (H)
(000) 000-0000 (O)

May 26, 1994

Mr. Daniel T. Barbour
Director, Human Resources
Broadbent Communications
30 Witherspoon Square
Princeton, NJ 00000

Dear Mr. Barbour:

Enclosed is my resume for your review. I am confident that my broad-based experience in telecommunications, marketing/management, and human resources would serve as an asset to your organization.

My career with MTI, New York, encompasses district management positions, product and project management, as well as technical operations and engineering. I am currently a Regional Manager in the International Business Communications unit (IBC) with responsibilities for profit and loss of the entire IBC unit. IBC provides telecommunications relay services. Working as a team, our division has reduced costs and improved customer quality by 5% within one year.

Additional functions have included the marketing of MTI computer products with support services for computer applications and telecommunications areas.

I look forward to speaking with you personally so that we may discuss my qualifications in greater detail. In the interim, thank for your consideration, attention, and forthcoming response.

Very truly yours,

Charles (Chuck) F. Nottingham

Enclosure

Beverly Baskin, CPRW, Marlboro, New Jersey.
The pattern for this letter is experience–career review/achievement–other functions–interest in meeting/thanks. Compare this letter with Letter 3 by the same writer.

CYNTHIA BARLOW
3222 Peach Street
Atlanta, GA 00000
(000) 000-0000

March 18, 1994

Ms. Carol R. Carrington
Carruthers Promotions, Inc.
1400 Wingate Road, N.E.
Millville, MD 00000

Dear Ms. Carrington:

As you suggested in your recent phone call, I am enclosing a copy of my resume for your consideration. I would like to call your attention to the skills and achievements in my background that are most relevant to the position you described.

For four years I have been a successful administrator, setting high standards and consistently achieving my goals. Since February, 1989, I have served in the United States Air Force as an Administrative Specialist/Assistant and acquired my training through the excellent programs the Air Force provides. I am highly motivated and will be a dynamic administrator for whatever company I represent.

I am confident of my administrative abilities and have already displayed effectiveness in managing an office and building customer relations.

I look forward to hearing from you again soon so that we may continue our discussion of your needs.

Sincerely,

Cynthia (Cindy) Barlow

CB/RSR
Enclosure

Rafael Santiago, Papillion, Nebraska.
The original version of this letter had a monogram, name, address, and phone number in a 1 7/8" left column. Administrative abilities are mentioned in the 2nd and 3rd paragraphs.

9

Jill L. Brock   3200 Green Place, Elva, OH 00000 ■ (000) 000-0000

April 11, 1993

Ms. Cynthia D. Ruttencutter
Akron Medical Group
3010 Some Street
Akron, OH 00000

Dear Ms. Ruttencutter:

I am seeking a part-time position with a physician's office or medical firm. If you need a self-motivated, conscientious individual with expertise in filing medical claims, I am the person you have been looking for.

As you can see from the enclosed resume, my expertise goes beyond simply filing medical claims. I have extensive experience in communicating with patients, doctors, and insurance companies. I am proficient in assigning ICD-9 and CPT codes to all insurance claims. While at Big Foot and Ankle Care, I performed all accounts receivable duties including tracking claims, contacting patients whose accounts were past due, posting receivables, and generating reports.

Should you have a position available that meets my qualifications, I would appreciate the opportunity to have an interview with you.

Thank you for your consideration, and I look forward to your reply.

Sincerely,

Jill L. Brock

JLB:jmt

Enclosure

10   *Susan Higgins, Amlin, Ohio.*
The pattern of this letter is purpose–experience/expertise–interest in an interview–thanks. To minimize use of the pronoun I, you or your is mentioned eight times.

JAMES ROBERT JONES

2400 Rising Trail   Atlanta, Georgia 00000   (000) 335-0000

October 14, 1993

Ms. Katherine B. Phelps, Principal
Augustana High School
2010 Ridley Road
Charlotte, NC 00000

Dear Ms. Phelps:

It is my goal is to secure a career-oriented position where I can contribute to the education of our youth.

As you can see from the enclosed resume, my education and experience have prepared me for this undertaking. During my career, I have functioned successfully in various assignments where my counseling, training, planning, and evaluation skills were sharpened. Additionally, the life experiences I will bring to the classroom include community involvement with both youth and senior citizens, the ability to speak German, and an understanding of German culture. My personal qualities—well-developed interpersonal skills, excellent communication abilities, integrity, and an exceptional work ethic— will allow me to contribute to any endeavor.

Should you wish to discuss potential employment, please call (000) 335-0000. I look forward to hearing from you.

Thank you for your consideration.

Sincerely,

James Robert Jones

For Resume 38. *Carol Lawrence, CPRW, Snellville, Georgia.*
Like Cover Letter 10, this letter's pattern is goal (purpose)–experience/expertise–interest in interview–thanks. Main paragraph emphasizes the person's skills for return from military life.

11

ANDY VINTON

985 Evergreen Court
Milledgeville, GA 00000
(000) 000-0000

May 12, 1993

Ms. Melanie G. Sandhurst, Sales Manager
FirstFruits Corporation
5241 Pine Drive
Macon, GA 00000

Dear Ms. Sandhurst:

Please consider this letter of introduction as an expression of my interest in exploring employment opportunities with your organization. I have enclosed my resume for your review.

My experience has helped me develop strong management abilities, excellent communication skills, and self-confidence, as well as the realization of the importance of customer satisfaction and top-quality service. I am an energetic team player, am intensely loyal, and have the ability to project effectively the image required. My self-motivation has allowed me to work my way into leadership positions. The experiences that I feel would benefit you the most are these:

- Food Service
- Quality/Inventory Control
- Purchasing, Shipping, Receiving
- Price Quotes/Auditing
- Sales
- Employee Supervision

If my qualifications correspond to your needs, I would appreciate meeting with you to discuss how I might contribute positively to your team.

Thank you for your time and consideration. I look forward to hearing from you.

Sincerely,

Andy Vinton

Carol Lawrence, CPRW, Snellville, Georgia.
The 1st of three four-paragraph letters with bullets. In each letter, the bullets appear with the 2nd paragraph. Here, the bullets call attention to relevant experiences.

COLLEEN M. ROSS
SALES/MARKETING

2335 Evanshire Court
Amlin, OH 00000

Home: (000) 000-0000
Work: (000) 000-0000

February 3, 1994

Mr. Norman D. Brunett
CD-ROM Innovations, Inc.
6201 N. Mission Road
Campbell, CA 00000

Dear Mr. Brunett:

I am presenting for your review my skills, achievements, proven leadership, work ethic, and straightforward approach to getting the job done, so that we can discuss my joining your organization as a member of your sales/marketing management team.

Although my entire career thus far has been in social work, I can assure you it has paralleled the skills required to sell a service or product. I have successfully executed the following in my present job:

- Maintained quotas
- Generated leads through cold calls, canvassing, telemarketing, and referrals
- Participated in trade shows, conferences, etc.
- Established new accounts
- Maintained and expanded existing accounts
- Negotiated business contracts

I am ready to turn these skills into a productive and profitable sales career. In my present job, 1 work for an organization that develops programs to sell companies on the hiring of economically disadvantaged youths. In this job, I have encountered several companies that have not been receptive to this concept. However, through perseverance and determination, I have been able to convince many companies to give these youths an opportunity. This same perseverance and determination will carry over to promote and sell all products or services.

I will work hard to achieve bottom-line results and look forward to discussing how I can contribute to your company's future success.

Sincerely,

Colleen M. Ross

CMR:amf

Enclosure: Resume

Susan Higgins, Amlin, Ohio.
The bulleted items call attention to transferable skills the person has for a career change from social work to sales/marketing management. The 3rd paragraph reinforces this interest.

13

SAMUEL WEINSTEIN

4000 East Shaw Avenue   Residence: (000) 222-2222
Fresno, CA 93000   Business: (000) 111-1111

December 14, 1993

Susan Whitcomb
ALPHA OMEGA SERVICES
12345 West Sheppard Avenue
Tustin, CA 91111

Dear Ms. Whitcomb:

Thank you for your time recently to discuss career opportunities available through Alpha Omega Services. Your organization's national reputation is impressive, and I have confidence in your ability to access companies that might benefit from my extensive retail management experience.

Qualifications I bring to your clients include these:

- A career that exceeds 28 years in retail management, marked by rapid advancement through increasingly responsible positions, including Regional General Merchandise Manager for a $400 million territory and presently Store Manager for a top-ranking store producing $40 million in annual volume.

- Track record for significant contributions to operations, sales, and profits, coupled with strengths in marketing, advertising, and promotions.

- Progressive and innovative industry outlook, evidenced by my ability to develop and market profitable new product lines.

- Management style that focuses on coaching, teambuilding, and empowering others.

Weighing the combination of these factors, I am confident I have much to offer your organization's clients who require an individual with vision, leadership, and a results-driven profit orientation.

I look forward to working with you and will follow up this letter with a telephone call during the week of December 22.

Sincerely,

Samuel Weinstein

Enclosure

14

For Resume 197. Susan B. Whitcomb, CPRW, Fresno, California.
In this letter, the bullets direct attention to the person's qualifications for a position in retail management. The 1st paragraph indicates a prior discussion—a sign of an active job search.

Gordon J. Thompson Jr.
PGA Professional
Fairfield County Club

P.O. Box 90
Fairfield, MI 49000-0000
(616) 555-5555

December 17, 1992

Search Committee
Saugatuck River Country Club
0000 River Road
Saugatuck, MI 00000

Dear Committee Members:

I received notice of your open position for a **Head Golf Professional** at Saugatuck River Country Club through the Michigan Section Employment Bulletin. I would like to take this opportunity to apply for this position. My resume is enclosed. This position especially interests me because the qualification requirements directly correlate with the experience and abilities I possess.

Of the many duties required by a golf professional and his staff, those that I hold in highest esteem are promotion of the game of golf and being responsive to the needs of the golfing population. With this commitment to golf, I can continue to provide the membership of Saugatuck River Country Club the excellent service the members deserve.

With seven years of experience as a Head Golf Professional and background in merchandising, golf instruction both at the private club level and community schools level, tournament management, and personal management, I would be an asset to the management team at Saugatuck River Country Club. With this knowledge and the ability to work in a team atmosphere, a smooth transition with minimum interruptions will be possible.

I would welcome the opportunity to discuss personally my qualifications and objectives with you at your earliest convenience. I can be contacted at Fairfield Country Club, P.O. Box 70, Fairfield, MI 49000-0000 or (616) 555-5555.

Sincerely,

Gordon J. Thompson Jr.
PGA Professional

For Resume 157. Patricia L. Nieboer, CPS, CPRW, Fremont, Michigan.
The 1st of four longer four-paragraph letters. The pattern in this letter is purpose–duties/skills –experience–interest in interview. The original had a graphic showing a golf ball on a tee.

15

Arthur S. Franklin
504 Cold Springs Circle
Amlin, OH 00000
(000) 000-0000    **CHEF**

May 11, 1994

Mr. Stephen J. Girard, Manager
The Paddock Inn
Keeneland, KY 00000

Dear Mr. Girard:

I am seeking a challenging position that will offer continued opportunity to develop further my knowledge and skills as an Executive Chef.

As you will note from my enclosed resume, I am a graduate of Johnson and Wales, a renowned college of cuisine. I am an experienced Chef and familiar with all aspects of operating a kitchen.

In my past two positions as Executive Chef, I would prepare all meals daily from scratch. The meat and fish would be filleted on the premises, and sauces, pastas, and stocks would also be prepared daily from scratch. As you know, this takes a great deal of organization and planning. While at Lone Star Steaks, I expanded the "all meat' menu to include classical chicken, fish, and veal dishes. I am constantly striving to make meals more appealing and nutritional while coordinating the kitchen staff to work efficiently as a team. Unfortunately, these past two positions were with start-up restaurants that did not survive in this highly competitive market.

If an opportunity exists within your organization for a highly motivated Executive Chef who is eager to develop his cuisine talents, please contact me at (000) 000-0000. I am available for an interview at your convenience to discuss my qualifications in greater detail.

Thank you for your consideration.

Sincerely,

Arthur S. Franklin

Enclosure

16   *Susan Higgins, Amlin, Ohio.*
Typically, the 2nd paragraph is the heavy-freight paragraph. Here, the 3rd paragraph carries the weight, indicating duties and achievements and explaining joblessness.

JESSICA L. JOHNSON
148 Washington Street
Lombard, IL 60000
(708) 000-0000

July 5, 1993

Ms. Carolyn R. Livengood
Human Resources Manager
Branson & Smith Products, Inc.
10100 Columbia Highway
Palo Verde, CA 00000

Dear Ms. Livengood:

I am writing in response to your advertisement for the Pacific Rim Sales position, which appeared in the June 27th Sunday edition of the *Chicago Tribune.* The enclosed resume details my qualifications.

I have functioned in marketing and customer service capacities for the past nine years in two companies that manufacture hardware used in the utility industry. My experience includes preparation of sales proposals presented to customers, development of promotions and sales materials, price determination, sales forecasting, and account management. My product and marketing knowledge, along with my commitment to top-quality customer service, has contributed to my success in these positions.

My most recent achievement was creation of a sales proposal that resulted in a $1 million order—the company's third largest ever. Other accomplishments include recommendation and implementation of systems that substantially increased efficiency and improved customer service. I am a hardworking employee with outstanding analytical, organizational, and interpersonal skills. I am adept at mastering new concepts and procedures and can quickly contribute to an organization.

I would appreciate an opportunity to discuss how my background and experience could benefit Branson & Smith Products, Inc. If you would like to schedule an interview appointment at your convenience, you may reach me at the telephone number listed above. Thank you for your time and consideration.

Sincerely,

Jessica L. Johnson

For Resume 178. Georgia Veith, Elmhurst, Illinois.
The pattern is purpose–experience–achievements–interest in interview. Notice in the 3rd paragraph the self-assessment, a feature sometimes found in a separate paragraph.

17

James B. Sellers
4300 Shier Rings Rd.
Amlin. OH 43000   (614) 000-0000

March 16, 1992

Mr. Harold T. Elkins
Triple Diamond Corporation
1234 Some Street
Cleveland, OH 00000

Dear Mr. Elkins:

I am a resourceful, results-oriented manager accustomed to P & L responsibilities and seeking a supervisory/management position, preferably in high-tech manufacturing or business at the national or international level.

I have extensive experience principally at the management level in the manufacture of precision components. My strengths lie in the development of production facilities and shipping operations, in addition to extensive supervisory skills. My distinguished record in management is outlined in the attached resume. I offer a solid background in managing the start-up and ongoing processes of production operations.

During my employment with ABC Industries Inc., I was responsible for getting the entire machine shop McDonald-Douglas-certified. This resulted in ABC's being awarded a contract for precision components. During the contract, ABC Industries received the maximum number of points from McDonald Douglas for the rating of A (excellent). While at DEF Corporation, I completely restructured its international shipping department, saving the company substantial money.

My former company, GHI Industrial Mfg., has experienced cost-cutting reorganizations due to management change. I am actively pursuing employment as a Supervisor or Quality Control Manager. I will be available at your convenience to discuss further my qualifications. Thank you for your time and consideration.

Sincerely.

James B. Sellers

Enclosure

18
For Resume 128. Susan Higgins, Amlin, Ohio.
The pattern is the same as that of Letter 17. The person is interested in a supervisory/management position, so these and related themes are mentioned repeatedly.

Dear Ms. Cavendish:

With a track record of success in the design field, I am exploring opportunities to utilize my creative design skills and contribute to your company's growth and expansion.

As you will note on my resume, I have a solid track record of accomplishments, using a variety of art media. This versatility is reflected in my distinctive accomplishments representing major corporations and community organizations.

With the emphasis on image in our society today, creative design can communicate an empowering message that translates into increased business or achievement of organizational goals.

If you are looking for a *"Designer with a Difference,"* I would appreciate an opportunity to meet with you to show you samples of the quality of my work. I can also provide professional references to verify my excellent client relations.

Thank you for your time and full consideration. I look forward to hearing from you in the near future.

Sincerely,

John Wilson

Julianne S. Franke, Lilburn, Georgia.
The 1st of three five-paragraph letters. In this short letter, you or your appears eight times. The pattern is purpose–accomplishments–personal philosophy–interest in meeting–thanks.

19

Thomas J. Allen, Ph.D., M.C.C.

6584 Pine Cove
Jefferson, MI 46000
(526) 000-0000

[Date]

A. Prospective Employer
Some Institution
1234 Some Street
Some City, ST 00000

Dear Mr./Ms. Employer:

I am seeking a position as a psychological counselor/therapist. I possess a Ph.D. in Counseling Psychology and have over 10 years of experience in one-on-one and group counseling.

During these years, I have been privileged to counsel others on a variety of human issues and emotions, including marriage, premarriage, depression, anxiety, grief work, codependency, divorce, single parenting, victimization, adultery, anger, self-control, thought life, and habits, to name a few.

I am experienced at using a variety of assessment tests and profiles to assist in diagnosing psychological difficulties as well as personality traits. I feel, however, that my best asset is my ability to listen well, communicate well, and be compassionate with individuals from a variety of backgrounds, thus helping individuals recover emotionally more quickly.

Enclosed is my resume for your consideration. To arrange a convenient time for an interview, please contact me at the telephone number listed above.

Thank you for your consideration.

Sincerely,

Dr. Thomas J. Allen, Ph.D.
Encl. Resume

20

For Resume 161. P. J. Margraf, New Braunfels, Texas.
The pattern for this letter is intention/credentials–experience–skills–interest in interview–thanks. Note the unique thick-thin lines in the letterhead.

HARLAN R. ELLIS
3845 Glencairn Road
Buffalo Grove, IL 00000
(000) 000-0000

December 14, 1993

Ms. Julie T. Northrup
Reece Retailers, Inc.
8185 Riverview Drive
Cincinnati, OH 00000

Dear Ms. Northup:

As an 20-year veteran in retail management, I understand that success depends on a strong commitment to *customer satisfaction* and a constant focus on the *bottom line*. Executing the basics and finding new solutions and business opportunities are key to increasing performance and market share. I believe that my background and accomplishments reflect a commitment and an ability to find solutions to these challenges.

My career in specialty retailing includes 17 years with my present organization, six of which have been as *Regional Manager*. I have supervised regions with up to 15 stores, over 300 employees, and total volumes to $53M. I have served as a troubleshooter, taking on many regional assignments, eventually having supervised one sixth of our company's 280 stores in the Midwest and Northwest. In addition, I have previous merchandising experience.

As a Regional Manager, I regard the following as my accomplishments:

- Recruiting and developing high-performance management teams, reducing turnover, and maintaining greater continuity in staffing

- Developing a new store opening manual for field operations

- Supervising renovation projects up to $1M in 17,000 sq. ft. units

- Consistently maintaining direct store expenses within targets

I approach my work with a strong sense of urgency, working well under pressure and change. I am a forward thinker and a team player who has a strong commitment to my people and the organizations I work for.

I look forward to meeting with you personally so that we may discuss my qualifications in greater detail. In the interim, thank you for your consideration, attention, and forthcoming response.

Very truly yours,

Harlan R. Ellis

Enclosure

Beverly Baskin, CPRW, Marlboro, New Jersey.
A substantial letter with bulleted items in the 3rd paragraph. The pattern is personal philosophy–experience–accomplishments–self-assessment–interest in meeting/thanks.

21

EDWARD K. IRVING
200 River Road
Tarrytown, NY 00000

September 23, 1993

Mr. William P. Jackson
Jackson & Jones Associates
1505 Cliff View Road
San Toma, CA 00000

Dear Mr. Lindgren:

Could one of your client companies use an ambitious, young accounting professional with an excellent record of growth and accomplishment as an accounting supervisor?

I am thoroughly trained and ready for my first supervisory assignment. I have a solid technical foundation in accounting fundamentals, which I gained during my last three years of employment at New Century Electronics, Inc. In addition, I have strong interpersonal, communications, and leadership skills, which should serve me well in a supervisory role.

Beyond my professional experience, I hold both a B.A. and an M.B.A. from New York University, where I majored in accounting. My resume attests that I was both a scholar and a campus leader.

Although I would prefer to remain on the East Coast, I will give serious consideration to other locations, should the opportunity be a good one.

If you can identify a suitable opportunity for me, Mr. Jackson, I can be reached confidentially at my office during evening hours. Both phone numbers are on the enclosed resume.

Thank you.

Sincerely,

Edward K. Irving

Enclosure

---

22 *Rafael Santiago, Papillion, Nebraska.*
The 1st of four six-paragraph letters. The original had a large, ornate monogram in the upper-left corner. The letter begins with a question and refers to the resume twice.

LESLIE WILEY
80 Johnson Road
Morganville, NJ 07000
(000) 555-3061

August 21, 1992

Dr. Thomas L. Bellingham, DMD
The Farmington Group
32000 West 10 Mile Road
Farmington Hills, MI 00000

Dear Dr. Bellingham:

Enclosed is my resume for your review. I graduated from Villanova University School of Dentistry with a DMD this past May. My undergraduate degree in Chemistry and Psychology was obtained at Yale University.

As an intern at the Villanova University Dental School Clinic, I am responsible for providing dental care to patients, including restorative procedures, oral surgery, periodontics, and endodontic therapy.

I have worked under the supervision of Oral and Maxillofacial Surgery Residents at several hospitals and participated in an Anesthesiology Rotation at Villanova University Hospital.

During the last eight years, I gained extensive business management skills as Business Manager and Supervisor of 20 retail stores at King's Dominion Amusement Park in Williamsport, Pennsylvania. During the spring and summer seasons, I am in charge of running all aspects of the businesses. My duties including supervising more than 200 employees, training of personnel, accounting, inventory control, and purchasing.

I look forward to speaking with you personally so that we may discuss my background and career opportunities in greater detail.

In the interim, I thank you for your attention, consideration, and forthcoming response.

Very truly yours,

Leslie Wiley

Enclosure

For Resume 80. Beverly Baskin, CPRW, Marlboro, New Jersey.
With the person's varied experience, the pattern is longer: education–experience (as intern)–experience (supervised)–experience (business)–interest in meeting–thanks.

23

Peter W. Canfield

38000 Lyndale Road • St. Louis, Missouri 63000 • (315) 555-5555

June 11, 1993

Mr. Lance P. Hollowell, Construction Manager
KIERKOFF CONSTRUCTION CO.
4420 N. Division Street
St. Louis, MO 00000

Dear Mr. Hollowell:

In response to your advertisement for a Construction Project Manager, I have enclosed my resume for your review.

I am currently Mechanical Inspector at the ABC Construction Company in Chicago, Illinois, where I am responsible for quality control, contract administration, cost estimating, and change order negotiations. Past responsibilities in this position and as Project Manager, Construction, at ACME Construction have included in-depth involvement in most of the areas where you require expertise— specifically, preparing site checks, cost estimates, and preliminary layouts; supervising construction plan preparation; obtaining and evaluating construction cost proposals and contract negotiation; remodeling and repairing existing buildings; and representing the company competently and professionally at contract negotiations and coordination meetings.

The following are highlights of my qualifications:

* 7 years of solid work experience in construction project management in a 14-year career in construction/engineering in the St. Louis area.

* Strong working relationships with St. Louis area contractors on numerous job sites.

* B.S. degree in Industrial Technology with emphasis in construction maintenance and management.

Also included for your review is a project addendum outlining significant construction projects I managed while at ACME Construction Corporation.

Salary is, of course, negotiable, but I am most interested in opportunities with salary/benefits packages starting in the low $40s.

I look forward to meeting with a Kierkoff representative personally to discuss how my background and experience may fit your needs. Thank you for your consideration.

Sincerely,

Peter W. Canfield

For Resume 151. Carla L. Culp, CPRW, Edwardsville, Illinois.
The number of paragraphs is increased to six because of two extra topics that require their own paragraphs: the reference to the project addendum and the indication of salary interest.

Arthur M. MacArthur

6830 Hermitage Road
Norristown, PA 00000   **(000) 000-0000**

November 15, 1993

Mr. J. Archibald Dunworthy, President
International TeleCOM Corporation
2055 New Town Pike
Princeton, NJ 00000

Dear Mr. Dunworthy:

Enclosed is my resume for your review. I am confident that my broad-based experience in various aspects of finance, accounting, contract administration, and management controls would serve as an asset to your corporation.

I am currently Manager of Contracts and Pricing for TransCOM Corporation. The following are some of my accomplishments in this position for TransCOM:

- Obtained the division's largest commercial training and services contract from a major optical retailer for 280 stores

- Administered a 36-month contract for disaster recovery and contingency management services

- Negotiated a $800K plus contract with the New Jersey State Department of Environmental Services

In addition, I implemented a telemarketing sales campaign to third-party priority software and negotiated contracts with seven vendors generating annual revenues between $700K and $1.5MM.

Former positions at TransCOM included Manager of Administrative Services and Manager of Computer Operations. As Manager of those divisions, I conceived and organized the organization's first formal computer training program, including handbooks, videotapes, and instruction modules. I also was in charge of a trainees housing program, which included a 120 – 2-bedroom apartment complex managed by my division.

I am familiar with redeployment of personnel, and I have performed extensive administrative services for a large Fortune 500 company.

Thank you for your consideration. I look forward to speaking with you personally so that we may discuss my qualifications in greater detail.

Very truly yours,

Arthur M. MacArthur

Enclosure

Beverly Baskin, CPRW, Marlboro, New Jersey.
The number of paragraphs is increased by the inclusion of an additional accomplishment, references to former positions, and the mention of experience with a Fortune 500 company.

25

Appendix

List of Contributors

Appendix

List of Contributors

The following persons are the contributors of the resumes and cover letters in this book. All of the contributors are professional resume writers. Except for one of these, all are current or former members of The Professional Association of Resume Writers. To include in this appendix the names of these writers and information about their business is to acknowledge with appreciation their voluntary submissions and the insights expressed in the letters that accompanied the submissions.

Alabama

Enterprise

Penny J. Rotolo
Laser Pages, Inc.
806 Boll Weevil Cir.
Enterprise, AL 36330
Phone: (205) 347-7468
Fax: (205) 347-7468

Montgomery

Don Orlando, MBA, CPRW
The McLean Group
640 South McDonough
Montgomery, AL 36104-5850
Phone: (205) 264-2020
Fax: (205) 264-9227

Alaska

Kodiak

Jacqueline K. Herter, CPS
Professional Word Processing
P.O. Box 3629
Kodiak, AK 99615
Phone: (907) 486-6221
Fax: (907) 486-6267

Arizona

Phoenix

Bernard Stopfer
Resumes Plus
2855 West Cactus Road, Suite 28
Phoenix, AZ 85029
Phone: (602) 789-1200
Fax: (602) 789-6014

Tempe

Fran Holsinger
Career Profiles
1726 E. Southern, Ste. 8
Tempe, AZ 85282
Phone: (602) 413-9383
Fax: (602) 345-9202

California

Aliso Viejo

Diane Y. Chapman
Words To Your Advantage
11 Mareblu, Suite 130
Aliso Viejo, CA 92656
Phone: (714) 248-8561
Fax: (714) 831-4432

Antioch

Margo Burkhardt
GHOSTWRITERS, Inc.
5048 Perry Way
Antioch, CA 94509
Phone: (510) 757-3438

Boulder Creek

Elaine Jackson
Sincerely Yours, Business Services
13140 Highway 9 (Central Avenue)
Boulder Creek, CA 95006
Phone: (408) 338-3000
Fax: (408) 338-3666

Fresno

Susan Britton Whitcomb, CPRW
Alpha Omega Services
1255 W. Shaw, #101
Fresno, CA 93711
Phone: (209) 222-7474

Placentia

Nita Busby, CPRW
Resumes, Etc.
2019 E. Orangethorpe
Placentia, CA 92670
Phone: (714) 528-3765
Fax: (714) 528-3720

Portola Valley

Ted Bache
Kingston-Bache Resumes
3130 Alpine Rd., Ste. 200-B
Portola Valley, CA 94028
Phone: (415) 854-8594
Fax: (415) 854-8594

San Diego

Ruth L. Binder, CPRW
The PDQ Typist... and More
11120 Madrigal Street
San Diego, CA 92129
Phone: (619) 672-3334
Fax: (619) 672-2018

San Jose

Gary E. Watkins
4970 Cherry Ave., #22
San Jose, CA 95118
Phone: (408) 267-1094

Sallie Young
The Wordsmith
2797 La Jolla Avenue
San Jose, CA 95124
Phone: (408) 978-7278

Colorado

Colorado Springs

Gina V. Bump
1432 Jetwing Circle
Colorado Springs, CO 80916
Phone: (719) 637-1729

Florida

Fernandina Beach

Rose Montgomery
P.O. Box 6013
2148 Sadler Road, Suite 224
Fernandina Beach, FL 32034
Phone: (904) 277-4366
Fax: (904) 261-0288

Gainesville

Steven M. Burt, CPRW
Resume House
P.O. Box 7172
Gainesville, FL 32605
Phone: (904) 371-8148
Fax: (904) 371-0673

Tampa

Diane McGoldrick
Business Services of Tampa Bay, Inc.
10014 N. Dale Mabry Highway, #101
Tampa, FL 33618
Phone: (813) 968-3131
Fax: (813) 960-9558

Georgia

Atlanta

T. Jabali, CPC
APRS Career & Resume Co., Inc.
1155 Hammond Drive, Ste. D-4260
Atlanta, GA 30328
Phone: (404) 393-3554
Fax: (404) 396-5911

Lilburn

Julianne Sutton Franke, M.S., Owner/Manager
Career Pro Resume Service of Lilburn
3955 Highway 29
Lilburn, GA 30247
Phone: (404) 381-9407
Fax: (404) 381-9981

Snellville

Carol Lawrence, CPRW
A-Plus Office Services, Inc.
2275 Oak Road, Suite E
Snellville, GA 30278
Phone: (404) 978-6000
Fax: (404) 978-0653

Tifton

Charles H. Styer
Styer's Editorial Services
Tifton, GA 31793
Phone: (912) 382-5589

Illinois

Chicago

Gerard Hosek
Résumés For Success
6830 N. Sheridan Rd., Suite 572
Chicago, IL 60626
Phone: (312) 262-0672

Edwardsville

Carla L. Culp, CPRW
The Word Center
One Mark Twain Plaza, Ste. 325
Edwardsville, IL 62025
Phone: (618) 692-9673
Fax: (618) 692-9718

Elmhurst

Georgia Veith
ABC Career Services
135 Addison Avenue, Ste. 216
Elmhurst, IL 60126
Phone: (708) 782-1222
Fax: (708) 279-5599

Flossmoor

Jennie R. Dowden, CPRW
Jenn's Resume Service
Flossmoor, IL 60422
Phone: (708) 957-5976

Springfield

Laura G. Lichtenstein
Lasting Impressions Resume & Writing Service
Springfield, IL 62701
Phone: (217) 528-5782
Fax: (217) 528-5579

Indiana

Evansville

Teresa Collins, CPRW / Erica Hanson
Quality Résumé
600 North Weinbach, Suite 810
Evansville, IN 47711
Phone: (812) 479-8380
Fax: (812) 473-4892

Indianapolis

Gayle Bernstein, CPRW
Typing PLUS
2710 East 62nd Street, Suite 1
Indianapolis, IN 46220
Phone: (317) 257-6789
Fax: (317) 479-3103

Carole Pefley, CPRW
TESS, Inc.
6214 Morenci Trail, Suite 200
Indianapolis, IN 46268
Phone: (317) 291-3574
Fax: (317) 291-3640

Richard L. Schillen
solutions by design
2105 N. Meridian, 101
Indianapolis, IN 46202
(317) 923-8868

Lafayette

Alan D. Ferrell
The Wabash Group
1001 Salem Street
Lafayette, IN 47904
Phone: (317) 423-2311

Iowa

Iowa City

Elizabeth J. Axnix, CPRW
QUALITY WORD PROCESSING
329 East Court Street
Iowa City, IA 52240-4914
Phone: (800) 359-7822
Fax: (319) 354-7822

Kansas

Lawrence

Linda Morton, CPRW
Transcriptions
1012 Massachusetts, Suite 200
Lawrence, KS 66044
Phone: (913) 842-4619
Fax: (913) 842-2846

Louisiana

Alexandria

Michael Robertson
Michael Robertson Resume Service
P.O. Box 5025
Alexandria, LA 71307-5025
Phone: (318) 443-3366

Maine

Auburn

Rolande L. LaPointe, CPC, CIPC, CPRW
  (President)
RO-LAN ASSOCIATES, INC.
86 Main Street
Auburn, ME 04210
Phone: (207) 784-1010
Fax: (207) 782-3446

Massachusetts

Hingham

Joseph C. Roper
A-Script Career Services
60 South Street
Hingham, MA 02043
Phone: (617) 749-2970
Fax: (617) 749-8583

Northampton

Shel Horowitz, Director
D. Dina Friedman, Co-Director
Accurate Writing & More
P.O. Box 1164
Northampton, MA 01061-1164, U.S.A.
Phone: (800) 683-WORD (683-9673)
or (413) 586-2388

Northboro

Steven Green, CPRW
CareerPath
242 Brewer Street
Northboro, MA 01532
Phone: (508) 393-5548

Oxford

Myla Clark
New Directions
10 East Main Street
Oxford, MA 01540
Phone: (508) 987-8443
Fax: (508) 987-2527

Springfield

Thomas Paul Gajda
Thomas Paul Resumes
108 Kathleen Street
Springfield, MA 01119
Phone: (413) 782-0401

Michigan

Fremont

Patricia L. Nieboer, CPS, CPRW
The Office
25 W Main St. B
Fremont, MI 49412-1135
Phone: (616) 924-6600
Fax: (616) 924-6694

Kalamazoo

Betty A. Callahan, CPRW
Professional Results
2415 S. Rose Street
Kalamazoo, MI 49001
Phone: (616) 382-2122

Minnesota

Willmar

Elizabeth A. Meyer
Executive Suites on First
Willmar, MN 56201
Phone: (612) 235-9512
Fax: (612) 235-8633

Mississippi

Oxford

Leo J. Lazarus
Mid-South Student Services
Oxford, MS 38655
Phone: (601) 234-6077

Missouri

Independence

Teresa Duey
The Word Specialist
4706 Shrank Drive
Independence, MO 64055
Phone: (816) 478-0406
Fax: (816) 478-6544

St. Louis

John A. Suarez, CPRW
The Impact Group
7935A Clayton Road
St. Louis, MO 63117-1373
Phone: (314) 721-3900
Fax: (314) 721-5805

Montana

Butte

Kathleen Y. McNamee, CPRW
Holdsworth & Associates, Inc.
P.O. Box 4555
Butte, MT 59702
Phone: (406) 782-1063
Fax: 1 (800) 281-1063

Nebraska

Omaha

Rafael Santiago
FIRST IMPRESSIONS INC.
1257 Golden Gate Drive, Ste. 10
Papillion, NE 68046
Phone: (402) 331-2112
Fax: (402) 733-0200

New Hampshire

Exeter

Stephen H. Mazurka
Resumes & Writing Services
12 Wentworth Street
Exeter, NH 03833
Phone: (603) 772-7087
Fax: (603) 772-7360

New Jersey

Cedar Grove

Robert H. Markman, President and Founder
RESUMES THAT WIN®
433 Route 23, Suite D
Cedar Grove, NJ 07009-1802
Phone: (201) 857-3200
Fax: (201) 857-FAXX (3299)

Fair Lawn

Vivian Belen, CPRW
The Job Search Specialist
1102 Bellair Avenue
Fair Lawn, NJ 07410
Phone: (201) 797-2883

Marlboro

Beverly Baskin, CPRW
Executive Director, Baskin Business and
  Career Services
Offices in Marlboro, Princeton, and
  Woodbridge, NJ
Phone: (800) 300-4079
Fax: (800) 300-5056

Stanhope

Shari Favela
Ki Resumes & Career Consulting
Stanhope, NJ 07874
Phone: (201) 691-0806

West Paterson

Melanie Noonan, CPS
Peripheral Pro
West Paterson, NJ /
    Business: Little Falls, NJ
Phone: (201) 785-3011 (Both addresses)
Fax: (201) 785-3071 (Both addresses)

New York

Elmira Heights

Lynda C. Grier
OMS
Elmira Heights, NY
Phone: (607) 734-3491
Fax: (607) 734-4099

Flushing

James Voketaitis
Resume Center of New York
39-15 Main Street, Suite 501
Flushing, NY 11354
Phone: (718) 445-1956
Fax: (718) 445-1291

New York

Margaret Lawson
Consult—Career & Educational Trends
Phone: (212) 862-4874

Yorktown Heights

Mark D. Berkowitz, N.C.C.C.
Career Development Resources
1312 Walter Rd.
Yorktown Heights, NY 10598
Phone: (914) 962-1548

North Carolina

Albemarle

Julie S. Thompson
TypeSet Plus
1718 Blanch Street
Albemarle, NC 28001
Phone: (704) 985-1315
Fax: (704) 985-1316

Asheville

Dayna Feist, CPRW
Gatehouse Business Services
265 Charlotte Street
Asheville, NC 28801
Phone: (704) 254-7893
Fax: (704) 245-7894

Charlotte

Barry Wohl and Lisa Wohl
Carolina Custom Resumes
8318 Pineville-Matthews Road, Ste. 280
Charlotte, NC 28226
Phone: (704) 541-7524

North Dakota

Bismarck

Claudia Stephenson
Bismarck Secretarial Service
206 E. Broadway
Bismarck, ND 58501
Phone: (701) 255-3141

Ohio

Amlin

Susan Higgins
Q Resume Services
6500 Shier Rings Road
Amlin, OH 43002-9742
Phone: (614) 889-1616
Fax: (614) 889-0459

Athens

Melissa L. Kasler
Résumé Impressions
5100 Marion-Johnson Road
Athens, OH 45701
Phone: (614) 592-3993
Fax: (614) 592-3993

Oregon

Aloha

Pat Kendall, CPRW
Advanced Resume Concepts
18580 S. W. Rosa Road
Aloha, OR 97007
Phone: (503) 591-9143
Fax: (503) 642-2535

Pennsylvania

Bethlehem

A ProActive Resume
Joanne C. Hughes, Ph.D.
1833 Calypso Avenue
Bethlehem, PA 18018
Phone: (215) 867-3094

Erie

Joseph A. DiGiorgio
Career Concepts
4504 Peach Street
Erie, PA 16509
Phone: (814) 868-2333
Fax: (814) 868-3238

Wendy A. Lowry
3223 West 12th, #2
Erie, PA 16505
Phone: (814) 833-3936

Greencastle

Barbara A. Adversalo, CPRW
Business Assistance Associates, Inc.
11371 Worleytown Road
Greencastle, PA 17225
Phone: (717) 597-2508

Huntingdon

Margaret M.Hilling, Owner
Huntingdon County Resume Service
RR 2, Box 385
Huntingdon, PA 16652-9209
Phone: (814) 643-1663

South Carolina

Columbia

Nancy P. Stein
St. Andrews Services
1345 Garner Lane, Suite 107
Columbia, SC 29210
Phone: (803) 798-3277
Fax: (803) 731-0737

Tennessee

Athens

Adelia Wyner, Owner
Secretarial Office Services
314 N. White Street
Athens, TN 37303
Phone: (615) 745-4513

Texas

Dallas

Loretta J. Barr
ACCESS! Seminars and Consulting
(f.k.a. Resume Clinic)
11500 Stemmons, Suite 109
Dallas, TX 75229
Phone: (214) 484-3266

Houston

Nell Turk
Superior Systems & Secretarial Services
7007 Gulf Freeway, Suite 133
Houston, TX 77087
Phone: (713) 645-9609

New Braunfels

P. J. Margraf
Margraf Innovative Services
New Braunfels, TX 78130
Phone: (210) 625-9515
Fax: (210) 625-3925

Virginia

Forest

Wendy S. Enelow, CPRW
The Advantage, Inc.
Route 6, Box 200
Forest, VA 24551
Phone: (800) 922-5353
Fax: (804) 525-2969

Virginia Beach

Susie Brady, CPRW
Letter Perfect
291 Independence Blvd., Ste. 442
Virginia Beach, VA 23462
Phone: (804) 473-0432
Fax: (804) 473-0709

Wyoming

Mills

Valerie Kulhavy
Business Professionals
Post Office Box 247
Mills, WY 82644
Phone: (307) 234-0138

Professional Association of Resume Writers

For those who would like to contact the Professional Association of Resume Writers, its address is as follows:

3637 Fourth Street North, Suite 330
St. Petersburg, FL 33704
Phone: (813) 821-2274
Fax: (813) 894-1277

Reader Response Form

If you would like to express your opinion of the Gallery of Best Resumes, please answer the questions on this page and return it to:

JIST Works, Inc. • Attn: Jim Irizarry, Publisher
720 North Park Avenue • Indianapolis, IN 46202-3431

Name: _____ Title: _____

Company: _____

Address: _____

City: _____ State: _____ ZIP: _____

Phone: (   ) _____ - _____ Ext.: _____

Please check the appropriate answers to the following questions:

1. Where did you buy this JIST book?
   - ☐ Bookstore (name): _____
   - ☐ Catalog (title): _____
   - ☐ Direct from JIST   ☐ Other: _____

2. How many JIST books do you own?   ☐ 1   ☐ 2-5   ☐ More than 5

3. What influenced your purchase of this JIST book?
   - ☐ Personal recommendation   ☐ Advertisement   ☐ Price
   - ☐ JIST catalog   ☐ Other: _____

4. How would you rate the overall content of the book?
   - ☐ Excellent   ☐ Very Good   ☐ Good   ☐ Satisfactory   ☐ Poor

5. What do you like best about this JIST book? _____
   _____

6. What do you like least about this JIST book? _____
   _____

7. Please feel free to list any other comments you may have about this book.
   _____
   _____

A Call for Resume Submissions

The creation of this book depended on the submissions of fictionalized resumes and cover letters from professional resume writers across the United States. If you live in the U.S. or Canada, are a professional resume writer, and would like to submit some of your best work for possible inclusion in future publications by JIST Works, Inc., please send your submission and cover letter to David Noble, Senior Editor, JIST Works, Inc., 720 North Park Avenue, Indianapolis, IN 46202-3431.

A Call for Job Search Manuscripts

JIST Works, Inc., a leading publisher and distributor of job search books in the United States, is looking for quality manuscripts on job searching and related topics. If you would like to submit a book proposal to JIST for consideration, please send a query letter with a SASE to Sara Adams, Managing Editor, JIST Works, Inc., 720 North Park Avenue, Indianapolis, IN 46202-3431.

THE COMPLETE GUIDE FOR OCCUPATIONAL EXPLORATION

By JIST Editorial Staff

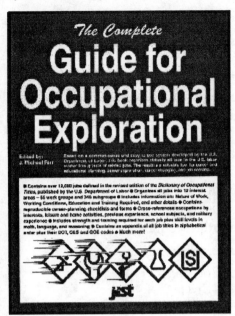

First revision since 1984! Based on the new *Dictionary of Occupational Titles, The Complete Guide* contains up-to-date information on today's occupations, many of which have been created or greatly changed by technology. More than 12,000 occupations are organized into:

- 12 major interests areas
- 66 work groups
- 348 subgroups of related jobs

Includes an alphabetical appendix listing almost 30,000 jobs.

OTHER INFORMATION

- A must book for career counselors, professionals, and school personnel
- The only book of its kind with up-to-date information
- One of the three major reference books used by job placement counselors

8-1/2 x 11, Paper, 936 pp.	8-1/2 x 11, Hardback, 936 pp.
ISBN 1-56370-052-2	**ISBN 1-56370-100-6**
$37.95 Order Code CGOE	*$47.95 Order Code CGOEH*

OCCUPATIONAL OUTLOOK HANDBOOK 1994-1995 Edition

By U.S. Department of Labor

This low-cost JIST edition of the U.S. Department of labor's popular career exploration guide describes the 250 jobs in which 85% of the American workforce is employed. Valuable information about each occupation includes a description of the work itself, employment outlook and opportunities, earnings, related occupations, training and advancement, and sources of additional information.

OTHER INFORMATION

- THE standard career reference book
- The most widely used and known career reference for professionals and schools
- Includes the latest Department of Labor statistics

8-1/2 x 11, Paper, 544 pp.	8-1/2 x 11, Hardback, 544 pp.
ISBN 1-56370-160-X	**ISBN 1-56370-161-X**
$15.95 Order Code OOH4	*$21.95 Order Code OOHH4*

*Look for these and other fine books from **JIST Works, Inc.**, at your full service bookstore or call us for additional information at 800-648-5478.*

THE RESUME and COVER LETTER BOOK

Write and Use an Effective Resume in Only One Day

By J. Michael Farr

First title in JIST's new Quick Guides series, by a best-selling author whose job search books have sold more than one million copies! Contains an "Instant Resume Worksheet" that enables job seekers to put together a basic, acceptable resume in less than one day. Provides helpful advice on creating job objectives, identifying skills, dealing with special situations, and getting a job.

OTHER INFORMATION

- Logical structure makes information easy to locate.
- Contains more than 50 sample resumes and cover letters.
- Crucial career planning and job search sections.

> 7 x 9, Paper, 288 pp.
> **ISBN 1-56370-141-3**
> **$9.95**
> Order Code RCLQG

THE QUICK INTERVIEW and SALARY NEGOTIATION BOOK

Dramatically Improve Your Interviewing Skill—and Pay—in a Matter of Hours

By J. Michael Farr

New, second title of JIST 's Quick Guide Series. J. Michael Farr's career books have sold more than 1 million copies. He has taught job search methods to trainers and instructors for nearly 20 years. In this informative book, he shares successful interview and salary negotiation techniques that have helped
thousands find jobs and get better salaries.

OTHER INFORMATION

- Outlines the three most important things to do in an interview
- Details how to make a $1,000 per minute in your negotiations
- Explains how to answer key problem questions

> 6 x 9, Paper, 160 pp.
> **ISBN 1-56370-162-6**
> **$9.95**
> *Order Code J1626*

*Look for these and other fine books from **JIST Works, Inc.**, at your full service bookstore or call us for additional information at 800-648-5478.*

THE VERY QUICK JOB SEARCH
Get a Good Job in Less Time

By J. Michael Farr

Based on years of experience and the experiences of thousands of job seekers. This is the only book proven to cut job search time in HALF. Covers ALL major career planning and job search topics in an interesting, thorough, and easy-to-follow way. Includes labor market trends, interviews, resumes, and more!

OTHER INFORMATION
- Proven techniques in finding a job in HALF the normal time
- This method, developed by Mike Farr, has been used by several million professional job trainers and job seekers
- Unique and results-oriented job search methods
- A proven classic, like *What Color Is Your Parachute?*

> 6 x 9, Paper, 260 pp.
> **ISBN 1-56370-181-2**
> **$12.95**
> *Order Code J1812*

THE RESUME SOLUTION
How to Write (and Use) a Resume That Gets Results

By David Swanson

Written by a former personnel director of a Fortune 500 company, *The Resume Solution* clues readers in to what employers really look for in a resume. Contains solid advice on how to produce an appealing, readable resume; more than 30 sample resumes and cover letters; and other insider tips not found in other resume books.

OTHER INFORMATION
- Step-by-step approach
- Lots of examples and activities
- Author is nationally recognized

> 8-1/2 x 11, Paper, 153 pp.
> **ISBN 1-56370-180-4**
> **$9.95**
> *Order Code J1804*

Look for these and other fine books from **JIST Works, Inc.,** *at your full service bookstore or call us for additional information at 800-648-5478.*

AMERICA'S TOP JOBS FOR COLLEGE GRADUATES

Detailed Information on Jobs and Trends for College Grads—and Those Considering a College Education

By U.S. Department of Labor and J. Michael Farr

Nearly 2 million graduates enter or reenter the job market each year. This newest addition to JIST's America's series explains why college graduates can expect to make more money and defines the latest labor market and career planning trends through the year 2005. Also includes information on the 500 most popular jobs, and details on employment trends by major industry.

OTHER INFORMATION

- Comprehensive appendices
- Based on the most current information from the Department of Labor
- Special section on job search and career planning

8-1/2 x 11, Paper, 300 pp.
ISBN 1-56370-140-5
$14.95
Order Code ATCG

America's Top 300 Jobs — *4th Edition*

A Complete Career Handbook

Praised by job search professionals as the most authoritative book of its kind on current and emerging jobs of the 1990s, it provides detailed descriptions of the 250 jobs in which more than 85 percent of the workforce are employed. Also includes information on more than 70 additional jobs.

OTHER INFORMATION

- Completely revised content
- The latest trends and salary projections based on U.S. Department of Labor information.

8-1/2 x 11, Paper, 544 pp.
ISBN: 1-56370-163-4
$17.95
Order Code T3004

---

*Look for these and other fine books from **JIST Works, Inc.**, at your full service bookstore or call us for additional information at 800-648-5478.*

THE CAREER CONNECTION FOR COLLEGE EDUCATION

A Guide to College Education & Related Career Opportunities

By Fred A. Rowe, Ed.D.

This easy-to-read reference for students and adults provides information on more than 100 college majors and the careers to which they can lead. Each college major description includes information on: types of degrees available, typical courses, prerequisite courses, and average starting salaries.

OTHER INFORMATION

- Includes self-assessment section
- Cross-references each degree to the *Dictionary of Occupational Titles*
- Latest projections of job growth and earnings
- 1,000 occupations cross-referenced to the DOT

> 6x9, Paper, 288 pp.
> **ISBN 1-56370-142-1**
> **$16.95**
> *Order Code CCCE*

THE CAREER CONNECTION FOR TECHNICAL EDUCATION

A Guide to Technical Training $ Related Career Opportunities

By Fred A. Rowe, Ed.D.

An easy-to-read reference for students and adults that provides information on more than 60 technical majors and the careers to which they can lead. Each degree description includes information on: educational requirements, typical courses, prerequisite courses, average starting salaries.

OTHER INFORMATION

- More than 750 occupations cross-referenced
- Includes self-assessment section
- Cross-references each degree to the *Dictionary of Occupational Titles*
- Covers all major technical careers

> 6x9, Paper, 192 pp.
> **ISBN 1-56370-143-X**
> **$14.95**
> *Order Code CCTE*

Look for these and other fine books from **JIST Works, Inc.,** *at your full service bookstore or call us for additional information at 800-648-5478.*

USING WORDPERFECT IN YOUR JOB SEARCH
(DOS/Windows)

By David F. Noble

This is a new type of focused computer book that shows readers how to use the power of WordPerfect to create best-quality resumes, cover letters, and other documents for job searching in the challenging job market of the 1990s. Explains the advantages of using WordPerfect to conduct an active job search compared to the more passive method of just sending resumes and cover letters in response to ads. The rest of the the book demonstrates how to use different versions of WordPerfect to produce customized resumes and other job search documents with ease.

OTHER INFORMATION

- Covers WordPerfect 5.0, 5.1, and 6.0 for DOS; and versions 5.1, 5.2 and 6.0 for Windows. Appropriate for beginning and advanced WordPerfect users.
- Contains many examples of resumes, cover letters, application letters, follow-up letters, acceptance letters, and thank-you letters.

> 7 1/2 x 9 1/2, Paper, 320 pp.
> **ISBN 1-56370-177-4**
> **$19.95**
> *Order Code J1774*

USING MICROSOFT WORD IN YOUR JOB SEARCH
(DOS/Windows)

By David F. Noble

This is a new type of focused computer book that shows readers how to use the power of Microsoft Word to create best-quality resumes, cover letters, and other documents for job searching in the challenging job market of the 1990s. Explains the advantages of using Microsoft Word to conduct an active job search compared to the more passive method of just sending resumes and cover letters in response to ads. The rest of the the book demonstrates how to use different versions of Microsoft Word to produce customized resumes and other job search documents with ease.

OTHER INFORMATION

- Covers Microsoft Word 5.0, 5.5, and 6.0 for DOS; and versions 5.0, 5.1 and 6.0 for Windows. Appropriate for beginning and advanced Microsoft Word users.
- Contains many examples of resumes, cover letters, application letters, follow-up letters, acceptance letters, and thank-you letters.

> 7 1/2 x 9 1/2, Paper, 320 pp.
> ISBN 1-56370-178-2
> $19.95
> *Order Code J1782*

To order call:
1-800-648-JIST
1-317-264-3720

Send your order today!
JIST Works, Inc.
720 North Park Avenue
Indianapolis, IN 46202-3431

Or FAX your order
1-317-264-3709 or
1-800-JIST-FAX

JIST publishes a variety of books on careers and job search topics. Please consider ordering one or more books from your dealer, local bookstore, or directly from JIST.

Orders from Individuals: Please use this information to order additional copies of this or other books listed on this page. Simply call or fax our *toll free* number. Our offices are open weekdays 7 a.m. to 7 p.m. eastern standard time.

QTY	BOOK TITLE			TOTAL $
	America's 50 Fastest Growing Jobs: The Authoritative Information Source	ISBN 1-56370-091-3	$11.95	
	Getting the Job You Really Want: A Step-by-Step Guide	ISBN 1-56370-092-1	$9.95	
	Job Strategies for Professionals: A Survival Guide for Experienced White-Collar Workers	ISBN 1-56370-139-1	$9.95	
	Mind Your Own Business: Getting Started as an Entrepreneur	ISBN 1-56370-083-2	$9.95	
	The Complete Guide for Occupational Exploration: *(soft cover)* Up-to-Date Informaton on More Than 12,000 Occupations *(hard cover)*	ISBN 1-56370-052-2 ISBN 1-56370-100-6	**$34.95** **$44.95**	
	Occupational Outlook Handbook 1994-1995 Edition *(soft cover)* *(hard cover)*	ISBN 1-56370-160-X ISBN 1-56370-161-8	$15.95 $21.95	
	The Quick Resume and Cover Letter Book: Write and Use an Effective Resume in Only One Day	ISBN 1-56370-141-3	$9.95	
	The Quick Interview and Salary Negotiation Book: Dramatically Improve Your Interviewing Skill and Pay in a Matter of Hours	ISBN 1-56370-162-6	$9.95	
	The Very Quick Job Search: Get a Good Job in Less Time	ISBN 1-56370-181-2	$12.95	
	The Resume Solution: How to Write and Use a Resume That Gets Results	ISBN 1-56370-180-4	$9.95	
	America's Top Jobs for College Graduates: Detailed Information on Jobs and Trends for College Grads — and Those Considering A College Education	ISBN 1-56370-140-5	$14.95	
	America's Top 300 Jobs — 4th Edition: A Complete Career Handbook *(trade version of the Occupational Outlook Handbook)*	ISBN 1-56370-163-4	$17.95	
	The Career Connection for College Education: A Guide to College Majors & Related Career Opportunities	ISBN 1-56370-142-1	$16.95	
	The Career Connection for Technical Education: A Guide to Technical Training & Related Career Opportunities	ISBN 1-56370-143-X	$14.95	
	Using WordPerfect in Your Job Search Create High Quality Resumes and Cover Letters Using WordPerfect	ISBN 1-56370-177-4	$19.95	
	Using Microsoft Word in Your Job Search Create High Quality Resumes and Cover Letters Using Microsoft Word	ISBN 1-56370-178-2	$19.95	

Check Out Our New Computer Skills Training Videos!

Computer skills have become essential for success in the work force. Many entry level jobs now require computer skills — over 90% of employers expect clerical candidates to have keyboarding skills as well as a working knowledge of one or more common business software programs. The same is true for experienced workers — over 70% of employers now seek managers with much higher levels of computer skills.

These low-cost, high quality videos can help you be more competitive in your current job and be a much more attractive job seeker.

You will easily master the latest versions of today's hottest software with the help of our easy-to-follow videos. Split screens show viewers what should be happening on their computer screens as they work through the commands and functions taught in the video. A 3 1/2" practice disk is included with most videos and reinforces the important concepts taught on-screen.

All this for only $34.95 each.
For more information call 1-800-648-JIST!

	POPULAR SOFTWARE TRAINING TITLES INCLUDE:				
	VIDEO TITLE	ISBN#	ORDER CODE	QTY	PRICE
1.	Quicken Made Easy	ISBN 1-57112-036-X	PV036X		
2.	Microsoft Word 6.0 Fast Editing	ISBN 1-57112-031-9	PV0319		
3.	PageMaker 5.0 Basics	ISBN 1-57112-032-7	PV0327		
4.	PageMaker 5.0 Advanced	ISBN 1-57112-033-5	PV0335		
5.	Excel 5 for Windows Basics	ISBN 1-57112-034-3	PV0343		
6.	Excel 5 for Windows Advanced	ISBN 1-57112-035-1	PV0351		
7.	MS-DOS Basics	ISBN 1-57112-003-3	PA160V		
8.	MS-DOS Intermediate	ISBN 1-57112-004-1	PA161V		
9.	MS-DOS Advanced	ISBN 1-57112-005-X	PA162V		
10.	MS-DOS 6.0/6.2	ISBN 1-57112-030-0	PV0300		
11.	Windows Basics	ISBN 1-57112-014-9	PA171V		
12.	Windows Advanced	ISBN 1-57112-015-7	PA172V		
13.	WordPerfect Basics	ISBN 1-57112-006-8	PA163V		
14.	WordPerfect Advanced	ISBN 1-57112-007-6	PA164V		
15.	WordPerfect 6 for Windows Basics	ISBN 1-57112-028-9	PV0289		
16.	WordPerfect 6 for Windows Advanced	ISBN 1-57112-029-7	PV0297		
17.	dBase Basics	ISBN 1-57112-008-4	PA165V		
18.	dBase Advanced	ISBN 1-57112-009-2	PA166V		
19.	Lotus 1-2-3 Basics	ISBN 1-57112-010-6	PA167V		
20.	Lotus 1-2-3 Intermediate	ISBN 1-57112-012-2	PA168V		
21.	Lotus 1-2-3 Advanced	ISBN 1-57112-011-4	PA169V		
22.	Lotus 1-2-3 Macros	ISBN 1-57112-013-0	PA170V		
23.	Lotus 4 for Windows	ISBN 1-57112-037-8	PV0378		
24.	Computer Basics	ISBN 1-57112-016-5	PA173V		
25.	Virus Protection & Computer Security	ISBN 1-57112-017-3	PA174V		
26.	PC Maintenance	ISBN 1-57112-018-1	PA175V		
27.	Computer Health Hazards	ISBN 1-57112-019-X	PA176V		
28.	Job Winning Resumes Using Your PC	ISBN 1-57112-020-3	PA177V		